Awakening Spirits
Wolves in the Southern Rockies

Awakening Spirits
Wolves in the Southern Rockies

Edited by Richard P. Reading,
Brian Miller, Amy L. Masching,
Rob Edward, and
Michael K. Phillips

FULCRUM
GOLDEN, COLORADO

Library of Congress Cataloging-in-Publication Data
Awakening spirits : wolves in the southern Rockies / edited by Richard P. Reading ... [et al.].
   p. cm.
 Includes bibliographical references and index.
 ISBN 978-1-55591-674-9 (pbk.)
 1. Gray wolf--Reintroduction--Rocky Mountains Region. I. Reading,
Richard P.
 QL737.C22A93 2010
 599.7730978--dc22

                        2009014273

Printed on recycled paper in the United States of America by Malloy, Inc.
0 9 8 7 6 5 4 3 2 1

Design by Jack Lenzo
Cover photograph © Shutterstock | Ronnie Howard
Interior photographs:
Page viii, courtesy of Tim Springer, © 2009, www.pbase.com/tspringer.
Page 12, courtesy of Doug Dance, © 2009, www.ddancenaturephotography.com.
Page 24, courtesy of Dan Drost, © 2009, www.pbase.com/ddrost.
Page 48, courtesy of Doug Dance, © 2009, www.ddancenaturephotography.com.
Page 60, courtesy of National Park Service/Bob Wesselman.
Page 78, courtesy of John Savage, © 2009, www.pbase.com/1229jr.
Page 102, courtesy of Doug Dance, © 2009, www.ddancenaturephotography.com.
Page 118, courtesy of Tim Springer, © 2009, www.pbase.com/tspringer.
Page 146, courtesy of Dan Drost, © 2009, www.pbase.com/ddrost.
Page 160, courtesy of Anne Edward, © 2009, www.pbase.com/yllstonewolf.
Page 186, courtesy of Larry Peterson, © 2009, lppphotography@gmail.com.
Page 196, courtesy of Doug Dance, © 2009, www.ddancenaturephotography.com.

Fulcrum Publishing
4690 Table Mountain Dr., Ste. 100
Golden, CO 80403
800-992-2908 • 303-277-1623
www.fulcrumbooks.com

Contents

Acknowledgments

A number of people and organizations made this book possible. First and foremost, we would like to express our gratitude to each of the authors of the chapters. Producing this volume took several years, and we appreciate the authors' patience and willingness to continually update their work. Each chapter also benefited from the accumulated knowledge and wisdom of other experts. In addition to the editors, we received thoughtful, well-written reviews from Dr. Joel Berger, Steve Forrest, Ty Gee, Dr. David Kenny, Dr. Berton Lee Lamb, Dr. Lauren McCain, Erin Robertson, Dr. Michael Soulé, Dr. Richard Wallace, and several chapter authors. Dr. Alyson Wiedenheft assisted us in putting technical medical terms into laymen's terms. Ed McPherson spent hours helping to format and edit several chapters. While reviewers' comments greatly strengthened the manuscript, we accept full responsibility for any errors that remain. Of course, research continues on several aspects of wolf restoration, and we expect that new insights will render inaccurate some of the conclusions we reached.

Producing a multiauthor, multidiscipline volume on a complex subject requires that contributors' organizations support their staff as they compile their chapters. We appreciate the contribution of organizations with which the individual authors are affiliated and for allowing them to work on this project. A few organizations provided substantially more support for this project and deserve special acknowledgment, including the Turner Endangered Species Fund, the Denver Zoological Foundation, the Wind River Ranch Foundation, Sinapu (which has since merged with another organization to become WildEarth Guardians), and the Southern Rockies Ecosystem Project (which no longer exists). We also recognize the support of several individuals within these organizations, including Craig Piper and the late Dr. Clayton Freiheit of the Denver Zoological Foundation.

Finally, we owe a debt of thanks to the wonderful people at Fulcrum Publishing for helping mold the rough draft of our book into the highly polished finished product you hold in your hands. First and foremost, we thank Bob Baron for finding merit in our manuscript and for providing excellent recommendations for improving our presentation, and Haley Berry for all of her wonderful guidance and expert assistance along the way. Many thanks also to Patty Maher, who helped this project reach fruition.

Introduction

A Comprehensive Approach to Evaluating the Potential for Wolf Restoration in the Southern Rockies

Richard P. Reading, Brian Miller, Amy L. Masching,
Rob Edward, and Michael K. Phillips

Wolves (*Canis* spp.) represent one of the most iconic species of wildlife. Until recently, people heavily persecuted wolves throughout most of their range, and in many areas of the world wolves remain the targets of eradication, or at least control. Yet there are people working to restore wolf populations.

Humans eliminated gray wolves (*Canis lupus*) from the Southern Rocky Mountains of the United States (figures I.1 and I.2) by the middle of the last century, but today wolf restoration proceeds in other portions of the species' range in North America. Some have begun to explore the feasibility and desirability of restoring wolves to the Southern Rockies, the region of mountains, foothills, and basins extending from southern Wyoming into northern New Mexico, or at least letting wolves reestablish themselves on their own in this area.

This book's authors include wildlife biologists, geographers, legal and policy experts, and conservationists whose common concern is the future of the wolf and the long-term ecological health of the Southern Rockies. Because of the wolf's absence from the Southern Rockies, these are not unrelated concerns. We organized this book to answer, or at least shed light on, the following questions:

1. Can we restore a viable wolf population to the Southern Rockies and reestablish the animal's role as a predator that benefits ecosystem integrity?
2. How might a restored Southern Rockies wolf population help to strengthen wolf population and recovery goals throughout the western United States and Canada?
3. What are the ecological, socioeconomic, political, and legal contexts that will influence restoring this species?

Due to simultaneously rapid human development of natural landscapes and locally expanding wolf populations, as well as battles over the wolf's status under the Endangered Species Act (ESA), there may not be a more appropriate time to attempt to answer these questions.

WHY RETURN THE WOLF?

The wolf instills in humans the deepest of emotions: spirituality, inspiration, awe, contempt, anger, and fear. At once a magnificent predator and dreaded outlaw, the wolf is an animal of legend. Many Native American tribes revered the wolf in their legends and religion. The European settlers who came to North America brought with them a culture of fear centered on the wolf, complete with familiar tales of cunning wolves attempting to trick and eat innocent children. From the seemingly practical standpoint of early settlers, the wolf was seen as a symbol of uncontrollable wildness, an animal that had to be eradicated in order for humans to survive and prosper. Over most of the wolf's former range, Euro-American settlers were successful at doing just that. Once found in relative abundance throughout Canada, every US state, and Mexico, and occupying nearly all ecosystem types, the wolf was driven to

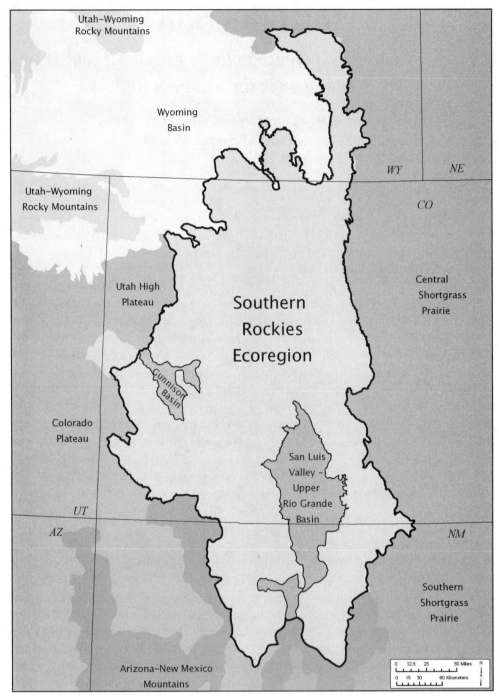

Figure I.2—Location of the Southern Rockies Ecoregion relative to surrounding ecoregions. Note that we include the Gunnison and San Luis Valley–Upper Rio Grande basins within the Southern Rocky Mountains Ecoregion.

Source: US Forest Service ECOMAP project and The Nature Conservancy

extinction south of the Canada-US border by the mid-1900s, with the exception of a small population in northern Minnesota.

Today, many people admire the wolf as an apex predator and a highly social animal, while others still see little to no value, purpose, or redeeming qualities in the animal. Yet within both of these views, the wolf is a symbol of wildness; it is this wildness that inspires the holders of the former view and creates antipathy in those who believe the latter. For those who recognize that wild places are few, dwindling, and increasingly diminished in native floras and faunas, wildness is no longer seen as something that must be destroyed in order for humans to prosper. Even more encouraging, perhaps, is the growing recognition that our willingness and ability to protect wild places and wildlife is a measure of our prosperity and wisdom.

It is due to these cultural transformations that the ESA was passed in 1973, and under this legislation the gray wolf was listed as endangered in 1974, providing the species with legal protection. As a result of ESA protection, the wolf has made a dramatic comeback in the upper Midwest, with more than 2,000 gray wolves now thriving in northern Minnesota and hundreds more expanding into northern Wisconsin and Michigan. The gray wolf also began to successfully recolonize northern Montana during the 1980s. Due to direct human intervention, in 1987 managers began returning the red wolf (*Canis rufus*) to portions of its former range in the southeastern United States, releasing the Mexican wolf to the southwestern United States in 1998, and, in 1995, returning the gray wolf to Yellowstone National Park and north-central Idaho under authority of the ESA.

In the Northern Rocky Mountains of the United States (i.e., the Rocky Mountains north of Colorado), wolf recovery has exceeded the expectations of federal, state, and tribal agencies involved in the effort. In 2000, there were an estimated 63 adult wolves in northwestern Montana, 177 in the Greater Yellowstone Ecosystem, and 192 in central Idaho (Bangs, Fontaine, Jiminez, et al. 2001), and by September 2008 these numbers had grown to 1,463 wolves in the Northern Rockies of the United States (US Fish and Wildlife Service 2008a). In addition, restored wolf populations have proven far more valuable to many local economies than predicted, due to increased interest in activities such as wolf viewing in Yellowstone National Park. Also of note, livestock depredations have been far lower than anticipated (Bangs, Fontaine, Jiminez, et al. 2001; Smith and Ferguson 2005).

The ESA mandates restoring populations of species listed as threatened or endangered where habitat exists and where restoration is feasible to meet recovery goals (Endangered Species Act 1973). As a result, other regions in the United States have been under consideration for wolf restoration by the US Fish and Wildlife Service (USFWS), the agency that implements recovery plans under the ESA. However, USFWS's recovery strategies, such as delineating distinct population segments (DPS) as biologically based wolf recovery zones and a recent proposal to reclassify and delist the gray wolf in portions of its former range under the ESA, make it unclear whether or not the law will be used to fulfill this objective (Phillips, Fascione, Miller, and Byers 2000; US Fish and Wildlife Service 2000a, 2008). However, the Southern Rockies stand out among potential candidate regions for repatriating the gray wolf, in part due to studies favorably measuring the region's ability to support viable populations of wolves (e.g., Bennett 1994; Phillips et al. 2000; Carroll et al. 2003; Carroll et al. 2006). There are also studies reporting general acceptance by people to bringing wolves back (Manfredo, Bright, Pate, and Tischbein 1994; Meadow, Reading, Phillips, et al. 2005).

WHY THE SOUTHERN ROCKIES?

We define the Southern Rockies landscape based on the US Forest Service ecoregion classification system (McNab and Avers 1994). Ecoregions are delineated based on similar patterns of topography, vegetation, soils, geology, species, and climate across a large landscape (Bailey 1995). We used the ecoregion classification boundaries with some minor modifications, such as adding major valleys classified as part of other ecoregions by the Forest Service, but which are surrounded by the Southern Rockies (figure I.2). The Southern Rockies Ecoregion as we define it is a large landscape, stretching north to south from the Laramie Mountains near Casper, Wyoming, along the Continental Divide in Colorado, and south to the Jemez, Sangre de Cristo, and Sandias of New Mexico to Albuquerque. The Great Plains are its eastern boundary and to the west, the red rock country of the Colorado Plateau. Politically, the area encompasses parts of Wyoming, Colorado, and New Mexico, sixty-four counties, and lands administered by federal agencies such as the US Forest Service, Bureau of Land Management, and National Park Service, as well as state, county, and local agencies. The area of the Southern Rockies covers about 166,818 sq. km (about 64,409 sq. mi.), or an area roughly equivalent to that of New England.

The Southern Rockies include the magnificent rugged mountains of Colorado, with fifty-four peaks higher than 14,000 ft. (4,267 m) in elevation, as well as countless other peaks of only slightly lesser stature. There is a less dramatic side to the Southern Rockies as well, including several vast intermountain basins, gently rolling foothills, and high, broad plateaus (Shinneman, McClelan, and Smith 2000).

The wide range in elevation and complex landforms comprising the Southern Rockies cause uneven distribution of moisture and significant differences in temperature—often over short distances—and thus lead to sharply contrasting local climates. These diverse climatic conditions help support fourteen ecological communities and native species (Shinneman, McClelan, and Smith 2000). The Southern Rockies region is also diverse because of its location as a biological meeting place where species converge from the boreal forests to the north, the grassland steppes (prairies) to the east, and the semiarid deserts to the south and west. Yet, as diverse as the patterns of ecosystems and landforms may be in the Southern Rockies, they are collectively unique and are distinguishable on the whole from surrounding ecoregions.

Via a long day hike, one can witness this tremendous variety in nature. Imagine a trek that descends a high-elevation peak in central Colorado: beginning at a cold, windswept mountain 13,000 feet (3,962 m) above sea level, a pika (*Ochotona princeps*) forages in an alpine meadow along the edge of a scree slope while a white-tailed ptarmigan (*Lagopus leucurus*) scurries into a stunted krummholz forest patch. At 11,000 feet (3,352 m), a pine marten (*Martes americana*) scurries across a trail and quickly disappears into a cool, dense subalpine forest of spruce (*Picea* spp.) and fir where a gray jay (*Perisoreus canadensis*) is perched and watching. When you reach 8,000 feet (2,438 m), a flammulated owl (*Otus flammeolus*) floats through a warm, dry forest of old ponderosa pines (*Pinus ponderosa*) and an Abert's squirrel (*Sciurus aberti*) hurriedly gathers pinecones. Down to 6,000 feet (1,828 m), white-tailed prairie dogs (*Cynomys lecurus*) bark at the sight of a ferruginous hawk (*Buteo regalis*), and a herd of pronghorn (*Antilocapra americana*) race across a broad, treeless valley of bunchgrasses and shrubs. At 5,000 feet (1,524 m), a desert bighorn (*Ovis canadensis*) takes a drink from a cool stream, keeping an eye out for a hungry puma (*Puma concolor*), and dozens of songbirds can be heard singing in the riparian forest of tall cottonwood trees (*Populus* spp.)

with lush undergrowth. Within the stream, a native Colorado River cutthroat trout (*Oncorhynchus clarki pleuriticu*) fights the current in search of stonefly nymphs.

For thousands of years, the gray wolf was also a part of these Southern Rockies ecosystems. Perhaps numbering in the thousands, the gray wolf functioned as a top-level predator in the region, preying upon herds of elk (*Cervus elaphus*), deer (*Odocoileus* spp.), and other species (Bennett 1994). The Southern Rockies biological communities evolved with the gray wolf. The animal's presence and regulatory role on prey was essential to the region's ecological function and integrity.

Yet, as with most other areas of the United States, decades of persecution by Euro-American homesteaders, government trappers, bounty hunters, and ranchers drove the wolf to extinction in the Southern Rockies; the last known wolf in the region was killed in 1945 by a state hunter in Conejos County, Colorado (Bennett 1994). These successful efforts, as with the native grizzly bear (*Ursus arctos*), were meant to make the West "safe" for livestock, people, and progress. During the early 1900s, the handful of wolves that remained were seen as marauding renegades, and they often took on legendary status, with nicknames like Three Toes and Old Lefty. Today, without the gray wolf, the Southern Rockies landscape is biologically incomplete. Yet, initial assessments of the region's prey base, wild landscapes, and human attitudes toward wolf restoration suggest that this need not be the case.

WHY AN ECOREGION APPROACH?

According to Noss and Cooperrider (1994), large natural landscapes such as ecoregions may be the most appropriate scale for conservation and land management activities. The myriad ecosystems comprising an ecoregion share ecological relationships, including corresponding natural processes, such as migrating species and the flow of

nutrients through a system, and natural disturbances, such as fire, drought, or disease outbreaks. Recognizing these relationships across large landscapes has become an essential component of conservation efforts and natural resource management activities. This approach contrasts sharply to past resource management and protection activities, which were largely carried out within politically defined landscape units, such as national parks, national forests, and states. Such political- and human-defined landscapes typically have little correlation with natural ecosystem boundaries, natural processes, or species habitat needs. For instance, in the Southern Rockies, in order to get to a reliable food source in winter, an elk may have to leave the protection of a national park, where hunting, logging, and livestock grazing are not allowed; cross a heavily logged and roaded multiple-use national forest where hunters abound; and finally settle in for the winter on its historical grassland wintering habitat, which may now be privately owned by cattle ranchers and second-home homeowners.

Only in recent years have land managers and conservation scientists successfully promoted a natural landscape approach to biodiversity conservation and natural resource management through concepts such as ecosystem management and land unit delineations such as greater ecosystems, an example being the Greater Yellowstone Ecosystem of northern Wyoming and parts of Idaho and Montana (e.g., Salwasser 1992; Grumbine 1990).

Only large landscapes fulfill the life history needs of gray wolves, such as their substantial prey requirements, expansive pack territory sizes, and long juvenile dispersal distances. To address the relevant factors affecting wolf restoration and the potential of the Southern Rockies to support such restoration requires examining large landscapes. Moreover, such an assessment must be placed within the even larger context of the Intermountain West. The Southern Rockies potentially provide a vital link between restored gray wolf populations just to the north, in the Greater Yellowstone Ecoregion, and to ongoing efforts to restore the Mexican wolf in the southwestern United States. (Phillips, Fascione, Miller, and Byers 2000). With all these factors in mind, this book evaluates the suitability of the Southern Rockies and surrounding landscapes for possible wolf restoration that would create a wild and natural legacy for future generations of people, predators, and prey.

COMPONENTS OF ASSESSING THE FEASIBILITY OF WOLF RESTORATION

Our objective is to determine if the Southern Rockies are suitable for restoring wolves in their former range. While the book's contributors support restoration, they evaluated the pros and cons objectively. It is in the best interest of wolves to ensure that any restoration effort is both biologically and socially feasible. The authors—experts in a number of disciplines—address the following question: Is wolf restoration in the Southern Rockies ecologically, socially, and legally rational, feasible, and justified? If this question cannot be answered in the affirmative, then it would be irresponsible to proceed, and if restoration did take place, it would likely fail.

With the above question in mind, the book is divided into three sections: Overview, Social Assessment, and Ecological Assessment, with multiple chapters in each section.

OVERVIEW

The first four chapters provide a historical and theoretical context for the social and ecological assessments that follow. Chapter 1 briefly surveys the long history of human interactions with nature; chapter 2 addresses human-wolf interactions over time in the

Lower 48 and recovery efforts in North Carolina, the Great Lakes, the Greater Yellowstone Ecosystem, and in New Mexico and Arizona; chapter 3 discusses why, from an ecological perspective, we should be concerned not only about the effect wolves and other large carnivores have on their prey but also about the associated ripple effects up and down the food chain; and chapter 4 suggests that if we are to restore wolves to the Southern Rockies, it will likely require translocating, or moving, animals into the region from elsewhere. Chapter 4 also explores the biological and social science variables that should be considered and addressed prior to translocation.

The book begins with two chapters that review the relationship between people and nature in North America from prehistory to the present. In chapter 1, Miller and Foreman explore the human-nature relationship broadly and over a time frame extending over millennia. They argue convincingly that Earth's current extinction spasm began with the arrival of humans into North America during the last ice age. Three waves of extinction characterize this extinction spasm, the first starting soon after people arrived and began killing wildlife unaccustomed to this new, highly efficient predator. The second wave of extinction followed the arrival of European colonists with their new "guns, germs, and steel" (see Diamond 1997). Finally, and most recently, economic globalization ushered in the present wave of extinction, which threatens to completely and permanently alter the ecological fabric of Earth.

Focusing in on wolves in chapter 2, Phillips and Miller describe the decline of wolves in the United States, the change in emphasis from extermination to conservation of the species, recent wolf recovery efforts, and the future prospects for continued recovery. They first describe the prevailing attitudes and rationale that led to the steady decline and near elimination of wolves south of Canada into the United States and Mexico. Fortunately, as Phillips and Miller describe, just as the United States was on the cusp of extirpating wolves from the Lower 48, human attitudes toward wolves shifted in the middle of last century. By the last few decades of the 1900s, people increasingly called for wolf restoration, eventually leading to large-scale, government-sponsored recovery programs. These programs continue today, with some enjoying spectacular success while others continue to struggle. Current debate rages over how extensive—both in numbers and geographically—wolf recovery should grow. Should and will wolf recovery extend to the Southern Rockies Ecoregion? The social and ecological feasibility and desirability of such an endeavor form the topics of the remainder of the book.

In chapter 3, Paquet, Miller, Kunkel, Reading, and Phillips discuss the importance of large carnivores to healthy, well-functioning ecosystems and to people. They explain how wolves, as predators at the top of the food chain, influence other species and ecosystem processes. Often termed "highly interactive" or "keystone" species, top predators frequently have disproportionately large impacts, especially given the relatively small size of their populations, that affect a broad array of other species, primarily through predation, the threat of predation (which affects behavior), or the direct killing of potential competitors. These impacts trickle down through the food chain. Yet, people value large carnivores for far more than their ecological role. Paquet and his colleagues also briefly discuss how large carnivores provide cultural, aesthetic, existence, and economic value to a growing number of people.

The final chapter in this section, chapter 4 by Miller, Reading, Ralls, Clark, and Estes, covers the broad array of biological and social variables that influence the success of animal translocations. Translocation programs form the core of wolf restoration efforts in the southeastern United States, southwestern United States, Idaho, and Yellowstone, and a similar program would likely be required to restore wolves to the Southern Rockies. Yet, most translocations fail because they fail to properly consider the full complement of factors discussed by Miller et al. Many of the variables introduced in chapter 4 are discussed in more detail in the chapters that comprise the remainder of this volume.

SOCIAL ASSESSMENT

Arguably the greatest challenges to wolf restoration are sociopolitical rather than ecological. The second section of the book focuses on nonbiological issues, with four chapters exploring the social aspects of potential wolf restoration in the Southern Rockies. Chapter 5 looks at the human landscape and land use within the Southern Rockies; chapter 6 reviews several studies that examine human attitudes toward wolves; chapter 7 addresses policy and legal issues; and chapter 8 looks at policy and policy making from a problem-solving approach, using a policy sciences framework first detailed by Harold Lasswell (1971; Lasswell and McDougal 1992).

ECOLOGICAL ASSESSMENT

The gray wolf is a highly adaptable species, as illustrated by the array of habitat types it historically occupied: from the Arctic tundra to the deserts of India, into high mountains, across expansive steppes, and through dense forests. Yet, certain habitat characteristics, such as an abundance of large ungulates, render some regions more amenable to wolf presence than others. In the book's final section, the contributors provide an ecological assessment of the potential of the Southern Rockies to support an ecologically meaningful population of wolves. Chapter 9 presents an overview of ecosystems comprising the Southern Rockies Ecoregion; chapter 10 reviews disease and other animal health considerations important to wolf restoration, and chapter 11 reviews past research and ecological modeling exercises that evaluate the current and projected future ability of the Southern Rockies to support wolves and discusses further the ecological implications of wolf restoration to the region.

The Southern Rockies Ecoregion covers a vast area, from southern Wyoming to northern New Mexico. Shinneman, Miller, and Kunkel provide an ecological overview of the ecoregion in chapter 9. They provide the context for the ecological assessment of the ecoregion for wolf recovery. After briefly discussing the geology, climate, and natural processes of the Southern Rockies, Shinneman et al. describe the composition and condition of the fourteen major ecological communities comprising the Southern Rockies, from high alpine to low-elevation riparian zones. The chapter ends with a review of the species and communities in the Southern Rockies that are currently most at risk. Shinneman and his colleagues conclude that despite significant human alteration, the ecoregion presents an excellent opportunity for protecting and restoring large landscapes and wide-ranging species.

From avian flu to the West Nile virus to chronic wasting disease, animal-borne diseases are receiving increasingly more attention. Any attempt at restoring wolves to the Southern Rockies requires a comprehensive assessment of disease and parasite risks. In chapter 10, Gillin and Hunter explore the various pathogens known to afflict wolves and the likely extent to which those pathogens would impact wolf restoration. They also briefly touch on some of the major diseases that affect the primary prey of wolves. Gillin and Hunter caution that any translocation would involve moving the whole suite of organisms associated with the individual animals being translocated, such as parasites and any diseases they may harbor. In addition, domestic animals within the restoration site present a potential source of pathogens to wolves. The extent to which pathogens control wolf populations remains poorly understood, but Gillin and Hunter provide guidelines for minimizing the risks to both translocated wolves and the community of animals at the translocation site.

Much of the Southern Rockies Ecoregion's vast area remains relatively wild. In the final chapter, Phillips, Miller, Kunkel, Paquet, Martin, and Smith review published research to evaluate the potential of the Southern Rockies to support wolves, and then they examine the ecological implications of wolf restoration. Past studies found that good habitat remains for wolves in the Southern Rockies. Phillips et al. report that the best estimates suggest that the ecoregion could support well over 1,000 wolves. Using biological and socioeconomic considerations, they suggest that the best sites for restoration are northern New Mexico, southwestern Colorado, northwestern Colorado, and west-central Colorado, in that order. Phillips et al. argue that research from other areas suggests that wolves would impact the populations of other carnivores and ungulate prey with cascading effects through the ecosystem, largely resulting in a healthier community. Although large ungulate populations like elk may decline, populations in the Southern Rockies currently remain higher than managers' objectives. As such, at least in the short-term, wolves likely would not affect hunter harvests. Moreover, a restored wolf population would predate upon livestock and pets in the region. Phillips et al. predict relatively low overall depredation, although individual ranchers may experience significant impacts. They recommend a mix of lethal control and nonlethal deterrents, as well as providing compensation for people impacted by depredation. Finally, Phillips and his colleagues find that fears over land use restrictions and human safety due to wolf restoration are generally overstated.

CONCLUSIONS

Wolves and wolf restoration are contentious. These wild carnivores inordinately influence the systems they inhabit—and the human psyches they infiltrate. After centuries of persecution, wolf supporters now outnumber wolf detractors (at least in the United States). In many rural areas, however, wolf detractors still outnumber wolf supporters. Yet, successful wolf restoration does not rely on a simple vote. Ultimately, wolf restoration will succeed where the biological context suggests that sufficient, high-quality habitat exists and where the sociopolitical context suggests that people will permit wolves to remain. In this volume, we recruited experts from a wide variety of fields to conduct a comprehensive assessment of pertinent biological and social considerations bearing on wolf restoration success in the Southern Rockies Ecoregion.

Wolves might eventually disperse to the Southern Rockies and establish a viable population, although the process would likely take decades. Given the ecological importance of wolves, waiting for them to (possibly) recolonize the region on their own seems inadequate. Active restoration efforts—namely, translocating wolves to the Southern Rockies—would expedite rekindling the vital ecological process of wolf predation to a region that is degrading ecologically in the absence of that process. If active restoration efforts are initiated, wildlife managers should consider the myriad biological and social factors that influence restoration success. The authors have outlined the most important of these variables and conducted biological and social assessments, and the results suggest that the Southern Rockies Ecoregion encompasses sufficient habitat to support a healthy population of wolves and that the public will support the project. Future projections of human development in the region paint a slightly less optimistic picture ecologically but point to growing support from the public. Still, some stakeholders, although a minority of the public, would likely oppose, perhaps strongly, any attempt to restore wolves.

If society wants to restore wolves to the Southern Rockies, managers must work to mitigate opposition by working to creatively and effectively address the concerns of those negatively impacted by wolf restoration. The success of wolf translocation programs in Yellowstone National Park and central Idaho underscore that restoration is possible, but the challenges that continue to face Mexican wolf restoration efforts in Arizona and New Mexico highlight the difficulties that could develop. Overall, based on the information provided in this book, we believe that wolf restoration would succeed in the Southern Rockies, and we look to the day when a viable population of wolves returns to the region to help restore its ecological health and wilderness character.

Overview

Chapter 1

A Brief History of Human–Nature Interactions

Brian Miller and Dave Foreman

INTRODUCTION

This chapter looks at North American extinction over the last 12,000 years. While the end of the Pleistocene may seem distant, and the causes of that epoch's extinctions difficult to discern, examining those causes may provide more accurate problem definitions for present crises and suggest paths for resolution.

There have been five great extinction spasms over the course of Earth's history, the most recent being 65 million years ago, at the end of the Cretaceous period (Jablonski 1995). Between these spasms, extinction rates were roughly in equal proportion to, or slightly lower than, creation rates of new species. We are now in a period where the rate of species loss is about a thousand times higher than this "background rate" of loss (E. O. Wilson 1992, 2002). While current extinction rates have probably not yet reached the intensity of those in the "great five," the present spasm has a unique causal agent.

During the first five extinction spasms, the causes were temporary perturbations such as asteroids, volcanic eruption, and climatic/atmospheric changes (Jablonski 1995). When causal events subsided, recovery proceeded. In the present spasm, however, the cause is one of nature's species, *Homo sapiens* (Soulé 1996). Some scientists speculate that our activities may result in our own elimination, and if that happens, perhaps recovery for surviving species from the present human-induced spasm will not be that different from previous recoveries.

Alternatively, humans have been called the ultimate weed species, and we may endure for quite some time (Quammen 1998). We have shown an incredible ability to invade, change, and inhabit every habitat type on Earth. Simply the sheer number of humans has overwhelmed our cospecies, and technology has heightened our capabilities. The species that survive are those adapted to the changes we make on land, sea, and in the air. Because evolution and recovery from an extinction spasm rely on filling vacant niches, the human species is not just eliminating life, it is greatly reducing the capacity of other species to recover from human onslaught (Soulé 1996).

Foreman (1999, 2004) categorized three causes for this ongoing extinction event in the Americas:

- Human arrival and climate warming
- Arrival of Europeans
- Global economic markets

HUMAN ARRIVAL AND CLIMATE WARMING

Two hundred-fifty million years ago, during the Paleozoic and Mesozoic eras, there was only one continent, Pangaea. The evolutionary play was enacted on one large, warm, and dry stage. The lack of variety in global conditions and the single landmass meant there was relatively little biological diversity until continental plates began to separate about 180 million years ago (Crosby 1986). Moving continents altered ocean currents and global wind patterns. As the plates separated and collided, mountain ranges pushed skyward and giant trenches formed in the ocean floor. The combination of these events created local and global climatic changes.

After an asteroid ended the Cretaceous period of the Mesozoic era, about 65 million years ago, mammals replaced reptiles as the dominant terrestrial organisms. During this time frame, the continents seemed to be separated by as much distance as at any time in history, and on the isolated fragments of Pangaea, species diversified rapidly and extensively (Crosby 1986). Land bridges allowed occasional faunal interchange between continents, but for the most part, life-forms evolved differently on their respective landmasses (Crosby 1986).

About 18,000 years ago, almost 48 percent of North America was locked in ice (McDonald 1984). The Bering land bridge connected Asia to an ice-free area in present-day Alaska, and the Laurentide and Cordillian ice sheets covered much of present-day Canada. These sheets formed a barrier between the ice-free areas of Beringia, the region of Alaska and the Yukon, and the ice-free areas covering much of the present-day Lower 48 of the United States (Agenbroad 1984; Flannery 2001). People crossed the Bering land bridge to inhabit Beringia, but glaciers blocked any ideas about southward expansion.

When the climate warmed, the glaciers melted, flooding the land bridge and opening a corridor between the Laurentide and Cordillian ice sheets (Agenbroad 1984). That corridor enabled humans to move south of the sheets. Paleo-Indians rapidly spread through the Americas (P. S. Martin 1984; Flores 1996; Ward 1997; P. S. Martin and Burney 1999). Within a short time after humans arrived, approximately 13,000 years BP, and the climate warmed, the continent lost 75 percent of its species weighing more than 45 kg, or roughly 100 lbs. (Ward 1997; Flannery 2001). The general

Rocky Mountain region lost at least twenty-three species of large herbivores, including five species of proboscidians (elephants) and five species of large carnivores (among them short-faced bears [Arctodus simus] and dire wolves, [Canis dirus]) (P. S. Martin and Burney 1999). The affected ecosystems may still be equilibrating from the shock of the extinctions that characterized the latter stage of the Pleistocene era, which ended 10,000 years BP (Flannery 2001).

A great deal of debate surrounds the cause of losing such large numbers of mammal species. Was it due to climate change or the human hand? Was it disease, as some speculate? Although data supporting or rejecting this latter idea would be hard to come by, new animals did arrive and could have easily carried their native microbes. Diamond (1997) proposed that virulent epizootics probably had their origins in the domestication of livestock and the development of agricultural economies; however, those developments did not occur until several thousand years after the Pleistocene extinction began. At present, evidence leans toward climate change and/or human predation as the causes of Pleistocene megafauna extinctions in North America (P. S. Martin and Klein 1984).

The evidence backing both theories largely shows one factor correlating with the other, but it does not indicate whether the correlation is by chance or due to a causal relationship. The two factors, climate and human predation, probably did not act in isolation. It seems likely that humans were a causative factor in the megafaunal extinctions. As we look at more recent extinctions, like the moas of New Zealand or the fauna of the Pacific Islands and Madagascar, the data indicate that the arrival of humans heralded the destruction of natural residents (A. Anderson 1984; Cassels 1984; Olson and James 1984; Trotter and McCulloch 1984; Ward 1987; Flannery 1996, 2001; P. S. Marten and Burney 1999).

The Pleistocene extinctions are blurred because a warming climatic event coincided with the arrival of humans in North America. Graham and Lundelius (1984) and Graham, Lundelius, Graham, et al. (1996) proposed that as North America warmed, the habitat became more homogenous. Species that overlapped because they could occupy different niches in the patchy habitats of a single area now began to compete, and some displaced others. Herbivorous pressures on a more homogenous plant environment could have caused an increase in toxic defenses by those plants. Thus, some herbivores were possibly poisoned out of existence (Graham and Lundelius 1984). While those authors attributed the changes in the mammal community to direct effects of climate, they also added that other factors such as habitat reorganization, biological interactions, and stochastic events may have played a role (Graham, Lundelius, Graham, et al. 1996).

Yet, enormous climatic turbulence marked the 2 million years of the Pleistocene, with at least twenty-seven episodes of rising and falling temperatures and seventeen ice ages and recoveries at roughly 100,000-year intervals (Ward 1997; Flannery 2001). None of these changes produced a mass extinction of the megafauna in North America like the one 10,000 years ago (Flannery 2001). And, the speed of climate change at the end of the Pleistocene was the same as the change during the glacial event 125,000 years earlier. In Africa, climate changed at the end of the Pleistocene, yet only about 15 percent of the megafauna on that continent was lost. In North America, however, where climate changed and humans entered concurrently, 75 percent of the megafauna vanished (P. S. Martin 1984; Flannery 2001).

By the time the large mammals disappeared, the climate had been warming for 5,000 years or so. Ice-free land increased by 78 percent with the retreat of the glaciers, plant photosynthesis was increasing, and migration corridors opened (McDonald 1984). Ecologically, these relaxing conditions (from the maximum ice of 18,000 years ago) should have enhanced the survival of large herbivores, and indeed, important diet items such as forbs, grasses, and broad-leafed plants were available in larger quantities (McDonald 1984).

The first people to travel southward through the ice-free corridor, the Clovis people, were extremely skilled hunters (P. S. Martin 1984; Flores 1996; Ward 1997; P. S. Martin and Burney 1999; Flannery 2001). From our sedentary and gadget-filled lifestyle, we are quick to label earlier cultures as primitive, particularly cultures that did not use metal. Yet, most of us could not survive for a day if we were transported back in time to the Pleistocene. We forget that obsidian, so elegantly crafted into spear and arrowhead points by one group of Paleo-Indians, the Clovis people, is being rediscovered for surgery because of its cutting edge, or that the basic design of canoes and kayaks has not been improved over several thousand years. Clovis points were not only artistic achievements, but were highly functional as well. And the people who made the points were very adept at using them.

Furthermore, many of the large mammals Paleo-Indians found were not like the large mammals of Africa that had evolved for several million years with hominids. Human development during the last 100,000 years is critical to this idea, because that is the time period during which humans made the "great leap forward" (Diamond 1997). Changes in brain size and skeletal structure along with advanced communication ability, about 50,000 years ago, converted humans into one of the most dangerous and effective predators in the world (Crosby 1986; Diamond 1997; Flannery 1996, 2001). Because mammoths entered North America 1.7 million years ago (Agenbroad 1984; King and Saunders 1984), they had never been confronted with this new and efficient predator.

What made megafauna vulnerable to human hunters? Predator avoidance behavior typically has a genetic and learned base. The level of each varies from species to species, but in combination, genes and learning decipher what is dangerous, when it is dangerous, and how it should be avoided. For example, fleeing an animal that is not capable of, or interested in, killing you only wastes valuable energy. Human hunters were much smaller than any threatening species previously faced by mammoths (Crosby 1986). Indeed, they were the first bipedal predator seen by the megafauna. Not only did mammoths and mastodons probably not recognize humans as a threat, but they had no appropriate evolutionary response to them. A more modern analogy is humans and whales. Two hundred years ago, humans using wind power and hand-thrown harpoons were able to decimate whale populations around the globe; this occurred even though whales were capable of defending themselves by capsizing boats and were being hunted in their vast native environment (Crosby 1986).

A strong piece of correlational data is found on Wrangell Island, an island off southeast Alaska's coast. The mammoths of Wrangell Island were isolated from mainland North American mammoths. About 13,000 years ago, the climate changed and humans crossed from Asia to what is now mainland Alaska; apparently they did not touch Wrangell Island. Eventually mammoths were extirpated from the mainland, but they survived on Wrangell Island until about 4,000 years ago, when humans arrived on the island and extinguished them (Ward 1997; Flannery 2001). Similarly, ground sloths, large rodents, and large birds survived the climate change on Cuba, but went extinct when humans peopled the island 6,000 years ago (Flannery 2001).

Some of the best evidence for human hunters ending the reign of North American megafauna comes from Dan Fischer, who analyzed mammoth tusks using a technique developed to assess nutritional and reproductive status in elephants (Ward 1997; Flannery 2001). If the climate change theory was correct, mammoths would have died in poor nutritional condition with low reproductive rates. However, all the mammoth tusks he analyzed showed that the carriers of those tusks were living in a healthy nutritional state. They also showed a high reproductive rate, indicative of a population facing heavy predation. Indeed, the reproductive rates Fischer estimated for mammoths paralleled reproductive rates of modern elephants that are heavily poached (Ward 1997).

Predation may have been the major factor in the decline of the mammoths, much as predation has driven snowshoe hare (Lepus americanus) cycles (Krebs, Boonstra, et al. 2001). In their study of hares, 95 percent of all mortality came via predators, and the mortality rate was unaffected when the hares were provided with supplemental feed. According to McDonald (1984), grasses and forbs should have been available to the grazing mammoths in larger quantities during the time of their decline. Thus it seems likely that mammoths would have gone extinct in the face of human hunters with or without climate change.

Yet, there are also ways climate could have played a role in the extinction of other species. Despite increasing productivity as the ice melted, the composition of plant species changed. Thus herbivores relying on a particular plant for food may have seen the supply decrease, even as total plant biomass increased with the receding glaciers. In those cases, the predation-sensitive hypothesis proposed by Sinclair and Arcese (1995) explains how vegetation changes and predation can interact to cause mortality. Unlike the example of snowshoe hares, where predation drove the system even in the presence of augmented food supplies, Sinclair and Arcese showed that as food supplies decreased, wildebeests (*Connochaetes taurinus*) increased their vulnerability in order to search for food. Thus, while the proximal cause of wildebeest mortality was often predation, the ultimate cause was declining food supplies.

The inexperience of large mammals with humans combined with the skill of Paleo-Indian hunters probably decimated the megaherbivores faster than they could reproduce. With the loss of the biggest megaherbivores, the next smaller size of herbivorous prey may have suffered increased predation pressures (Janzen 1983). That smaller size range of prey still had their traditional predators, but now they were also supporting the suite of larger predators along with the newly arrived Paleo-Indian hunters. As large prey populations crashed, the large carnivores of the Pleistocene most certainly followed.

The megaherbivores likely played an important role in regulating ecosystem functions before humans arrived (Owen-Smith 1989; P. S. Martin and Burney 1999). Habitat changing from patchy to homogeneous has been attributed to climatic shifts, with the homogeneous habitat then causing the loss of smaller species (Graham and Lundelius 1984; Graham, Lundelius, Graham, et al. 1996). Such changes, however, could also be due to the loss of giant mammals (Owen-Smith 1989).

If the Pleistocene megafauna behaved like modern elephants (and the genus *Mammuthus* is closely related to the genus *Elephas* [Ward 1997]), the ancient proboscideans would dig for water and create a matrix of patches by grazing and pushing over shrubs and trees (Owen-Smith 1989). Therefore, when the megafauna disappeared, forage quality may have declined and habitat dwindled for other, smaller species. Reduced patch diversity meant that sedentary animals depending on such habitat became more vulnerable to human predation, interspecific competition, and stochastic events

(Owen-Smith 1989). Following the loss of such large keystone species, there was undoubtedly a wave of secondary extinctions (Owen-Smith 1989; P. S. Martin and Burney 1999). Vegetation changes also may have occurred when large herbivores ceased to disperse plant seeds, as Flannery (1996) proposed for the Australian flora of 50,000 years ago.

If some combination of climate change, human hunting, and other environmental stresses facilitated extinctions of megafauna in North America at the end of the Pleistocene, there are important lessons that we moderns can learn (E. Anderson 1984). Today's humans not only still eliminate species, but our bulging population and sophisticated technology mean that we are doing so at ever-increasing rates (E. O. Wilson 2002). And, humans are now manufacturing another climate change. The International Panel on Climate Change estimates that during the next century, global temperatures will increase 2 to 6 degrees Celsius (roughly 4 to 11 degrees Fahrenheit), significantly altering ecosystems (Raven 2001; E. O. Wilson 2002).

Why did some megafaunal species survive the human invasion and climate change? The half-dozen surviving ungulates in North America tended to migrate over large areas or move seasonally to higher and lower elevations (Owen-Smith 1989). Migrating animals make use of food over a wider area, and if predators are unable to easily follow such prey, the animals are only vulnerable for part of the year. Thus, predators (including human predators) have less impact on such prey (Fryxell, Greever, and Sinclair 1988).

In addition, most of the large mammals that now define the Great Plains were of recent Eurasian origin and became dominant following the extinction of the megafauna (Kurtén 1971 in Crosby 1986; Flores 1996). Indeed, some surviving species entered the continent at the same time or even slightly after Paleo-Indians (Flannery 2001).

Loss of megafauna along with vegetation changes allowed new species to achieve dominant evolutionary roles. The keystone role of the megaherbivores that existed during the Pleistocene in North America likely passed to the remaining carnivores in the Holocene (11,700 years BP to present). Wolves (*Canis lupus*) were one of the carnivores that inherited that dominant and keystone role in the Southern Rocky Mountain region, and ecological processes adjusted accordingly.

Following the loss of megafauna in North America, the Clovis culture disappeared, possibly because it was too specialized to survive without these large animals (Flores 1996). The people of the Great Plains had to adapt to the new situation that offered less accessible resources and more stringent ecological conditions. After benefiting from seemingly boundless natural resources during the late Pleistocene, people were forced to live within the different ecological conditions of the Holocene. In the north, there was a succession of nomadic groups specializing in hunting bison (Flores 1996). Bison (*Bison bison*) of the Great Plains lived in large nomadic herds, and thus could sustain hunting pressure—particularly before the horse reentered North America. What is now the southwestern United States suffered a 2,000-year drought that began about 9,000 years ago and eliminated about 50 percent of the plant diversity (Flores 1996). Humans largely abandoned the area during this drought, underscoring the fragility of the drought-driven plains of this region. Many people moved into the mountains of the Southern Rockies (Elias 2002). When humans later recolonized the area, they consciously kept their numbers small and their economies diverse. Similar to the Maori of New Zealand after they hunted the moa to extinction, the people of the southern plains became generalist hunters and gatherers who spread their impact across a wide range of resources (Flores 1996).

In contrast, urbanized and agricultural peoples such as the Ancestral Puebloans (sometimes called Anasazi), Hohokum, Cahokia Moundbuilders, Toltecs, and Aztecs began to rely more heavily upon cultivation. Cultivation began to dominate the Ancestral Puebloan lifestyle about 2,500 years ago (Elias 2002). Blessed by a friendly climate, their population grew to its highest level about AD 1000 (Elias 2002). From 1150 to about 1450, what is now the southwestern United States was rocked by severe droughts that coincided with the Medieval Warm Period in Europe (Elias 2002). As a result, the Ancestral Puebloan population, bolstered by the good times, may now have been too numerous for the food supply to support (see also Wright 2005; Diamond 2005). In combination with the drought affecting agriculture, the Utes arrived in the area around 1200, and their presence may have helped to displace the Ancestral Puebloans (Anonymous n.d.). At any rate, the Ancestral Puebloans abandoned their towns (Elias 2002).

From the end of the Pleistocene until 500 years ago, the humans of North America lived in varied ways with untold numbers of cultures and languages. The subsequent conquest of those cultures by Europeans, and attempts to erase them, was a horrific act (Wright 1992). Urban and agricultural cultures in North America produced civilizations rivaling or exceeding those in Europe in astronomy, mathematics, and architecture. But they also faced many of the same problems that city-states around the world faced as they grew and sought to extend their influence into neighboring areas (Wright 2005).

Over the last 10,000 years, nomadic cultures were in far better balance with their new environment than urban and agricultural cultures. Although Kay (1994, 1995, 2007) and Martin and Szuter (1999, 2002) contend that predation by humans limited the distribution of some ungulates throughout the Intermountain West before the arrival of Europeans, on the whole there were no more major extinctions until Europeans entered the continent. Until then, wolves, grizzlies, and bison thrived.

ARRIVAL OF EUROPEANS

The arrival of Europeans to North America in 1500 brought on the second phase of the current extinction spasm (Foreman 1999). This phase was characterized by the introduction of new technologies that intensified hunting and agricultural pressures. In general, the level of technology rendered European invaders another new predator. In addition, their agricultural technology made it far easier and faster for them to destroy and change habitats. Europeans also introduced a market economy based on cash and commodities. Because that market traded in animal parts, it fueled extinction. In short, European colonial expansion played a pervasive and fundamental role in creating conditions leading to the modern biodiversity crisis (Crosby 1986; Burger 1987; Bodley 1990; Isbister 1993; Middleton, O'Keefe, and Moyo 1993).

Although European expansion over the last 500 years most directly affected the present situation, the phenomena of imperialism has been unrestricted to culture, time, or location in our world. Throughout human history, the processes of conquest and expansion have changed societies and the environment to various degrees, so it would be naive to think of the concept as uniquely European. Indeed, the expansion of humans has had dramatic effects every time they enter a region that is new to them (Flannery 1996, 2001; Ward 1997).

That said, the budding industrial nations of Europe were a global force 500 years ago. They required access to raw materials and markets. They often secured that access by military conquest, but also conquered by dominating trade routes, both intentionally

and inadvertently through introduced diseases, and purposefully transforming religious practices (Baran 1957; Magdoff 1969; Crosby 1986; Burger 1987; Lewis 1988; Nash 1989; Bodley 1990; Isbister 1993). Such practices destroyed many cultural links indigenous peoples had to nature that had evolved over the previous 10,000 years. Once such restructuring occurred, people who formerly lived in a more or less self-sustaining fashion often fell into poverty as measured by a European-based market economy. A market economy, combined with poverty, is a powerful force that can, and did, override indigenous taboos against exploitation of natural resources.

The loss of Pleistocene keystone species due to climate changes and human predation undoubtedly contributed to waves of secondary extinctions (Owen-Smith 1989; P. S. Martin and Burney 1999). The second invasion of Europeans did the same. Essentially, European weaponry and horses made them a new predator. Guns and mounts also made Native Americans more efficient hunters before their numbers were reduced (Flores 1996). The animal species that survived the first invasion now faced new threats.

By the 1840s, the beaver (*Castor canadensis*) nearly went extinct because of overharvesting by trappers. Before this commercially driven onslaught, beavers numbered 60 million (Forman 2000). With extirpation of the beaver, wetlands dried, stream dynamics changed, and flooding increased (Foreman 2004). There is no way to know the impact of these habitat changes on species associated with systems driven by beavers, because no baseline data for comparisons exist.

By 1900, three of the five remaining species of large carnivores were functionally extinct in the western United States and northern Mexico—the wolf, jaguar (*Panthera onca*), and grizzly bear (*Ursus arctos*). Only pumas and black bears (*Ursus americanus*) survived. Bison, another keystone species, once numbered more than 30 million individuals, but by the 1880s they were reduced to only a few hundred (Licht 1997).

By the early twentieth century, ungulates were so few in number that government agencies began imposing legal hunting restrictions (US Fish and Wildlife Service 1987b). Such restrictions may have been a pattern throughout human history. It is likely that taboos against exploiting a resource probably came into effect in most cultures after the resource went into a steep decline and humans realized its vulnerability.

The people inhabiting the Great Plains, who had been living with the same floral and faunal structure for the previous 10,000 years, were nearly exterminated and were forced to reside on smaller and smaller sections of land the government designated for them. The 1887 Dawes Act alone transferred 10.4 million hectares (about 25.7 million acres) of reservation land to corporate and private owners (Foreman 2004). Black Elk, a famous medicine man of the Oglala Lakota (Sioux), put it succinctly when he said,

Once we were happy in our own country and we were seldom hungry, for the two-leggeds and the four-leggeds lived together like relatives, and there was plenty for them and for us. But the whites came, and they made little islands for us and other little islands for the four-leggeds and always these islands are becoming smaller. (Neihardt 1972, 7–8)

Reducing and confining the Native American population and virtually eliminating grizzly bears, wolves, and bison opened the West to the introduction of Eurasian cattle (*Bos taurus*). Eliminating native peoples and bison—and the subsequent introduction of exotic cattle—was not serendipitous. When a bill to limit bison hunting was introduced to the Texas legislature in 1877, US General Phil Sheridan went to Austin, Texas, to

oppose it for military reasons (Cook 1989). According to Cook, Sheridan said:

These men [bison hunters] have done in the last two years and will do more in the next year, to settle the vexed Indian question, than the entire regular army has done in the last thirty years. They are destroying the Indian's commissary; and it is a well-known fact that an army losing its base of supplies is placed at great disadvantage...for the sake of a lasting peace, let them kill, skin, and sell until the buffaloes are exterminated. Then your prairies can be covered by speckled cattle, and the festive cowboy, who follows the hunter as a second forerunner of an advanced civilization. (1989, 113)

The West was forever changed. The plains were resilient to grazing and had been home to millions of herbivores wandering in large herds since the spread of the Pliocene (5.3 to 1.8 million years BP) grasslands. But Europeans replaced bison with cattle and sheep, domesticated stock that had evolved in the wetter climate of Europe, at an unsustainable level; they intensified the effect of these animals by fencing them into parcels of land, forcing them to graze the same areas.

Thus, overgrazing, particularly in the late 1800s, became a serious threat to ecological health and biodiversity throughout the West (Vale 1975; US General Accounting Office 1988). Overgrazing has helped exotic plants invade, altered grass composition, degraded riparian habitat, and reduced forage quality and quantity (Vale 1975; US General Accounting Office 1988; Flores 1996).

With the extension of agriculture to the Great Plains and areas farther west, ranchers began to persecute wolves, coyotes (*Canis latrans*), and prairie dogs (*Cynomys* spp.) to facilitate livestock management. By 1915, the federal government began to financially subsidize and organize predator eradication campaigns (Bishop and Culbertson 1976). Despite the warnings of leading naturalists such as Ernest Thompson Seton, Victor Shelford, S. Charles Kendeigh, and Aldo Leopold during the early part of the twentieth century, these programs grew and, in modified form, continue today. Soon, the government and its agents poisoned or trapped on millions of acres each year—with taxpayer money. By 1929, these efforts were significant enough to require the formation of the Division of Predatory Animal and Rodent Control (DiSilvestro 1985). This new division was part of the US Biological Survey (precursor to the US Fish and Wildlife Service, which, since 1973, has been mandated to restore wolves and other endangered species).

The sheer quantity of cattle, combined with practices such as fencing and persecution of carnivores (Bishop and Culbertson 1976; DiSilvestro 1985; McIntyre 1995) and prairie dogs (Marsh 1984; E. Anderson, Forrest, et al. 1986), changed the plant and animal composition of the Southern Rocky Mountains and has left the black-footed ferret (*Mustela nigripes*) dangerously close to extinction (Miller et al. 1996). Overstocking cattle also produced the grazing collapse of the 1880s–1890s, which ruined a large number of ranchers and created many of the arroyos that we see today (Flores 1996). Later, the Dust Bowl of the 1930s again devastated homesteaders. The erosion of that period continued the "degrassing" of the prairie (Flores 1996). Perhaps more alarming yet, the critically important Ogallala Aquifer is being used at an unsustainable rate. If this trend is not reversed, the aquifer may run dry (Flores 1996).

At higher elevations, the 1872 Mining Law and 1873's Timber Culture Act encouraged extraction and altered the face of the mountains (Foreman 2004). Contamination from mines (cyanide, mercury, etc.) eliminated freshwater flora and fauna, and stream dredging and slag heaps altered habitat. Today, according to Shinneman, McClelan, and Smith (2000), more than 9,000 abandoned mines in Colorado continue to contaminate the land. Additional pressures on the environment occurred as professional hunters harvested wildlife to feed the miners, causing a large impact, as several mining towns temporarily rivaled Denver in size (chap. 5).

In addition, the federal government granted nearly a quarter of a million acres to railroad companies so that rails could connect the Pacific and Atlantic oceans (Foreman 2004). Subsequently, wildlife was killed to feed the rail crews (Crosby 1986). When completed, the railways carried goods to the east and west, and hunters sent tons of meat, hides, bones, and feathers to both coasts. In fact, the industry centered on selling bison bones continued a full decade after the extirpation of bison (Flannery 2001). While many species had been declining throughout the 1800s, the effects of the railroad may have been their coup de grâce.

The European settlement of North America eliminated key species that survived the collapse of 10,000 years ago. Both the Paleo-Indians and the western Europeans came to the New World from Eurasia (albeit from different directions), and both arrived in a short time span (within 13,000 years). Both groups took resources that they found initially easy to harvest, but following the loss of the megafauna, many of the first peoples developed a way of life within the carrying capacity of the remaining flora and fauna. Similarly, though some current laws protect game animals and some threatened species that survived European settlement, some elements of the present population have not comprehended that an economic ideology of constant growth, consumption, and mass production is at the expense of our natural heritage.

GLOBAL ECONOMIC MARKETS REVIVE PANGAEA

Global economic markets, a one-world concept, re-create the era of a single continent. Establishing such markets has been a particularly strong component of US economic policy (Isbister 1993; Korten 1995). Market pressures force competing firms to reduce costs, often by trying to get society as a whole to pay for as many of their costs as possible, creating what economists refer to as "externalities." Ludwig, Hilborn, and Walters (1993) documented how the market economy has produced and rewarded unsustainable practices in fisheries, forestry, and agriculture. The "discount rate," or the value of having money today rather than in the future, is generally about 10 percent a year and makes it economically more advantageous to overharvest slow-reproducing resources in the short-term rather than harvest them sustainably so that some of those resources can be used in the future (see Caughley and Sinclair 1994 for detail). In short, markets can determine whether something is profitable, but not whether it is sustainable—which is particularly useful to companies that are only interested in maximizing profits (Middleton, O'Keefe, and Moyo 1993).

Agribusiness has been seen as an attempt to achieve modernity in many poorer countries (Sonnefeld 1992). The development of international agribusiness has affected the Southern Rocky Mountain region, where the economy was once based in agriculture, particularly livestock, but is now dominated by the service industry (see chap. 5). Livestock production on the arid lands of this region has not been able to compete effectively with that of richer agricultural land in other parts of the globe where livestock are raised for export.

Much of the livestock in the Southern Rockies rely on public lands at least part of the year (see chap. 5). Yet, less than 5 percent of the livestock consumed in the United States is produced on western public lands (US General Accounting Office 1988). Increased competition from livestock producers around the globe may reduce that percentage further. Indeed, the proportion of Colorado's gross state economic product contributed by farming and ranching has steadily declined since at least the early 1970s. In analyzing statistics from the US Department of Commerce (2008), the contribution by farming and ranching fell from 3.1 percent of the Colorado economy in 1969 to 1.1 percent in 2006, and that decline has been regular and steady. This has produced a new threat to wildlife of the region, particularly on privately owned ranches and farms whose acreage has been sold off for housing developments. When agriculture falters economically, developers offer landowners a lucrative alternative. The resulting exurban housing developments come with fences, pets, roads, and demands for water, sewers, and electricity, all of which adversely affect the landscape for most other species living there.

At present, the most significant opposition to wolf reintroduction into the Southern Rockies Ecoregion comes from the livestock industry (see chap. 6). Wolves are seen as another threat to the ranching way of life. As a federally protected species, the wolf is a pawn in the struggle of states' rights against the federal government (chap. 6). Wolves have become a scapegoat for the ranching industry, which has been steadily declining, even when wolves were not present. We propose that private landholders may be able to increase their chances of solvency by exploring creative options for cooperation with wildlife restoration.

CONCLUSIONS

We all understand history in a given time frame, largely gleaned from our personal experiences (chap. 6). But to really understand the processes that exist in the present, we advocate that it is necessary to consider what North America looked like before humans arrived. The impact of people cannot be separated from ecological history in the Southern Rocky Mountains.

On our present path, the global economic market is reuniting the fragments of Pangaea and setting the stage for evolution. The play will be written and directed by one actor, *Homo sapiens*. The only other species to survive will be those that somehow escape our technological prowess and cultural whims. But that path is not the only option.

Much can be gleaned from the performance thus far—namely, how the confluence of climatic events and the human footprint upon the landscape has and will continue to alter the abundance, diversity, and distribution of flora and fauna (Wright 2005; Diamond 2005). With that knowledge, goals can be based on answers to the question "Where can we go from here?" What can we do to restore wildlands to a state where they are "self-willed," where ecological and evolutionary processes—not the economic policies of humans—dictate their direction and pace? What philosophies, attitudes, and beliefs do we need to change? Investigating the possibility of restoring wolves to the Southern Rocky Mountains is one step in determining where we can go.

The ecological drama unfolding on the stage of the North American landscape undoubtedly has many more acts yet to be performed. We have the opportunity to make decisions that will affect future generations. We can integrate the wisdom of our biological and ecological understanding of the world into management policies and lifestyle choices, or we can choose to ignore that wisdom and proceed as if the dominion of *Homo sapiens* will last forever.

Chapter 2

Extermination and Recovery of the Red Wolf and Gray Wolf in the Conterminous United States

Michael K. Phillips and Brian Miller

As recently as 150 years ago, the gray wolf (*Canis lupus*) lived throughout most of the conterminous United States, except for the Gulf Coast region east of Texas, where the red wolf (*Canis rufus*) occurred (Young and Goldman 1944; Nowak 1983) (figure 2.1). This wide distribution is especially noteworthy because conflict with agrarian interests resulted in government-supported wolf eradication campaigns as early as 1630, in the Massachusetts Bay Colony (Young and Goldman 1944; McIntyre 1995). Over the next three centuries, eradication campaigns were extended throughout the conterminous United States, resulting in the near extermination of both species there. In recent decades, there has been considerable effort to recover the red and gray wolf. Wolves are now more widely distributed than at any time since probably the 1920s. This chapter summarizes extermination and recovery efforts for wolf species in the conterminous United States.

EXTERMINATION OF THE RED WOLF AND GRAY WOLF

Historically, wolves were the most widely distributed large mammals in North America (figure 2.1). The species was likely represented by several hundred thousand individuals that occurred wherever large ungulates were found. Tolerant of environmental extremes, wolves inhabited areas from latitude 15° north in central Mexico to the Arctic (Hall 1981; Nowak 1995).

For about 13,000 years, the first peoples arriving on the North American continent lived with wolves as part of the landscape. Wolves were hunted, but Native Americans also imitated the wolf's style of hunting and viewed the species as a role model (Lopez 1978). The relationship between people in North America and wolves changed drastically when Europeans arrived 500 years ago with their culture, customs, and religion (Lopez 1978; McIntyre 1995). They came with attitudes about nature that were largely negative, dominating, and utilitarian (Kellert 1993). Thus, to understand the wolf's extermination in North America, it is important to understand the European history of attitudes toward the species (McIntyre 1995; see also chap. 1).

Religion played an integral role in the relationship between Europeans and wild places and wild things. Medieval religion held that wilderness was useless land inhabited by evil, whereas agricultural landscapes were godly, orderly, and subdued beneath human control (Primack 1998). By the fifth century AD, the Roman Catholic Church had adopted the view that the wolf was a dangerous predator, a symbol of religious heresy, and "deceitful and lascivious" (i.e., lustful) (Boitani 1995, 8). This view persisted for more than a thousand years and spawned the first version of "Little Red Riding Hood" in 1600. Boitani (1995, 8) writes, "This fable is a perfect example of a culture detaching itself from the biological reality of an animal in order to construct an image for its own use."

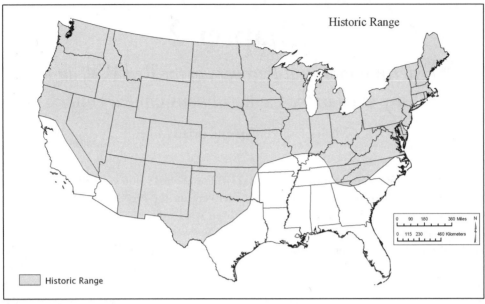

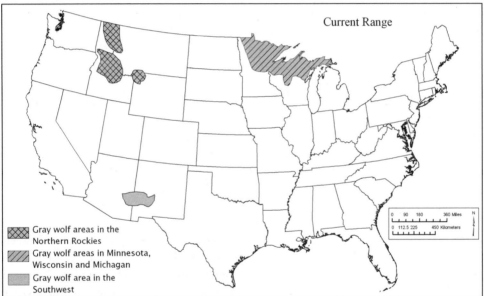

Figure 2.1—Historic and current ranges of the gray wolf (Canis lupus).
Source: US Fish and Wildlife Service

In central Europe, around AD 800, Charlemagne authorized and formed a special wolf hunting corps (Boitani 1995). Any member who killed a wolf had a legal right to collect money from all people living within two leagues (8 to 15 km or 5 to 9 mi.) of the spot where the wolf was captured and killed. In Sweden, killing predators was a public obligation after about 1350, and in 1442 all Swedish farmers were required by law to place and maintain wolf nets (Gilbert 1995). The last wolf disappeared from England during the early 1500s, although Celts had been hunting wolves intensively for the previous 1,800 years. Early kings of England allowed criminals to pay their fines in wolf heads or scalps if they were low on money. One Scottish king, James VI (1566–1625), declared that all men would join the organized wolf hunts (Boitani 1995). Age was not an issue in this decree, and young and old alike were mandated to participate. Wolves were eliminated in Scotland by 1684 and in Ireland by 1770.

With this history, colonists came to the New World. Don Juan de Oñate brought 7,000 head of livestock into what is now New Mexico in 1599, when he was searching for a channel linking the Atlantic and Pacific oceans (Dary 1974). The English brought livestock in 1609, two years after settling in Jamestown, Virginia. Livestock husbandry in both the West and East was lax, and domestic animals ranged freely (McIntyre 1995). Conflict between agrarian colonists and wolves thus began, and by 1630 the settlers in the Massachusetts Bay Colony proclaimed the first bounty (Matthiasson 1987; McIntyre 1995). McIntyre writes:

> Beginning in 1630, just 10 years after landing in the New World, the settlers in the Massachusetts Bay Colony passed a series of laws offering a cash reward to any resident who killed a wolf. The money to pay for those bounties initially came from assessments placed on livestock owners: one penny for every "beast (cow) and horse" and a half cent for each "swine and goat." In later laws, the colony paid bounties, as high as 40 shillings per wolf, directly out of the public treasury. A 1638 law fixed the minimum wage for a laborer at 18 cents per day, so 40 shillings (one shilling equaled 12 cents) was equivalent to 27 days of a laborer's wages. Such high prices tempted many to seek out and kill wolves. (1995, 29)

A utilitarian view of nature, religious philosophy, and livestock production all influenced the destruction of wolves and many other species of wildlife. For example,

in 1638, King Charles I of England decreed that hats *had* to be manufactured from beaver (*Castor canadensis*), and by the early 1800s that species had disappeared from the eastern United States (Matthiasson 1987). The last bison (*Bison bison*) east of the Appalachian Mountains was killed in 1801 and the last one east of the Mississippi in 1825 (Matthiasson 1987). The last elk (*Cervus elaphus*) east of the Mississippi disappeared in 1867 (Matthiasson 1987). Eastern ungulates were soon reduced to one species, the white-tailed deer (*Odocoileus virginianus*), which could thrive on the edge of human civilization. The eastern United States were effectively "tamed" within a century. Afterward, settlers set their sights on the western United States.

Wolf persecution in the West reached a zenith in the late 1800s and early 1900s, a time when the wolf's natural prey of bison, elk, and deer had been greatly reduced due to unregulated exploitation by hunters striving to satisfy demand by East Coast consumers (Schmidt 1978; US Fish and Wildlife Service 1987a). Bison were also killed as part of federal efforts to force Indians to submit to the reservation system (Isenberg 1992; see also quote by General Sheridan, chap. 1, page 20). In response to reduced prey populations, wolves increasingly ate domestic livestock.

Consequently, the US government and private citizens intensified control efforts. Of this time, Barry Lopez (1978, 180) wrote, "The wolf was not the cattleman's only problem—there was weather, disease, rustling, fluctuating beef prices, hazards of trail drives...But the wolf became an object of pathologic hatred."

Some control was affected with religious fervor. In 1900, Benjamin Corbin, "boss wolf hunter" of North Dakota, wrote:

> In the New Testament, the parable of the Good Shepherd shines like a star. If Jesus did not disdain to call himself the

Good Shepherd, why should any man in North Dakota not be proud to be called by that name, or be associated as I am, with the men who are feeding their flocks on the rich and abundant pastures of this great commonwealth? Largely, my life has been spent in protecting these flocks against the incursions of ravenous beasts of prey. I know it is but a step and the first step, which counts in the march of civilization…

That's why I am here. The wolf is the enemy of civilization, and I want to exterminate him. (1900, 4)

Hatred for wolves was fueled by stories of individual wolves that performed great feats of destruction against the settlers' herds. Some of these animals were named, and they achieved celebrity status. The roster included Old Two Toes, Custer Wolf, Rags the Digger, Old Three Toes of the Apishapa, Blanca and her mate Lobo, the King of the Currumpaw (Caras 1966; McIntyre 1995, 144–147, 217–252). The stature of the most famous wolves was heightened because of their purported tendencies to kill large numbers of livestock and their supernatural abilities to avoid capture. For example, naturalist E. T. Seton wrote:

Old Lobo, or the king, as the Mexicans called him, was the gigantic leader of a remarkable pack of gray wolves, that had ravaged the Currumpaw Valley for a number of years…Old Lobo was a giant among wolves, and was cunning and strong in proportion to his size…

Old Lobo's band was but a small one… Several of the band, besides the two leaders, were especially noted. One of these was a beautiful white wolf, that the Mexicans called Blanca; this was supposed to be a female, possibly Lobo's mate…

…There was not a stockman on the Currumpaw who would not readily have given the value of many steers for the scalp of any one of Lobo's band, but they seemed to possess charmed lives, and defied all manner of devices to kill them. They scorned all hunters, derided all poisons, and continued, for at least five years, to exact their tribute from the Currumpaw ranchers to the extent, many said, of a cow each day. According to this estimate, therefore, the band had killed more than two thousand of the finest stock, for, as was only too well-known, they selected the best in every instance. (1898, 1–2)

In 1998, Gipson et al. (1998) evaluated the credibility of early literature about famous wolves. In the course of their research they calculated kill rates for fourteen such wolves and determined that, according to historical accounts, each wolf had an average of 48 kg (about 100 lbs.) of cattle flesh available per day. They considered several possible explanations for the extremely high kill rates that would be required to generate such a bounty and concluded that early authors fabricated information. Such misinformation continues today. Ron Gillett, a former outfitter and hunting guide who tried to start a ballot initiative for the 2008 election that, if passed, would have eliminated all wolves from Idaho, stated:

Once you put wolves into an area, they kill everything that moves. They kill all of the prey first, whether that be squirrels, deer, elk, or mountain sheep. Then they kill other predators, and when they get down to wolves, they are cannibals. (Wilkerson 2007, 48)

Accuracy notwithstanding, stories about famous wolves fueled the country's desire to eradicate the species, and by the early 1900s the livestock industry had become a very effective advocate of the need for more government intervention in wildlife control (i.e., killing). In 1915, Congress began funding a federal wolf control program and assigned the mission of implementing it to the US Biological Survey. The early contributions made to this program by the livestock industry gave them considerable influence over policy (Leopold 1964; Dunlop 1988). Indeed, the Biological Survey's internal reports revealed that the goal of policy was the "absolute extermination" of the wolf, and poisoning was the main method used (McIntyre 1995, 18).

By 1929, this federal program was exterminating wolves and other species so extensively that the Biological Survey formed a new division to coordinate those activities, the Division of Predatory Animal and Rodent Control (DiSilvestro 1985; Dunlop 1988). In 1931, the Animal Damage Control Act authorized trapping, poisoning, and shooting of wildlife on federal or private lands (Dunlop 1988). It also indirectly sanctioned the partnership between this new division and the livestock industry (Bean 1983).

Eradication efforts were carried out everywhere, on private and public land alike. Wolf eradication efforts were even carried out in Yellowstone National Park from 1872, the year of the park's establishment, until the mid-1930s. Records indicate that from 1918 to 1935 government hunters killed 114 wolves in the park (Phillips and Smith 1996, 15).

Various and ingenious methods were used to kill wolves (Mech 1970, 325–333; McIntyre 1995). They were shot, trapped, poisoned, roped from horseback, and dismembered (Gilbert 1995). Puppies were dug from dens and clubbed to death. Steel traps usually had teeth to help hold the animal until the trapper arrived (Gilbert 1995). Some trappers welded nails to the jaws for a better grip on the leg (H. Rangel, former trapper from Mexico, pers. comm.). Strychnine and Compound 1080 were placed in meat and broadcast by horseback and later by airplane (Gilbert 1995). Like trapping, poisoning was

indiscriminate, and the death of nontarget species was considered acceptable.

The "wolfers" (professional wolf killers) were effective and enjoyed widespread support. Even Aldo Leopold took an active part in wolf control early in his career, writing,

> In those days we had never heard of passing up a chance to kill a wolf. In a second we were pumping lead into the pack, but with more excitement than accuracy... When our rifles were empty, the old wolf was down, and a pup was dragging a leg into impassable slide-rocks. (1966, 138)

CONSERVATION OF THE RED WOLF AND THE GRAY WOLF

During the 1930s, concern arose among biologists about the wholesale slaughter of wolves. In the late 1930s and early 1940s, some biologists conducted field studies on the gray wolf (Olson 1938; Murie 1944). These studies sparked significant interest in the ecology and conservation of the wolf. For example, in 1944 Stanley Young and E. A. Goldman wrote, "There still remain, even in the United States, some areas of considerable size in which we feel that both the red and the gray wolf should be allowed to continue their existence without molestation." (1944, 385)

Aldo Leopold (1944) stated that, unless government agencies did something to protect the wolf in at least some areas, the species would disappear from the United States.

Later he articulated an important ecological insight:

> We reached the old wolf in time to watch a fierce green fire dying in her eyes. I realized then and have known ever since that there was something new to me in those eyes—something known only to her and the mountain. I was young then and full of trigger itch. I thought that less wolves would mean more deer,

and that no wolves would mean hunters' paradise. But after seeing the green fire die, I sensed that neither the wolf nor the mountain would agree with such a view. (1966, 138–139)

Despite credible scientific evidence and changing public attitudes toward wildlife control (in general) and wolves (in particular), the policy of extermination continued, probably because the viability of any policy is determined by the momentum of the status quo, access to funding and internal resources, and the preferences of key individuals in the decision-making process (Miller et al. 1996). Consequently, the entrenched policy of wolf control that generated jobs, funding, and power was not to be abandoned simply because of new and contradictory information.

By the 1940s, wolves were essentially absent from the conterminous United States (Young and Goldman 1944; Young 1970; Brown 1983; Nowak 1983). In the early 1950s, government trappers turned efforts to northern Mexico and the few wolves from there that dispersed to the United States. This influx was eliminated by the end of the decade, when wolf numbers were at an all-time low (McIntyre 1995). Then, fewer than 1,000 wolves persisted in the remote regions of the Gulf Coast (red wolves) and the forests of northeastern Minnesota (gray wolves). Additionally, probably fewer than twenty wolves inhabited Isle Royale National Park, a 546 sq. km (210 sq. mi.) island in Lake Superior located about 32 km (20 mi.) from the Minnesota mainland (Stenlund 1955; Mech 1966; Peterson 1977; Fuller et al. 1992; Thiel 1993). In addition to being persecuted by humans, remnant red wolf populations were threatened with extinction because of hybridization with coyotes (*Canis latrans*) (McCarley 1962; Nowak 1972, 1979). By 1980, the red wolf was considered extinct in the wild (McCarley and Carley 1979; US Fish and Wildlife Service 1984).

From the 1950s through the 1970s, studies provided insights into gray wolf ecology (Stenlund 1955; Mech 1966, 1970; Mech and Frenzel 1971; Pimlott 1966, 1967; Peterson 1977; Rabb et al. 1967; Van Ballenberghe 1972) and fostered a growing public desire to conserve the species. Those advocating wolf conservation rather than eradication were pioneers of a new paradigm. Quite simply, advocating for wolf conservation represented a significant change in how Americans viewed themselves in relation to nature. Nothing less than a major shift in public attitude was required before one could imagine wolves persisting in the wildlands of the conterminous United States.

In the conclusion of his seminal book *The Wolf*, L. David Mech wrote:

Once blinded emotionally by such hate, the anti-wolf people fail to see that the wolf has no choice about the way it lives: that it cannot thrive on grass or twigs any more than a man can. To them the wolf pack is a cowardly assemblage of wanton slayers, the animal's howl a bloodcurdling condemnation of all the innocent big game of the country. These people cannot be changed. If the wolf is to survive, the wolf haters must be outnumbered. They must be out-shouted, out-financed, and out-voted. Their narrow and biased attitude must be outweighed by an attitude based on an understanding of natural processes. Finally their hate must be outdone by a love for the whole of nature, for the unspoiled wilderness, and for the wolf as a beautiful, interesting, and integral part of both. (1970, 348)

EFFORTS TO RECOVER THE RED WOLF AND GRAY WOLF

By the early 1970s, the environmental movement was real and had significant momentum. The Endangered Species Act (ESA) of

1973 (Public Law No. 93–205, as amended) provided significant protection for the wolf. In response, nongovernmental conservation organizations such as the National Wildlife Federation and Defenders of Wildlife launched efforts to recover wolves. Such efforts were opposed by agribusiness, led by the American Farm Bureau, stockgrower associations, and their state affiliates.

Shortly after passage, the US Department of the Interior's US Fish and Wildlife Service, charged with administering the ESA, initiated efforts to recover wolves. The first list of endangered species included the red wolf, eastern timber wolf (*C. l. lycaon*), and the northern Rocky Mountain wolf (*C. l. irremotus*) (US Fish and Wildlife Service 1974). In April 1976, the Mexican wolf (*C. l. baileyi*) was listed as endangered (*Federal Register* 41, 17740), and in June of that year, the Texas wolf (*C. l. monstrabilis*) was listed as endangered (*Federal Register* 41, 24064). At this time, the red wolf was probably extinct in the wild, and gray wolves were only represented by a remnant population in northeastern Minnesota and a few animals on Isle Royale National Park.

Because listing several subspecies created myriad problems, and because the trend among taxonomists was to recognize fewer subspecies of wolves, in 1978 the US Fish and Wildlife Service combined the subspecific listings for the gray wolf and reclassified it at the species level (i.e., *Canis lupus*) as endangered throughout the conterminous United States and Mexico, except for Minnesota, where the gray wolf was reclassified to threatened (Nowak 1978). As the service finalized this reclassification, some voiced concern that eliminating subspecific differentiation could jeopardize efforts to locate and maintain subspecific stocks. In response, the service indicated that efforts would continue to recognize valid subspecies for purposes of research and conservation (Nowak 1978). Shortly after the listing action was completed, the service formed recovery teams charged with developing and implementing plans for recovering wolves. The red wolf has a recovery plan, and the gray wolf has three plans that cover three separate geographic areas: the Great Lakes, the Northern Rockies, and the southwestern United States. There is no recovery goal for wolf numbers throughout the entire Lower 48.

Recovery planning and implementation are critically important components of the ESA. Unlike some of the act's other provisions, recovery planning and implementation are intended to promote increases in the populations of listed species, rather than simply limiting further declines. Section 4(f) of the ESA clearly indicates that the objective of recovery plans is to identify and catalyze activities necessary to restore listed species to a point where they are secure, self-sustaining components of their ecosystem and, thus, to allow delisting (US Fish and Wildlife Service 1996a; see chap. 7). The courts have determined that development and implementation of recovery plans are mandatory under the ESA, unless the secretary of the interior determines that such plans would not promote conservation of the species (see chap. 7).

THE RED WOLF

By the time the ESA was passed and a red wolf recovery program launched in 1984, the species was nearly extinct in the wild. Consequently, recovery had to rely on captive breeding and reintroductions. In 1973, a federally supported captive-breeding program was established at the Point Defiance Zoological Gardens in Tacoma, Washington. By November 2001, the founding stock of 14 wolves had spawned a captive population that included 160 animals maintained at 32 facilities. Management of captive breeding is guided by a Species Survival Plan (SSP) initiated in 1984 and implemented by the Association of Zoos and Aquariums.

The origins of the red wolf are enigmatic and have been debated since persistence of the species became a conservation concern nearly forty years ago. Some authorities have considered the red wolf to be a full species (Nowak 1992), while others have considered that it might be a subspecies of the gray wolf (Lawrence and Bossert 1967; Phillips and Henry 1992) or a hybrid resulting from interbreedings of gray wolves and coyotes (Mech 1970; Wayne and Jenks 1991; Roy et al. 1996). The debate harmed the red wolf recovery program and served as rationale for the American Sheep Industry to petition the secretary of the interior to remove the red wolf from the list of endangered and threatened species (Gittleman and Pimm 1991). The service denied the petition (Henry 1997).

Recent genetics work suggests that the red wolf and eastern timber wolf share a close taxonomic relationship and both evolved in North America, sharing a common lineage with the coyote until 150,000 to 300,000 years ago (Wilson et al. 2000). The service continues to recognize the red wolf as a valid species distinct from the gray wolf and coyote. However, based on historical taxonomic classifications, Wilson et al. (2000) contend that the red wolf and the eastern timber wolf require the classification *Canis lycaon*.

A red wolf recovery plan was finalized in 1984 (US Fish and Wildlife Service 1984), but it did not present criteria for removing the species from the list of endangered and threatened species (i.e., delisting). The plan did establish the foundation for reintroducing up to fifteen wolves for five consecutive years to the Alligator River National Wildlife Refuge in northeastern North Carolina (US Fish and Wildlife Service 1984). The released wolves and their offspring were to be designated as members of an experimental-nonessential population per Section 10(j) of the ESA (Parker et al. 1986; see chap. 7). The designation allows the service to relax the restrictions of the act to facilitate wolf management (Parker and Phillips 1991).

The Alligator River National Wildlife Refuge reintroduction is notable for several reasons, including being the first attempt ever to restore an extinct-in-the-wild carnivore species. From 1987 through 2001, eighty-three red wolves were released on thirty-eight occasions. These animals gave birth to at least 214 pups in the wild. By December 2001, the population included approximately 100 red wolves distributed in 20 packs across a 6,912 sq. km (2,668 sq. mi.) recovery area that was 60 percent private land and 40 percent public land, mostly comprised of three national wildlife refuges (Bud Fazio, red wolf recovery coordinator, pers. comm.). By 2008, the numbers of individuals and packs remained approximately the same; recovery requires 550 wolves with at least 220 in the wild (US Fish and Wildlife Service 2009a).

In 1989, a revised red wolf recovery plan called for additional reintroduction projects and indicated that for the foreseeable future it would not be feasible to down-list (change species' classification from endangered to threatened) or delist (remove species from the list of threatened and endangered species) the red wolf (US Fish and Wildlife Service 1989). In 1991, a second reintroduction project was initiated in Great Smoky Mountains National Park with the experimental release of one family (US Fish and Wildlife Service 1992a). Results suggested that restoration was feasible. Consequently, the service released thirty-seven wolves there from 1992 through 1996 to establish a second experimental-nonessential population. Of the released animals, twenty-six died or were recaptured after traveling outside the park. Of twenty-eight pups born in the wild and not removed, none survived its first year. In 1998, the service terminated that project because the wolves tended to establish home ranges that included nonpark lands, had a low pup survival rate, and experienced low winter prey availability (Henry 1998).

From 1987 through 1994, it seemed that the red wolf reintroduction project at Alligator River National Wildlife Refuge was succeeding (Phillips et al. 1996). During the mid-1990s, the situation changed because hybridization between red wolves and coyotes became increasingly common (Kelly and Phillips 2000). A comprehensive population and habitat viability assessment in April 1999 generated a management plan to reduce hybridization (Kelly et al. 1999). By November 2001, the plan, which called for very intensive fieldwork to prevent or significantly limit red wolf–coyote interbreeding by removing or sterilizing coyotes, promoting the formation and maintenance of wolf breeding pairs, and euthanizing known and suspected hybrids, was beginning to show progress.

Few conflicts with humans have arisen since red wolves were released at Alligator River National Wildlife Refuge. White-tailed deer are abundant in northeastern North Carolina, and hunter harvest has remained heavy despite the presence of red wolves. Very few depredations from red wolves have been reported or documented. Through November 2001, only three depredations were documented, and every complaint was investigated exhaustively; the three confirmed cases involved one chicken, one hunting dog, and a few domestic ducks. No cases of livestock depredations have been reported for the recovery area.

Despite the chronic challenge of hybridization, the Alligator River National Wildlife Refuge restoration project is showing limited success due to intensive wolf and coyote management. Overall, the project illustrates that the values and successes of reintroduction efforts often have the potential to extend beyond the immediate preservation of the reintroduced species to positively affect local citizens and communities, larger conservation efforts, and other imperiled species (Phillips 1990).

A Cornell University study concluded that on average the Alligator River National Wildlife Refuge red wolf project generates an annual regional economic impact of about $37.5 million (Rosen 1997). Public opinion polls conducted as part of the Cornell study and by North Carolina State University revealed that the majority of local residents strongly favor red wolf recovery in northeastern North Carolina (Quintal 1995). Such support derives partly from the ecological effects generated by red wolves. Local landowners credit red wolf predation on raccoons (*Procyon lotor*) as benefiting populations of bobwhite quail (*Colinus virginianus*) and turkey (*Meleagris gallopavo*). Food habits data and observations by local landowners reveal that red wolf predation on nutria (*Coypu myocaster*) reduces damage to water-control levees. Rosen (1997) predicted that because of such benefits the public would strongly support and materially benefit from efforts to reestablish red wolves elsewhere.

It seems likely that the red wolf could be recovered via reintroduction of captive-born animals were it not for the species' predilection to hybridize with coyotes. Data collected during intensive fieldwork are beginning to suggest that coyotes and red wolves can be managed to greatly reduce the frequency of hybridization. Confirmation of these preliminary results will, however, require several more years of work. Of course, hybridization would not be a problem if red wolves could be reintroduced to areas that were not inhabited by coyotes. Historically, coyotes were not in the red wolf's range, but they have now moved in. Consequently, long-term prospects are bleak for the species to be restored to a significant portion of the southeastern United States.

THE GRAY WOLF IN THE
GREAT LAKES REGION

The gray wolf recovery plan was written for the Great Lakes region and approved by the service in May 1978 (US Fish and Wildlife Service 1978). However, the plan does not include goals or criteria for the wolf population on Isle Royale, because it is not considered an important factor in the long-term survival of the species. The population on the island is small (usually including twelve to twenty-five wolves and never more than fifty) and almost completely isolated from other wolf populations (Peterson et al. 1998). While assigning no "recovery value" to the Isle Royale population, the service recognized the population's importance as the focus of long-term research and recommended that it be completely protected (US Fish and Wildlife Service 1992b).

A revised plan, approved in January 1992 (US Fish and Wildlife Service 1992b), included two delisting criteria. The service considered wolves in the Great Lakes region as a single population that would be considered recovered once the survival of the Minnesota population was secure and an additional viable population lived outside of Minnesota.* Although these criteria had (arguably) been met by 2001, as of this writing, attempts to delist the species in the region have been defeated twice in federal court. The effort to delist the species in the Great Lakes region continued in early 2009, when the US Fish and Wildlife Service again attempted to delist the species (US Fish and Wildilfe Service 2009b). However, conservation groups again have threatened to sue.

Prior to the ESA, wolves in Minnesota were not protected and could be hunted and trapped. The state sponsored a control program that included aerial gunning until 1956 and bounty payments until 1965 (Minnesota Department of Natural Resources 2001). Until 1973, the year the ESA was enacted, some wolves were killed for fur, while others were killed under the state's predator control program. Various surveys conducted from the late 1950s to 1973 indicated that the Minnesota wolf population did not exceed 1,000 animals and dropped as low as 350 to 700 individuals. Wolves that have since populated the region originated in Minnesota.

After wolves were included on the list of threatened and endangered species, the population in Minnesota began to grow and expand into Wisconsin and Michigan. Historically, Wisconsin held about 3,000 to 5,000 wolves, but from about 1830 to 1960 that number dropped to zero (Thiel 1993; Wydeven et al. 1995). Until the mid-1970s, occasional sightings were reported, but there was no evidence of reproduction (Wisconsin Department of Natural Resources 1999). By the mid-1980s, Wisconsin's wolf population numbered fifteen to twenty-five animals (Wydeven et al. 1995). By 1997, the wolf population had exceeded the state's endangered criteria, and its status was changed to threatened, meaning there were eighty or more wolves for three successive years.

In Michigan, the last known breeding population of wolves (outside of Isle Royale) was reported in the mid-1950s. While numbers continued to decline through the 1970s, it is possible that wolves were never

---

* In 1996, the US Fish and Wildlife Service and the National Marine Fisheries Service adopted a policy for recognizing distinct population segments (DPS) for purposes of listing, reclassifying, and delisting vertebrate species (Fay and Nammach 1996). This policy may allow the service to protect and conserve species and the ecosystems upon which they depend before large-scale declines occur that would necessitate listing a species or subspecies throughout its entire range. For a group of vertebrates to be recognized as a DPS, they must be "discrete" and "significant." Discreteness requires that the population segment be delimited by physical, physiological, ecological, or behavioral barriers or by an international boundary that coincides with differences in the degree of protection. Significance requires that the population segment inhabit an unusual or unique ecological setting, exhibit marked genetic differences from other populations of the parent taxon, or inhabit an area that, if devoid of the species, would result in a significant gap in the range of the taxon.

completely extirpated from the state (Michigan Department of Natural Resources 1997). During the 1980s, reports of wolves in the Upper Peninsula increased, and a pair produced pups there in 1991. In 1997, the Department of Natural Resources finalized a comprehensive management plan for Michigan's wolf population. In 1999 and 2001, Wisconsin's and Minnesota's natural resources departments did the same (respectively). Together, those three state plans should ensure the long-term survival of wolves in the Great Lakes region.

By 2001, the wolf population in Minnesota included more than 2,500 animals distributed over about 40 percent of the state, Wisconsin's wolves numbered 251 animals over about 40 percent of the state, and Michigan had 249 animals distributed over about 30 percent of the state. As of 2006, there were 3,020 wolves in Minnesota, 465 in Wisconsin, and 434 in Michigan, not counting Isle Royale's 30 wolves (US Fish and Wildlife Service 2007a). In general, the rural people of the Great Lakes region have been more tolerant of wolves than the rural people of the Northern Rockies and the southwestern United States.

THE GRAY WOLF IN THE NORTHERN ROCKY MOUNTAINS

In 1974, the US Fish and Wildlife Service started an interagency wolf recovery team, which compiled the Northern Rocky Mountain Wolf Recovery Plan (US Fish and Wildlife Service 1980). A revised plan in 1987 focused recovery on northwestern Wyoming, western Montana, and central Idaho, an area characterized by large tracts of public land, healthy populations of native ungulates, and relatively little livestock (US Fish and Wildlife Service 1987a). The 1987 plan identified several criteria for downlisting and delisting the species and predicted that about 300 wolves in 30 packs would inhabit the region at the time of

recovery. The plan promoted natural recovery for Montana and Idaho if two packs had become established in Idaho by 1992. If two Idaho packs did not exist by 1992, then reintroduction would become a tool for Idaho and Yellowstone National Park. The plan recognized that reintroduction was the surest way to restore wolves to the Greater Yellowstone Ecosystem.

During the 1960s, the stage was set for wolves to naturally recolonize northwestern Montana as the Canadian government greatly reduced human-caused mortality in southwestern Canada (Carbyn 1983). By the 1970s, dispersing wolves were traveling through northwestern Montana, and by 1982 a pack inhabited Glacier National Park (Ream and Mattson 1982). In 1986, the first litter of pups in more than fifty years was born there (Ream et al. 1985; Ream et al. 1989). By 1993, the number of wolves in northwestern Montana had increased to fifty-five (Fritts et al. 1995). By December 2001, the population included eighty-four wolves (US Fish and Wildlife Service et al. 2002). By 2003, there were 183 wolves and the population essentially stopped growing; by 2006, there were 159 individuals in Montana (US Fish and Wildlife Service 2007b). Northwestern Montana has lower ungulate densities and higher levels of livestock than central Idaho and Yellowstone, thus wolves may be closer to their carrying capacity there—particularly the capacity of human tolerance (Bangs et al. 2001; US Fish and Wildlife Service 2009b).

By the early 1990s, two naturally occurring packs had not materialized in Idaho, and interest in restoring wolves to Yellowstone National Park had intensified. While Leopold (1944) had first discussed wolf restoration to the park in the 1940s, it was not until 1972 that the Department of the Interior officially considered the idea. That stimulated a study to determine if any wolves remained in Yellowstone; infrequent sightings were occasionally reported to park officials. The study concluded that wolves were absent from the park and recommended that the species be restored through reintroductions (Weaver 1978).

In 1989, Congressman Wayne Owens (D-UT) introduced a bill in the US Congress that required the service to prepare an Environmental Impact Statement (EIS) on wolf reintroduction to Yellowstone National Park. The bill prompted numerous discussions, but Congress did not authorize an EIS. Congress did, however, fund two reports aimed at answering the many questions surrounding wolf restoration (Yellowstone National Park et al. 1990; Varley and Brewster 1992). In 1992, Congress directed the service to prepare an EIS on wolf reintroduction to Yellowstone and central Idaho.

The reintroduction EIS initiated what would become one of the most extensive public processes ever conducted for a national environmental issue. The EIS took two and a half years to complete and covered all aspects of reintroducing wolves to Yellowstone and central Idaho. After releasing the draft EIS, government officials held more than 130 public hearings and meetings and considered 160,000 public comments from all 50 states and 40 foreign countries (US Fish and Wildlife 1994). The final EIS was published in April 1994, and by July 1994 the secretaries of the interior and agriculture had signed a Record of Decision and Statement of Findings on the Environmental Impact Statement, effecting the final EIS as the federal government's official policy.

The final EIS recommended reintroducing about fifteen wolves annually to both Yellowstone and Idaho. This would continue for three to five years, and the wolves would come from Canada. It also recommended that released wolves and their offspring be designated as members of experimental-nonessential populations per Section 10(j) of the ESA (Bangs 1994). Such a designation,

as with the red wolves in North Carolina, allows the service to relax the restrictions of the act when managing wolves (Parker and Phillips 1991; Bangs 1994; see also chap. 7).

The restoration plan called for releasing wolves in Idaho immediately after they were moved from Canada (a "hard" release), whereas in Yellowstone the wolves would be acclimated for several weeks in large pens at the site of release before being set free (a more labor-intensive, "soft" release). Because hard releases are easier, they have been commonly used to reintroduce wildlife throughout North America (Griffith et al. 1989). While the overarching objective was to establish populations of wolves in the Greater Yellowstone Area and central Idaho as quickly and cost effectively as possible, the service did decide to test hard releases versus soft releases to refine and optimize subsequent releases and to gain information to benefit future wolf reintroductions (Fritts et al. 1997).

In January 1995, fifteen wolves from Alberta, Canada, were released in Idaho, and a year later twenty wolves from British Columbia, Canada, were released (Bangs and Fritts 1996; Fritts et al. 1997). In March 1995, the Nez Perce signed a cooperative agreement with the service (Agreement No. 14-48-0001-95-538) authorizing the tribe to assume responsibility for recovery and management of the Idaho gray wolves. By September 1995, the tribe completed a plan to guide such activities (Jimenez et al. 1995). The overall goal of the plan was to establish a wolf population in central Idaho that would contribute to the recovery of the species in the Northern Rocky Mountains.

During March 1995, fourteen wolves from Alberta were released in Yellowstone National Park, and in January 1996, seventeen wolves from British Columbia were released (Phillips and Smith 1996). Furthermore, as part of wolf population control activities, ten pups were transferred from northwestern Montana to an acclimation pen in the park in late 1996. These wolves were under the jurisdiction of the National Park Service and the US Fish and Wildlife Service.

Both wolf opponents and proponents filed several lawsuits over the experimental-nonessential designation for reintroduced wolves. Wolf proponents claimed that the designation illegally reduced ESA protection for naturally occurring wolves inhabiting northwestern Montana and possibly central Idaho. In December 1997, wolf opponents won the day when a Wyoming federal judge in the US District Court of Wyoming determined that the designation had been illegally applied and ordered the service to remove the already reintroduced wolves and their offspring. Given the ramifications of his determination, the order was stayed pending appeal. The appeal was settled in January 2000 when the Tenth Circuit Court of Appeals (Denver, Colorado) reversed the Wyoming court order. The losing parties did not appeal to the US Supreme Court.

The reintroduced wolves adapted better than predicted, establishing their population two years after reintroduction rather than the predicted three to five years (Fritts et al. 1997). Compared to predictions in the EIS, the wolves produced more pups, survived at a higher rate, and had fewer conflicts with humans (Phillips and Smith 1996; Bangs et al. 1998; Smith et al. 1999; Fritts et al. 2001).* Additionally, by 2001 more than 70,000 visitors to Yellowstone had observed wolves (Fritts et al. 2003), and public interest in recovery remains high.†

Both hard- and soft-release techniques established wolf populations. Fritts et al. concluded:

> It appears that if landscape conditions, prey availability, wolf restoration stock, and early release management are suitable…the choice of hard versus soft release seems to matter little. Nonetheless, hard releases may be advantageous if the size of the area can accommodate wolves wandering without encountering people or killing livestock. The technique is relatively inexpensive as well, and involves less husbandry. If the size of the area is restricted, however, then a soft release should be used to limit post-release movements. Because few areas are as extensive as central Idaho, soft releases are likely to be preferred in future wolf restoration efforts. (2001, 144)

From the original 31 Canadian wolves of 1995 and 1996 (plus the 10 pups from northwestern Montana in 1996), the wolf population inhabiting the Greater Yellowstone Area grew to 189 individuals by December 2001; by 2006, the number was 371 (US Fish and Wildlife Service 2007a). Under Nez Perce management, there were 251 wolves in Idaho by the end of 2001 and 713 by 2006 (US Fish and Wildlife Service 2007a). By mid-September 2008, the service estimated that there were 360 wolves in Montana, 771 in

---

* The frequency of wolf control belies the actual magnitude of the wolf-livestock problem. For example, only about 1 percent of farms in wolf range in Minnesota suffer verified wolf depredations (W. J. Paul, unpublished report, 1998, as cited by Mech et al. 2000). Similarly, average annual confirmed losses in the Northern Rockies have been slight: four cattle and twenty-eight sheep (and four dogs) in the Greater Yellowstone Area and nine cattle and twenty-nine sheep (and two dogs) in Idaho during the first five years. These rates are one-third to one-half of the rates predicted in the EIS. In contrast, livestock producers in Montana annually report losing about 80,000 cattle and 90,000 sheep (Bangs 1998). Financial compensation for livestock losses has proven useful for minimizing animosity toward wolves (Fischer 1989; Fischer et al. 1994). In North America, encounters that have ended in contact between wolves and humans have been rare.

† The above summary of the Yellowstone project is complemented well by several books that provide additional details, including Fischer (1995), Ferguson (1996), Phillips and Smith (1996), Schullery (1996), McNamee (1997), and Smith and Ferguson (2005).

Idaho, and 332 in Wyoming, for a total of 1,463 wolves in the Northern Rockies (US Fish and Wildlife Service 2008a).

The recovery goal set in 1987 was for ten or more breeding pairs in each of the three recovery areas for three consecutive years, for a total of more than 300 wolves throughout the region (Refsnider 2000, 43454, 43457). By 1999, the service indicated that they might change the objectives for recovery, likely due to ceaseless political controversy, early rapid growth of wolf populations in the Greater Yellowstone Area and central Idaho, and the relatively slow growth of the wolf population in Montana. The new objective for recovery came from Appendix 9 of the EIS for the reintroductions (USFWS 1994, 6–75). It stated: "Thirty or more breeding pairs comprising some 300+ wolves in a metapopulation with genetic exchange between subpopulations should have a long-term probability of persistence."

In November 2001, the service queried dozens of professionals familiar with wolf recovery about population viability. By February 2002, the service had determined that the official recovery goal for the Northern Rockies would be maintaining a viable wolf population for three consecutive years, defining a viable population as "Thirty or more breeding pairs (an adult male and an adult female wolf that have produced at least 2 pups that survived until December 31 of the year of their birth, during the previous breeding season), comprising some 300+ wolves in a metapopulation with genetic exchange between subpopulations" (Bangs 2002, 1).

The wolf population no longer had to be distributed equally, and the recovery objective was reached by December 31, 2002. So the service proposed that the gray wolf in the distinct population segment for the Northern Rocky Mountains should be removed from the list of threatened and endangered species. In addition to the Greater Yellowstone Ecosystem, northwestern Montana,

and central Idaho (areas having wolves), this distinct population segment included the eastern parts of Washington and Oregon, north-central Utah, and the rest of Montana, Idaho, and Wyoming—areas of former range where wolves no longer exist (US Fish and Wildlife Service 2007a).

One hurdle remained. Wolves could not be delisted in the Northern Rockies' distinct population segment until the state governments of Wyoming, Idaho, and Montana each submitted management plans assuring that adequate regulatory mechanisms existed to protect wolves at or above recovery levels after federal protection was removed; the plans had to be approved by the US Fish and Wildlife Service (US Fish and Wildlife Service 2007a). There was no point in removing federal protection from a threatened or endangered species if the subsequent local management would then mismanage the species to the point that it was again threatened.

In January 2002, the US Fish and Wildlife Service accepted the Montana Fish, Wildlife, and Parks Department's conservation and management plan. In March 2002, the Idaho Legislative Wolf Oversight Committee finalized its plan (Idaho Legislative Wolf Oversight Committee 2002). This plan was developed and approved by the state legislature and the US Fish and Wildlife Service. After delisting, the Nez Perce would turn management responsibilities over to the Idaho Department of Fish and Game. Because of the tribe's expertise, the Idaho Department of Fish and Game intended to consult with the tribe when the state assumed management authority.

Even though the 2002 Idaho legislature's wolf management plan was acceptable to the US Fish and Wildlife Service, the 2001 legislature previously had passed House Joint Memorial No. 5, which demanded "that wolf recovery efforts in Idaho be discontinued immediately and wolves be removed by whatever means necessary" (Legislature of the State of Idaho 2005). As indicated in the 2002 management plan, House Joint Memorial No. 5 continues to be the state's official position. The official position notwithstanding, Memorial No. 5 does not carry the weight of law. Nevertheless, Idaho governor Butch Otto spoke at Idaho Sportsman's Day on January 11, 2007, and vowed to kill more than 80 percent of Idaho's wolves, perhaps shooting the first one himself; he promised to begin the moment wolves were removed from the federal endangered species list (Woodruff 2007). Montana's plan for wolf management is much more sensible than the Idaho governor's.

Wyoming did not complete a wolf management plan until 2004, and the US Fish and Wildlife Service rejected it because it was inadequate to maintain wolves at recovery level (US Fish and Wildlife Service 2007b). Wyoming litigated this decision in the Wyoming federal district court, but the case was dismissed on procedural grounds (US Fish and Wildlife Service 2007b). Wyoming appealed, but in April 2006 the Tenth Circuit Court of Appeals (in Denver, Colorado) agreed with the Wyoming federal district court. Thus, on August 1, 2006, the US Fish and Wildlife Service determined that wolves in the Northern Rockies could not be delisted, because Wyoming did not provide the necessary regulatory mechanisms to conserve their share of the wolf population (US Fish and Wildlife Service 2006). In short, Wyoming declared the wolf a predator if it ranged outside of the northwestern section of the state; this meant that a wolf could be shot on sight, and the US Fish and Wildlife Service thought that was a threat to the species (Smith and Ferguson 2005).

At the time of this writing, the US Fish and Wildlife Service had unsuccessfully attempted, for the second time, to remove the gray wolf in the Northern Rocky Mountains from the list of threatened and endangered species and continued to try to delist the species (US Fish and Wildlife Service 2008a). In October 2008, the service abandoned trying to delist wolves regionally and adopted a new tactic by delisting the wolf only in Montana and Idaho because federal courts repeatedly rejected Wyoming's management plan (US Fish and Wildlife Service 2009b). Conservation groups and the state of Wyoming have already threatened to sue the service again.

One of the primary arguments against wolf delisting in the Northern Rocky Mountains and the Great Lakes region is that the species presently occupies less than 5 percent of its range. Conservationists argue that such a wide-ranging species must occupy a significant portion of its range in order to meet the definition of recovery as defined by Congress.

THE MEXICAN GRAY WOLF IN THE SOUTHWEST

The Mexican wolf, a subspecies of the gray wolf, was extirpated from the southwestern United States by the 1940s. Between 1977 and 1980, under an agreement between the United States and Mexico, five Mexican wolves were captured in the Mexican states of Durango and Chihuahua. These four males and one pregnant female were transported to the Arizona-Sonora Desert Museum in Tucson, Arizona, to establish a captive-breeding program. In 1979, the service formed a Mexican Wolf Recovery Team; the team finalized a binational recovery plan with Mexico in 1982. The prime objective of the plan was to maintain a captive-breeding program and to reestablish a population of at least 100 Mexican wolves within their historic range (US Fish and Wildlife Service 1982). The plan called for reestablishing at least two wild populations, but it did not specify a population goal for the second one. The recovery team considered the objective to be necessary for the survival of the Mexican wolf, but did not propose a numerical objective for full recovery and delisting (from the ESA) of the Mexican wolf (US Fish and Wildlife Service 1982).

Given the absence of wild Mexican wolves, captive breeding is essential to recovery. In the mid-1990s, two captive lineages of Mexican wolves were found to be of pure wild strains and were included in the captive-breeding program. This increased the number of founders of the captive-bred population to seven. Thus, all known Mexican wolves in existence today stem from just these seven animals, a true brush with extinction. By July 31, 2008, the captive-breeding program included 327 animals maintained at 47 facilities in the United States and Mexico (Siminski 2008a). The Mexican Wolf Species Survival Plan guides the captive-breeding program, and its goal is to retain at least 300 Mexican gray wolves in captivity to protect the subspecies from extinction while producing additional animals for reintroduction (Siminski 2008b). Wolves are bred and managed for reintroduction at three US facilities: the Sevilleta National Wildlife Refuge and Ladder Ranch (owned by Ted Turner) wolf management facilities, both in New Mexico, and Wolf Haven International, in Tenino, Washington.

Wolves with potential for reintroduction are managed with minimal human contact to promote behavior to avoid humans and maximize pair bonding, breeding, pup rearing, and pack formation. Wolves are selected for reintroduction by genetic makeup, reproductive performance, behavior, and physical prowess (US Fish and Wildlife Service 2006).

In the early 1990s, as the species became increasingly secure in captivity, the US Fish and Wildlife Service began to develop an EIS for reestablishing a wild population. After considering nearly 18,000 comments on the draft EIS, the service recommended reintroducing Mexican gray wolves to the Blue Range Wolf Recovery Area on the Arizona–New Mexico border (US Fish and Wildlife Service 1996b). The record of decision was signed in March 1997, and the specifics for reintroduction and management were published shortly thereafter (Parsons 1998). Similarly, the Arizona Game and Fish Department (AGFD) concluded that the Arizona portion of the Blue Range Wolf Recovery Area was best suited for a reintroduction project; in 1995, AGFD developed a reintroduction plan for this area (Groebner et al. 1995).

The Blue Range Wolf Recovery Area encompasses 17,752 sq. km (6,852 sq. mi.) of the Gila National Forest in New Mexico and the Apache National Forest in Arizona and New Mexico. The service's final administrative rule authorizes them to reintroduce wolves only in the "primary recovery zone" of the Blue Range Wolf Recovery Area, an area that encompasses 2,664 sq. km (1,028 sq. mi.) of the Apache National Forest (Parsons 1998). The remainder of the Blue Range Wolf Recovery Area comprises the "secondary recovery zone," and the service is authorized only to conduct rereleases in the secondary recovery zone. Wolves travelling from the primary recovery zone can inhabit the secondary zone, but wolves living entirely outside the boundaries of the Blue Range Wolf Recovery Area are required to be captured and brought back to the primary zones or returned to captivity (US Fish and Wildlife Service 1998b).

This is the only endangered species reintroduction project we are aware of where hard boundaries legally limit the area that can be occupied by the species in the wild, even though suitable areas exist on public lands outside the boundary.

At the beginning of the project, the New Mexico Game Commission officially opposed the Blue Range Wolf Recovery Area project. On March 29, 2002, the commission unanimously reaffirmed its opposition to the reintroduction of wolves in the Gila National Forest portion of the Blue Range Wolf Recovery Area. Citing a study by the state's game and fish department, the commission claimed that no potential wolf release sites in the Gila National Forest would provide the biological and societal characteristics necessary for success. A new game commission, appointed by incoming governor Bill Richardson, reversed the position, deciding at a meeting on April 4, 2004, to support wolf reintroduction and recovery. Early opposition to the Blue Range Wolf Recovery Area project notwithstanding, New Mexico Game and Fish (NMGF) has provided a field biologist to serve on the Interagency Field Team since 1999, and it is now one of six coleading agencies. In addition, although the White Mountain Apache and San Carlos Apache initially showed little interest in the reintroduction, the White Mountain Apache became a member of the six coleading agencies in 2002 and began allowing wolves to occupy tribal lands in 2003.

In contrast, the Arizona Game Commission has never opposed the Blue Range reintroduction project, and the AGFD has become a leader in managing the wild population and in the decision-making process. The AGFD promoted a 2003 memorandum of understanding that formed the multiagency Adaptive Management Oversight Committee, which it leads. The AGFD has a much larger budget (from lottery proceeds) than does NMGF.

Ninety-nine Mexican gray wolves were released from 1998 through 2006—four years beyond the anticipated need to release wolves. The US Fish and Wildlife Service (1996b) estimated that it would take nine years (1997 to 2005) to reach a population of 100 wolves with 18 breeding pairs. Although the reintroduction did not actually begin until 1998, the 100-wolf prime objective was not met in nine years—by 2006—as planned. By the end of 2006, just fifty-nine wolves and six breeding pairs (using the definition of "breeding pair" from the 1998 final rule) survived in the wild. By the end of 2008,

those numbers had fallen to fifty-two wolves and just two breeding pairs. Importantly, the 2008 official population count showed that fewer individual wolves and fewer breeding pairs existed in the wild than did at the end of 2003.

Despite encouraging first efforts in captive breeding and reintroduction, the service has failed to reach any basic benchmark for recovery in the wild since the Mexican gray wolf reintroduction project began. Instead, the population of Mexican gray wolves in the Blue Range Wolf Recovery Area has suffered significant human-caused losses from both illegal killings and authorized removal actions by the service. Average litter size for the reintroduced population during its first five years was 2.1, compared to 4.2 to 6.9 elsewhere, and the average pack size was 4.8 (Fuller 2003).

A telling finding in the five-year review from 1998 to 2003 was an average annual failure rate of 64 percent (Mexican Wolf Blue Range Adaptive Management Oversight Committee and Interagency Field Team 2005). The failure rate is the sum of wolf mortalities plus wolves killed or removed from the wild by deliberate management actions carried out by the agencies (e.g., because a wolf preyed on livestock three times). Such a high failure rate is unsustainable without continually supplementing the population through releases, especially given the lower than average litter sizes. This explains why releases have been continued beyond what was initially anticipated.

Most Mexican wolf deaths have been caused by humans. From March 1998 through January 2009, there have been thirty-one illegal shootings, twelve wolves killed by vehicles, and nineteen deaths from natural or unknown causes (US Fish and Wildlife Service 2009c). An additional 144 wolves were lethally and nonlethally removed from the wild from 1998 to 2008 (US Fish and Wildlife Service 2008b); from a population dynamics perspective, non-lethal removal is equivalent to mortality (Paquet et al. 2001).

Rather than redouble its wolf conservation efforts in light of this daunting record, in 2003 the service delegated authority over wolf recovery to the Mexican Wolf Management Oversight Committee, directed by the AGFD. Since then, control issues have surfaced resulting in unproductive conflict.

The Management Oversight Committee adopted Standard Operating Procedure 13 (SOP 13) in 2005, which requires the service to permanently remove every Mexican wolf that preys on livestock three times or more within 365 days. This caused permanent wolf removals to spike: of the seventy Mexican wolves removed by the service for conflicts with livestock since reintroduction began, forty-five were removed under the SOP 13 mandate between 2005 and 2008. As a result, the Mexican gray wolf is not currently on a positive trajectory toward recovery. Wild Mexican gray wolves declined by 12 percent from 2006 to 2007, despite a goal of a 10 percent population increase. Thus, the service fell 22 percent short of its most recent goal. More seriously, the number of breeding pairs as defined in the final rule declined from six at the end of 2006 to only three at the end of 2007. This reverse population trend may portend the Mexican gray wolf's second extinction in the wild.

The EIS predicted livestock depredation rates of 1 to 34 head per 100 wolves. Between 1998 and 2004, confirmed kills of livestock (cattle) by Mexican wolves averaged 14 per an adjusted population of 100 wolves (Mexican Wolf Blue Range Adaptive Management Oversight Committee and Interagency Field Team 2005; US Fish and Wildlife Service 2006). In 2005, the rate increased to 45 head per 100 wolves. One factor contributing to livestock depredation in the Blue Range Wolf Recovery Area is the practice of year-round grazing with open range calving on a significant portion of the area.

The Mexican Wolf Recovery Plan, approved and adopted in 1982, is, according to the service's policy, supposed to be updated or revised every five years if it is out of date or not in compliance with the ESA. The Mexican Wolf Recovery Plan has never been updated or revised, even though it does not contain "objective, measurable criteria which, when met, would result in a determination…that the species be removed from the list" (ESA Section 4(f)(2)(B)(ii)) nor a detailed plan for fully recovering Mexican wolves throughout a significant portion of their historic range to a population status that warrants delisting from the ESA. The current Mexican Wolf Recovery Plan has been in effect, in its original form, for twenty-five years and needs revision. Following the listing of a southwestern gray wolf distinct population segment, the service initiated a process for revising the recovery plan in October 2003, but it suspended that effort in January 2005 after a federal court ruling vacated the distinct population segment listing (*Defenders of Wildlife v. Norton*, 03-1348-JO).

Though the Mexican wolf remains listed as endangered in the Southwest under the 1978 listing rule for the entire gray wolf species, the service has not reinitiated the recovery planning process for the critically endangered Mexican gray wolf subspecies. As such, in late 2008 conservationists filed a petition to compel the US Fish and Wildlife Service to expedite revision of the Mexican Wolf Recovery Plan.

The final rule for the reintroduction project required the service to conduct a comprehensive review of the project at the end of three years, in March 2001, and after five years, in March 2003 (Parsons 1998). The service contracted the 2001 review to the Conservation Breeding Specialist Group (CBSG) from the International Union for

Conservation of Nature–Species Survival Commission (IUCN-SSC), and the 2003 review was conducted internally (Mexican Wolf Blue Range Adaptive Management Oversight Committee and Interagency Field Team 2005).

The 2001 review was conducted by a team of scientists led by renowned wolf ecologist Dr. Paul C. Paquet. They found that (1) survival and recruitment rates were far too low to ensure population growth and persistence; (2) livestock producers using public lands could make a substantive contribution to reducing conflicts with wolves through improved husbandry and better management of carcasses; and (3) dispersal of wolves outside the recovery area boundaries is required if the regional population is to be viable (Paquet et al. 2001). They recommended that regulations for the Blue Range reintroduction project be modified to allow wolves that are not management problems to establish territories outside the Blue Range Wolf Recovery Area boundary, and that livestock operators on public land be required to take some responsibility for carcass management or disposal to reduce the likelihood of wolves becoming habituated to feeding on livestock. None of the substantive recommendations in the Paquet report has yet been implemented or initiated.

The internal five-year review completed in 2003 made thirty-seven recommendations, many of which are burdened by required bureaucratic processes of government agencies (Mexican Wolf Blue Range Adaptive Management Oversight Committee and Interagency Field Team 2005). While some recommendations could improve the status of the Blue Range reintroduction project in the next two to five years, four provisions are worrisome from a conservation perspective. These four would (1) specify that new regulations will not address wolf habituation to livestock or attraction to the vicinity of livestock through scavenging on untended livestock carcasses, one of the principal reasons wolves are trapped or shot (Recommendations 12.b. and 29); (2) allow private individuals to kill wolves in broader circumstances than presently permitted (Recommendation 10); (3) mandate that current management protocols apply to all new areas made available for wolf occupation, even though those protocols result in an unsustainable failure rate (Recommendation 5.c); and (4) allow Arizona, New Mexico, and tribal authorities to cap the wolf population in the bistate area at 125 individuals and permit wolves in excess of that number to be killed (Recommendation 11). The population figure of 125 as an adequate recovered population has no scientific justification and no relationship to the recovery of wolves in the Southwest. The Mexican gray wolf is not currently on a firm trajectory toward recovery.

WHAT IS RECOVERY?

Unfortunately, the ESA provides no clear answer to a question of great importance: What is recovery? Service policy states, "The goal of this process [recovery] is to restore listed species to a point where they are secure, self-sustaining components of their ecosystem and, thus, to allow delisting" (US Fish and Wildlife Service 1996b, 2).

Recent developments in conservation biology show that species interactions contribute greatly to ecosystem health, and the loss of species that are highly interactive degrades composition, structure, and diversity in ecosystems (Soulé et al. 2005). Thus, increasing understanding of interactions and webs means that the older definitions of recovery based on taxonomic representation and population viability are outdated. For highly interactive species, species that play driving roles in their ecosystems, achieving functional (ecological and evolutionary) densities over a significant portion of range is particularly important. Without functional densities and distributions of species that are ecological drivers, biodiversity will continue to decline despite the best of intentions (Soulé et al. 2003a, 2005). Examples of such species include prairie dogs (*Cynomys* spp.), beavers, elephants, and wolves.

The concept of restoring functional densities of a species over a significant portion of suitable habitat within a species' historic range means recovery must strive for numbers that are higher than what is deemed taxonomically viable (Tear et al. 1993; Rohlf 1991; Shaffer and Stein 2000; Miller et al. 2000; Soulé et al. 2003b, 2005). For example, wolves in the Greater Yellowstone Ecosystem may exist in viable numbers, but they do not affect elk numbers and behavior in Colorado. A complex of prairie dog colonies covering 1,000 hectares (2,471 acres) may hold 10,000 or more prairie dogs, enough to be considered viable, but that complex may only hold 15 black-footed ferrets, a population at risk. Minimal recovery goals may keep a taxonomic representation, but such minimal goals for highly interactive species will continue to erode biodiversity.

The ESA does not discuss the role of highly interactive species in endangerment or recovery, probably because the act was written and last revised before much was known of these complexities. But, the act does state that decisions need to be based on the best scientific knowledge available, and there is enough flexibility to incorporate knowledge about how a species affects the broader ecosystem (Soulé et al. 2005).

Goals to restore a species' density and distribution across as much of its former range that holds suitable habitat as possible seem consistent with the act's definitions of *endangered species* (any species which is in danger of extinction throughout all or a significant portion of its range) and *threatened species* (any species which is likely to become an endangered species within the foreseeable future throughout all or a significant portion

of its range). Vucetich et al. (2006) argued that such an approach would mean that the species should be recovered to at least 75 percent of its range, where *range* is defined as "historic range that is currently suitable or can be made suitable by removing or sufficiently mitigating threats to the species." In 2001, the Ninth Circuit Court of Appeals reinforced these definitions when it implied that recovery must consider a significant portion of a species' historic range, at least where suitable habitat exists (*Defenders of Wildlife v. Norton*, 258 F.3d 1136, 1145).

Since passage of the ESA, conservation measures initiated by the service and other federal and state agencies have led to thirteen delisting actions involving nine species, two subspecies, and two distinct population segments (Enbring 1985; Jacobs 1985; Neal 1987a, 1987b; Swem 1994; Mesta 1999; Anderson and DeGange 2001). In each of the thirteen cases, the service emphasized that delisting was justified because evidence indicated that the species was distributed throughout its former range at near original abundance and was faced with no foreseeable threats.

In these cases, decisions on delisting seemed to be guided by Aldo Leopold's maxim:

> There seems to be a tacit assumption that if grizzlies survive in Canada and Alaska, that is good enough. It is not good enough for me…Relegating grizzlies to Alaska is about like relegating happiness to heaven; one may never get there (1966, 277).

CONCLUSIONS

As recently as 1850, the gray wolf and the red wolf lived throughout most of the conterminous United States (Young and Goldman 1944; Nowak 1983). Conflict with agrarian interests resulted in government-supported wolf eradication campaigns as early as 1630 in the Massachusetts Bay Colony, which then expanded throughout the contermi- nous United States, resulting in the near extermination of red and gray wolves (Young and Goldman 1944; McIntyre 1995).

The conservation status of red and gray wolves has greatly improved since the 1950s, when both species approached extinction in the Lower 48. This improvement is a direct result of a rising conservation consciousness in the public and implementation of recovery activities under the ESA. The status of each species would not have improved if not for the ESA.

At present, the red wolf is limited to North Carolina, and its future is threatened because of hybridization with coyotes—a species formerly not present in the south- eastern United States. Gray wolf recovery efforts are centered in three regions: the Great Lakes states, the Northern Rockies, and the Southwest. The Great Lakes popu- lation of wolves has responded very well and now holds around 4,000 wolves. The Great Lakes area once held a population of wild wolves, and changing management prac- tices allowed them to expand. The North- ern Rockies population holds around 1,200 individuals, with all but about 150 of those wolves in Yellowstone and Idaho, and with both populations started by reintroduc- ing wolves from Canada. The population in northern Montana came from coloniz- ing wild wolves. The Mexican wolf popula- tion in Arizona and New Mexico holds only about fifty individuals and was started by the release of animals raised in captivity.

In the Northern Rockies and the south- western United States, there has been signifi- cant opposition to wolf recovery, largely from agrarian interests. Farmers and livestock pro- ducers of the Great Lakes region, however, have lived with increasing wolf numbers for forty years and are much more tolerant.

The US Fish and Wildlife Service has attempted to remove protections from wolves

despite repeated legal defeats and despite the fact that wolves occupy only about 5 per- cent of their original range in the Lower 48. There are several areas of former range in the Lower 48 that could provide excellent habi- tat for wolves, but where wolves are absent. Expanding recovery efforts to include pres- ently unoccupied wolf habitat, such as the Southern Rocky Mountains, would contrib- ute mightily toward recovery of the species. (See Vucetich et al. 2006 for a robust discus- sion of this subject.)

There are presently no efforts by the US Fish and Wildlife Service to restore wolves to areas with good habitat that lack wolves, despite a scientific, ESA, and court empha- sis interpreting recovery as occurring in a "significant portion of the former range" (*Defenders of Wildlife v. Norton*, 258 F.3d 1136, 1145). Recent studies show that habi- tat could support 1,000 or more wolves in the northeastern United States, from New York to Maine (Harrison and Chapin 1998; Mladenoff and Sickley 1999). The Southern Rockies Ecoregion contains almost 1.5 to 1.8 times more public land than is available to wolves in the Yellowstone area and central Idaho, and 6 times the amount of public land available to Mexican wolves in the Blue Range Wolf Recovery Area. A 1994 con- gressionally mandated study concluded that the Colorado portion of the ecoregion could support more than 1,000 wolves, mostly on public land (Bennett 1994). Mech (2000) proposed that because the ecoregion is nearly equidistant from the Northern Rockies and the Blue Range Wolf Recovery Area, it is possible that a Southern Rockies population, through the production and movement of dispersers, would contribute to establishing and maintaining a metapopulation of wolves extending from the Arctic to Mexico. Car- roll et al. (2004) rate the Grand Canyon area (Arizona into southern Utah) as potentially able to support the largest regional popula- tion in the southwestern United States; the area offers a low probability of extinction and high resilience to potential change.

By not trying to place wolves in such high-quality habitats, the US Fish and Wildlife Service is allowing de facto no-wolf zones. Such a policy prevents wolves from connecting across a landscape and fulfilling their ecological function. While wolves may persist in a few locations, they will remain at higher risk because opportunities to disperse and colonize new habitat will be artificially limited. That will affect not just ecological function but also evolutionary potential. There are, however, local efforts by nongovernmental organizations to return wolves to these and other areas.

Significant credit for gains in wolf conservation is due to citizens, members of nongovernmental conservation organizations, elected and appointed officials, and individuals working for state, tribal, and federal governments who, despite political controversy, recognize the key role wolves play in ecosystems and in our nation's natural heritage.

Chapter 3

The Importance of Large Carnivores

Paul C. Paquet, Brian Miller, Kyran Kunkel, Richard P. Reading, and Michael K. Phillips

INTRODUCTION

Aldo Leopold (1966, 190) wrote that "the last word in ignorance is the man who says of an animal or plant: 'What good is it?' To keep every cog and wheel is the first precaution of intelligent tinkering." Despite this sage advice, we have not kept every cog and wheel. Today, the scythe of extinction cuts 1,000 to 10,000 times faster than historical background rates (i.e., average historical extinction rates), and its pace is increasing (E. O. Wilson 2002). A healthy ecosystem requires a full complement of native species and biological processes such as structure and function associated with the species.

Finely tuned interactions among species, physical environments, and ecological processes form the webs of life on our planet. Ecosystems, species, and systems have evolved over time within a range of variability (Noss 1999). When cogs or wheels are lost, the variability range that species can tolerate exceeds their ability to adapt, causing secondary waves of extinction that amplify instability.

Among animals, the pollinators, seed dispersers, ecosystem engineers such as beavers, and a host of other organisms are critical to the structure and function of biological communities (Owen-Smith 1989; E. O. Wilson 1987; Buchmann and Nabhan 1996; Detling 1998). We believe self-sustaining populations of gray wolves (*Canis lupus*) within their native range indicate healthy ecosystems. When wolves are eliminated, ecological and evolutionary relationships are distorted far beyond the obvious effect of changes in the number and behavior of ungulates, their principal prey. Wolves perform important functions at and above the community level, whether through pathways of energy flow, widespread coevolutionary adaptations with other organisms (e.g., prey species, mesopredators, parasites), or by affecting standing plant biomass and production. Today, in the absence of wolves, the Southern Rocky Mountains suffer from ecological imbalances such as too many elk (*Cervus elaphus*) and the effects of their overpopulation on the flora and fauna of the region. Accordingly, restoring an ecologically viable wolf population in the Southern Rocky Mountains should restore a significant level of ecological health to the region.

Large carnivores, including wolves, are important for more than just their ecological value, however. For many people, such animals represent strong cultural and aesthetic values, and the importance of these values appears to be increasing (Kellert 1996). The strong values large carnivores invoke lead to substantial economic value as more people spend money to see carnivores in the wild and purchase related products. Simply put, large carnivores matter to a vast and growing number of people.

HOW CARNIVORES AFFECT ECOSYSTEM HEALTH

When scientists discuss ecological interactions affecting abundance, distribution, and diversity across "trophic levels," or the food chain, they often talk about top-down or bottom-up control. In the ecological sense, control means a qualitative or quantitative effect on an ecosystem's structure, function, and diversity (Menge 1992).

Reducing trophic interactions to sharp categorizations of either top-down or bottom-up is counterproductive. It is clear that forces flow in both directions simultaneously and interact while doing so (Menge and Sutherland 1976; Fretwell 1987; Hunter and Price 1992; Menge 1992; Power 1992; Estes et al. 2001). While the number of trophic levels in a top-down cascade affects plant biomass, the productivity from the bottom-up also affects the number of trophic levels (Fretwell 1987; Power 1992). For example, wolves may limit the number of elk and moose (*Alces alces*) in an area and thus permit more willows to persist in a riparian area, but the amount of plant productivity also determines if enough elk and moose can survive in a region to support a population of wolves. Scientists quickly recognized the qualitative and quantitative role that food has on consumers. Until recently, however, knowledge about how carnivores affect a system remained obscure.

As a simple example, if bottom-up control dominates a system, energy moving up the food chain regulates the system. An increase in the biomass of consumers is directly related to increases in productivity of their resources. Species richness and diversity are maintained by defenses of both plants and herbivores, or because competition forces species to specialize and use discrete niches (Pianka 1974; Hunter and Price 1992; Polis and Strong 1996). Because large carnivores sit at the top of the food chain, bottom-up theories leave them with little ecological role (Estes et al. 2001). Under the bottom-up model, they receive more than they contribute. Implicitly, this can justify politically based management strategies that hold carnivore numbers artificially low,

thereby "protecting" domestic livestock and increasing large-game populations to benefit sport hunters.

In a system with top-down regulation, herbivores can reduce the biomass of plants, but in turn, carnivores check the numbers of herbivores (Hairston et al. 1960; Fretwell 1977, 1987; Oksanen et al. 1981; Oksanen and Oksanen 2000). Predation also produces indirect impacts that flow through the system far beyond the direct effect of a predator on prey. For example, too few carnivores allow ungulate numbers to increase, which changes the plant community in ways that affect diversity, abundance, and competition among many other organisms. Top-down regulation implies strong interactions among three general trophic levels: plants, herbivores, and carnivores.

At very low levels of productivity, there will be only one trophic level: plants (see Oksanen and Oksanen 2000). Factors limiting plant biomass are available resources and competition with other plants for the same resources. As productivity increases, so does plant biomass, until there is enough to support a second trophic level, the herbivorous consumers (Oksanen and Oksanen 2000). With two trophic levels, herbivore biomass increases with increasing productivity until a third trophic level can be supported, the carnivorous consumers (Oksanen and Oksanen 2000). Carnivores now limit the number of herbivores, reducing the amount of pressure that herbivores place on plants. The plants and carnivores now flourish (first and third trophic levels), whereas the herbivores (second trophic level) are held in check by carnivores.

Plants flourish under odd numbers of trophic levels, but growth is limited under even numbers. In contrast to bottom-up theory, under top-down regulation neither plant nor herbivore biomass increases linearly with increases in productivity. Instead, there will be an incremental accrual as the food chain lengthens; herbivores limit the expansion of plants and carnivores do the same to herbivores (see Oksanen and Oksanen 2000).

Sometimes a species with low biomass can have an ecological effect that is disproportionate to its abundance, as with a highly interactive species such as beavers (*Castor canadensis*) (Soulé et al. 2003a, 2005). Under top-down regulation, such species maintain diversity, although a numerically dominant species may also serve that function (Paine 1966; Estes et al. 2001). If a carnivore such as a wolf checks a prey species that is competitively superior, or changes the prey's behavior in some way, then it is erecting ecological boundaries that protect weaker competitors from competitive exclusion (Paine 1966; Terborgh et al. 1999; Estes et al. 2001). Under this paradigm, carnivores play an important role in regulating interactions, and predation can cause indirect impacts that affect flora and fauna ecologically distant from the carnivore (Terborgh 1988; Terborgh and Estes forthcoming).

THE IMPACTS OF PREDATORS ON PREY

Carnivores control prey directly and indirectly. While predation may directly reduce numbers of prey (Terborgh 1988; Terborgh et al. 1997, 2001; Estes et al. 1998; Schoener and Spiller 1999), it may also indirectly cause prey to alter their behavior so that they become less vulnerable, by choosing different habitats, different food sources, different group sizes, different times of activity, or limiting the amount of time spent feeding (Kotler et al. 1993; Brown et al. 1994; FitzGibbon and Lazarus 1995; Palomares and Delibes 1997; Schmitz 1998; Berger et al. 2001b).

If a predator preys on a wide range of species, its presence may cause all prey species to reduce their respective niches and thus may reduce competition among those species. Removing the predator dissolves the ecological boundaries that check competition. As a result, prey species may compete for limited resources, and superior competitors may displace weaker competitors, thus leading to less diversity through competitive exclusion (see Paine 1966; Terborgh et al. 1997; Henke and Bryant 1999). The impact of carnivores extends beyond the objects of their predation. By changing distribution, abundance, and behavior of herbivores, carnivores have far-reaching effects. For example, because herbivores eat seeds and plants, predation on herbivores influences the structure of the plant community (Terborgh 1988; Terborgh et al. 1997, 2001; Estes et al. 1998). The plant community, in turn, influences distribution, abundance, and competitive interaction within groups of birds, mammals, and insects.

We briefly introduced the idea above that plants suffer or thrive when there are even or odd numbers of trophic levels, respectively. Direct evidence for this is the overexploitation (through the fur trade) of sea otters (*Enhydra lutris*) in the North Pacific for their fur (see Estes 1996; Estes et al. 1978, 1989, 1998; Estes and Duggins 1995). This system evolved with three trophic levels: carnivorous sea otters, herbivorous macroinvertebrates such as sea urchins, and kelp forests. Following the decline of sea otters, marine invertebrate herbivores increased in number and devastated kelp forests, thus reducing the food chain from three levels to two. This in turn produced a cascade of indirect effects, including reducing diversity among a host of fish, shorebird, invertebrate, and raptor species (see Estes 1996; Estes et al. 1978, 1989, 1998; Estes and Duggins 1995).

Gradual recovery of the sea otter in recent years has restored the third trophic level. Invertebrate grazers then declined, and the kelp forests and associated fauna recovered (Estes et al. 1978, 1989, 1998). When killer whales (*Orcinus orca*) entered the area, they imposed a fourth trophic level (Estes et al. 1998). The killer whales reduced numbers of sea otters, allowing the invertebrate grazers to increase, and that reduced the biomass of the kelp forest. At a 2001 presentation in Denver, Colorado, J. A. Estes emphasized the importance of long-term studies; he stated that analyzing any five-year block of time from their thirty years of data would produce different results.

Similarly, Krebs, Boonstra, et al. (2001) synthesized forty years of studies on the snowshoe hare (*Lepus americanus*) cycle. Some ecology textbooks highlight the observed ten-year oscillation as a predator-prey cycle between Canada lynx (*Lynx canadensis*) and hare. Studies by Krebs, Boonstra, et al. (1995) and Krebs, Boutin, et al. (2001), however, revealed that one can only understand the process by analyzing all three trophic levels. Krebs, Boutin, et al. wrote (2001, 34), "The hare cycle is caused by an interaction between predation and food supplies, and its biological impacts ripple across many species of predators and prey in the boreal forest." When examining these interactions, Krebs, Boutin, et al. (2001) stated that the dominant factor regulating the hare cycle was predation. Cycle dynamics did not change with the addition of nutrients, and the immediate cause of death in 95 percent of the hares was predation. Furthermore, lynx were not the only predator of hares. Other predators included coyotes (*Canis latrans*), goshawks (*Accipiter gentilis*), great-horned owls (*Bubo virginianus*), smaller raptors, and small mammals, particularly red squirrels (*Tamiasciurus hudsonicus*) and ground squirrels (Krebs, Boutin, et al. 2001). Absent lynx, the hare cycle continued unchanged because of "compensation," in this case increased predation by these other predators (Stenseth et al. 1998).

Both the sea otter and snowshoe hare investigations demonstrate the importance of long-term studies and accentuate the need to investigate predator-prey interactions over more than just two trophic levels, let alone examining the interactions between only one species of predator and one species of prey.

In Venezuela, Terborgh et al. (1997, 2001) took advantage of a hydroelectric project that formed Lago Guri, a reservoir 120 km (74 mi.) long and up to 70 km (43 mi.) wide with islands scattered throughout. After seven years of isolation on the islands, nearly 75 percent of the vertebrate species have disappeared; the islands are too small to support populations of jaguars (*Panthera onca*) and pumas (*Puma concolor*) (Terborgh et al. 1997, 2001). The few animal species remaining are hyperabundant and have had devastating effects on the plant communities. On these islands there is little regeneration of the canopy trees (Terborgh et al. 1997, 2001).

In another example, researchers working on grasslands in Texas found that nine months after coyote removal, rodent species' richness and diversity declined compared to that of areas with coyotes (Henke and Bryant 1999). Twelve months after coyote removal, the Ord's kangaroo rat (*Dipodomys ordii*) was the only rodent species captured on the study area (Henke and Bryant 1999). Removing coyotes eliminated the ecological boundaries among species of rodents, and the Ord's kangaroo rat was a superior competitor, increasing in number and displacing other rodent species.

Wolves are a highly interactive species. Long-term monitoring data from the boreal forest of Isle Royale indicate that predation by wolves on moose plays a role in ecosystem function by changing the number and behavior of moose (McLaren and Peterson 1994). The number and movements of moose then affects the balsam fir (*Abies balsamea*) forest (and other woody plants) by regulating seedling establishment, sapling recruitment, sapling growth rates, litter production in the forest, and soil nutrient dynamics (Pastor et al. 1988; Post el al. 1999 and references within).

When the wolf population declined, moose reached high densities and suppressed fir growth. This top-down trophic cascade regulation is apparently replaced by bottom-up influences only when forest stand–replacing disturbances such as fire or large windstorms occur at times when moose density is already low (McLaren and Peterson 1994). This is strong evidence that wolves exert top-down control of a food chain.

Research in the Greater Yellowstone Ecosystem and elsewhere suggests elk populations not regulated by large predators negatively affect the growth of aspen (*Populus tremuloides*) (Kay 1990, Kay and Wagner 1994). Wolves, a significant predator of elk, may positively influence the aspen canopy through a trophic cascade caused by the wolf reducing elk numbers, modifying elk movement, and changing elk browsing patterns on young aspen (White et al. 1998; Ripple and Betscha 2003, 2004). Elk proliferated and aspen recruitment ceased when wolves disappeared from Yellowstone National Park (Ripple and Larson 2000).

Similarly, Berger et al. (2001a) showed that moose increased their numbers when wolves and grizzly bears (*Ursus arctos*) were absent. Because moose reduced the quality and quantity of willow, neotropical migrant birds fared better in areas where wolves and bears preyed on moose. These factors are being reversed with the reintroduction of wolves into Yellowstone in 1995 (Ripple and Betscha 2004). Today there are fewer moose and more willows, and birds are faring better.

RELATIONSHIPS BETWEEN LARGE CARNIVORES AND SMALLER PREDATORS

Large carnivores directly and indirectly affect smaller carnivores, or mesopredators, and therefore the community structure of small prey (Terborgh and Winter 1980; Soulé et al. 1988; Bolger et al. 1991; Vickery et al. 1994; Palomares et al. 1995; Sovada et al. 1995; Crooks and Soulé 1999; Henke and Bryant 1999; Schoener and Spiller 1999).

Small prey distribution and abundance affect ecological factors such as seed dispersal, soil porosity, soil chemistry, plant biomass, plant nutrient content, and epizootics (Whicker and Detling 1988; Hoogland 1995; Detling 1998; Keesing 2000).

In California, Soulé et al. (1988) and Crooks and Soulé (1999) documented more species of scrub-dependent birds in canyons with coyotes than in canyons without coyotes. The absence of coyotes allowed opossums (*Didelphis virginianus*), foxes (*Vulpes* spp.), and house cats to proliferate. These species preyed heavily on songbirds and native rodents. Other researchers have observed the effects of mesopredator release in grasslands (Vickery et al. 1994; Henke and Bryant 1999), wetlands (Sovada et al. 1995), and Mediterranean forest (Palomares et al. 1995).

We think mesopredator release can manifest in at least three ways: population increases of smaller predators, modified niche exploitation, and altered community structure (largely because of the first two factors). An excellent example comes from Yellowstone. Wolves were extirpated from the park in the early part of the last century. In the absence of competition from wolves, coyotes assumed some of the ecological characteristics and functions of the larger canid, including forming packs and preying on large ungulates (R. L. Crabtree, pers. comm.). However, because they are smaller than wolves, coyotes could only partially fill the role of the apex predator. The dynamics of the predator/prey system were modified. Interspecific associations such as mutualistic relationships and coevolved food webs were disrupted. This in turn may have markedly altered the diversity and composition of the natural community, causing secondary extinctions or other unanticipated ripple effects, such as the loss of aspen, willow, beavers, and neotropical migrant bird species.

When wolves were reintroduced, they changed the distribution and abundance of coyotes, as they have done elsewhere (Paquet 1989, 1991, 1992; Crabtree and Sheldon 1999). In addition to these obvious competitive interactions, wolves also provide a regular supply of carrion, which is exploited by smaller carnivores.

MACROECOLOGICAL EVIDENCE FOR TOP-DOWN FORCES

The previous sections outlined some mechanisms through which the presence of carnivores can control ecosystems. How widespread are their impacts? Historically, many natural resources managers and biologists held the view that bottom-up forces drove ecosystem interactions (Polis and Strong 1996). Obviously, resource abundance and competition play important roles, but modern evidence shows that top-down effects function simultaneously (see Terborgh et al. 1999; Estes et al. 2001; Ray et al. 2005; Terborgh and Estes forthcoming). To ignore the indirect effects exerted by carnivores on diversity, structure, and function of an ecosystem could fatally flaw management strategies.

There is a growing body of macroecological (i.e., ecology at large geographic and spatial scales) evidence to support the impact of carnivores on ecosystems. For example, Oksanen and Oksanen (2000) compared areas with herbivores to areas without herbivores to determine differences in plant biomass and primary productivity. They studied fifty-one locations in Arctic or Antarctic regions. In areas with herbivores, as plant biomass increased, productivity remained about the same, whereas in areas without herbivores, as plant biomass increased, productivity increased rapidly (Oksanen and Oksanen 2000). These observations support their hypothesis of top-down regulation.

Beyond the Arctic and Antarctic, most macroecological evidence for impacts of carnivores on ecosystems must be viewed with caution because humans have altered a large percentage of temperate and tropical biomes.

This complicates our ability to separate the effects of carnivores from those of humans. Nevertheless, evidence suggests that carnivores are important.

Crête and Manseau (1996) compared the biomass of ungulates to primary productivity along a 1,000 km (620 mi.) north–south latitudinal gradient on the Québec-Labrador peninsula, and Crête (1999) did the same over North America. At the same latitude, there were five to seven times more ungulates in areas where there were no wolves compared to where wolves were present. In areas of former wolf range but where no wolves currently exist, the ungulate biomass regressed to primary productivity, producing a positive slope (Crête 1999).

In Poland, red deer (elk) irrupted after persecution eliminated wolves, and roe deer (*Capreolus capreolus*) irrupted when humans extirpated European lynx (*Lynx lynx*) (Jedrzejewska and Jedrzejewski 1998 in Jedrzejewski et al. 2002). Eliminating carnivores from an area that evolved with strong predator-prey interactions may have a severe impact through a trophic cascade.

Having reviewed both qualitative and quantitative evidence across a number of different ecological systems, Terborgh et al. (1999) concluded that top-down control was stronger and more common than previously thought. Schmitz et al. (2000) conducted a quantitative meta-analysis of trophic cascades in terrestrial systems using data from sixty independent tests in forty-one studies. Their analysis, limited to invertebrates and small vertebrates, detected trophic cascades in forty-five of the sixty tests. They showed that predator removal had a significant, direct impact on herbivore numbers and on plant damage (positive) and reduced plant biomass and plant-reproductive output (negative). Schmitz et al. concluded that trophic cascades were present under a variety of conditions with different types of predators and occurred more frequently than is currently believed.

Another quantitative meta-analysis examined forty scientific papers on terrestrial trophic cascades in arthropod-dominated food webs (Halaj and Wise 2001). They reported extensive evidence supporting terrestrial trophic cascades. Indeed, 77 percent of the 299 experiments showed a positive response on the part of herbivores when predators were removed (Halaj and Wise 2001).

Finally, Estes et al. (2001) reviewed the impacts of predation in a variety of ecosystems, including rocky shores, kelp forests, lakes, rivers and streams, oceanic systems, boreal and temperate forests, coastal scrub, tropical forests, and on islands with exotic predators. They concluded that predation has dramatic impacts at organizational levels ranging from individual behavior to system dynamics and on time scales ranging from ecological to evolutionary (Estes et al. 2001).

Failing to recognize the role of carnivores can produce drastic changes in ecosystems (Terborgh and Estes forthcoming). For example, wildlife managers have reduced carnivore numbers to keep ungulates at artificially high levels for recreational hunting. Yet, an overabundance of white-tailed deer has been shown to reduce numbers of native rodent species, produce declines in understory nesting birds, obliterate understory vegetation in some forests, and even eliminate regeneration of the oak (*Quercus* spp.) canopy (Alverson et al. 1988, 1994; McShea and Rappole 1992; McShea et al. 1997).

If we continue to manage carnivores by reducing their numbers without considering the indirect effects that will cascade through a system, we will undoubtedly continue to alter the structure and function of native ecosystems in ways that we may later regret. We believe that it is not a question of whether or not carnivores play an important role; it is a question of how they play their role in trophic interactions.

RELATIVE STRENGTH OF INTERACTIONS UNDER VARIOUS CONDITIONS

While carnivores such as wolves exert top-down influences on communities, those influences vary significantly under different environmental conditions. The level of influence is a complex and situational event. Abiotic, or nonbiologic, factors such as type, frequency, and scale of natural disturbance (e.g., fire, flood, windthrow) can influence the relative importance of top-down or bottom-up forces (see Connell 1978). Disturbance over large geographic areas shortens food chains (at least temporarily) and thus changes interaction dynamics among trophic levels (Menge and Sutherland 1976). As Sanford (1999) found, climatic patterns such as El Niño or La Niña affect the ability of highly interactive predators to regulate prey in aquatic systems. Ballard and Van Ballenberghe (1997) and Post et al. (1999) found the same for terrestrial systems. Seasonally driven mechanisms can alter rates of compensatory mortality and natality, or birthrates, and thus adjust the impact of predation on the population size of prey (Boyce et al. 1999b). A region's productivity level can influence what threshold of distribution and abundance for the predator allows that predator to exert its role in an ecosystem.

Behaviors such as migration enable animals to make use of food over a larger area (Fryxell et al. 1988). If terrestrial predators such as wolves are unable to follow migrating ungulates such as caribou (*Rangifer tarandus*) over a long distance, then they will have less relative impact on population numbers of the migrants (Fryxell et al. 1988; Fryxell 1995). Migratory wildebeests (*Connochaetes taurinus*) fit the hypothesis of predation-sensitive foraging, where food supplies and predation interact to regulate populations (Sinclair and Arcese 1995). Like the earlier example of snowshoe hares, predation is the final agent of mortality. Unlike the case of the hares, however, food supply plays a driving role in mortality of wildebeests by predation: as food supply decreases, wildebeests increase their risk to find food (Sinclair and Arcese 1995).

The physical habitat in which an animal lives imposes adaptive pressures that mold behaviors and population structures, in turn affecting the role of predation. Behavior of a predator is important: Is it social or solitary? Is it a cursorial hunter or a sit-and-wait hunter? Is it a generalist or a specialist? Among prey species, sociality and large body size enhance predation-avoidance capabilities.

The strength of interaction between species is complex and situational. Even within the same species, it can be difficult to extrapolate results from one part of the range to another (Soulé et al. 2003a, 2005).

CARNIVORES AND MANAGEMENT

Scientific data increasingly indicate that carnivores play an important controlling role in an ecological system (see Terborgh et al. 1999; Ray et al. 2005; Terborgh and Estes forthcoming). Yet, carnivore control as institutionalized by several government agencies has historically been the center of management solutions. Intensive management regimes often do not fully consider the circumstance, season, behavior, or other conditions that affect the complex role of carnivores in the system.

Short-term control and hunting restrictions may be necessary when a system is highly perturbed, or fluctuating outside its normal bounds of variability. Just as heavy human harvest can influence prey numbers, so too can predators, particularly when prey densities are low (Boyce et al. 1999b). However, rather than focusing solely on symptoms, we need to ask deeper questions about why our systems are perturbed.

What indirect effects ripple through a system if managers or hunters reduce carnivore numbers below the bounds of their natural variation? What will happen to vegetation and nongame species diversity if we try to hold ungulate numbers at unnaturally constant and high numbers for recreational hunting? Can we manage populations of predator and prey in ways that more closely resemble natural patterns? (Indeed, managing ungulate production for hunter success philosophically differs little from managing livestock for meat production.) A quote in W. B. Ballard et al. (2001, 107) is telling:

> Biologists continue to debate whether predation is a regulatory or a limiting factor, but to wildlife managers who are responsible for managing deer populations to provide hunting and viewing opportunities, the distinction between these terms may not matter.

It should. Evidence indicates that our lack of understanding (or lack of caring) about the role of carnivores in ecosystem processes has damaged the systems we try to manage. Eradicating and reducing carnivores such as wolves and pumas has, by removing a critical element, simplified systems by reducing biodiversity, largely by eliminating the carnivores' keystone role of ungulate predation.

Not only have we reduced carnivore numbers, but we have also managed for unnaturally high numbers of ungulates. The elk population in Colorado currently exceeds the carrying capacity of the range. In 2001, the Colorado Division of Wildlife wanted to reduce elk numbers from about 260,000 to 190,000 (Meyers 2002). After an elk count showed that numbers had swelled to 305,000 in the spring of 2002, the Division of Wildlife raised its target population to 230,000. Adjusting target goals after the fact does not change the land's productivity, and the winter of 2001–2002 was very dry. We would do well to remember the experience of the Kaibab Plateau, where the mule deer (*Odocoileus hemionus*) population grew so large in the absence of predation that the animals depleted their food base, eventually leading to mass starvation.

None of these questions is new. Aldo Leopold asked many of them a half century ago. Yet, as long as we think mainly from paradigms of hunter harvest—or silviculture, or livestock production—and fail to think in terms of ecosystem function, we will continue to lose diversity despite good intentions, higher budgets, and increasing human effort.

In short, wildlife management policies based on reducing carnivore numbers have caused, and will continue to cause, severe harm to many other organisms that seem distantly removed from the apex trophic layer (see Terborgh 1988; Terborgh et al. 1999; Terborgh and Estes forthcoming). For these reasons, we believe that carnivore policy and ungulate management must be driven by sound ecological science at the ecoregion, or landscape, scale.

IMPORTANCE TO PEOPLE

Nature and the wildlife it contains provide physical, emotional, and intellectual benefits to people (Kellert 1996; Decker et al. 2001). Large carnivores epitomize the so-called charismatic megafauna; that is, large, charismatic species such as wolves and polar bears (*Ursus maritimus*) that tend to enjoy greater support among most people (Kellert 1996). People appreciate large carnivores for the cultural, aesthetic, existence, economic, and other values they represent (Kellert 1993, 1996). Other people disdain large carnivores based on fears for human, livestock, or pet safety; the negative economic impact they sometimes cause; and issues of private property rights and government actions that they believe large carnivores represent (Kellert 1996; Kellert et al. 1996; Meadow et al. 2005; see chap. 6).

The significance of some species from a historical or other human-centered perspective leads to strong personal and symbolic values (Shepard 1978; Kellert 1986b, 1996; Reading 1993). Large carnivores such as wolves and bears provide symbolic, religious, and historical values to many people (Rolston 1985; Hardy-Short and Short 2000). These animals often invoke a feeling of awe and enlivened senses among humans (Kellert 1996; Hardy-Short and Short 2000). As a result, in many cultures people revere or revered large carnivores (Luckert 1975; Campbell 1988; Nelson 1993). Hoping to tap into the admired attributes of large carnivores, such as hunting prowess, stealth, strength, and speed, people created religious and social societies centered on these among other animals (Levi-Strauss 1963, 1966; Campbell 1988). Large carnivores continue to symbolize such traits today, as any list of sports teams' and luxury products' names attest.

The beauty and symbolic nature of large carnivores inspires many people (Kellert 1993, 1996; Kellert et al. 1996). That inspiration often stimulates the mind and results in an artistic outpouring (van Diern and Hummelinck 1979; Rolston 1981; Reading 1993). As a result, animals like bears, tigers (*Panthera tigris*), and wolves often form the foci of literature, poems, paintings, sculptures, and dance. These animals and the art they inspire provide a source of satisfaction, well-being, and contentment to many people who view them (Kellert 1996).

People also develop strong emotional attachments to large carnivores based on moral and ethical considerations (Kellert 1980, 1996; Reading 1993). Many of these people will never see a polar bear or grizzly bear in the wild, but they want these animals to exist. To these people, such intrinsic "existence values" are important and influential (Rolston 1981; Brown et al. 2001). People donate substantial sums of money to ensure the conservation of large carnivores and often vote to further their protection. For some, the animals are not only important to themselves, but they also want to ensure that their children or grandchildren have the opportunity to see them in the wild. Social scientists dub these "bequest values" (Brown et al. 2001). Other people embrace altruistic values toward carnivores—they simply recognize that other people want to see them, whether or not they relate to them.

Large carnivores head the list of species people want to see when they engage in wildlife-based recreation, and people often expend great effort in trying to catch a glimpse of them in natural settings (van Dieren and Hummelinck 1979; Rolston 1981; Reading 1993). As a result of the satisfaction many people obtain from direct experiences with large carnivores, they spend money traveling to view them and purchase products featuring these animals (Kellert 1996).

Large carnivores also add value to outdoor recreation that is not wildlife-based, because people often place additional value on seeing these animals or simply knowing they are around (Rolston 1981; Shaw 1987; Brown et al. 2001). The economic impact of wolf restoration to Yellowstone National Park, for example, generates an additional $35 million per year in revenue for the region surrounding the park, and, because those dollars turn over in the local communities, the wolves have created an overall impact of $70 million per year to the local economy (Duffield et al. 2006; Stark 2006; Anonymous 2007). Indirect recreational values accrue from books, television shows, and magazines devoted to these animals (Bryan 1980; Kellert 1996). Product branding (Tony the Tiger, Mercury Cougar, Chicago Bears) helps companies sell products from cars to sports teams to corn flakes to camping gear to sporting event tickets.

Not all values ascribed to large carnivores are positive, however. Some people dislike large carnivores because they represent a threat to the safety of humans, pets, or livestock (Kellert 1980, 1995; Reading 1993; Hardy-Short and Short 2000). That

dislike often extends well beyond concerns for safety. As Kellert (1996, 105) stated with respect to wolves:

> As the extent and viciousness of the killing often reached irrational proportions, one suspects the wolf may have performed roles beyond the merely utilitarian. Destroying the wolf may have also reflected the urge to rid the world of an unwanted and feared element in nature, perhaps even the settler's atavistic potential to succumb to the allure of wildness and the absence of civilizing control.

Kellert (1996, 110) goes on to suggest that for some people, "the wolf, grizzly bear, puma, and other large predators remain a vivid reminder of the necessity to combat and repress wild nature in the never ending struggle to render the land safe and productive." To other people, large carnivores have come to symbolize governmental interference in how they manage private property or interact with wildlife (Kellert 1996; Meadow et al. 2005). For centuries, governments helped people to control or eradicate large carnivores (Lopez 1978; Dunlap 1988; Kellert 1996), so it is not surprising that the recent shift by many government agencies from control to conservation has been met with bewilderment and anger by some sectors of society.

Despite some of the negative values they engender, overall, large carnivores stimulate the imagination and inspire a sense of awe and wonder for many people, making them among the most highly valued of all species. It is difficult to place a monetary figure on many of the values ascribed to large carnivores (Brown et al. 2001). The result is that they often go underappreciated in traditional economic analyses and therefore governmental policies. Yet, that is slowly changing as decision makers increasingly recognize that not all parts of a cost-benefit analysis are easily captured using traditional methods (Brown et al. 2001; Loomis 2004).

CONCLUSIONS

Large carnivores are ecologically important, often disproportionately important, to the ecological systems they inhabit. Yet they are also important to people for a variety of other reasons, including cultural reasons, aesthetics, their right to exist, and the economic benefits they sometimes accrue. These animals often exert strong influence on ecological systems through top-down regulation, in which they affect herbivores that in turn affect vegetation. The mechanisms of top-down regulation include direct effects, through predation, and indirect effects, in

which large carnivores influence the behavior of their prey. By controlling populations of smaller predators, large carnivores also reduce pressure on the prey of these mesopredators.

Evidence for the importance of large carnivores to the ecological systems they inhabit continues to mount. Many people value the role that these charismatic animals play in the systems they inhabit, but people value large carnivores for a variety of other reasons as well, including symbolic, existence, aesthetic, recreational, and other values. Of course, many people also hold negative values and attitudes toward large carnivores. Thus, the human dimensions of large carnivore management may rival or surpass the ecological challenges of their management.

Chapter 4
Variables Influencing Carnivore Translocation

Brian Miller, Richard P. Reading, Katherine Ralls,
Susan G. Clark, and James A. Estes

INTRODUCTION

Humans have had major impacts on the earth's ecosystems and have eliminated large mammals, particularly carnivores, over extensive areas through a combination of habitat destruction, prey reduction, and direct persecution. Yet large mammals, especially carnivores, often play key roles in maintaining ecological communities. Through predation, large carnivores send indirect effects rippling through the trophic levels of an ecosystem, affecting organisms that exist at several scales (Terborgh 1988; Terborgh et al. 1999; Estes et al. 2001; see chap. 3).

When humans remove large carnivores from ecological systems that the carnivores helped mold and maintain, those systems simplify and degrade (Terborgh et al. 1999). Research clearly documents degradation of such systems following the loss of top carnivores. As a result, ecologists label such species "highly interactive" (Soulé et al. 2003a, 2005). One type of highly interactive species is the keystone species, a species that greatly affects the ecological system it inhabits, and its effect is much greater than might be expected by its abundance. Although more data on how systems decline after removing such highly interactive species are always beneficial, we suggest that the real question now is, What happens when we try to restore ecological processes by returning an extirpated keystone species?

Restoring species usually involves active human intervention, such as releasing wild-born individuals or captive-born animals

into an area where they no longer exist or where they exist at low numbers (Griffith et al. 1989; Wolf et al. 1997). If natural recolonization of a carnivore occurs at a reasonable rate, protecting important corridors and habitat is usually preferable (and cheaper). However, with the present rates of habitat loss, the chances of natural recolonization for many carnivore species become less likely with each passing day.

Successfully restoring large carnivores can aid larger conservation efforts in several ways. Large carnivores play important roles, often functioning as umbrella species (species with huge habitat requirements, such that conserving them will protect enough habitat for many other species with small needs), indicator species (species more sensitive to ecological change than other species, and thus indicators of ecosystem health), or keystone species (Miller et al. 1998). Therefore, restoring them contributes to the design and management of protected areas (Noss and Cooperrider 1994; Lambeck 1997; Soulé et al. 2005). Perhaps most importantly, returning carnivores can restore ecological processes that are important to the health of an ecosystem (Soulé et al. 2003b, 2005).

We first discuss how attention to some important biological considerations can affect the success of a translocation. Next, we consider human variables. A successful program requires a holistic and truly interdisciplinary approach that integrates social and biological sciences. We emphasize reintroduction, returning species to areas where their populations were extirpated, because restocking (releasing animals to augment an existing population) and introduction (releasing animals outside their historical range) may be inadvisable, although those tactics may be useful under special circumstances (IUCN 1987).

BIOLOGICAL CONSIDERATIONS

Many biological factors affect the ease of translocating an animal. Understanding genetics, demography, behavior, disease, and habitat requirements can produce methods that greatly increase success (Stanley Price 1989; Kleiman 1989; Reading and Clark 1996; Wolf et al. 1997; Miller et al. 1999; Seddon et al. 2007; Jule et al. 2008). That information is often lacking. Schaller (1996) reported that only 15 percent of terrestrial carnivore species had been the subject of at least one field investigation by the early 1990s, and even the status of most species remains obscure.

A translocation program should include a feasibility study, a preparation phase, a release phase, and a monitoring phase (IUCN 1987). The planning team should address several biological questions during the feasibility study (Reading et al. 1991; Kleiman et al. 1993; Miller et al. 1999), including:

+ Is there a need to reintroduce or restock a wild population?
+ Did the species occur as a viable population in the proposed release area?
+ If restocking is possible, would it pose a threat to the existing wild population, or might it benefit the population by reducing inbreeding depression?
+ Have policies eliminated, curbed, or mitigated the causes of the population decline or extirpation (i.e., local extinction)?
+ Is there sufficient protected habitat for the animals to survive?
+ Are there suitable animals available that are surplus to the genetic and demographic needs of the source population?
+ Is there sufficient knowledge to formulate a plan of action and evaluate its success?

If a feasibility study gives the green light, the planning team should address myriad additional biological considerations. In the following paragraphs, we discuss selecting animals, genetics, demography, behavior, health and disease, habitat evaluation, rejuvenating ecological processes by translocation, and other technical considerations (following B. Miller, Ralls, et al. 1999).

SELECTING ANIMALS FOR TRANSLOCATIONS
Taxonomy

Animals chosen for translocation should be as similar as possible to those that originally inhabited the release site. However, the planning team should examine existing subspecific frameworks closely because they may not reflect the true distribution of genetic variation and genetic discontinuities within species (Ryder 1986; Avise 1989). Early taxonomists created numerous subspecies within most species of carnivores, and they often based their classifications on a small number of physical (called morphological) characters from a small number of specimens. Because morphological traits result from the influence of genetics and the environment, such early subspecific designations often overestimated the number of genetically based subspecies.

Wolves provide a good example. Hall and Kelson (1959) listed thirty-two worldwide subspecies of gray wolves (*Canis lupus*). This probably represents an inflated number of wolf subspecies, because minor transitions in physical traits along distributions (known as clines) may not merit subspecific status (Carbyn 1987). In fact, Nowak (1995) revised wolf taxonomy to include five subspecies. Wolves can disperse over long distances, and the vast expanse of boreal areas probably facilitated gene flow, particularly in North America before European settlement (Carbyn 1987; Wayne and Vila 2003). Genetic diversity of wolves is better explained as a pattern of differentiation with distance rather than subspecific geographic boundaries (Forbes and Boyd 1987).

Genetic studies using modern molecular techniques can help define appropriate genetic subdivisions. A translocation team must carefully interpret molecular genetic differentiation among populations, because it does not always reflect historical barriers to gene flow. For example, widely separated populations of coyotes (*Canis latrans*) show little mitochondrial DNA differentiation (Lehman et al. 1991). However, in kit foxes (*Vulpes macrotis*), a small canid with limited dispersal capabilities, significant genetic differences exist between populations, and those differences reflect geographical barriers (Mercure et al. 1993). While the Mexican wolf (*C. l. baileyi*) is considered a genetically unique subspecies of the gray wolf (Garcia-Moreno et al. 1996), Wayne et al. (1992) believed that apparent genetic differences among other extant gray wolf populations reflected population declines and habitat fragmentation rather than a long history of genetic isolation. Thus, if carnivores range over large areas, like wolves do, spatial heterogeneity in the genetic structure of a population is probably not much of a concern, but it can be for animals with limited capability to disperse. Size may not always be an indicator of dispersal ability. For example, grizzly bears (*Ursus arctos*) are more limited in dispersal capability than one would expect for an animal of that size.

Wild versus Captive Animals

Wild-born animals usually survive longer than captive-born animals in translocations (Griffith et al. 1989; Snyder et al. 1996; Jule et al. 2008), and we recommend releasing captive carnivores only when there are no other alternatives (Miller et al. 1999). That said, it is important to note that captive breeding and reintroduction have saved some species from extinction, including the red wolf (*Canis rufus*) and the black-footed ferret (*Mustela nigripes*) (Miller et al. 1996; Phillips et al. 2003). In addition, captive animals can be used in education and research—whether or not they are ever released into the wild. For example, some questions important to conservation, such as understanding energetic needs or reproductive behavior, are difficult to answer using wild animals.

There are several reasons that we recommend moving wild-born animals over captive-bred animals. Captive breeding for translocation is expensive in terms of time, space, and money, and it can be risky. The captive environment may erode the genetic basis for important morphological, physiological, and behavioral traits via the artificial selection that inevitably occurs in captivity (Snyder et al. 1996; Jule et al. 2008). For example, while captive-born animals may still exhibit the correct behavior in a given situation, they may not perform it at the level of efficiency needed to survive in the wild. Indeed, during a captive-breeding program, learned behavioral traits can degenerate much more rapidly than genetic diversity (May 1991). Examples of behavioral traits that the captive environment may adversely affect include searching for food, killing, predator avoidance, recognizing home sites, movement patterns (such as seasonal migrations), methods of raising young, ability of young to follow mothers to kill sites, and negative response to human presence (Miller et al. 1996; Snyder et al. 1996; Beldon and McCown 1996; Jule et al. 2008). As a result, post-reintroduction mortality rates for captive-born animals are often high. Reducing the impact of these problems during reintroduction is often time-consuming and expensive.

Different species respond variably to captive conditions, but more generations in captivity likely increases the degeneration of survival skills. As a result, translocation programs using captive-reared animals should employ substantial prerelease preparation and postrelease training. While Seddon et al. (2007) mention that this idea has had little experimental testing, experimentally compared releases of black-footed ferrets demonstrated that animals raised in seminatural outdoor pens had higher survival rates (Biggins et al. 1999).

But even such preparation and training may not be able to restore survival traits to full efficiency. Effectively developing behaviors often requires the correct environment for learning (including a skilled parent) or, in the case of critical periods—also called imprinting, in which animals only learn during a particular window of time during their development—the correct stimulus at the proper time during development. In social animals that learn by mimicking, developing a behavior requires a group member with skill and experience. Captive conditions often make it difficult to provide these requirements. Furthermore, selecting for tameness and other genetic adaptations to the captive environment can create serious problems for populations maintained in captivity over several generations (Snyder et al. 1996; Frankham et al. 2002).

Experimental releases of captive-raised and wild-born individuals of the same species often demonstrate that captive-raised animals exhibit different behaviors and lower survival rates than their wild-born counterparts (Schadweiler and Tester 1972; Cade et al. 1989; Griffith et al. 1989; Beck et al. 1991; Wiley et al. 1992; Beldon and McCown 1996; Miller et al. 1996; Jule et al. 2008). Captive-raised pumas (*Puma concolor*) in Florida had less fear of humans and were more likely to engage in puma-human and puma-livestock encounters than wild-caught animals (Beldon and McCown 1996). Similarly, orphan sea otter (*Enhydra lutris*) pups

raised in captivity and released into the wild often approached people; two released pups allegedly attacked humans (J. A. Estes, pers. obs.). Such interactions between wildlife and people or their domesticated animals often end badly for wildlife.

Age-sex Categories

Erickson and Hamilton (1988) recommended releasing animals in sex ratios similar to those exhibited by wild populations to help ensure reproductive encounters. This often means releasing more females (Short et al. 1992). Differences between male and female behaviors, as well as age, may influence release considerations. Young animals often display greater plasticity in behavior than adults and are less important to the source population. Some translocations release mixed sexes and ages that replicate natural social groups, such as wolf packs (Bangs and Fritts 1996).

In many cases, the availability of animals from the source population limits both genetic and demographic considerations. This is especially true when the source population is a captive-breeding program. In many such situations, managers should give priority to the genetic and demographic management of the source population rather than the group scheduled for release. This is especially true at the beginning of a program, when there is often high mortality (Miller et al. 1999; Frankham et al. 2002).

Puma translocations illustrate several of these points. In Florida puma releases, wild-caught females with kittens did not move far from their release sites, and the kittens behaved normally; however, wild-caught and released males covered large areas until they located females (Beldon and McCown 1996). Ruth et al. (1998) found that sex, age, and social status affected the success of moving wild-caught pumas in New Mexico. The best results came when pumas were between twelve and twenty-seven months of age; these animals moved the shortest distance from the release site and quickly established areas of use. Pumas of this age group (dispersal age) may settle more quickly because they are predisposed to accept an unfamiliar area (Ross and Jalkotzy 1995; Ruth et al. 1998). In addition, females of this age group moved less and had higher survival rates than males. Removing pumas less than twenty-seven months of age from a self-sustaining population would probably not jeopardize the source population genetically or demographically (Logan et al. 1996), an important consideration (Kleiman 1989; Stanley Price 1989). Adult translocated pumas (twenty-eight to ninety-six months of age) taken from established territories traveled the farthest from their release site, often showing homing tendencies (Ruth et al. 1998). Indeed, two pumas in this age class returned to their original home territories, more than 400 km (248 mi.) away. Older pumas (more than ninety-six months of age) showed high, immediate risk of death (Ruth et al. 1998). Similarly, adult male sea otters had a greater risk of death during capture and translocation than individuals in other age-sex classes (J. A. Estes, pers. obs.).

In general, puma translocation increased mortality over that observed in the source population (Ruth et al. 1998). The risks were long-term, and a number of deaths occurred in the second year after release. Chronic stress may have contributed to the deaths, particularly for adults. Combining suggestions for puma translocation from Ruth et al. (1998) and Beldon and McCown (1996), it is preferable to first release dispersal age females. After female pumas establish areas of use, the program could release young males in the presence of those females to keep them from wandering long distances. We caution, however, that it is sometimes difficult to determine optimum ages for translocation. For example, in some species, juveniles may exhibit higher survival rates after translocation, but the planning team should balance future reproductive potential against immediate reproductive capacity of any adults that establish in the release area.

Homing behavior and excessive movement from the release site has been a major problem in past translocations of ursids (bears), canids (dogs), felids (cats), and mustelids (weasels and allies) (Linnell et al. 1997). For example, when biologists moved 139 California sea otters to San Nicolas Island (about 100 km, or 60 mi., west of Los Angeles), the majority dispersed away from the island, and a minimum of 30 individuals, including juvenile and adult females, returned to their capture location (G. Rathbun, pers. comm.).

Excessive movement from the release site is a major reason for low survival and poor reproductive rates of translocated carnivores. Movement distances after release often directly correlate with mortality rates (Ruth et al. 1998). Linnell et al. (1997) suggested holding animals on a release site for a time prior to release to reduce postrelease movements, and moving large carnivores far from their capture site to reduce homing. This very approach was successful in establishing the gray wolf population in the Greater Yellowstone Area (Fritts et al. 2001).

Many wolves translocated to Yellowstone left their release site and headed in the direction they knew as home (summarized by Fritts 1993). Fourteen wolves released in Yellowstone during 1995 were held at the release site in enclosures for three months while fifteen wolves released into central Idaho were released immediately upon arrival. Wolves from Yellowstone traveled a mean of 22 km (14 mi.) from their release site, whereas wolves in Idaho traveled a mean of 82 km (51 mi.) from their release site (Fritts et al. 1997). Wolves released in Idaho headed in a general northward direction, because they originated in Canada (Fritts et al. 1997). Yellowstone wolf packs that acclimated in enclosures tended to stay together in packs (Fritts et al. 1997).

Genetics

Genetic considerations are important to translocation, yet biologists performed genetic screening in only 37 percent of reintroduction projects using captive-raised animals that Beck et al. (1993) reviewed. As discussed above, translocated animals should be as genetically diverse as possible because of the potential for founder effects (in which genetic diversity in a population is constrained by the diversity of the few individuals that survive to found a new population) and inbreeding depression within the small populations typical of translocation programs (Frankham et al. 2002). This is especially true in the early stages of a program. Researchers have documented inbreeding depression, that is, reduced reproductive fitness due to mating between close relatives (Ralls et al. 2001; Frankham et al. 2002; Keller and Waller 2002) in a large number of captive mammals (Ralls et al. 1988; Lacy 1997), including wolves (Laikre and Ryman 1991) and various wild populations of animals and plants (Keller and Waller 2002). Inbreeding depression can create problems in small reintroduced populations of large mammals because these populations probably had low inbreeding rates in North America prior to the arrival of European colonists (Ralls et al. 1986; Frankham 1995). Genetic problems may contribute to declining numbers in translocated herds of bighorn sheep (*Ovis canadensis*) (Fitzsimmons et al. 1997). Wildt et al. (1995) demonstrated that felid populations with reduced genetic diversity ejaculate lower total sperm counts and extraordinarily higher numbers of malformed spermatozoa than populations of the same species with high levels of genetic diversity. They also showed that homozygous populations showed physiological defects, including cardiac and immune system problems.

Outbreeding depression (reduced reproductive fitness due to mating between genetically dissimilar individuals) is much less likely to be a problem than inbreeding depression (Ballou 1997; Ralls et al. 2001; Frankham et al. 2002). Evidence for outbreeding depression comes primarily from plants and animals with extremely limited dispersal and appears to be more common in plants than animals (Ballou 1997; Ralls et al. 2001). In fact, a review by Arnold and Hodges (1995) found that even hybrids between species are not uniformly unfit, but they usually had either equivalent fitness to the two parental taxa or higher levels of fitness than at least one of the parents. So far, studies of captive animals have failed to find evidence of outbreeding depression in mammals (Smith et al. 1987; Jaquish 1994; Ballou 1997; R. C. Lacy, pers. comm.).

Many conservationists caution against simply trying to bolster numbers or maximize genetic heterogeneity by translocating animals into an area with a remnant population (IUCN 1987). The result could be "contamination" or even swamping of unique remnant genetic stocks by the translocated animals (Berg 1982; Stanley Price 1989). For example, when biologists released hatchery coho salmon (*Oncorhynchus kisutch*) into streams of the lower Columbia Basin, the released stock replaced native populations of coho salmon (Johnson et al. 1991). On the other hand, small remnant populations may suffer from severe inbreeding depression expressed as poor survival or reproductive success.

Planners can quickly reverse inbreeding depression in such populations by reintroducing a few individuals from another population (Frankham et al. 2002; Keller and Waller 2002). There are now several dramatic examples that demonstrate these benefits in small wild populations, including desert topminnow fish (*Poeciliopsis monacha*) (Vrijenhoek 1996), adders (*Vipera berus*) (Madsen et al. 1999), prairie chickens (*Tympanuchus cupido*) (Westemeier et al. 1998), and pumas (Hedrick 2001). Thus, the planning team should consider the probable genetic costs and benefits of introducing new individuals into a small remnant population on a case-by-case basis.

For most species, it is probably best to maximize genetic diversity among release animals. Haig et al. (1990) suggested that biologists select captive-bred animals in an attempt to balance the genetic contribution from each founder (by maximizing an index called the founder genome equivalent). This approach has been used for red wolves and Mexican wolves (M. Phillips, pers. comm.; see chap. 2). However, this strategy should not jeopardize the genetic integrity of the source population (Kleiman 1989). Greater genetic diversity among released animals would reduce the chances for founder effects and inbreeding depression, which may be important in a small population struggling to become established. Greater diversity may also enable the population to better adapt to its habitat.

Demography

Colonies of translocated animals must become large enough, as quickly as possible, to withstand fluctuations in the environment and their population size, because vacillations in either can drastically increase chances of extinction in small populations (Gilpin and Soulé 1986; Beissenger and McCullough 2002). To understand these population dynamics, biologists must analyze demographic parameters such as fecundity (i.e., birthrate), mortality, population growth rate, age structure, sex ratio, and life expectancy in natural populations (Stanley Price 1989). Comparing demographic traits of reintroduced populations with wild populations will help managers determine when a translocated population has become established and viable.

Demographic characteristics are also important for defining habitat quality, which is the foundation of any good conservation management plan. Van Horne (1983) discussed misleading conclusions about habitat quality when planners used simple density

estimates and presence/absence data without knowledge of age structure or social structure. For example, a team might conduct density surveys during warm months, when winter habitat may act as the limiting factor for species survival (Van Horne 1983). Additionally, social interactions can push juvenile dispersing animals into poorer quality habitat or even habitat sinks (in which death rates exceed birthrates), because a stable population of territorial adults occupies all good habitat. Even though individuals exist in temporarily high numbers in the poor habitat, very few of those animals will survive to reproduce (Van Horne 1983).

In polygynous carnivores (one male breeding with several females), adult females with young often center their activities where critical resources are concentrated and easiest to obtain. When caring for offspring, females may be restricted to optimal habitat because they must satisfy elevated energetic requirements with minimum time away from their young. Male carnivores, on the other hand, sometimes wander over extensive areas searching for females. Their movements are highly variable and often related more to reproductive needs and social status than habitat quality. For that reason, adult females, which form the demographic base of a population, often best represent the habitat needs of a carnivore species. Alternatively, in monogamous species such as the kit fox, pair-bonded males and females share the same home range (White and Ralls 1993).

Without paying attention to demographic factors, such as age structure, mortality, reproduction, and behavioral information such as social structure, one cannot truly differentiate the quality and usefulness of various habitat types for a reintroduced population.

Behavior

Candidates for translocation must perform behavioral traits efficiently in a variety of situations. The environment and a host of simultaneous behaviors necessary for survival directly influence the expression of a given trait. Several authors suggest using behavior as a measure of success in translocation projects (Kleiman 1989; Miller et al. 1996). Knowledge of hunting, killing, caching, predator avoidance, reproduction, parenting, imprinting periods, social organization, communication, territoriality, locomotion, daily movements, seasonal movements, and habitat choices all affect the selection of individuals for release, timing of translocations, method of release, and choice of sites. We discussed many of these factors in previous sections.

As mentioned earlier, site fidelity and homing are important behavioral traits affecting large-carnivore translocation success (Linnell et al. 1997). Habituating animals to release sites appears to help reduce dispersal following translocation for many species (Stanley Price 1989; Fritts et al. 1997; Linnell et al. 1997). Permitting animals to acclimate to release sites in a group setting also permits them to hone behavioral skills such as pack formation, social interaction, and foraging ability (Bangs and Fritts 1996).

Health and Disease

Translocation programs should carefully assess the health and physical condition of animals selected for release (Scott 1988; Cunningham 1996; see chap. 10). Despite Griffith et al. (1989) finding no correlation between success and physical condition of animals at time of release, we believe biologists should use only animals in good physical condition for translocations. Canada lynx (*Lynx canadensis*) in poor condition experienced high rates of starvation during a reintroduction in Colorado (Kloor 1999). Holding lynx in captivity until their physical condition improved appeared to help alleviate this problem (Shenk 2006).

In addition, translocations should not introduce diseases to the release site

(Cunningham 1996; see chap. 10), yet only 46 percent of translocation programs using captive-born animals conducted medical screening before release (Beck et al. 1993). Veterinary intervention at the founder site and screening at the proposed release site—through vaccination or postrelease monitoring—can help minimize risks (Woodford and Rossiter 1993). Papers by Ballou and Lyles (1993) provide mechanisms for assessing the risk of disease.

Capturing and holding animals until release likely induce stress, particularly for wild-born animals, that can increase susceptibility to new or latent infectious diseases (Woodford and Rossiter 1993). Logan et al. (1996) speculated that stress contributed to the deaths of some translocated wild-born pumas, particularly adults older than twenty-seven months of age. In contrast, none of the wild-born gray wolves reintroduced to Yellowstone National Park suffered from any apparent adverse effects of their translocation and subsequent confinement for acclimation (Phillips and Smith 1996).

HABITAT EVALUATION

It is critically important to determine the extent of suitable habitat and causes for the original decline of the species. If an area lacks sufficient habitat or if changes in human activity and behavior have not eliminated the original cause of decline, it is nearly impossible to justify a translocation (Kleiman 1989; Stanley Price 1989; Short et al. 1992; Miller et al. 1999). Effectively halting harvest or excessive control programs on the species may be enough for many large carnivores (e.g., gray wolves), but other species (e.g., grizzly bears) may be much more sensitive to human presence and disturbance.

We should evaluate translocation sites in terms of the species' habitat requirements, spatial characteristics of the area, and management considerations. We caution, however, that while it is relatively easy to determine a priori if habitat is inadequate (by demonstrating that one or more critical elements is missing), it is much more difficult to demonstrate that habitat is adequate (determining that all critical elements are present). Ideally, the translocation team should at least find sufficient evidence that the species once thrived in the target habitat, and biologists should analyze current factors that may act against translocation success.

Important factors to consider when comparing sites quantitatively include prey, cover, den sites, water sources, competitors, predators, and the presence of exotics (Miller et al. 1999). It is more difficult to assess ecosystem resilience and the effects of disturbances such as fires, droughts, catastrophic storms, etc., although these too are sound considerations (Kleiman 1989; Stanley Price 1989). Such disturbances often cause scale-dependent responses, and issues of scale are difficult to understand and interpret. This is especially so for large carnivores that, due to their extensive movements, require managers to evaluate conservation issues across a landscape. Because landscape-level (ecoregion) conservation is important to regional biodiversity, and because habitat fragmentation affects landscapes on a drastic level, large carnivores function as good indicators of wilderness quality (Miller et al. 1998).

With an adequate and constant prey base, carnivores maintain smaller home ranges and wander over less territory, thus exposing fewer animals to the high mortality associated with reserve and other natural area boundaries (Woodroffe and Ginsberg 1998; see chap. 2 for Mexican wolves). Adequate prey densities can also reduce livestock depredation and its consequent conflicts (Chellam and Saberwal 2000). Reduced conflicts with livestock are more likely if prey populations remain at relatively high levels. If prey populations crash when livestock arrive, a common occurrence, livestock represent the only option for carnivores, and livestock can become an ecological replacement for traditional prey. Thus, even if prey populations rebound to former levels, livestock predation may persist, particularly if livestock numbers are high. Under those circumstances, it may be difficult to induce predators to return to native prey.

Important spatial considerations include the degree of isolation, size, shape, and site location (in the context of historical range). Habitat area is especially important for large carnivores because they exist at the top of the food chain, and therefore their densities are lower than species living at other trophic levels. As such, large carnivore populations are among the first to disappear when the area of habitat declines through fragmentation and alteration (Crooks 2002).

Conflict with people on reserve borders is the major cause of mortality of large carnivores living in reserves, representing roughly 89 percent of grizzly bear mortality (Woodroffe and Ginsberg 1998). Because large carnivores in small reserves more often encounter the population sink that exists at a reserve boundary, they are most vulnerable (Woodroffe and Ginsberg 1998). The same situation exists on the edges of natural areas outside of reserves. Even if large animals survive in fragmented habitats for long periods, the reality of such "edge effects" diminishes their evolutionary potential. Genetic drift, random changes in gene frequency due to chance alone, can overwhelm the forces of natural selection in small, isolated populations (Soulé 1995, 1996).

Corridors often help mediate the effects of habitat fragmentation, yet they remain a complex issue. Different types of connections among habitats could benefit carnivores (Crooks 2002). For example, corridors can connect habitat patches within a protected area or other natural areas in the immediate region. Some large carnivores, like pumas, can negotiate intrareserve corridors even if given an occasional bottleneck in the connection, although individuals vary substantially in their proclivity to do so (Beier 1993; B. Miller, pers. obs.) On the other hand, corridors that facilitate long-distance interchange between populations of a metapopulation (i.e., a linked network of populations) often must support residents of the focal species within the corridors (Noss and Cooperrider 1994). Though records exist of large mammalian carnivores dispersing and covering hundreds of kilometers, these individuals are often juvenile males. Conversely, juvenile females usually establish territories relatively close to their area of birth (Greenwood 1980). If we wish to maintain the capacity to naturally reestablish populations that have "winked-out," we must create habitat connections that allow females to move.

REJUVENATING ECOLOGICAL PROCESSES BY TRANSLOCATION

Currently, we are missing a critical element for ecological planning: we lack information on how quickly or to what extent restoring an extirpated (locally extinct) keystone carnivore rejuvenates ecological processes. We know results vary according to temporal and geographic scales, how long the keystone has been absent, the complexity of the system, the level of natural cycles in populations, whether alternative states of ecosystem stability exist or not, timing and type of disturbance regimes, generation time, dispersal capabilities, and ecological changes that occurred since the species was extirpated (exotic invasion, new diseases, vegetation changes, etc.). Breitenmoser et al. (2001) and Soulé et al. (2003a, 2005) identified the ecosystem effects of large-carnivore translocations as an important research need.

The loss of a large carnivore can perturb a system by removing a factor that limits ungulate and mesopredator population numbers; by changing ungulate behavior, movement patterns, and habitat use; by altering

community structure; and by modifying habitat exploitation by the remaining fauna (see chap. 3). A surrogate species that tries to occupy the role of the former top predator most likely will not be able to fill that niche in the same way (e.g., coyotes replacing wolves in Yellowstone). Thus, mutualistic relationships, competitive interactions, and food webs may change even with a surrogate species and possibly result in effects that ripple through the system and cause secondary extinctions in other species.

The level, duration, and type of ecological changes that a keystone species induces affect how easily it can return to an ecosystem and perform its former function. In some cases, restoring a critical missing piece of an ecosystem can restore both structure and function, albeit slowly. When humans harvested sea otters to near extinction, marine invertebrate herbivores increased in number and devastated kelp forests. This produced a cascade of indirect effects that reduced the diversity of a host of fish, shorebirds, invertebrates, and raptors (Estes 1996; Estes and Duggins 1995; Estes, Duggins, and Rathbun 1989; Estes, Smith, and Palmisanto 1978; Estes, Tinker, et al. 1998). Following reintroduction of the sea otter, invertebrate grazers declined, and the kelp forests and associated fauna recovered (Estes, Smith, and Palmisanto 1978; Estes, Duggins, and Rathbun 1989; Estes, Tinker, et al. 1998).

Alternatively, translocation may not overcome the cascade of indirect changes triggered by the loss of a keystone species. For example, in Africa in 1954 humans introduced the Nile perch (*Lates nilotica*) into Lake Victoria to benefit the fishing industry, causing a series of ecological events that eliminated nearly 400 native species of fish from the lake (Goldschmidt 1996). The catch of Nile perch rose from less than 2 percent of annual harvest in 1978 to almost 80 percent in 1986 (Kaufman 1992). Being much larger than the native cichlids and tilapias, cooking Nile perch meant burning more wood. Growing human numbers and less forest led to more agriculture and agricultural runoff. Runoff increased nutrients in the lake, and with the decline of native herbivorous fish, the shallower waters experienced algal blooms. Lake Victoria once had high oxygen levels at all depths, but the algal blooms depleted oxygen below 25 m (80 ft.), with a trend toward total anoxia (Kaufman 1992). Such eutrophic (low-oxygen) conditions caused exotic water hyacinths (*Eichornia crassipes*) to choke important breeding areas in shallow water (Primack 1998). Restoration of Lake Victoria thus requires much more than just the reintroduction of tilapia and cichlid species.

TECHNICAL CONSIDERATIONS

Technical considerations of translocations closely relate to the biological factors we just discussed. The planning team should consider all difficult management issues during the feasibility study. Questions posed by Kleiman et al. (1993) included:

+ What legal framework exists, and does the program comply with laws?
+ Is there an active research program to devise translocation tactics?
+ Are there sufficient fiscal and intellectual resources to maintain the program?
+ Will agencies with oversight adequately monitor the program?

To these questions, Miller et al. (1999) added:

+ What are the goals of the translocation?
+ What logistic challenges must planners overcome?

Biologists should carefully monitor the translocation to determine causes of mortality, movements and behaviors of released animals, life history attributes, and changes in habitat. The results of monitoring should guide future releases; therefore, records require detailed information, and monitoring should extend to the offspring of released animals (Beck et al. 1993). Unfortunately, monitoring is one of the first things many organizations eliminate in order to reduce expenses (Noss and Cooperrider 1994). Far too many translocation efforts remain poorly documented (Breitenmoser et al. 2001).

Planners should define goals carefully to facilitate accurate evaluation. Defining success solely by survival is often misleading because mortality is often high during early releases. Alternatively, analysis of behavioral traits during early releases may provide clues as to how animals respond to their new environment, and thereby improve techniques (Kleiman et al. 1986; Miller et al. 1996). Knowledge that helps improve translocation methodologies may be the most important goal of early releases (Phillips 1990; Miller et al. 1996). High mortality is not necessarily a failure unless biologists do not learn enough to increase survival in future translocations. For that reason, careful planning with a sound scientific approach and effective monitoring often will offer the most efficient path toward successful recovery.

Funding and physical resources always pose a problem in conservation efforts, and translocation programs are expensive. Because resources are always limited, cost-benefit analyses are important. Miller et al. (1999) suggested comparing techniques based on cost per successfully reproducing female.

In summary, several general biological guidelines can facilitate translocating carnivores, including issues of taxonomy, genetics, demographics, behavior, health, habitat, and technical considerations. Carnivores often play a strong role in regulating interactions among trophic levels, and their restoration represents a large step toward restoring ecosystem health across a landscape. While some general concepts likely apply to translocation across carnivore species, we stress that individual species vary in their responses, and the translocation team should test ideas scientifically.

SOCIAL SCIENCE CONSIDERATIONS

The social challenges of carnivore translocation are perhaps more daunting than the biological ones (Reading and Clark 1996; Fritts et al. 1997; Reading et al. 1997; Clark et al. 2001; Breitenmoser et al. 2001). Schaller (1996) commented that we know how to protect carnivores, but not how to live with them. To begin doing so first involves an in-depth understanding of culture, knowledge, beliefs, opinions, attitudes, and values; economic trends; formal and informal organizational structures; the social context of the project; the distribution and use of power and authority; and how we make choices and decisions. Chapters 6 and 8 cover much of this information, so we provide only a brief overview here.

HUMAN VALUES, ATTITUDES, BELIEFS, AND OPINIONS

Human values toward carnivores and the variables influencing those values factor heavily into the success or failure of carnivore translocations (Reading et al. 1997; Breitenmoser et al. 2001; Clark et al. 2001). However, biologists rarely give sufficient treatment to these considerations in carnivore programs (see chap. 6). As Fritts et al. (1995, 1997) clearly state, biologically there is no problem reintroducing wolves successfully; the problem lies in addressing human opposition.

Developing local support, or at least successfully addressing local opposition, is especially crucial to translocation efforts (Bath 1991; Reading and Kellert 1993; Reading et al. 1997). As such, prior to translocating carnivores into an area it is vital to examine local values, attitudes, beliefs, and opinions

to determine local people's concerns. This permits developing appropriate public relations campaigns designed to inform, build support, and, to the extent possible, address opposition (Reading and Kellert 1993; Reading et al. 1997). Attempting translocations into areas with unsupportive or antagonistic local publics can have disastrous results, such as the ill-fated attempt to reintroduce wolves into northern Michigan in 1974 in which local opposition led to all of the reintroduced wolves being killed and the program terminated (Hook and Robinson 1982). No less important is the need to understand values held by those people who are part of a decision-making team (Reading et al. 2006; see chap. 6).

Not appreciating the full range of human values and attitudes toward carnivores lies at the heart of many conservation problems. Several values that people attribute to carnivores, such as ecological (i.e., the role they play in their ecosystems), aesthetic (i.e., appreciation of their beauty or prowess), or existence (i.e., their "right" to exist), fall outside traditional economic analyses (Kellert 1996). When forming policy, planners usually ignore or override these values in favor of the more easily measured costs of a program, such as livestock predation (see chap. 8). The importance of being inclusive in conservation and management programs cannot be overemphasized.

In chapter 6, we define values, attitudes, beliefs, and myths and discuss how they have guided actions and decisions. Value differences result from variability in education, personal experiences, cultures, the influence of important social institutions (like schools and religious groups), and more, and are often reflected in differences among demographic groups.

Kellert (1996) identifies three broad demographic trends. First, people with greater dependence on land and natural resources generally express strong utilitarian values (i.e., use of wildlife for human benefit) and want to dominate nature. As a result, these people usually favor exploiting and subjugating wildlife for human benefit. Second, people with more formal education and higher incomes usually voice higher naturalistic and ecological values and attitudes toward wildlife. This suggests a strong interest in outdoor recreation and support for wildlife conservation. Third, younger people and women tend to demonstrate high moral and humanistic values and attitudes toward wildlife (although some studies that examined attitudes toward wolves found no significant differences between women and men; see chap. 6). These people would likely display greater affection for individual animals and oppose consumptive uses.

Trying to change attitudes, behaviors, and values is difficult, especially if those values are strongly held (see chap. 6). A number of factors influence attitudes and values toward carnivores and carnivore translocation. The most important variables include real and perceived characteristics of the species, such as ferociousness, size, sentient capacity, phylogeny, and degree of relatedness to humans; the animal's symbolic nature; the relationship between the animal and humans; and how people use the animal (Kellert 1996). It is far easier to garner support for charismatic species than for smaller, lesser-known species. Many species, like giant pandas (*Ailuropoda melanoleuca*), bald eagles (*Haliaeetus leucocephalus*), and gray wolves, represent powerful cultural or symbolic values for many people.

Several important aspects of the relationship between people and the carnivore species proposed for translocation strongly influence attitudes (Bath 1991; Reading and Kellert 1993; Kellert 1996; Reading et al. 1997). First, the population and conservation status of the species, such as being rare, threatened, or endangered, affects how many people will view a translocation effort.

People's attitudes and opinions in such situations will often depend on how they view conservation programs in general and pertinent laws and regulations in particular. For example, status as a threatened or endangered species under the US Endangered Species Act (ESA) elicits concern, fear, and hostility among certain sectors of society, such as agricultural interests concerned about land use and other restrictions, and compassion and support among others, such as members of conservation organizations concerned with species preservation (Bath 1991; Bath and Buchanan 1989). People often base negative attitudes on real or perceived fears of the restrictive elements in the ESA that many people believe represent a threat to their livelihoods and lifestyles, on negative attitudes toward wildlife in general, and on real or perceived effects of past recovery programs (Kellert 1990; Reading and Kellert 1993). Positive attitudes often stem from concern over the loss of biodiversity and positive attitudes toward wildlife (Kellert 1996).

A second important aspect of the relationship between people and carnivores are real and potential human-wildlife conflicts (Bath 1991; Reading and Kellert 1993; Kellert 1996). Concerns over threats to humans and domestic animals (both pets and livestock) can strongly influence values and attitudes. Third, many people base their attitudes and opinions toward translocations on whether or not the translocation will lead to future opportunities for future wildlife use, such as trapping and hunting. Exploiting a translocated population is often controversial, especially for a newly established population. Human-wildlife property relations represent a fourth issue affecting attitudes and opinions, because people often fear land use and other restrictions. Finally, the perceived worth of an animal strongly influences values and attitudes toward it. A carnivore's perceived worth is influenced by all of the variables already mentioned, as well as knowledge, moral and ethical issues (e.g., animal rights), traditional market values (e.g., pelts, tourist attractions), and extra-market values (e.g., rodent control, ecosystem regulator or indicator roles). As a result, people value carnivores in many different, complex ways.

Planners can improve program performance and effectiveness by addressing human values during carnivore translocation programs. Understanding the diversity of values at play in a translocation program and how people form those values (and associated attitudes, beliefs, opinions, and behaviors) facilitates developing stronger public relations programs (Reading and Kellert 1993). Effective public relations programs are crucial if a translocation program hopes to develop support for and mitigate opposition against carnivore translocations.

ORGANIZATIONAL CONSIDERATIONS

Because several different government, non-profit, and private organizations implement carnivore translocations, often cooperatively, it is important to consider organizational dimensions of the program (Reading et al. 1997; Breitenmoser et al. 2001; see chap. 8). Although the kind of organizational system employed in a translocation program strongly influences success, this dimension is probably the least appreciated and addressed variable in carnivore conservation (Reading and Clark 1996; Reading et al. 1997). A swift fox (*Vulpes velox*) recovery program in Alberta, Canada, illustrates the importance and evolution of a solid organizational structure (Breitenmoser et al. 2001).

We believe that carnivore translocations often fail due to a variety of organizational reasons, including organization structures poorly matched to the translocation task, delegating implementation to an individual (or organization) lacking the necessary

expertise, issuing conflicting directives, over-dependence on other organizations, poor leadership, and excessive discretion (Yaffee 1982; Clark et al. 1994; Clark and Cragun 1994; Reading et al. 1996, 1997). Understanding the organizational environments, structures, and cultures helps explain organizational and individual behavior in carnivore translocations, often accounting for program failures (Moosbruker and Kleiman 2001).

An organization's external and internal environments influence the way in which it operates. The external environment, including the larger social setting, the operating environment, and the power setting of the organization, act to influence the program's goals and the value systems of the individuals involved (Warwick 1975). Perrow (1986) suggests that organizations usually move continually toward centralized control, and that hostile, more complex, and more rapidly changing environments lead to more rigid organizations with more rules. Yet, to be most effective in the highly complex, diverse, uncertain, and changing environments that typify carnivore translocations, organizations should adopt less rigid, less centralized structures (Gordon 1983; Perrow 1986).

An organization's internal environment is composed of three main elements: structure, culture, and power/authority relations. We discuss these components in chapter 8, along with the need for organizational specialists on interdisciplinary teams. Good ideas and valid concerns can emanate from any source. So, all opinions should be heard and respected equally, but we also caution that opinions without factual support are not equivalent to reliable scientific evidence to the contrary, and therefore should not carry equal weight in decision making (Noss 1999).

Several factors affect individual and organizational goals, including the task at hand, power and authority issues, and knowledge or assumptions about alternative strategies and their consequences (Yaffee 1982;

Westrum 1988). Differences among individuals, groups, and organizations can lead to multiple, conflicting goals in a program. Goal displacement occurs if nontask goals, such as gaining or maintaining program control (e.g., obtaining or retaining lead-agency status), dominate over a program's task goal, such as reestablishing populations of carnivores.

In summary, understanding the biological and technical aspects of a carnivore translocation is crucial, but is insufficient if we hope to maximize efficiency and success rates. People involved in translocations must also understand the importance of the social science dimensions to the translocation challenge. This requires an interdisciplinary approach that understands values, organization, and power and authority. By better understanding how these variables influence success, participants can streamline their programs, reduce unproductive conflict, and ultimately improve overall performance.

Social
Assessment

Chapter 5

The Human Landscape

Hannah Gosnell and Doug Shinneman

INTRODUCTION

Carnivore restoration efforts require careful consideration of habitat and ecological conditions, but equally important are the human dimensions of wildlife management. Attitudes among the human population must be considered (see chap. 6), and socioeconomic trends should be assessed to help understand and predict the social impacts of natural resource decisions (chap. 11). A solid understanding of a region's culture, politics, and history can provide wildlife managers with insight into local attitudes regarding wildlife issues, help them identify key stakeholders, and prepare them to deal with potential allies and adversaries.

In this chapter we describe the human landscape of the Southern Rockies, which includes concrete "things" on the land, like people, buildings, roads, dams, and mines, as well as less tangible anthropogenic influences, like political boundaries, land management regimes, and local economies. We describe the region as a whole, but pay special attention to the four subregions identified by wolf biologists as prime reintroduction areas in chapter 11: northern New Mexico, southwest Colorado, west-central Colorado, and northwest Colorado.

In the following sections we consider the ways in which humans have organized and subdivided the land in terms of ownership, management, protection, and roads, and we look at historical and current uses of the land and associated ecological impacts. We describe the cultural landscape, past and present, focusing on the subregions of interest for wolf (*Canis lupus*) reintroduction. Finally, we look at population, land development, and economic trends in the region as a whole, as well as in the subregions of interest.

THE LAY OF THE LAND

LAND OWNERSHIP

The Southern Rockies exhibit a complex pattern of public and private land ownership (table 5.1, figure 5.1). This pattern is the result of changes in federal land policy over time, beginning with an era of acquisition, followed by a period of land disposition to settlers during the homestead era in the mid- to late nineteenth century, and then a period of retention, when remaining federal lands were set aside for public ownership (Wilkinson 1992). Those lands, concentrated in the West and interspersed with private lands in many places, are now managed by federal agencies such as the US Forest Service, the National Park Service, and the Bureau of Land Management. The federal government also granted western states "school trust" lands—millions of acres (usually in separate square-mile sections) intended to raise money for public education.

In the Southern Rockies, the federal government owns roughly 56 percent of the land. Adding state lands to that total, about 60 percent of the region is under public ownership. The US Department of Agriculture's US Forest Service is the single largest landowner in the ecoregion, responsible for more than 71,680 sq. km (27,668 sq. mi.). Approximately 37 percent of the Southern Rockies region is privately owned, and the remaining 3 percent is Native American tribal land. In addition, local governments are responsible for managing a relatively small amount of public land in the form of city and county open space systems (Theobald et al. 1998).

The Southern Rockies' ecosystems (see chap. 9) are not evenly distributed across this complex pattern of land ownership. Many lower elevation ecosystems, such as grasslands and shrublands, occur mainly on private, Bureau of Land Management (BLM), or state lands, while the higher elevation ecosystems, such as subalpine forests and alpine tundra, are more prevalent on national forest lands. Moreover, single functioning ecosystems, defined at almost any scale, regularly transcend land ownership boundaries, complicating efforts to manage them in a comprehensive, holistic way.

Because private land is concentrated in lower elevations and valleys throughout the West, these ecosystems have seen the greatest impacts related to commercial and residential development. Such development not only fragments habitat on private lands but also impacts habitat on adjacent public lands.

While the Southern Rockies have seen significant development, much of the region remains intact due to the large, contiguous swath of public land at the region's core, connecting the Medicine Bow Mountains in south-central Wyoming to the southern end of the Sangre de Cristo Mountains in north-central New Mexico, and the Front Range at the western edge of the Great Plains to the eastern edge of the Colorado Plateau (figure 5.1). This public land pattern provides a basis for maintaining habitat connectivity essential to native species living in the region.

The distribution of cities, towns, and counties in and around the ecoregion represents another human-created landscape pattern with implications for native ecosystems.

These cultural and political entities influence land use and development patterns through changes in population, local economies, and land use planning policies, though there is significant spatial variation in the degree of impact various human settlements have on the land. For instance, while some Colorado counties and cities pursue ambitious open space acquisition programs and growth control measures, others prioritize development (Shinneman et al. 2000).

LAND MANAGEMENT AND PROTECTION

The Southern Rockies have witnessed numerous conservation milestones, beginning with the establishment of the US forest reserves in the 1890s. The federal government established Rocky Mountain National Park in 1915, and in 1919 the Trapper's Lake area on the White River Plateau became the first national forest land managed for wilderness values. Since those early conservation accomplishments, the Southern Rockies have added nearly fifty federally designated wilderness areas and six national parks and monuments that collectively protect 16,598 sq. km (6,406 sq. mi.). Add other strictly protected lands to that total, such as US Forest Service research natural areas, and the figure grows by another 395 sq. km (153 sq. mi.), to at least 16,993 sq. km (6,559 sq. mi.), or roughly 10.5 percent of the ecoregion's land base. More than 1,976 sq. km (763 sq. mi.) have somewhat lower levels of protection, such as state wildlife areas, national wildlife refuges, and Bureau of Land Management Areas of Critical Environmental Concern. In addition, the region contains less-formally protected lands with various levels of stewardship, such as county and city open space, private nature reserves, and private land protected from development with conservation easements (Theobald et al. 1998).

Compared to most regions in the United States, the land comprising the Southern

Rockies has a relatively high level of protection. The strictly protected federal lands of national parks and monuments, wilderness areas, and natural research areas, however, do not represent the full diversity of ecosystems and species in the region. Congress typically chose these landscapes for their scenic, historic, and recreational values, their charismatic wildlife (e.g., elk, *Cervus elaphus*), or their low economic value. Biologically rich landscapes, such as low-elevation riparian areas and shrublands, are not well represented in the current system of strictly protected nature reserves (e.g., see Scott et al. 2001). Shinneman, Miller, and Kunkel (see chap. 9) determined that only three of twelve major terrestrial ecosystem types in the Southern Rockies have more than 10 percent of their total area within strictly protected lands.

Protection is still possible for additional areas in the Southern Rockies, a move that would remedy existing conservation gaps. The US Forest Service has identified 19,760 sq. km (7,627 sq. mi.) of roadless lands on national forests in the Southern Rockies (US Forest Service 2000). While these areas received protection under the Roadless Area Conservation Rule established by the Clinton administration in 2001, under the subsequent Bush administration several legal challenges and administrative revisions to this rule leave the protection of these areas in question. Furthermore, existing Wilderness Study Areas (roadless areas with interim protection) and additional roadless areas that the US Forest Service and BLM do not yet officially recognize have been proposed for permanent wilderness protection, and the US Congress may again consider wilderness legislation to protect roughly 6,500 sq. km (2,509 sq. mi.) of primarily BLM roadless areas in Colorado, as it did in 2002. If these wild lands do eventually receive permanent protection, when combined with the existing system of protected areas, roughly 40,000 sq. km (about 15,500

sq. mi.) of the Southern Rockies would be highly protected—or roughly 25 percent of the region. Moreover, many roadless lands contain biologically significant lower elevation ecosystems, which are now poorly protected. By adding these areas, Shinneman et al. (2000) predict that nearly ten of the twelve major ecosystem types they analyzed would enjoy at least 10 percent of their total area protected, and five of the twelve would enjoy protection levels above 25 percent.

Despite the uncertain status of most of these lands, several recent land conservation achievements have substantially improved ecosystem protection in the Southern Rockies. In 1999, The Nature Conservancy acquired the 405 sq. km (156 sq. mi.) Medano-Zapata Ranch and later the 393 sq. km (152 sq. mi.) Baca Ranch in Colorado's San Luis Valley. The latter substantially expanded park acreage for Great Sand Dunes National Park and Preserve. In 2000, the US Forest Service acquired the 360 sq. km (139 sq. mi.) Baca Ranch in northern New Mexico and established Valles Caldera National Preserve, bridging a gap between protected lands in Santa Fe National Forest and Bandelier National Monument. Additional US Forest Service areas that have gained more protection are the recently designated wilderness areas of Spanish Peaks Wilderness in southern Colorado (72 sq. km; 28 sq. mi.) and James Peak Wilderness, east of Denver and Boulder (57 sq. km/22 sq. mi.) on national forest land, and in southwestern Colorado, the 72 sq. km (28 sq. mi.) Gunnison Gorge Wilderness and the Black Ridge Canyon Wilderness on BLM land (305 sq. km; 118 sq. mi.). In addition, as of late 2008, the Great Outdoors Colorado program—funded primarily through the sales of lottery tickets—has protected roughly 3,440 sq. km (1,328 sq. mi.) in the state.

Local and regional land trusts that buy private properties and establish conservation easements with willing landowners have become numerous in the region. The

Colorado Coalition of Land Trusts now includes ten regional and national land trusts and thirty-two local member organizations working throughout the Colorado portion of the Southern Rockies; they have protected more than 1.95 million acres in the state (Colorado Coalition of Land Trusts 2007).

Ubiquitous roads fragment the landscape, compromising the ecological value of protected land in the Southern Rockies. Starting with the mining boom of the mid-1800s, a steady progression of wagon roads, stagecoach routes, and railroads soon spanned the region. During this settlement period, railroads in particular were instrumental in moving valuable minerals out of the region and importing resources, new industries, new residents, and tourists into the Southern Rockies. Cities such as Greeley, Colorado, and Laramie, Wyoming, sprang up and prospered along railroad lines, and railroads helped transform the Southern Rockies from a frontier region into a modern industrial economy. Between 1860 (sixteen years before statehood, in 1876) and 1900, Colorado's population grew from 34,277 to 539,700 (Noel et al. 1994).

During the early to mid-1900s, the construction of paved roads changed the region even more. In Colorado, paved roads expanded from roughly 800 km to 6,400 km (500 mi. to 4,000 mi.) between 1930 and 1940 (Noel et al. 1994). By the 1950s, the interstate highway system and the modern automobile made it easier to reach formerly difficult-to-access mountain locations. This spurred further population growth, tourism, and new development industries, including the region's famed ski resorts.

Today, more than 121,600 km (76,000 mi.) of primary and secondary roads cross the Southern Rockies, not including most residential streets and the thousands of miles of poorly mapped primitive roads (Shinneman et al. 2000). The region's public lands are also heavily roaded; there are more than 27,742 km (17,339 mi.) of inventoried roads on national forest lands in Colorado alone (Finley 1999). Local road densities vary greatly within the region, but they are often much higher than expected, even in relatively undeveloped areas. For instance, one study in New Mexico found that Bandelier National Monument and the surrounding area averaged more than 2.5 km (1.5 mi.) of roads per square kilometer (4 miles per square mile) (Allen 1994). In contrast, several large areas in the Southern Rockies are relatively devoid of roads, especially those centered on large wilderness areas, such as in portions of the San Juan Mountains and on the White River Plateau. However, except for these large wildlands, few areas in the Southern Rockies are more than 6.4 km (4 mi.) from the nearest road (Shinneman et al. 2000). Further, although alpine and subalpine habitats generally contain few roads, lower elevation and more biologically diverse habitats are usually heavily roaded (Shinneman et al. 2000).

Roads are a concern for many land managers, biologists, and conservationists due to their impacts on native species and ecosystem function (Schoenwald-Cox and Buechner 1992; Trombulak and Frissell 2000). Some of the ecologically deleterious impacts of roads include:

- Increased mortality due to automobile collisions (Bangs et al. 1989; Fuller 1989)
- Reduced mobility of both small and large animals due to barrier effects (Fahrig et al. 1995; Foster and Humphrey 1995)
- Increased dispersal of edge-adapted, weedy, aggressive, predator, and parasitic species due to travel corridor effects (Tysor and Worley 1992; Parendes and Jones 2000)
- Greater human access to habitat interiors and activities, such as fuel-wood gathering, hunting, poaching, plant gathering, and recreation in those areas (Lyon 1983; Trombulak and Frissell 2000)

+ Increased sediment and pollution runoff into nearby streams and wetlands (Bauer 1985; Forman and Deblinger 2000)

+ Increased likelihood of severe erosion of roads on steep slopes (Trombulak and Frissell 2000)

Combined, these factors fragment and isolate natural habitat by subdividing formerly intact vegetation patches and creating a "road-effect zone" that changes the habitat conditions and species compositions well into the interiors of adjacent natural habitat (Reed et al. 1996; Shinneman and Baker 2000; Forman 2000).

Various factors influence the relative impact that roads have on landscapes and ecosystems. For instance, a lightly used, primitive dirt road may not restrict some species from crossing the road, but a busy, paved four-lane highway may represent an impermeable barrier to many wildlife species. Species such as elk, pumas (*Puma concolor*), wolves, black bears (*Ursus americanus*), and grizzly bears (*Ursus arctos*) may not persist in areas of high road densities due to an aversion to roads and/or negative impacts from increased human hunting, poaching, and harassing (Lyon 1983; Van Dyke et al. 1986; McClellan and Shackleton 1988). For instance, wolves generally do not persist where road densities exceed 0.58 km/sq. km (1.5 mi./sq. mi.) (Thiel 1985; Mech et al. 1988), although Mech et al. indicated that their results probably do not apply to areas with different human populations or road use. Later, Mech (1989) concluded that a road-density threshold of 0.58 km/sq. km (1.5 mi./sq. mi.) is useful for predicting the likelihood of wolf persistence if the area under consideration is not adjacent to large reservoirs of occupied wolf range. He further explained that relatively small areas of high road density could sustain wolves so long as suitable roadless reservoirs exist nearby.

HISTORICAL AND CURRENT LAND USES

Mining, livestock grazing, logging, and water use have significantly altered the natural ecosystems of the Southern Rockies. While resource extraction no longer forms the basis of the Southern Rockies' economy (Power 1996), these activities still play a major role in the shape and condition of the current landscape.

MINING

Mining put the Southern Rockies on the map for many Americans during the mid- to late 1800s, promoting westward migration and settlement in the region. With hundreds of active mines currently operating in the region, mining still has a significant impact on the landscape. In addition, there are at least 9,700 abandoned mines in the Southern Rockies, many of which continue to pollute terrestrial and aquatic ecosystems (Shinneman et al. 2000). One of the worst offenders is the now bankrupt Summitville Mine in the San Juan Mountains. This open-pit, cyanide heap-leach gold mine leaked significant quantities of acidic, metal-rich drainage and cyanide solutions into the Wightman Fork of the Alamosa River, destroying all aquatic life for 27 km (17 mi.) downstream (Shinneman et al. 2000; Hinchman and Noreen 1993).

LOGGING

Although logging has never been economically prosperous in the region as a whole, 150 years of Euro-American settlement and localized logging booms have significantly altered the forests of the Southern Rockies Ecoregion. Timber cutting, road building, and fire suppression affect most of the 93,859 sq. km (36,230 sq. mi.) of forest and woodlands in the Southern Rockies, which constitutes 59 percent of the land cover (Shinneman et al. 2000). Ponderosa pine (*Pinus ponderosa*) and Douglas fir (*Pseudotsuga menziesii*) forests—both central to the region's foothill forest ecosystems—have been the hardest hit by logging activities, which often focus on harvesting the largest, oldest trees. Less than 5 percent of the remaining ponderosa pine stands in Southern Rockies national forests are considered to be in an old-growth structural stage, a potentially problematic situation for species that depend on old-growth habitat (Shinneman et al. 2000; see chap. 9). Further, clear-cutting in the spruce-fir and lodgepole pine (*Pinus contorta*) forests on the Medicine Bow National Forest in Wyoming fragmented that region significantly more than clear-cutting of similar areas of the Pacific Northwest (Reed et al. 1996). Highly fragmented forests may lead to declines in populations of forest-interior dependent species in the Southern Rockies, including boreal owls (*Aegolius funereus*), goshawks (*Accipiter gentilis*), and pine martens (*Martes americana*).

WATER USE

Water in the Southern Rockies enabled the region to flourish, largely through irrigated agriculture. Today, industrial and urban uses divert an increasing portion of water originating in the Southern Rockies via the region's myriad dams, ditches, and tunnels that store and redirect millions of acre-feet of water every year. But 90 percent of the water diverted from streams still goes to agricultural crops such as hay and alfalfa, grains, vegetables, and fruit, rather than residential use (Riebsame 1997). This is not to say that the sprawling subdivisions along the Front Range are inconsequential. In Denver, for example, more than half the water consumed is attributable to outdoor landscaping (Riebsame 1997). Other ecological impacts related to water use in the Southern Rockies result from dams and reservoirs, loss and degradation of stream habitat and riparian areas, loss of groundwater function, and alterations in stream hydrology (Shinneman et al. 2000).

AGRICULTURE

Agricultural practices have played a major role in transforming the Southern Rockies landscape by converting native vegetation and natural communities to croplands and rangelands. While only 5 percent of the region, or 7,904 sq. km (3,051 sq. mi.), is currently classified as either dry land or irrigated cropland, this 5 percent tends to be some of the most biologically important land in the ecoregion (valley bottoms, riparian areas, and wetlands). The Southern Rockies Ecosystem Project found that approximately 82 percent of all croplands in the ecoregion sat below 2,438 m (8,000 ft.) in elevation, and 10 percent fell within 152 m (500 ft.) of a river or perennial stream (Shinneman et al. 2000).

Agricultural landscapes throughout the region, however, are experiencing rapid rates of conversion to residential and commercial uses. The total area of farm- and rangelands in the region decreased between 1987 and 2002, with losses in Colorado leading the way at 8.7 percent (US Department of Agriculture National Agricultural Statistics Service 1997, 2002).

LIVESTOCK GRAZING

Livestock grazing started in the seventeenth century in northern New Mexico and now occurs in nearly all locations and ecosystem types throughout the region. Ranching's contribution to the region's economy has declined dramatically over the last half century, but its effects on the land remain extensive and significant. Rangeland managers play a significant role in determining the ecological conditions of the region, on both public and private land.

Most ranchers in the Southern Rockies depend at least partially on public lands for grazing their animals at different times of the year. Active grazing allotments exist on Forest Service and BLM public lands throughout the region. The US Forest Service manages 70,740 sq. km (27,306 sq. mi.)

in the ecoregion, and nearly 70 percent of that has active grazing allotments. Similarly, the BLM grazes 93 percent of the 32,801 sq. km (12,661 sq. mi.) it oversees in Colorado. Of Colorado's 11,856 sq. km (4,576 sq. mi.) of state-owned land, grazing occurs on roughly 80 percent (Shinneman et al. 2000). Similar figures exist for BLM and state land in the Wyoming and New Mexico portions of the ecoregion. In addition, all three national wildlife refuges in the region allow grazing on portions of their land. Given these numbers, Shinneman et al. (2000) estimate that livestock grazing is available on roughly 80 to 90 percent of state and federal public lands in the ecoregion, and grazing actually occurs on 70 to 80 percent.

The BLM monitors the condition of its rangelands using various range condition classification systems. In 1998, the BLM in Colorado rated the forage condition of 72 percent of the 30,529 sq. km (11,784 sq. mi.) that are subject to grazing as fair or poor (US Bureau of Land Management 1996). Given that even fair condition means that the land supports less than one-half its historical carrying capacity, these numbers are cause for concern. But most land managers agree that, for a variety of reasons, the overall condition of the region's rangelands is improving.

Wilcove et al. (1998) estimated that livestock grazing in the United States contributed to the imperiled status of 33 percent of federally listed threatened species and 14 percent of endangered species. Since cattle preferentially congregate along stream banks and riparian areas, water quality and stream hydrology are often negatively impacted (Schultz and Leininger 1990). Grazing is also associated with both intentional and unintentional vegetation change. Rangeland managers introduce nonnative grasses such as crested wheatgrass (*Agropyron desertorum*) because they provide good forage for livestock (Noss and Cooperrider 1994). Grazing can also unintentionally

cause changes in plant species' structure and composition, such as the proliferation of weeds like cheatgrass (*Bromus tectorum*), and can lead to increased soil erosion (D'Antonio and Vitousek 1992). Grazing can negatively affect large ungulates, predators, and other native animals as well. Fences to control roaming livestock interfere with animal movements, especially pronghorn (*Antilocapra americana*), but also deer (*Odocoileus* spp.) and elk (Noss and Cooperrider 1994). Livestock compete with native herbivores for forage, water, and space, and livestock managers often eliminate "pests" like prairie dogs (*Cynomys* spp.) and predators like coyotes (*Canis latrans*) (Peek and Dalke 1982). Federal and private efforts on behalf of the livestock industry eliminated wolves and grizzly bears in the Southern Rockies by the mid-1900s (Fitzgerald et al. 1994). The absence of these large carnivores has contributed to unnaturally large elk populations (Colorado Division of Wildlife 2001) throughout much of the Southern Rockies, which in turn has led to overbrowsing of native vegetation, like aspen (*Populus* spp.), in some places (Baker et al. 1997).

RECREATIONAL USES

Every year, millions of people visit the public lands of the Southern Rockies for recreation. Many of them come at least in part to see wildlife, bringing significant tourist dollars to the region. Their presence helps the economy but challenges wildlife managers.

Most outdoor recreationists in the Southern Rockies target one of the six national parks and monuments in the region, or one of the eight national forests. Recreation on BLM land is on the rise, especially with the growth of off-road vehicle recreation, but it does not rival use of the parks and forests.

The White River, Pike and San Isabel, and Santa Fe are the most popular national forests in the region (Shinneman et al. 2000). Popularity is measured in "recreation visitor days" (RVDs). RVDs are the total number of days each visitor used the national forest multiplied by the number of visitors. Thus, if a group of ten people visited a national forest for two days, that would be twenty recreation visitor days.

The White River National Forest, recognized throughout the world for its exceptional outdoor recreation opportunities, was ranked fifth in the nation in 1995 in terms of visitor days. Although the White River National Forest contains only 16 percent of the Forest Service lands in Colorado, it hosts about 30 percent of the state's national forest recreation (US Forest Service 1999). Its 8,892 sq. km (3,432 sq. mi.) surround major ski resorts such as Aspen, Vail, and Breckenridge, and host 13 percent of all ski visits in the nation. Only two to four hours west of Denver on Interstate 70, this national forest is the primary target of Front Range recreationists. The Front Range Pike and San Isabel area is popular for mountain bikers and backpackers. In New Mexico, many people visit the Santa Fe National Forest because of its close proximity to Santa Fe and Albuquerque (US Forest Service 1999).

Data vary with respect to the number of annual visitor days estimated for each recreational activity. Bowker et al. (1999) predicted higher rates of growth in user days for activities such as cross-country skiing (242 percent), downhill skiing, and backpacking, and slower rates for hunting (22 percent), fishing (59 percent), snowmobiling, and off-road driving (54 percent). Not surprisingly, the overall patterns are similar for data concerning numbers of recreationists.

The biggest impacts associated with recreation in the Southern Rockies relate to the ski industry and the extensive land development associated with ski areas (e.g., parking lots, second homes, condos, resorts, golf courses, and shopping centers). The ski areas themselves fragment high-elevation forests with ski runs, chairlifts, and mountain lodges. The recent expansion of Vail Resort ski area into lynx (*Lynx canadensis*) habitat in the White River National Forest provides an example of how controversial ski area impacts can be (Thompson and Halfpenny 1991). Even though 180 sq. km (70 sq. mi.) of the White River National Forest are currently under permit for skiing, the US Forest Service is contemplating plans for further expansion.

According to the Forest Service, Summit County, Colorado, has the highest potential to provide additional capacity for skiing on national forest lands. If industry growth rates stay the same, the combined daily capacity in 2010 must rise to 53,070 skiers a day to meet the projected demand of 5 million skiers per year. This will require an additional 5.7 sq. km (2.2 sq. mi.) of national forest lands. By 2030, the US Forest Service estimates demand for skiing will require an additional 34 sq. km (13 sq. mi.), resulting in a total of 102 sq. km (39 sq. mi.) of national forest land allocated to skiing in Summit County (US Forest Service 1999).

Though studies do not project that mechanized recreation, such as all-terrain vehicle (ATV) use, will grow as fast as downhill and cross-country skiing over the next fifty years, this activity still has a significant and growing presence on the landscape. In Colorado, the number of registered ATVs more than tripled during the 1990s, and snowmobile numbers increased by 64 percent (Finley 1999). Off-road vehicle use on fragile desert lands and wetlands is of particular concern.

Even hiking and backpacking, seemingly low-impact activities, can produce negative ecological effects. Trails often traverse riparian areas and nesting areas and can harm native species and damage delicate natural communities. Heavy traffic in high-elevation tundra causes damage that takes years to repair. The Colorado Fourteeners Initiative works throughout the state to improve trail systems and minimize human impact on fragile mountain ecosystems.

The main impacts associated with recreation on public lands in the Southern Rockies include direct disturbance of wildlife, modification of habitat through vegetation damage, introduction of exotic species, erosion, and air and water pollution (Knight 1995).

THE CULTURAL LANDSCAPE: MAJOR SUBREGIONS AND COMMUNITIES

The Southern Rockies constitute a socially and culturally diverse landscape. In this section we look at the region in terms of race, ethnicity, educational attainment, and political affiliation. We then examine the four major subregions: northern New Mexico and southern Colorado; the Front Range; Colorado's Western Slope; and southern Wyoming and northwestern Colorado.

County boundaries obviously do not conform to ecoregion boundaries, but they do offer the most convenient subdivision for socioeconomic analysis. There are sixty-four counties in or near the Southern Rockies with significant socioeconomic ties to the region: six in south-central Wyoming, forty-eight in Colorado, and ten in northwestern New Mexico (US Department of Commerce 2000) (figure 5.2). Because socioeconomic data are only available by county, we used county boundaries for these analyses. It is important to note that the socioeconomic region we analysed therefore encompasses 349,450 sq. km (134,887 sq. mi.), an area larger than that delineated by the biophysical boundaries of the Southern Rockies Ecoregion.

In terms of race and ethnicity, the Southern Rockies have a higher percentage of white people, Hispanics, and Native Americans than the nation as a whole. Thirty-one of the region's sixty-four counties—almost half—were more than 95 percent white in 2007. San Juan County in New Mexico had the highest proportion of Native Americans (36.7 percent) due to its overlap with the Navajo Reservation and many pueblos located nearby. Rio Arriba County, New Mexico (15.4 percent), Sandoval County, New Mexico (13.9 percent), and Montezuma County, Colorado (14.0 percent), where the Colorado Ute Mountain Ute Reservation is located, all have significant Native American populations as well. The highest percentages of people with ancestry from Africa or Asia occur in the urban counties along Colorado's Front Range and around Albuquerque (US Census Bureau 2007a).

In terms of educational attainment, Colorado, New Mexico, and Wyoming all fell close to national averages. (County data were not available.) According to the US Census Bureau (2007b), estimates for 2006 indicated that 28 percent of all Americans over the age of twenty-five had a college degree; Wyoming, at 20.8 percent, was well below that average, while New Mexico, at 26.7 percent, was slightly below the national average, and Colorado, at 36.4 percent, had the second highest level of education of all states.

The percentage of people below the poverty level nationally was 12.5 percent in 2005–2006. Colorado (10.6 percent) and Wyoming (10.3 percent) were both below the national average, while New Mexico, at 17.4 percent, was the second highest of any state (US Census Bureau 2007b).

Political affiliations for the region were fairly evenly split in 2008, with 37.0 percent of registered voters listed as Democrat, 34.2 percent listed as Republican, and 28.8 percent as other or not affiliated. This represents a trend toward becoming more Democratic, because the breakdown in 2001 was 33.8 percent registered as Democrat, 35.8 percent registered as Republican, and 30.5 percent registered as other. In 2008, New Mexico was more Democratic (50.0 percent to 37.1 percent Republican) (New Mexico Secretary of State 2008), Wyoming was more Republican (63.1 percent to 26.5 percent Democratic) (Wyoming Secretary of State 2008), and Colorado was more

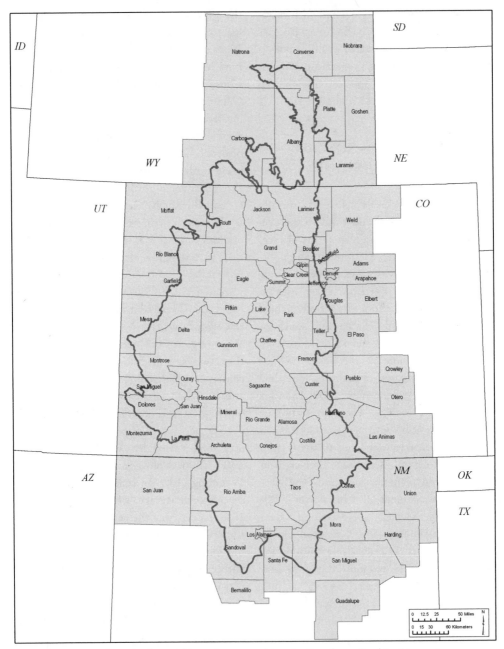

Figure 5.2—Counties located in and surrounding the Southern Rockies Ecoregion.
Source: Southern Rockies Ecosystem Project

evenly split with 33.2 percent Republicans and 32.9 percent Democrats (Colorado Secretary of State 2008).

The most Democratic counties in the Southern Rockies coincide with concentrations of Hispanics in New Mexico and southern Colorado, and in the Front Range urban areas. Large numbers of Republicans live in Colorado's Front Range as well, with the highest number in El Paso County, where Colorado Springs, the US Air Force Academy, and Focus on the Family are located.

The highest concentrations of Republican voters are located in the counties of southern Wyoming and northern Colorado (US Department of Commerce 2008; New Mexico Secretary of State 2008; Wyoming Secretary of State 2008; Colorado Secretary of State 2008).

We divided the Southern Rockies into the four subregions cited earlier, based on cultural, political, economic, and demographic data. The boundaries are not distinct and generalizations are difficult, but we believe this breakdown helps rather than hinders regional understanding. The following is a brief consideration of the history and nature of each of these subregions.

NORTHERN NEW MEXICO AND SOUTHERN COLORADO

The northern New Mexico and southern Colorado subregion was the first part of the Southern Rockies to be settled by human societies. Today's cultural landscape is a product of the southward movement of Native Americans over the course of thousands of years, followed by the northward movement of the Spanish-American empire from the sixteenth to nineteenth centuries, and finally the westward movement of Anglo-Americans in the nineteenth century (Abbott et al. 1982).

Prior to permanent Spanish settlements such as Santa Fe, settled in 1609, and the later Anglo migrations into the subregion, the Southern Rockies were home to native peoples who lived in permanent habitations as well as on the land as hunters and gatherers. Beginning with the Paleo-Indians, who inhabited the Southern Rockies around 11,000 years ago, the ecosystem gradually became home to the pueblo (village) peoples, who located and harvested crops in valleys and on mesa tops.

The most highly developed culture in prehistoric Colorado and northern New Mexico was the Ancestral Puebloan, prevalent in the Four Corners region from the eleventh through thirteenth centuries. Many of the complexes they inhabited are now popular national parks and monuments: Mesa Verde, Chaco Canyon, Canyon de Chelly, and others. By 1300, the Ancestral Puebloans had disappeared. Likely descendents of the Ancestral Puebloans, the Pueblo Indians remain an important culture of the region today (Abbott et al. 1982).

From the fifteenth to the seventeenth centuries, hunting and gathering tribes such as the Apache, Ute, Comanche, Arapaho, and Cheyenne moved into the Southern Rockies. In the fifteenth century, the Utes came into the region from the Great Basin of what is now Nevada. Also, the Jicarilla Apache settled in the area after migrating from Canada to the Southwest between AD 1300 and 1500.

The seventeenth century saw extensive colonization and missionary efforts by the Spanish. New Mexicans migrated north to the San Luis and Arkansas valleys in the early eighteenth century. French trappers and traders began moving into the region in the 1700s as well, creating new dimensions in the ongoing conflicts between the Spanish and the Indians (Abbott et al. 1982).

Anglos began flooding the area following the discovery of gold in 1858 on Cherry Creek, the start of the Colorado gold rush of 1859. The town of Trinidad became an important point of contact between eastern Hispano settlements and Anglo Coloradans. Abbott et al. characterized the early history of this region as follows:

> Since the early 1700s, the southern Rockies, the San Luis basin, and the Arkansas Valley had been zones of contact among dissimilar peoples—Utes and Apaches, Comanches and Spaniards, Frenchmen and Spaniards, and above all, New Mexicans and Americans—competing for control of the same territory...The lands of

Colorado were one of the major frontiers of world history, a zone of interpenetration between the expansive societies of Hispanic and Anglo America. (1982, 49)

The arrival of Europeans heralded the beginning of innumerable challenges for the native peoples of the Southern Rockies and throughout North America, both natural, in the form of disease and elimination of critical game, and cultural, in the form of forced relocation and imposition of European religion and culture. Ongoing tensions among Anglo, Hispanic, and Indian cultures continue to dominate the landscape in northern New Mexico and southern Colorado today.

THE FRONT RANGE OF COLORADO

The Eastern Slope of the Colorado Rockies, the region east of the Continental Divide, first saw large numbers of settlers in the late 1850s and 1860s with the first gold rush. Following the miners were the town builders and boosters, seeking to get rich by supplying the miners. The gold in the South Platte played out quickly, but coal mining in Jefferson and Weld counties during the 1870s and 1880s kept the economy going and towns growing. Railroads came to southern Colorado in the 1870s and helped make Pueblo the "great iron and steel city of the New West" (Abbott et al. 1982, 88). This initial period of booms petered out after about 1910, followed by a period of depression through the 1930s.

Footloose industries (those that are easily moved), especially those in the high-tech sector, began relocating to Colorado as early as the 1950s. Martin Marietta came to Littleton in 1956, followed by IBM, Honeywell, Kodak, Hewlett-Packard, and others throughout the 1960s and 1970s. The energy boom in the 1970s was a major impetus for growth in Colorado, but people fled the West and East coasts for the Colorado lifestyle as well (White 1991; Travis 2007).

COLORADO'S WESTERN SLOPE

The Western Slope, the region west of the Continental Divide, first attracted Anglos because of its mineral wealth. During the 1870s, a silver boom brought hordes of people to Leadville, which became Colorado's second largest city in the early 1880s. Mining, banking, and saloons were the three biggest moneymakers in the region. Other boomtowns included Gunnison, Aspen, Rico, Telluride, Ouray, Creede, Silverton, and Durango—known as "the Denver of Southern Colorado" (Abbott et al. 1982, 112).

Following the miners came the cattle barons, who dominated rural landscapes throughout the region from the 1880s to the present. Large and small cattle ranchers and nomadic sheepherders shared the public land. Lawlessness on the public domain resulted in cutthroat competition and extreme overgrazing (Foss 1960). Drought, depression, and the dismal conditions of the range in the 1930s led to the Taylor Grazing Act of 1934, assigning management of public rangelands to the federal government.

During the 1930s, farming and mining made up roughly a third of total employment in Colorado. By 1962, farming and mining had shrunk to 9 percent of total employment, while manufacturing and government grew to 14 percent and 60 percent, respectively. The region had shifted from an extractive economy to a service economy (Abbott et al. 1982). During the 1950s and 1960s, tourism was the third ranking industry in the state, and many of today's ski areas were established during the 1960s.

The mineral economy persisted, however, and the 1950s saw a uranium boom in the Gunnison-Uncompahgre and Durango regions that lasted until the mid-1960s. During the 1960s and 1970s, coal production in the region increased by a factor of six, largely replacing natural gas as a means for producing electricity. The discovery of oil shale deposits in New Mexico and Colorado fueled growth in the 1970s, spurring a 40 percent increase in the population of Grand Junction during that decade. The 1980s energy bust hit the Western Slope hard, but the 1990s saw astronomical growth related to tourism, the ski industry, the real estate market, and the underlying service economy. In *Atlas of the New West*, Riebsame writes:

> Population growth turned the West's early 1980s housing glut to a shortage by the early 1990s...Building began anew. West coasters rushed in, capital gains cash burning a hole in their pockets. And right behind, a rush of construction workers began taking the place of miners and oil riggers. (1997, 102)

Today's major issues in the region include exurban development, sprawl, the conversion of ranches to subdivisions and "ranchettes," the loss of affordable housing, erosion of traditional communities, and increased pressure on national forests because of the boom in recreation.

SOUTHERN WYOMING AND NORTHWESTERN COLORADO

In many ways the northern part of the ecoregion resembles the Western Slope. The region's economy was historically driven by cattle ranching and mining—coal in the Intermountain region from New Mexico up through Wyoming to Montana; oil and gas in the Overthrust Belt near the Wyoming-Utah border; and later, uranium, oil shale, and synfuels.

During the 1860s, cowboys drove cattle herds north along the Texas Trail to the prairies of eastern Wyoming. Huge cattle operations owned land holdings measuring in the millions of acres throughout the southern part of the state. In addition, sheepherders grazed their flocks in the high, semidesert country of south-central Wyoming (www .tracksacrosswyoming.com/default.aspx).

The Union Pacific Railroad advanced west in 1868, and the railroad towns of Cheyenne, Laramie, Rawlins, Green River, and Evanston were established. These towns provided shipping and supply services for the surrounding ranches and industries. Vast fields of coal supplied jobs for hundreds of workers and fuel for the locomotives. Homesteaders and entrepreneurs soon followed and turned the railroad towns into communities (www .tracksacrosswyoming.com/default.aspx).

The petroleum industry got its start in Wyoming in 1884, building the first refinery in Casper in 1895. When oil and natural gas prices rose swiftly in the late 1970s and early 1980s, they set off a wave of exploration and development (Power 1996).

Wyoming maintains a significant petroleum industry today, employing approximately 17,000 people for a payroll of more than $600 million. Although the ranching industry affects local economies, the state economy now depends more on service industries (Petroleum Association of Wyoming 2002).

CURRENT POPULATION TRENDS

The Southern Rockies are an attractive destination for migrants, a fact demonstrated by significant rates of population growth over the last century. In this section, we examine past and present population trends gleaned from the US Census and discuss the varied reasons for the region's long-standing popularity.

The tide of natural resource exploitation that began with the gold rush in 1859 continued into the first decade of the twentieth century. Thus the late 1800s and early 1900s saw significant population growth correlated with railroads, silver booms, cattle ranching, coal mining, and town-building efforts. Between 1900 and 1920, Colorado's population increased by 74 percent, but then dropped 20 percent in the next two decades because of an economic downturn (Abbott et al. 1982).

The most significant population growth in the region occurred during and after World War II, in what some call the beginning of the New West (Riebsame 1997; Travis 2007). Commenting on the West as a whole, White (1991) attributes this westward movement to the federal bureaucracies that devoted a disproportionate share of their resources to western development. The economy of the Southern Rockies remained strong after the war, due in large part to military expenditures on the Western Slope and in the Four Corners region (Wilkinson 1999). However, people came to the region as much for quality of life as for jobs and the opportunity to make money.

The 1970s saw another population increase related to the energy boom. The Arab oil embargo resulted in American energy policy shifting its focus to domestic sources: coal throughout the Intermountain region, between New Mexico and Montana; oil and gas in the Overthrust Belt, near the Wyoming-Utah border; and uranium in Colorado, New Mexico, and Wyoming. Later, oil shale and synfuels in northwest Colorado and southern Wyoming would contribute to the boom, which helped make Denver second only to Houston among energy capitals of the country (Riebsame 1997; Wiley and Gottlieb 1982). During the 1970s, Grand Junction's population increased by 40 percent, while the Southern Rockies region as a whole increased by a third—nearly three times the national growth rate.

National prosperity fueled by a bullish market, the growing popularity of the region, and the continued growth of the high-tech sector fueled the population boom of the 1990s. Wealth and spending on luxuries, such as second homes in the mountains, characterized this boom. From the 1970s to the present, counties with federally designated wilderness areas grew two to three times faster than all other counties in the country, rural or urban (Riebsame 1997).

As of 2007, counties within the Southern Rockies hosted a combined population of over 6 million people. The Denver metropolitan area was (and is) the largest urban center, with roughly 2.5 million people. Seventy-seven percent of the population for the entire region lives in the Front Range counties of Colorado (the cities of Denver, Colorado Springs, Fort Collins, etc.) and Santa Fe and Bernalillo counties in New Mexico (the cities of Santa Fe and Albuquerque). Because county political boundaries differ from the ecoregion boundaries, a significant portion of this urban population falls outside physiographic elements of the Southern Rockies Ecoregion. The least populous counties in the region lie mainly in the southwestern corner of Colorado, an area considered for possible wolf reintroduction in chapter 11 (table 5.2).

In terms of population density, in 2007 the urban Front Range counties ranked highest, with Denver County leading the way with 2,090 people/sq. km (5,350 people/sq. mi.) (figure 5.3). The least densely populated counties occur in southwestern Colorado, with average densities of 0.4 people/sq. km (1 person/sq. mi.). The northwest part of the ecoregion and portions of the San Luis Valley and Sangre de Cristo were also lightly populated (around 1 person/sq. km, or 2.5 persons/sq. mi.). Colorado's average population density was 16.4/sq. km (42/sq. mi.), New Mexico's was 5.9/sq. km (15/sq. mi.), and Wyoming's was 2/sq. km (5/sq. mi.). Fifty-four of the sixty-four counties in the region had population densities lower than the national average of 31/sq. km (80/sq. mi.) (US Department of Commerce 2000).

Notably, population distribution statistics at the county level do not accurately demonstrate patterns of human population. In the Southern Rockies, population centers are typically concentrated in lower elevations and mountain valleys as a result of a vast public land system and past settlement patterns. Thus, large portions of heavily

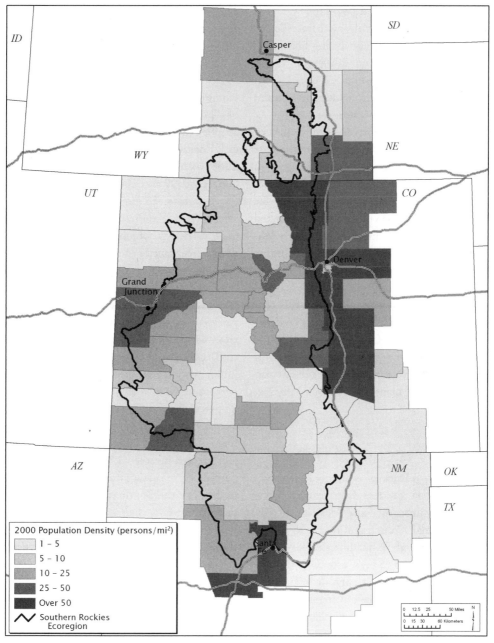

Figure 5.3—Human population density of counties within and surrounding the Southern Rockies Ecoregion.
Source: 2000 US Census

populated counties are often relatively devoid of development.

Between 1990 and 2000, the West was the fastest growing region in the United States, with 10.4 million new people and an overall growth rate of 19.7 percent (US Department of Commerce 2000). This trend has slowed a bit but continued, with the West growing by 10.9 percent, or 6.9 million people, from 2001 to 2007—faster than any other region.

Wyoming, Hawaii, and Montana were the only western states with growth rates lower than the national average during both periods. Between 1950 and 2007, the West's share of the national population grew from 13 percent to 22 percent, making more than one in five Americans westerners.

Human population in the Southern Rockies increased 28 percent over the past decade, with some of the highest growth rates occurring in southwestern Colorado. Colorado ranked third in the nation for growth during the 1990s, and it ranked eighth for growth this decade. The neighboring states of New Mexico and Wyoming increased their populations in the 1990s by 20.1 percent and 8.9 percent, respectively, and by 8.3 percent and 5.9 percent this century, respectively (US Department of Commerce 2008; US Census Bureau 2008). Population projections for the region suggest that high growth rates and the current patterns of development will continue, albeit at a slower rate.

CURRENT ECONOMIC TRENDS

The Southern Rockies' economy has evolved over the past century from extraction of natural resources such as gold, silver, oil, gas, uranium, coal, timber, and forage to service industries, retail trade, finance, insurance, and real estate. Today's economy is more diverse and complex, with significant portions of the region's income coming from small footloose businesses and nonlabor sources (US Department of Commerce 2008; see also T. M. Power 1996; Travis 2007).

Population growth, personal income, and employment (number of new jobs) are commonly used as economic growth indicators. For the Southern Rockies, these indicators were significantly higher than the US average, and job creation has stayed ahead of population growth. While population in the region nearly doubled between 1969 and 1999, personal income swelled 250 percent (in 1999 dollars) and jobs increased 187 percent (2.3 million new jobs created). Jobs in the United States as a whole increased by only 80 percent (US Department of Commerce [REIS] 1999; US Department of Commerce, County Business Patterns 1999). Numbers of new jobs in the Southern Rockies continued increasing through 2006, with an additional 453,662 jobs added between 1999 and 2006 (table 5.4).

In addition to number of jobs, an important economic indicator related to employment is the type of job being created; that is, what percentage of the workforce is made up of wage and salary workers (those who work for someone else) versus proprietors (self-employed business owners). In the Southern Rockies, wage and salary earners dropped from 85 percent of the workforce in 1969 to 81 percent in 1999 and to 77 percent in 2006, while proprietors increased from 15 percent in 1969 to 19 percent in 1999 and to 23 percent in 2006 (table 5.3). These changes closely mirror changes in the national workforce (table 5.3). Twenty-two percent of new jobs created between 1969 and 1999 and 48 percent of the new jobs created from 1999 to 2006 in the Southern Rockies were proprietors running their own businesses (compared to 20 percent and 54 percent during these periods in the United States as a whole) (US Department of Commerce [REIS] 1999; US Department of Commerce, County Business Patterns 1999) (table 5.3).

Most of the new businesses cropping up in the region are small, with few employees. More than half of the 164,280 Southern Rockies business establishments in 1999 employed fewer than five people, and 87 percent employed fewer than twenty people. This indicates a stable, diverse economy. When one or two large employers dominate a community (as with mining- or timber-dependent communities), much of the economic risk lies in the hands of one employer. That risk is more spread out with several smaller companies in a community (Rasker 1994).

A closer look at the type of proprietorship reveals that almost all new business owners are non–farm related, and many represent growing, footloose industries. People who can take their businesses anywhere increasingly choose the Southern Rockies for quality of life reasons (Power 1996). Many of these new small businesses are in the service sector (table 5.4). Perhaps most significant, the percentage of jobs in government declined from 24 percent to 14 percent between 1969 and 1999 and then remained stable until 2006, while the share of jobs in the private sector increased from 73 percent in 1969 to 85 percent in 2006 (table 5.4).

In terms of population and economic growth, the Southern Rockies, like the rest of the West, has seen steady growth since the late 1980s. That said, because the majority of counties evaluated are in Colorado, the picture masks the sixteen counties of Wyoming and New Mexico, many with less vibrant local economies. It is important to recognize spatial variation in socioeconomic conditions in the different subregions of the Southern Rockies, especially when considering potentially controversial wildlife management activities. For example, although Denver and Boulder counties (along the Colorado Front Range) each had under 2 percent of 2006 jobs in extractive industries, counties in southern Wyoming, southwestern Colorado, and northern New Mexico remain somewhat more dependent on "Old West" economies. The four counties with more than a quarter of their jobs in extractive industries (defined as farming, mining, agricultural services, forestry, fishing, and other) in 2006 were all in southern Colorado and northern New Mexico: Mora (32 percent), Union (29 percent), Jackson (28 percent), and Rio Blanco (27 percent).

Many counties in the proposed wolf reintroduction areas retain significant extractive economies. In the northwest Colorado site (Rio Blanco and Moffat counties), 27 percent and 17 percent of 2006 jobs, respectively, were in extractive industries. In the west-central site, Delta (9 percent) and Montrose (8 percent) counties stand out. In the northern New Mexico wolf reintroduction site, Costilla (19 percent) and Las Animas (12 percent) counties (both in Colorado just north of the New Mexico border) are significant, while in the southwest Colorado site, none of the counties had more than 7 percent of their 2006 jobs in extractive industries.

Much of the livestock production in the Southern Rockies relies on public lands grazing. Yet less than 5 percent of the livestock eaten in the United States is produced on western public lands (US General Accounting Office 1988; Wuerthner and Matteson 2002). Increased competition from livestock producers around the globe likely will further reduce that percentage. While ranching may be an important contributor to certain local economies, figures from the US Census Bureau's Bureau of Economic Analysis indicate that the contribution by farming and ranching to the overall Colorado economy fell from 3.1 percent in 1969 to 1.1 percent in both 1999 and 2006 (table 5.4). At present, the livestock industry presents the most significant opposition to restoring wolves to the Southern Rockies (see chap. 6). In the opinion of many ranchers, wolves are simply another threat to a livelihood that is being replaced in local economic importance by the service sector.

CURRENT LAND DEVELOPMENT TRENDS

Population and economic growth inevitably spur land development. Interestingly, the physical expansion of residential housing in the Southern Rockies exceeds population growth for three reasons: an increase in lower-density suburban development, the boom in exurban and "ranchette" rural development, and the growth in second-home ownership in the Southern Rockies, which is twice the national average and not reflected in population statistics (Theobald 2000). Thus, the impact of urban sprawl and expansion of low-density housing developments on natural landscapes in the Southern Rockies and surrounding areas is even greater than the high population growth rates suggest, and it is among the most significant agents of landscape change.

Moreover, the negative impact of housing expansion on ecosystems and species is actually much greater than the total area developed. Scattered low-density development fragments habitat. In many mountain valleys and foothill forests, low-density exurban developments occur along public-private land ownership boundaries, and can block wildlife movement. This can isolate wildlife habitat on surrounding public lands (Theobald 2000).

Developed areas also create "disturbance zones" that extend beyond the actual development and into adjacent natural habitat. Predation by household pets (cats are particularly destructive), the spread of noxious weeds, increases in aggressive human-adapted species (e.g., raccoons [*Procyon lotor*], striped skunks [*Mephitis mephitis*], or starlings [*Sturnus vulgaris*]), introduction of detrimental wildlife attractions (e.g., trash cans), and increases in recreational activity surrounding developed areas greatly affect ecological integrity (Knight 1995). The extended zone of negative effect for songbirds and medium-sized mammals is similar around low-density housing development and dense development; indeed, low-density housing may produce a greater overall impact due to the larger landscape area required (Odell and Knight 2001).

Moreover, human communities often suppress important natural disturbance processes such as fires and floods around developed areas in order to protect houses

and businesses. The proximity of much of the region's housing developments to forest-land restricts options for managing natural disturbance on public lands, in particular the ability to allow natural and ecologically beneficial forest fires to burn (Shinneman et al. 2000; Theobald 2000). This situation recently manifested itself in policy and introduced legislation to aggressively thin over-grown forests around urban areas, as well as far into the backcountry, via increased logging levels, streamlined environmental review, limited public participation, and scant attention to perpetuating natural fire regimes (e.g., see the George W. Bush administration's Healthy Forest Initiative, US Department of Agriculture 2003).

Using housing-unit data from US Census Block Groups, Theobald (2000, 2001) calculated historical and future spatial trends in development patterns for the region. Looking specifically at the Southern Rockies Ecoregion (and not the county-defined region), land within urban (less than 1 housing unit per hectare or 1 per 2.5 acres) and suburban (1 unit per 1 to 4 hectares or 1 per 2.5 to 10 acres) development grew from roughly 415 sq. km (160 sq. mi.) in 1960 to 1,729 sq. km (667 sq. mi.) by 1990. Research suggests that this area will grow to roughly 3,853 sq. km (1,487 sq. mi.) by 2020 and to 5,434 sq. km (2,098 sq. mi.) by 2050. Exurban development (1 unit per 4 to 16 hectares or 1 per 10 to 40 acres), grew from roughly 1,877 sq. km (725 sq. mi.) to 5,928 sq. km (2,288 sq. mi.) between 1960 and 1990, and it is projected at roughly 8,398 sq. km (3,242 sq. mi.) by 2020 and 11,065 sq. km (4,271 sq. mi.) by 2050. Exurban, suburban, and urban developments collectively covered about 7,508 sq. km (2,898 sq. mi.) (4.6 percent of the ecoregion) in 1990 and are projected to grow to 16,598 sq. km (6,407 sq. mi.) (10 percent of the ecoregion) by 2050.

This pattern of development is mainly concentrated in mountain valleys, foothills, and lower elevation valleys (Shinneman et al. 2000; Theobald 2000). These areas often include valuable agricultural lands and species-rich wildlife habitat such as ponderosa pine forests, oak shrublands, montane grasslands, riparian areas, and wetlands (Shinneman et al. 2000).

CONCLUSIONS

The Southern Rockies have witnessed several boom periods of human influx and prosperous economies, punctuated by brief periods of economic downturn or stagnation. The net result has been an expanding human population that has extensively modified the natural landscape. These ecological changes have arisen from land uses representative of the Old and New West: from cattle grazing to mountain biking, gold mining to luxury second-home development, predator control to downhill skiing. Yet, despite dramatic ecological changes since Euro-American settlement, quite remarkably the region retains significant stretches of wildlands with suitable habitat for the gray wolf and other large carnivores. Indeed, the region's wild landscapes and substantial public land base are significant reasons why it continues to attract so many new people and businesses.

The presence of these wildlands, combined with a human population less dependent on natural resource extraction and increasingly favoring environmental protection, bodes well for wolf restoration efforts. Yet, while some elements of the New West promote and favor ecological restoration, other New West trends do not. Urban and exurban housing development in particular threaten key habitats and the larger integrity of the landscape, especially when development and road construction occur in critical wildlife corridors. For instance, the highly traveled Interstate 70 in Colorado with its rapidly developing counties (e.g., Eagle County experienced a 90 percent human

population growth rate in the 1990s) would pose significant challenges to the long-term viability of a restored wolf population. Yet as communities continue to shift from extraction-based economies to service economies, which often rely on marketing local natural amenities, they increasingly recognize the economic benefits of restored and healthy ecosystems. In fact, studies linked economic growth in the 1990s in western communities to a demand for wildlife amenities (Ingram and Lewandrowski 1999). Thus, one key to successful wolf restoration is to link economic prosperity to the region's wildlife and ecological health in the minds of the public.

It is also important to recognize that a one-size-fits-all approach to wolf restoration in the Southern Rockies is unlikely to succeed. As wildlife managers begin to focus on specific areas for restoration, they will need to consider local cultures, attitudes, politics, and socioeconomic conditions (see chap. 4). Being aware of local conditions will aid in forging allies in these communities. In northern New Mexico, for example, it will be important to recruit leaders in the Hispanic and Native American communities to help with education and public relations. In northwestern Colorado, managers must be sensitive to the concerns of relatively large, close-knit, and politically powerful ranching communities.

Moreover, local situations must be considered within the larger human landscape context in order to determine how socioeconomic and cultural factors might interplay across the Southern Rockies landscape as a whole. For instance, successfully restoring wolves in one well-studied and well-prepared subregion may ultimately lead to an expanding wolf population that creates significant political and cultural problems in unprepared adjacent subregions. Such a scenario could threaten the overall viability of any wolf restoration effort. Yet, this cultural diversity may also be seen as a strength. Because the region is not a cultural monolith, there are more opportunities to win support for a restored wolf population in key subregions, which may then provide momentum for a successful restoration project overall.

If local issues are strongly integrated into a wolf restoration program and if expanding development can be channeled away from the most critical habitats, wolf restoration in the Southern Rockies will most likely be successful. These are significant but not insurmountable challenges. Recent restoration of the Canada lynx in the Southern Rockies and wolf restoration in other ecoregions provide examples of workable approaches. They also indicate where improvements, further research, and innovations are still needed. However, these models should be readily adaptable to wolf restoration in the Southern Rockies. It is an ecologically suitable region that contains a human population increasingly favorable to environmental protection and restoration.

Owner	Hectares	Acres	% SRE
Tribal	456,149	1,127,168	2.70%
US Bureau of Land Management	2,002,323	4,947,848	12.00%
US National Park Service	164,617	406,776	1.00%
US Forest Service	7,142,617	17,649,792	42.80%
US Fish and Wildlife Service	17,056	42,147	0.10%
Other federal lands	18,689	46,182	0.10%
State lands	645,596	1,595,302	3.90%
Private/Other	6,234,816	15,406,565	37.40%
Totals	**16,681,863**	**41,221,780**	**100.00%**

Table 5.1—Major land ownership in the Southern Rockies Ecoregion and surrounding areas, with percent and acres by ownership. State land includes state parks, state wildlife areas, state land board lands, and state forest.

Source: Land Stewardship/Ownership data from New Mexico Gap Analysis 1996 and Wyoming Gap Analysis 1996; US Bureau of Land Management 1996)

Most Populous Counties	Least Populous Counties
Bernalillo, NM: 615,099 (Albuquerque)	San Juan, CO: 578
El Paso, CO: 576,884 (Colorado Springs)	Hinsdale, CO: 819
Denver, CO: 566,974 (Denver)	Mineral, CO: 929
Arapahoe, CO: 537,197	Jackson, CO: 1,406
Jefferson, CO: 526,994	Dolores, CO: 1,911
Adams, CO: 414,338	Costilla, CO: 3,378
Boulder, CO: 282,304	Custer, CO: 3,926
Larimer, CO: 276,253 (Fort Collins)	Ouray, CO: 4,307
Douglas, CO: 263,621	Gilpin, CO: 5,042
Weld, CO: 236,857	Mora, NM: 5,151
Pueblo, CO: 152,912	Rio Blanco, CO: 6,180
Sante Fe, NM: 142,407	Saguache, CO: 7,006

Table 5.2—The most and least populous counties in the Southern Rockies Ecoregion in 2006.

Source: US Department of Commerce, Bureau of the Census, http://quickfacts.census.gov/qfd/states/08000.html)

	1969	% of 1969	1999	% of 1999	New Jobs, 1969–1999	% of New Jobs	2006	% of 2006	New Jobs, 1999–2006	% of New Jobs
Southern Rockies										
Wage and Salary	1,050,143	85%	2,849,619	81%	1,799,476	78%	3,084,265	77%	234,646	52%
Proprietors	180,146	15%	682,287	19%	502,141	22%	901,303	23%	219,016	48%
Farm Proprietors	22,298	2%	27,876	<1%	5,578	<1%%	31,841	1%	3,965	1%
Nonfarm Proprietors	157,848	13%	654,411	19%	496,563	22%	869,462	22%	215,051	47%
Total Employment	1,230,289	100%	3,531,906	100%	2,301,617	100%	3,985,568	100%	453,662	100%
United States										
Wage and Salary	78,726,000	86%	136,617,000	83%	57,891,000	80%	143,249,000	80%	6,632,000	46%
Proprietors	12,331,200	14%	27,140,900	17%	14,809,700	20%	35,083,900	20%	7,943,000	54%
Farm Proprietors	2,751,000	3%	2,249,000	1%	-502,000	-1%	2,116,000	1%	-133,000	-1%
Nonfarm Proprietors	9,580,200	11%	24,891,900	15%	15,311,700	21%	32,967,900	18%	8,076,000	55%
Total Employment	91,057,200	100%	163,757,900	100%	72,700,700	100%	178,332,900	100%	14,575,000	100%

Table 5.3—Changes in employment by type, Southern Rockies Ecoregion and the United States, 1969–2006.

Source: US Department of Commerce, Bureau of Economic Analysis, Regional Economic Information System 2008). Percentages do not always add up due to rounding.

Job Sector	1969	% of 1969	1999	% of 1999	New Jobs, 1969–1999	% of New Jobs	2006	% of 2006	New Jobs, 1999–2006	% of New Jobs
Farm and ranch	37,933	3%	40,726	1%	2,793	0%	45,161	1%	4,435	1%
Nonfarm	1,192,356	97%	3,491,180	99%	2,298,824	100%	3,940,407	99%	449,227	99%
Private (non-farm)	892,596	73%	2,984,901	85%	2,092,305	91%	3,411,898	85%	426,997	94%
Ag. services, forestry, fishing and other	7,759	1%	38,406	1%	30,647	1%	6,527	0%	-31,879	-7%
Mining	24,466	2%	26,051	1%	1,585	0%	36,269	1%	10,218	2%
Construction	67,375	5%	253,270	7%	185,895	8%	335,920	8%	82,650	18%
Manufacturing	133,109	11%	245,275	7%	112,166	5%	201,336	5%	-43,939	-10%
Transportation and public utilities	67,788	6%	189,511	5%	121,723	5%	114,968	3%	-74,543	-16%
Wholesale trade	55,842	5%	141,156	4%	85,314	4%	136,829	3%	-4,327	-1%
Retail trade	194,752	16%	607,289	17%	412,537	18%	439,457	10%	-167,832	-37%
Finance, insurance, and real estate	99,513	8%	335,903	10%	236,390	10%	440,197	10%	104,294	23%
Services	241,992	20%	1,148,040	33%	906,048	39%	1,700,395	40%	552,355	122%
Government	299,760	24%	506,279	14%	206,519	9%	528,509	14%	22,230	5%
Federal, civilian	61,788	5%	73,534	2%	11,746	1%	73,704	2%	170	0%
Military	76,630	6%	54,361	2%	-22,269	-1%	53,746	1%	-615	0%
State and local	161,342	13%	378,384	11%	217,042	9%	401,059	10%	22,675	5%
Total full-time and part-time employment	1,230,289	100%	3,531,906	100%	2,301,617	100%	3,985,568	100%	453,662	100%

Table 5.4—Employment by industry, Southern Rockies Ecoregion, 1969–2006.
Source: US Department of Commerce, Bureau of Economic Analysis, Regional Economic Information System 2008). Percentages do not always add up due to rounding.

Chapter 6
Public Attitudes toward Wolves and Wolf Recovery

Brian Miller, Richard P. Reading, and Hannah Gosnell

INTRODUCTION

Perhaps no species polarizes opinions in the United States more than wolves (*Canis* spp.). Some people love wolves, others loath them, and few are ambivalent. This polarization complicates wolf conservation and management, often eliciting strong responses from particular interest groups, or stakeholders. As such, it is crucial to examine public and stakeholder attitudes toward wolves and the implications of those attitudes to gray wolf (*C. lupus*) recovery in the Southern Rockies Ecoregion.

In this chapter, we define attitudes and related values, beliefs, perceptions, and knowledge. We next review what we know about public attitudes and beliefs toward wolves. This body of literature is relatively large and is growing as social scientists and others attempt to understand the reasons for polarized attitudes toward wildlife and how best to address the unproductive conflict and polemics surrounding wolf recovery. We finish by applying what we know to prospects for wolf recovery in the Southern Rockies.

DEFINING VALUES, ATTITUDES, AND BELIEFS

Values, attitudes, and beliefs help define who we are as individuals and what we do. They serve to impose order and consistency to the complex and chaotic world in which we live (Tessler and Shaffer 1990; Olson and Zanna 1993). Many people use the terms *values*, *attitudes*, and *beliefs* almost interchangeably.

Although these terms all interact, they do differ (Bright and Barro 2000). So we offer some definitions for clarification (Bem 1970; Rokeach 1972).

A value is a preferred mode of behaving (e.g., honesty) or existing (e.g., equality). Values influence attitudes, or an attraction toward or rejection of an entity (in this case, wolves), and they are often based on intellectual evaluation of a situation (e.g., what we know, or think we know, about wolf ecology and behavior) (Williams 1979). Values are thus affected by perception, context, and knowledge of a situation (Rokeach 1972; Williams 1979; Brown 1984; Brown and Manfredo 1987).

There are many types of values (see table 6.1) (Lasswell 1971; Kellert 1984, 1995; Steinhoff 1980). It is important to note that when people have multiple values, the values vary in strength (Rokeach 1972; Brown 1984). Sociologists often group values into categories, some of which are specific to wildlife and nature (table 6.1). Because the relative strengths of values are not equal, people arrange them in a hierarchical fashion. Thus, when a person is faced with a situation in which two or more values clash, that individual usually relies upon more strongly held values (core values) over less strongly held ones (peripheral values) (Williams 1979).

Attitudes as we define the term are affinities or aversions toward something (e.g., wolves), and that affinity/aversion is based on beliefs (Bem 1970; Rokeach 1972). A belief, in turn, is based on our perception of how an entity affects a given situation. Context is thus important. An example might be a livestock owner's belief about the predatory nature of wolves after discovering a fresh livestock kill (Bem 1970; Rokeach 1972). Extreme attitudes tend to be based on more simple belief systems than moderate attitudes (Bright and Barro 2000). Indeed, in many ways it is easier to be a zealot.

Perceptions are formed by what a person senses and understands about an issue. Perceptions evolve from information, cultural values, and personal experiences (Brown 1984). Context describes a person's situation, for example how frequently someone is exposed to an issue and the social setting. Traditional customs, peer pressure, level of socialization by institutions, and other factors interact to determine the social setting (Brown and Manfredo 1987; Chaiken and Stangor 1987). Finally, a person's mood (e.g., level of satisfaction) and physical state (e.g., physical or economic health) can also be important.

Knowledge is the acquisition, comprehension, and retention of information, and it depends on exposure, receptivity, perception, interpretation, and memory (Petty et al. 1997). While knowledge is an important determinant of values, attitudes, and beliefs, its importance is often overestimated, especially among people who value knowledge greatly, such as biologists and conservationists (Reading 1993; Kellert et al. 1996). Knowledge is only one of several factors influencing values, attitudes, and beliefs, and its influence is often relatively weak.

When values, attitudes, and beliefs are strongly held, new knowledge is often selectively received (accepting only the parts of the information with which one already agrees) and selectively interpreted (Tessler and Shaffer 1990; J. A. Olson and Zanna 1993). In other words, people often focus on facts that support their attitudes. For example, people with negative attitudes toward wolves may focus on the fact that wolves sometimes begin to eat their prey before it is dead. Alternatively, people with positive attitudes toward wolves often focus on the species' sociality and high levels of parental care. Indeed, values, attitudes, and beliefs can even affect memory, with information supporting a preexisting opinion memorized and remembered more easily than information contradicting such an opinion (Tessler and Shaffer 1990; J. A. Olson and Zanna 1993). These interactions are strengthened if information is poor, ambiguous, or too complex to be easily understood (Tessler and Shaffer 1990; J. A. Olson and Zanna 1993).

MYTH AND WOLVES

Strongly entrenched attitudes and beliefs toward wolves, whether positive or negative, can be viewed as components of people's larger worldviews. Social scientists refer to such worldviews as myths. Our broad use of the word *myth* follows from Lasswell and Kaplan (1950, 116–117), who define myth as "the pattern of the basic political symbols current in a society" consisting of "the political perspectives most firmly accepted" in a community. Thus, myths are based on a number of fundamental assumptions, regardless of their truth (Dicey 1926, in Lasswell and Kaplan 1950). Over time, these assumptions are no longer questioned. For example, in American society, most people never question the assumption that economic growth is good, they simply operate in a manner that takes this assumption as a given.

Myths are therefore powerful belief systems based on unquestioned assumptions, and they are supported by powerful symbols. In the United States, for example, bald eagles (*Haliaeetus leucocephalus*) symbolize freedom. Myths developed because the world is far too complicated for any person to fully understand. Simon (1976) referred to our inability to comprehend all aspects of a problem or situation as "bounded rationality."

As such, people create myths to help them understand, relate to, and operate in a complex world. Myths promote solidarity among people who share them. Problems arise when people refuse to accept that perspectives different from their own are valid; thus, their own subjective experience becomes a substitute for reality (Arendt 1958).

Because myths and their symbols rest on assumptions that are not challenged, they enter the realm of belief. They are typically not defended with logic but often elicit emotional responses. Many people may be able to hold an intellectual conversation about the pros and cons of a given technique, but they can become quite irrational when a fundamental myth they embrace is challenged. Emotional responses can even become violent. For this reason, leaders use and manipulate myths to further their political agendas, usually by associating loyalty to their agenda with loyalty to the dominant myth (and its symbols). The use of patriotism, nationalism, and religion by those in power has produced mass followings for many historical events that do not reflect well on our species.

Opposition to wolves and wolf restoration has been viewed as an outgrowth of a larger western myth about resource use called the Cowboy Myth or Frontier Myth (Slotkin 1992; McCain et al. 2002). This myth is an outgrowth of philosophies and assumptions associated with Judeo-Christian heritage, libertarian political and economic thought, early American notions of agrarian societies, and European settlement of the West (Locke 1690; Smith 1902; White 1967; Wallace et al. 1996). It is frequently applied to help define human relationships to the land and environment in the rural western United States. Some of the key symbols include barbed wire, cowboys on horseback, the open range, and guns (Slotkin 1992). This myth includes a strong belief that human dominion over nature is good and vested in God's will. It also includes a distrust of outsiders, a

strong belief in libertarianism, and the presence or threat of violence to support one's position (Slotkin 1992; Reading and Kellert 1993). In other words, proponents of this Cowboy or Frontier Myth do not like other people telling them what to do, especially if those people come from outside their county, state, or region (in that order).

To those who embrace the Cowboy or Frontier Myth, wolves often symbolize a contemptible enemy, representing a reversion to the wilderness that early European settlers fought to tame, in part by killing wolves. Further, wolves support the perception of a loss of control over public and even private land, an economic hardship, and a threat to traditional western lifestyles. Seen in this light, we can understand why incentive programs that simply pay ranchers for livestock killed by wolves are insufficient to develop support for the species. Indeed, such programs may even reinforce antithetic responses.

Supporters of wolves also embrace a myth, which we will refer to as the Wilderness Myth. This myth has its roots in assumptions and philosophies associated with ecological and conservation thought, the right to existence for all organisms, and changing human relationships to the natural world (Kellert 1996). Powerful symbols of this myth include wilderness, awe-inspiring vistas, endangered species, and charismatic animals. The myth challenges popular notions that define quality of life in solely economic terms, instead arguing that society should sacrifice economic growth for a healthy environment. Proponents largely distrust and often vilify big business, corporate America, and natural resource extractors, including many if not most ranchers. Additionally, proponents argue that industries that rely on extracting or using natural resources should be willing to change management practices to restore ecological health to the land.

To supporters of the Wilderness Myth, the wolf represents a strong symbol of wildness and pristine nature. Proponents focus on the wolf's complex social structure and its role as a keystone species that is crucial to a well-functioning ecosystem (see chap. 3). Supporters of the Wilderness Myth also believe that wolves symbolize the extent to which society is willing to go to conserve nature and natural processes. To adherents of the Cowboy or Frontier and Wilderness myths, wolves symbolize a struggle over who controls public land. People who embrace the Wilderness Myth believe that natural resource extractors have dominated, mismanaged, and sacrificed the public good for private profit on public lands for far too long.

Although we have reduced the large number of myths associated with wolves into two broad, somewhat oversimplified camps, we believe that this dichotomy helps illustrate the conflict surrounding wolf recovery in the Southern Rockies. Obviously, these myths are based on different value systems and worldviews. Managing the resulting conflicts between proponents of each is difficult. However, there are similarities between proponents of each myth, including a professed love for open spaces, wildlife, and natural beauty. Focusing on these similarities offers the best prospects for productively managing the conflict between wolf lovers and haters.

ATTITUDES WITHIN PUBLIC INSTITUTIONS TOWARD WOLVES

The attitudes people hold may be the most important factor influencing the success of wolf recovery. These attitudes are affected by level of knowledge, human-animal relationships, personal experience with the species, real and perceived impacts of the species on economies or lifestyles, and the species' economic or cultural value (Reading 1993; Kellert 1996). The challenges faced by a recovery program are heightened when opinions about a species are highly polarized (Chaiken and Stangor 1987; Reading 1993; Kellert 1993).

Challenges become particularly difficult if opposing interest groups, or stakeholders, are powerful, wealthy, and influential. Our political system is a representative democracy where, although one person represents one vote, all votes are not equal. For example, people residing in rural regions enjoy de facto stronger representation because senators from rural regions representing fewer constituents have equal standing with senators from urban regions, who represent more constituents. The same is true for rural states and the electoral college.

Any level of federal protection for a wildlife species often increases polarization, especially if certain stakeholders perceive economic or political consequences from such protections. In addition, many species represent powerful symbols that characterize traits or issues extending well beyond their ecological role. Thus, because wolves symbolize far more than the animals themselves, we must also consider opinions and attitudes toward the Endangered Species Act, issues of state vs. federal control, the decision-making power and goals of stakeholders, wilderness, traditional landowner control over public and private land, and more. Indeed, reintroducing wolves combined with their federal legal protection may imply a loss of political power to ranchers, loggers, and miners, who once held that power almost undisputedly throughout the West. Much of that power has recently shifted to urban recreationists and conservationists, even though the extent of this shift is debated (Reading et al. 1994). Thus, wolves, endangered species, and proposals for wilderness areas are straw men for the real issue: who controls the land.

ATTITUDES WITHIN WILDLIFE MANAGEMENT AGENCIES

We will now explore the results of surveys taken to help understand the attitudes of the general public and key stakeholder groups toward wolves. We note, however, that in any kind of recovery effort, it is also important to consider the attitudes of people within the managing agencies (Reading et al. 2006). After all, individuals in federal, state, and local government agencies make decisions that dictate the future of the species. We often assume that everyone in a management body assigned with recovering a species holds the same, or at least similar, values. That is usually not true. And even if all members of an agency share similar values, they may not hold those values in the same order of preference. Differences in value hierarchies are usually even more pronounced between individuals from different organizations. Members representing a nongovernmental conservation organization may place wolf recovery at the top of their list of goals, whereas representatives of an agency with a multiuse mandate may have to balance wolf recovery against other goals, some of which may even compete with wolf recovery.

The US Fish and Wildlife Service is legally responsible for evaluating the status of species and listing them as threatened or endangered under the US Endangered Species Act (see chap. 7). The service must prepare recovery plans, coordinate recovery programs, and enforce laws. While many service biologists are dedicated to wolf recovery, it is largely a regulatory agency and does not directly control much of the land where wolf recovery might occur. Thus, it seems to us that politics forces the service to accommodate uses of land that may interfere with wolf recovery. Biologists who favor an action benefiting wolf recovery may be overruled at higher levels of the bureaucracy if there is resistance to the recommendation by powerful opponents. In some cases, biologists with a naturalistic or scientific philosophy (table 6.1) may be faced with threats to career advancement (PEER 1997). In emotionally charged programs, the level of political influence from above can lead to self-censorship,

fatigue (burnout), and frustration in dedicated field biologists.

The National Park Service supports wolf restoration in national parks (especially Yellowstone) because their mission includes maintaining and restoring the original flora and fauna of areas they manage (Fritts et al. 1995). This is part of their larger mission to maintain natural processes and diversity (US National Park Service 1988). Park service employees tend to embrace a naturalistic value (table 6.1).

The US Forest Service and US Bureau of Land Management are multiple-use agencies. Those uses include recreation; wildlife protection; grazing; mining; oil, natural gas, and timber extraction; and wilderness protection (Fritts et al. 1995), and the uses often conflict with one another. The US Forest Service and the BLM control much of the land where wolves would live if recovery proceeds in the Southern Rockies. If a species is threatened or endangered, both agencies must consult with the US Fish and Wildlife Service to ensure that proposed activities do not injure that population (see chap. 7). The multiple-use mandate of these agencies, however, means, according to studies, that many members of these organizations likely embrace human dominion over nature (table 6.1).

Wildlife Services (formerly the Division of Animal Damage Control) is in the US Department of Agriculture and is responsible for controlling wildlife that causes economic damage (Fritts et al. 1995). This includes protected species, and control is accomplished using lethal means, translocation, aversive conditioning, or protection (such as guard dogs). This agency played a major role in wolf eradication and historically served agricultural interests when they conflicted with ecological interests. Studies suggest that employees of the division tend toward an ethic of domination over nature and view wolf recovery in a more negativistic, or at least tightly controlled, manner than other agency personnel discussed thus far (table 6.1).

State governments are concerned that: (1) federal protection will restrict their management options; (2) wolves may not be quickly delisted after recovery; (3) local interests may not be sufficiently considered in the planning process; and, (4) traditionally powerful constituents in rural areas (especially hunter and agricultural interests) may believe that wolf reintroduction threatens their interests (Fritts et al. 1995). State agencies tend to be dominated or influenced by a mix of scientific, dominion over nature, and utilitarian beliefs (table 6.1). For example, state wildlife agencies rely, in part, on hunting license sales for income. These agencies also need the goodwill of ranchers for hunter access. Thus, state wildlife agencies face a conflict if a threatened or endangered species interferes with hunting success and their license income. Hunting and ranching interests often dominate the state commissions that oversee state wildlife agencies. Other local agencies, especially agricultural agencies, are even more hostile toward carnivores. While many state-level wildlife biologists may favor restoring wolves to the Southern Rockies, political pressures likely prevent them from expressing their views.

ATTITUDES WITHIN STATE LEGISLATURES

Rural interests are overrepresented within state legislatures because of the way legislative district boundaries are drawn (e.g., a rural district may represent only 6,000 people, versus an urban district of the same size, which might represent 60,000 people). This rural bias leverages the antipredator sentiment, which is more prevalent in rural areas. Compounding this bias is the fact that most legislatures send any bill dealing with predator management directly to committees dealing with agricultural issues (and thus dominated by rural representatives). The result is an antipredator bias that contrasts starkly with the attitudes of the general population. In 1991, for example, Idaho and Wyoming passed legislative resolutions opposing wolf reintroduction. Nevertheless, the US Fish and Wildlife Service successfully reintroduced wolves to Yellowstone National Park and north-central Idaho.

Following successful reintroduction of the wolf in Yellowstone, all three states wanted the wolf removed from federal protection to allow them to manage wolves under their own nongame and endangered species legislation, and they produced individual state management plans as required by the US Fish and Wildlife Service (Fritts et al. 1995; Montana Fish, Wildlife, Parks 2004). Although the service delisted the wolf in the Northern Rockies in 2007 (US Fish and Wildlife Service 2007b), a federal court found that action illegal and ruled that they must restore the wolf's federal protection. Part of the court's ruling stemmed from the judge's dissatisfaction with Wyoming's plan, which included maintaining pest status for wolves over most of the state. Interestingly, Wyoming's wolf management plan was at first rejected by the service, then accepted by them (US Fish and Wildlife Service 2007b). Rejection of the plan by the federal judge forced the service to yet again change its stance (US Fish and Wildlife Service 2008). In late 2008, the US Fish and Wildlife Service (2008) accepted management plans for wolves from Montana and Idaho and proposed delisting the species in those two states only. In 2009, the US Fish and Wildlife Service delisted the species in Montana and Idaho, but not Wyoming (US Fish and Wildlife Service 2009b) and was promptly sued by Wyoming and several conservation organizations.

Colorado recognized the need to address wolf management at the beginning of this century, and in 2005 the state's wildlife commission adopted a set of management recommendations made by a working group of ranchers, conservation activists, biologists, hunters, and local officials to manage any wolves that might disperse into the state (Colorado Wolf Management Working Group 2004). However, the state's Agricultural Department still maintains a wolf bounty in defiance of federal law (Colorado Wolf Management Working Group 2004).

TRIBAL ATTITUDES

Official tribal positions on wolves can change frequently because they vary with the composition of tribal councils (Fritts et al. 1995). Some Native Americans view the return of the wolf as an important cultural and religious event, while others view it as restoring ecological systems and still others fear economic losses (Fritts et al. 1995). Traditional tribal members possess cultural, aesthetic, and moral values toward wolves. Other Native Americans hold values similar to those of ranchers. Tribal sovereignty and management responsibility for the wolf are major concerns of tribal agencies and governments (Fritts et al. 1995).

RESULTS OF ATTITUDE SURVEYS ABOUT WOLVES

To people who dislike them, wolves are strong, negative symbols of wildness, danger, reduced political power, economic loss, and a deterioration of the civilization they have built (Kellert 1985a, 1995; Clark et al. 1996). Older, less-educated respondents and men disliked wolves more than women under twenty-five with a college education (Kellert 1996). The best predictors of negative attitude toward wolves were fear and a general negative attitude toward animals (Hook 1982).

Positive attitudes toward wolves are highly correlated with affection for animals and desire to protect wildlife habitat (Kellert 1996; Clark et al. 1996; Meadow 2001). Wolves are embraced as symbols of wilderness, nature, ecological integrity, and a level

of commitment to conservation. Regional differences revealed that Alaskan respondents had the most positive perceptions of the wolf (Kellert 1985a). Demographic trends for positive or negative attitudes toward wolves were consistent throughout studies across the United States.

MIDWESTERN UNITED STATES

A few studies were conducted on attitudes toward wolves in Minnesota and northern Michigan. In 1974, Van Ballenberghe (1974) reported that the Minnesota wolf population was doing better than it had since the 1940s and 1950s, but that there was no real attempt to manage the species or habitat. He speculated that unless there was some form of management of wolf populations rather than of individual wolves, the more negative attitudes that existed before the 1960s could return. Before the 1960s, about 100 wolves suspected of preying on domestic livestock were killed each year and another 100 to 200 were killed annually by trapping, poaching, and incidental taking (Van Ballenberghe 1974).

In 1985, Kellert found that sample groups among Minnesota's residents, with the exception of farmers, had a strong positive perception of the wolf, and that all groups agreed that the wolf was symbolic of nature's wonder and beauty. Support existed for wolf populations, but that support did not supersede human needs. Thus, to most respondents it was acceptable to kill wolves that attacked livestock or to extract minerals in areas where wolves were protected. In contrast, limiting hunting was the favored method of increasing deer numbers—not reducing the number of wolves (Kellert 1985b).

In 1999, Kellert again surveyed attitudes of Minnesota's northern residents, non-northern residents, and farmers. About 50 percent of all three groups indicated they cared a great deal for wolves, whereas only about 20 percent said they cared very little for the species. More than 70 percent thought the wolf symbolized the beauty and wonder of nature, and 60 percent said they would not be afraid to live near wolves. A majority of farmers, however, did not want to live near wolves. Most residents favored protection for the wolf but preferred wolf management by the state instead of the federal government (Kellert 1999).

Kellert further found that while most residents and farmers favored compensating farmers for livestock lost to wolves, non-northern residents thought financial compensation should occur only if farms were managed in ways that discouraged wolf attacks. Farmers disagreed, citing the expense as prohibitive (Kellert 1999).

The majority of people responding to Kellert's survey expressed no concern that wolves would negatively impact deer hunting. If deer numbers dropped, a majority thought that wolves should be reduced, but a strong minority thought human hunting should be limited (Kellert 1999). This last finding contrasted somewhat with answers to a similar question in 1985 (Kellert 1985b).

Kellert (1990) also surveyed public attitudes toward wolves in Michigan. Of residents in the Upper Peninsula, 64 percent favored wolf restoration, 15 percent opposed it, and 21 percent were uncommitted. Of residents in the Lower Peninsula, 57 percent favored restoration, 9 percent opposed it, and 34 percent were uncommitted (Kellert 1990). This generally agreed with an earlier study by Hook (1982) showing that Michigan residents supported wolves and that hunters were more positive than the general public (Hook 1982).

As pointed out by Refsnider (2000), Kellert's public attitude surveys in Minnesota and Michigan (Kellert 1985b, 1990, 1999) and citizen input to a wolf management plan in the state indicate strong public support for wolf recovery if adverse impacts on recreational activities and livestock producers can be minimized (Michigan Department of Natural Resources 1997; Minnesota Department of Natural Resources 1998; Wisconsin Department of Natural Resources 1999).

NORTHERN ROCKY MOUNTAINS

Several studies have explored public attitudes toward wolves in and around the Greater Yellowstone Ecosystem. In 1985, McNaught (1985) found that visitors favored reintroducing wolves into Yellowstone National Park by a ratio of three to one, and that six to one believed that adding wolves would improve the Yellowstone experience. Duffield et al. (1992) found that visitors to Yellowstone showed a two to one margin favoring wolf restoration.

Bath (1987a) found that 91 percent of Wyoming stock growers did not favor wolf reintroduction into Yellowstone National Park, but members of Defenders of Wildlife and the Wyoming Wildlife Federation favored reintroduction (89 percent and 67 percent, respectively). Around the park, 51 percent of the public opposed and 39 percent favored wolf reintroduction; however, across the entire state of Wyoming, 49 percent favored reintroduction and 35 percent opposed it (Bath 1987b, 1987c). These results were very similar to results from a Wyoming Game and Fish Department survey (Thompson 1991) and a survey by Bath and Buchanan (1989).

In Montana, 65 percent of the public believed that wolves belonged in the state, with stronger support in populous counties (78 percent) than rural counties (54 percent) (Lenihan 1987). In the same study, 52 percent thought wolves should be reintroduced into Montana, Idaho, and Yellowstone National Park, while 56 percent of those from rural counties did not approve of the idea. Lenihan (1987) found that support for wolf reintroduction was based on perceptions that wolves were important to the ecological community (41 percent) and that wolves were historically present (40 percent).

Loss of livestock was the most important rationale for opposition (57 percent). Tucker and Pletscher (1989) found that 72 percent of residents living in northwestern Montana and 58 percent of hunters in Flathead County hoped that wolves would continue to inhabit the area and should be allowed to expand. Tucker and Pletscher (1989) speculated that support for wolves might dwindle if recovery meant restrictions on recreational and commercial uses.

A survey conducted by the Idaho Environmental Science Teachers (1987) found that 78 percent of the Idaho public would like to see wild populations of wolves living in Idaho, while 12 percent disagreed and 10 percent had no opinion. Freemuth (1992) found that 72 percent of the Idaho public favored wolves, while 22 percent opposed them.

Bath and Phillips (1990) noted that the primary reason some Idaho and Montana residents opposed wolf reintroduction was the cost of the program, which agreed with Bath's (1987c) survey of Idaho residents. There was also concern among ranchers that wolves would kill their livestock and that any losses were unacceptable to them.

Bath and Phillips (1990) asked if opinions would change under three conditions: livestock losses were kept to less than 1 percent, ranchers were financially compensated for those losses, and wolves stayed in the park or surrounding wilderness areas. They found that three out of four people who did not favor wolf reintroduction would not change their opinion, regardless of the options. If wolves could be monitored effectively and be restricted to within the park and surrounding wilderness areas, only 27 percent (Montana) and 25 percent (Idaho) of those originally opposed would favor wolf reintroduction. Thompson (1991) found that 14 percent of those opposed to wolf restoration would change their opinion if there were a compensation program. This reluctance to change viewpoints regardless of the options

presented reinforces the earlier discussion about the difficulty of changing values, especially when well developed, and the importance of myth in comparison to opinions.

There was strong support among the general public for a compensation program to protect livestock owners from financial losses due to wolf depredation. In addition, Thompson (1991) and Lenihan (1987) found that 57 percent and 59 percent of the public, respectively, thought that wolves should be killed for taking livestock.

There was some public concern that wolves might attack people. McNaught (1995) found that 20 percent of respondents he surveyed would be afraid to hike in Yellowstone National Park if wolves were present. Eisenstein (1992) reported gross misunderstandings and misconceptions about wolves, with many people responding that they knew for a fact that wolves kill people. The surveys conducted around Yellowstone do not agree on whether or not the public perceived wolves as a serious threat to wildlife populations, but they did show a level of concern over possible impacts to hunter harvest (US Fish and Wildlife Service 1994).

SOUTHWESTERN UNITED STATES

Recent studies of attitudes toward wolves were conducted in the southwestern United States in association with a planned reintroduction on the Arizona–New Mexico border. According to those studies, people who were urban, younger, and who had attained a higher level of education tended to support wolf reintroduction (Duda et al. 1995; Duda and Young 1995). Voters favoring wolf reintroduction into the Blue Range Primitive Area of Arizona were more commonly registered as independents (85 percent), and there were more Democrats (73 percent) than Republicans (64 percent), but support ranged across political affiliation (Duda et al. 1995). The findings for the proposed reintroduction into the Blue Range were nearly identical to those from similar questions about a potential reintroduction into the White Sands Missile Range of New Mexico (Duda et al. 1995). A survey by Groebner et al. (1995) in Arizona found that 61 percent of those surveyed supported wolf reintroduction. Seventy-three percent of New Mexico residents thought that maintaining wolves in the wild would not threaten economic prosperity (Duda et al. 1995; Duda and Young 1995).

The most important reasons people gave for supporting the reintroduction of wolves into Arizona and New Mexico were to save the wolf from extinction, because wolves lived in the southwestern United States historically, and because wolves play a part in a functioning ecosystem (Duda et al. 1995; Duda and Young 1995; Meadow et al. 2005). Opposition was founded on fear of lost livestock, reduced deer (*Odocoileus* spp.) and elk (*Cervus elaphus*) populations, and threat to human safety (Duda et al. 1995; Duda and Young 1995; Meadow et al. 2005).

SOUTHERN ROCKY MOUNTAINS

While the Southern Rockies include parts of southern Wyoming and northern New Mexico, we focus primarily on Colorado. Some Colorado surveys have evaluated the public's attitudes toward wolves and the possibility of reintroducing them into the state. In general, rural residents of Colorado tend to support traditional forms of wildlife management (e.g., trapping and hunting), whereas urban residents are more likely to oppose these practices and support greater rights for animals (Kellert 1984; Manfredo et al. 1993; Teel et al. 2001). Some evidence suggests that longtime residents of a state or area are more likely to support traditional forms of wildlife management, such as wolf control, than are newer residents (Zinn and Andelt 1999).

At the request of the US Fish and Wildlife Service, Colorado State University conducted a study titled "Colorado Residents'" Attitudes and Perceptions toward Reintroduction of the Gray Wolf into Colorado" (Manfredo et al. 1993). They found that the public generally supported the idea of wolf reintroduction, and 71 percent indicated they would vote for reintroducing wolves. Eastern Slope (largely urban/suburban) residents were more supportive than Western Slope (largely rural) residents, with 74 percent versus 65 percent, respectively, saying they would vote yes if given the opportunity. Most people considered wolf reintroduction at least as important as protecting several other endangered or threatened species in the state (e.g., peregrine falcons [*Falco peregrinus*], greenback cutthroat trout [*Oncorhynchus clarki somias*], and river otters [*Lutra canadensis*]), but not more important than protecting bald eagles. The majority of respondents did not view wolf reintroduction as more important than other major wildlife management activities in the state (e.g., providing opportunities for fishing, hunting, and wildlife viewing; wildlife education in schools; and protecting and improving wildlife habitat).

In a recent poll of registered voters in Colorado, New Mexico, and Arizona, Meadow et al. (2005) found that 64 percent of respondents favored wolf restoration to the Southern Rockies, whereas 31 percent opposed it (Colorado and Arizona reported 68 percent in favor and 28 percent opposed, while New Mexico reported 59 percent in favor and 38 percent opposed). Similarly, a December 2002 poll involving 600 residents from outside the Southern Rockies in Utah's most populous counties (accounting for 77 percent of the state's population) found 61 percent in support of restoring wolves to Utah, with 27 percent opposed, and 12 percent undecided (*Salt Lake City Tribune*, Tuesday, December 31, 2002). In the Meadow et al. (2005) study, people registered as Democrats showed the highest support (80 percent), followed by independents (68 percent) and Republicans (56 percent) (see also Meadow 2001).

There was little difference in levels of support between women (67 percent) and men (66 percent) or between hunters (61 percent) and nonhunters (70 percent) (Meadow et al. 2005). Further, voters wanted restoration and management based on science, and showed strong support for large, interconnected lands that were managed for wildlife (Meadow et al. 2005).

According to Manfredo et al. (1993), Pate et al. (1996), Meadow (2001), and Meadow et al. (2005), individuals who support wolf restoration do so because they believe that restoration will preserve the wolf, balance deer and elk populations, increase people's understanding of the importance of wilderness, and restore the natural environment. Those opposed to restoration believe that ranchers will lose money; wolves will attack humans, pets, and livestock; and wolf predation will reduce deer and elk populations (Manfredo et al. 1993; Pate et al. 1996; Meadow 2001). Proponents and opponents to wolf recovery believe that ranchers will shoot wolves (Manfredo et al. 1993).

The survey results demonstrate that there is general public support for wolf reintroduction in the Southern Rockies—indeed throughout the entire Southwest—increasing the likelihood that such an undertaking might be feasible, at least from a public opinion perspective. Surveys show that most people support wildlife on many different fronts. In addition, the demographics and economics of the region—increasingly urban, well-educated people not connected to livelihoods involving livestock—continue to move in directions that would seem to increase support for wolf reintroduction over time. Still, approximately 30 percent of the public opposes reintroduction, and such individuals could present a formidable challenge to a reintroduction project, especially if they hold strongly opposing views, are politically powerful, and are motivated to act (Reading and Clark 1996).

MITIGATING OPPOSING VALUES

The findings from these past studies show strong general support for wolf reintroduction throughout the Southern Rockies, the West, and the nation. Indeed, throughout all the studies we reviewed, approximately two-thirds of the general population supported wolf conservation and restoration. But, the studies also showed intense polarization among stakeholders, with some interest groups strongly disliking wolves and opposing restoration. This polarization poses a significant threat to the success of wolf restoration programs, and efforts to mitigate strongly polarized positions should be given high priority in the initial stages of any restoration effort.

The studies by Bath (1987c) and Thompson (1991) revealed that three out of four ranchers opposed to wolves would not change their minds about reintroducing wolves into Yellowstone regardless of their being offered different options for mitigation. Similarly, Meadow et al. (2005) found that persuasive arguments did little to change the attitudes of respondents (supporters or opponents to wolves) other than to increase the extremity of the views. Such deeply rooted feelings suggest that these attitudes are based on wolves as symbols of larger, powerfully influential societal issues and will likely impede the role of science and information in decision making. It will also make common ground harder to find, decrease dispute resolution options, and increase the chances that stakeholders will forge decisions primarily by power brokering.

Any wolf recovery program must adequately address the hostility and antagonism of ranchers, some hunters, and some local residents toward reintroduction while simultaneously maintaining the support and addressing the almost diametrically opposite concerns of the larger general population (including conservationists). Decreasing opposition and developing a supportive public for a wolf management plan are neces-sary whether or not society decides to rein-troduce wolves into the Southern Rockies, because any decision would likely alienate some stakeholders. This requires devoting substantial attention to addressing current conflict among polarized stakeholders in the wolf restoration controversy.

Public relations and education programs have successfully developed support for some reintroduction programs, but such programs usually worked with largely uninformed publics with poorly developed attitudes and species that are less controversial. Programs directed at changing attitudes and values are rarely successful, especially if those attitudes are strongly held (Chaiken and Stangor 1987; Meadow et al. 2005). The data suggest that beliefs toward and the symbolism of wolves (based on associated cultures, perceptions, and values) may be the most important fac-tors influencing attitudes, as very few people now have personal experience with the spe-cies. With myth playing such a strong role, it will be difficult to reach consensus.

Attitudes based on unchallenged assumptions highlight the difference between knowledge and attitudes discussed earlier. Indeed, for both wolves (Bath 1989; Kellert 1990) and black-footed ferrets (*Mustela nigripes*) (Reading 1993) the two groups of people who scored highest on general knowledge of the species had diametrically opposed attitudes. Conservation groups and ranchers both scored well on knowledge of both species, but conservation groups most fervently supported conservation of those species and ranchers most strongly opposed it (Reading 1993). Education is important, but because knowledge is only one of sev-eral factors influencing attitudes, changing the attitudes or behaviors of people with strongly held attitudes is difficult or impos-sible. Changing attitudes, especially strongly held attitudes, requires more than simply providing information.

Values, attitudes, and behaviors can change over time as situations, knowledge, and experiences change (Sinden and Worrel 1979; Williams 1979). Understanding why and how values, attitudes, and behaviors change is important if one hopes to develop more or less supportive publics for wolf con-servation. But changing attitudes, and espe-cially values, is difficult.

Most social scientists agree that the best chances for attitude change occur when indi-viduals become aware of internal contradic-tions between different values or between values, attitudes, and behaviors (Williams 1979; Olson and Zanna 1993; Petty et al. 1997). For example antilittering campaigns often succeed by playing on people's patrio-tism and love of nature. People will seek to reduce the discomfort they experience from these inconsistencies by changing more dis-sonant, peripheral values and attitudes and behaviors to better reflect core values (Wil-liams 1979; Tessler and Shaffer 1990). This is why it is so difficult to change strongly held attitudes. They reflect core values.

Effective persuasion requires that people both receive and acquiesce to a persuasive message (Olson and Zanna 1993). Recep-tivity depends on several factors, including motivation, the identity of the messenger, the strength and frequency of the message, the clarity of the message, and the state of the recipient (Chaiken and Stangor 1987; Petty et al. 1997).

Peer pressure can play a large role in maintaining or changing values, attitudes, and behaviors (Chaiken and Stangor 1987; Tessler and Shaffer 1990). In addition, changes are more likely to occur when alter-native choices are provided that facilitate attitude or behavior change or permit people to reach the same or similar goals differently (Tessler and Shaffer 1990; Petty et al. 1997). For example, people are more likely to throw trash into a garbage can than on the street when garbage cans are made easily available.

When a value is strongly intertwined with other values or is the product of personal experience, it is more difficult to change (Williams 1979; Olson and Zanna 1993).

APPROACHES

More successful education and public relations programs generally seek to change opposition, to develop support among uninformed or undecided individuals, and to conserve and strengthen supporters. There are three basic methods for accomplishing these goals: pressure, purchase, and persuasion (Cutlip and Center 1964). Ideally, all three methods should be integrated into a public relations program.

First, law enforcement can be used to apply pressure, but the pressure should be very carefully employed. To be truly successful, education and public relations programs should rely on carrots more than sticks, so programs should also entice with incentives (i.e., purchase). Finally, education and public relations programs should persuade people to support program goals or at least not actively oppose them. Receptivity can be enhanced if the message is delivered by someone with the same socioeconomic characteristics or by someone who is trusted (Reading 1993).

Duda and Young (1995) recommended that groups favoring reintroduction of wolves should hire a local advocate at the earliest stages of planning. They suggested drawing trusted and credible people from retired fish and wildlife agency personnel, trappers, hunters, ranchers, or other individuals considered residents and not associated with outside interests. Meadow (2001) concluded the same. It is also important to target key groups with education programs (using spokespeople within the target groups), integrate human and ecological concerns, and design species-specific education initiatives (Kellert et al. 1996). Of course, groups opposing wolf recovery could follow the same tack of developing spokespeople who have an intimate knowledge of the issue and connection with members of target audiences. Similarly, if agency personnel or conservationists decide after studying the issue that wolf reintroduction should not occur for biological and/or social reasons, they may well need an education and public relations program to explain the decision to wolf supporters.

Another effective way to change attitudes is through the social institutions that form and reinforce values (Reading 1993). All major social institutions are important, but education and religious institutions may be the most influential (Reading 1993). Yet social institutions are often comprised of people espousing the values a program hopes to change, and they are largely responsible for maintaining the currently dominant values of society. People with a vested interest in maintaining these values often control the institutions (Reading 1993). Nevertheless, institutional values can and do change. To affect this transformation, those working for change should apply pressure both externally and internally.

Some people argue that we should not try to influence other people's values and attitudes. Usually, but not always, these are individuals who disagree with a value or attitude being promoted and strive to make it seem as though they are taking the moral high ground. In reality, such a stance promotes the status quo and allows it to continue influencing values and attitudes. While we should respect the right of people to hold values and attitudes that differ from our own, it is also important to recognize that humans are constantly striving to influence others' values and attitudes. Because everyone believes his or her value system is superior (otherwise an individual would change his or her values or value hierarchy), everyone is trying to convince others to embrace his or her values. Indeed, every expression of an opinion, every behavioral decision, and even the selection of "objective" information to provide to others reflects a person's values and attitudes and serves to influence others to some degree.

Developing support for a position on a controversial wildlife program like wolf recovery is a large, complicated undertaking, and the responsibility should not fall on people untrained in public relations and who are already burdened by other tasks. An education and public relations program should be implemented by the appropriate branches of the key agencies involved, conservation organizations, or preferably both, in collaboration with social scientists and professionals trained in education and public relations.

Finally, most people understand that favorable attitudes among the general public are important to success in a public program such as wolf recovery. We stress that it is also important to understand the attitudes of the participants in the public program (Miller et al. 1994; Clark 1997; Reading et al. 2006). We often assume that all people working toward a recognized end share the same goals. That may or may not be true, and even if it is true, all participants may not weigh the same goals equally. For example, one organization may have a sole goal of wolf recovery, whereas an organization with multiple goals may value wolf recovery, but it may also embrace other goals for other constituents, some of which may even conflict with wolf recovery. And, two organizations may value a goal equally, but one organization can be task-oriented and accustomed to acting quickly, the other may be process-oriented and determined to follow its internal procedures, regardless of the pace.

A large and growing body of evidence indicates that the public is strongly supportive of efforts to conserve wildlife (including wolves), but also that the public has a poor factual understanding of wildlife and conservation issues (Kellert 1976, 1995). Unfortunately, many education programs have fallen far short of informing citizens about the real issues facing conservation programs and instead offer chatty newsletters that highlight organizational achievements or reinforce the dominant philosophy (Alvarez 1993). Education programs should not only provide the fundamentals of environmental and wildlife conservation, but should also give citizens the tools necessary to make government work (Alvarez 1993).

Value	Definition
Basic Values	
Power	Support in making decisions, even against opposition
Wealth	The opportunity to control resources, including money, people, etc.
Enlightenment	Knowledge and information
Skill	Talents in all realms, including professions, arts, vocations, etc.
Well-being	Personal safety, health, and comfort
Affection	Friendship, loyalty, love, and intimacy in interpersonal relationships
Respect	Recognition in a profession, trade, or community
Rectitude	Responsible or ethical conduct
Values toward Wolves	
Aesthetic	Emotional, spiritual, or artistic inspiration from wolves
Negative	Fear of and aversion toward wolves
Utilitarian	Practical and commodity interest in wolves (consumptive use)
Moral	Ethical and moral desire to protect wolves (e.g., right to exist)
Naturalistic	Outdoor recreational interest in wolves (nonconsumptive use)
Scientific	Factual and ecological interest in wolves
Humanitarian	Strong affection for wolves
Domination	Interest in dominating and controlling wolves for human benefit
Cultural	Historic, religious, or symbolic importance of wolves

Table 6.1—Some basic values and attitudes toward wildlife/wolves.
Sources: *Lasswell 1971; †Kellert 1993, 1996

Chapter 7

The Legal Framework for Wolf Recovery in the Southern Rockies

Jay Tutchton and Melissa Hailey

INTRODUCTION

Among the many laws that could influence wolf recovery in the Southern Rocky Mountains, some are much more important than others. This chapter focuses on the important laws first: the Endangered Species Act of 1973 and the National Environmental Policy Act of 1969.

The Endangered Species Act (ESA)[1] is our nation's primary law designed to protect and recover endangered species, and it is administered by the US Department of the Interior's US Fish and Wildlife Service. In the Southern Rockies, the gray wolf is listed as an endangered species and thus protected by the ESA. Currently, because there are no gray wolves in the area, the gray wolf in the Southern Rockies is likely to remain listed and protected under the ESA for the foreseeable future. Accordingly, until there is a secure gray wolf population in the Southern Rockies, the ESA will provide the key legal framework governing any wolves that attempt to reoccupy the Southern Rockies naturally and any wolves reintroduced by humans. The ESA's recovery planning and reintroduction provisions are also likely to drive any wolf recovery efforts.

The National Environmental Policy Act (NEPA)[2] applies to all major federal actions that could significantly impact the quality of the environment. Numerous federal actions, including those that could impact gray wolf recovery, must comply with NEPA. Importantly, any federal actions designed to directly facilitate gray wolf recovery, such as

reintroduction efforts, would trigger the federal government's obligations under NEPA. Together the ESA and NEPA comprise the most important and immediately relevant laws influencing wolf recovery in the Southern Rockies.

Secondly, this chapter briefly looks at two other laws, both enacted in 1976: the National Forest Management Act and the Federal Land Policy and Management Act, which govern the management of federal lands likely to be critical to wolf recovery. The National Forest Management Act (NFMA)[3] is the more significant of the two because it governs management of the national forests by the US Forest Service, an agency of the US Department of Agriculture. The national forests of the Southern Rockies contain the majority of suitable gray wolf habitat (see chap. 11). Accordingly, the quality of the Forest Service's management of these lands will impact wolf recovery.

The Federal Land Policy and Management Act (FLPMA)[4] governs the management of lands controlled by the US Bureau of Land Management (BLM), an agency of US Department of the Interior. Because the BLM controls a large amount of land in the greater Southern Rockies Ecoregion, particularly in low-lying corridor areas, the BLM's land management could also influence wolf recovery. However, because both the Forest Service and the BLM are also bound by the ESA and NEPA, these agencies' specific land management statutes (NFMA and FLPMA) are of lesser importance than the ESA and

NEPA, because both statutes guide the actions of all federal agencies.

Third, and finally, this chapter looks briefly at state and local laws that could influence gray wolf recovery. Presently, the influence of these laws is only theoretical. So long as the gray wolf remains protected by the ESA, all conflicting state and local laws are preempted by the US Constitution. Simply put, state and local laws are trumped by the ESA and will remain so until the gray wolf in the Southern Rockies is sufficiently recovered to be delisted from the ESA. In the meantime, state and local governments are free only to offer the gray wolf more protection than offered by the ESA, but not less. If a state or local law offers less protection to wolves than that provided by the ESA, the state or local law is illegal and will be struck down by a court if challenged.

THE FEDERAL LAWS MOST APPLICABLE TO WOLF RECOVERY: ESA AND NEPA

THE ENDANGERED SPECIES ACT

The ESA is our most significant environmental law focusing directly on species preservation and recovery. Accordingly, any discussion of species recovery must begin with the law specifically designed by Congress for this purpose. Unlike NEPA, the ESA is not limited to major federal actions. Instead, the ESA governs all federal, state, and local government actions, as well as actions taken by private citizens and other private entities. Additionally, unlike NFMA and FLPMA, the ESA is not limited to the management of federal lands, but it protects endangered species wherever they are found, on anyone's land. The breadth and power of the ESA make it the single most important law influencing wolf recovery in the Southern Rockies.

Strength and Policy

In passing the ESA, Congress found that "as a consequence of economic growth and development untempered by adequate concern and conservation" human activities had rendered various species extinct or so depleted in numbers that they were threatened with extinction.[5] Congress declared these vanishing species were of "esthetic, ecological, educational, historical, recreational, and scientific value to the Nation and its people"[6] and set out to save them from extinction.

Accordingly, Congress designed the ESA "to provide a means whereby the ecosystems upon which endangered species and threatened species depend may be conserved" and to provide "a program for the conservation of such endangered species and threatened species."[7] Congress further declared it "to be the policy of Congress that all Federal departments and agencies shall seek to conserve endangered species and threatened species and shall utilize their authorities in furtherance of the purposes of this Act."[8]

In considering these explicit congressional directions and statements of policy, the US Supreme Court held in a case decided in 1978 that the ESA is "the most comprehensive legislation for the preservation of endangered species ever enacted by any nation."[9] The Supreme Court specifically noted "the plain intent of Congress in enacting this statute was to halt and reverse the trend towards species extinction, whatever the cost" and found this intent was "reflected not only in the stated policies of the Act, but in literally every section of the statute."[10]

Section 4 of the ESA: The Magic List

For terrestrial species like the gray wolf, the ESA is administered by the secretary of the interior, acting through the US Fish and Wildlife Service.[11] The service implements the ESA based on a "magic" list of protected species.[12] Officially listed species are protected. Those that are not listed enjoy no ESA protection.[13] As a result, Congress aptly described Section 4 of the ESA,[14] the section that sets out the listing process, as "the cornerstone of effective implementation of the [ESA]."[15] Currently, besides the small "experimental, nonessential" population of Mexican gray wolves[16] in New Mexico and Arizona, the gray wolf is listed as an endangered "species" throughout the Southern Rockies.

The use of the word *species*, however, is a bit of a misnomer. In the ESA, Congress broadly defined the term *species* to include "any subspecies of fish or wildlife or plant and any distinct population segment of any species of vertebrate fish or wildlife which interbreeds when mature."[17] Accordingly, the ESA is more accurately characterized as a law protecting full species, subspecies, and distinct population segments of vertebrate fish or wildlife. Congress did not explain what it meant by the phrase *distinct population segment* (DPS), but the service defines a DPS as an "evolutionary significant unit of a biological species" that is both discrete and significant.[18]

Discreteness includes either being "markedly separated from other populations of the same taxon as a consequence of physical, physiological, ecological, or behavioral factors" or "delimited by international governmental boundaries within which differences in control of exploitation, management of habitat, conservation status, or regulatory mechanisms exist that are significant."[19] Significance includes but is not limited to "persistence of the DPS in an ecological setting unusual or unique for the taxon; evidence that loss of the DPS would result in a significant gap in the range of the taxon; evidence that the DPS represents the only surviving natural occurrence of a taxon that may be more abundant elsewhere as an introduced population outside its historic range; or evidence that the DPS differs markedly from other populations of the species in its genetic characteristics."[20]

Accordingly, in considering the prospect that gray wolves in the Southern Rockies will remain listed under the ESA for the foreseeable future, it is important to note that even if the "species" gray wolf is recovered elsewhere, it will likely remain listed in the Southern Rockies as a "species" or as a "DPS of a species" that is distinct from the Northern Rockies gray wolf populations[21] and significant in that its absence would result in a significant gap in the range of the taxon.

Additionally, it is important to note that the ESA sets out two separate categories of listed species reflecting their relative degree of imperilment. A species is "endangered" if it "is in danger of extinction throughout all or a significant portion of its range."[22] A species is "threatened" if it "is likely to become an endangered species within the foreseeable future throughout all or a significant portion of its range."[23] Thus, if gray wolf populations in the Southern Rockies begin to recover, the service could take an intermediate step and down-list the gray wolf from endangered to threatened in this area. In that instance, gray wolves would remain protected by the ESA until they no longer meet the definition of a threatened species.

The Section 4 listing process can be initiated by either the service acting of its own accord or by a citizen petition.[24] The process is a two-way street governing both decisions to list or delist a species.[25] In reaching any listing decision, the service is governed by five listing factors.[26] If any of the five factors indicate the species is threatened or endangered, the service must list, or alternatively refuse to delist, the species.[27] The five factors are:

+ the present or threatened destruction, modification, or curtailment of its habitat or range;
+ over-utilization for commercial, recreational, scientific, or educational purposes;
+ disease or predation;
+ the inadequacy of existing regulatory mechanisms; or
+ other natural or manmade factors affecting its continued existence.[28]

The Legal Framework for Wolf Recovery 121

The Service must make its decision on whether or not to list or delist a species solely on the basis of the best scientific and commercial data available.[29] All service listing decisions are subject to judicial review.[30]

Section 4 of the ESA: Critical Habitat

Section 4 contains a second provision that could, if used, facilitate wolf recovery in the Southern Rockies: the requirement to designate critical habitat for listed species. The service has never designated critical habitat for the gray wolf because the original listing of the gray wolf predated Congress's addition of the critical habitat requirement to the ESA. However, Congress provided that "critical habitat may be established for those species now listed as threatened or endangered species for which no critical habitat has heretofore been established."[31] This means that the service has the power to designate critical habitat for the gray wolf in the Southern Rockies of its own accord. Alternately, any citizen could force the service to consider designating critical habitat by filing a petition requesting the designation of critical habitat under the Administrative Procedure Act of 1946 (APA).[32] As explained below, designating critical habitat would have important legal and practical benefits for the wolf.

In creating the ESA, "Congress started from the finding that 'the two major causes of extinction are hunting and destruction of natural habitat.'"[33] Of these two threats, "Congress was informed that the greatest was the destruction of natural habitat."[34] Congress chose to protect the ecosystems on which endangered species depend through the designation of critical habitat. Congress placed great value on the protection of a species' critical habitat equating the designation of a species' critical habitat as being of equal or more importance than the listing of the species under the Act in the first instance. Classifying a species as endangered or threatened is only the first step in insuring its survival. Of equal or more importance is the determination of the habitat necessary for the species' continued existence. Once a habitat is so designated, the Act requires that proposed federal actions not adversely affect the habitat. If the protection of endangered species depends in large measure on the preservation of the species' habitat, then the ultimate effectiveness of the Endangered Species Act will depend on the designation of critical habitats.[35]

Accordingly, in amending the ESA, Congress required that "concurrently" with listing a species as threatened or endangered, the service must designate critical habitat for the species "to the maximum extent prudent and determinable."[36] If the service determines that critical habitat is "not determinable," it may extend this deadline for one year.[37] However, at the close of that additional year, the service must publish a final critical habitat regulation based on the data then available.[38] Thus, the "not determinable" exception only allows the service an additional year to figure out what habitat should be designated as critical.

Congress did not explain the "not prudent" exception further, but it did indicate this exception was to be used sparingly. "It is only in rare circumstances where the specification of critical habitat concurrently with the listing would not be beneficial to the species."[39] According to the service's regulations, it may determine that a critical habitat designation is "not prudent" only when: (1) the species is threatened by taking[40] or other human activity, and identifying critical habitat can be expected to increase the degree of such threat to the species, or (2) designation of critical habitat would not be beneficial to the species.[41] The courts have consistently rejected claims by the service that designating critical habitat for a species is "not prudent" because it would not be beneficial to the species.[42]

Congress did, however, make the critical habitat designation process flexible. The service "may, from time-to-time thereafter as appropriate, revise"[43] any critical habitat designation. The service must base its critical habitat determinations on the basis of the best scientific data available and take into consideration the economic impact, the impact on national security, and any other relevant impact of specifying any particular area as critical habitat.[44] Accordingly, the critical habitat designation process differs from the listing process in that it requires the service not only to consider the best available science, but to also consider economic and other factors specifically excluded from consideration in listing decisions.

The ESA defines a species' "critical habitat" as:

> (i) the specific areas within the geographic area occupied by the species, at the time it is listed in accordance with the provisions of [the ESA], on which are found those physical or biological features (I) essential to the conservation of the species and (II) which may require special management considerations or protections; and
> (ii) specific areas outside of the geographic area occupied by the species at the time it is listed in accordance with the provisions of [the ESA], upon a determination by the Secretary that such areas are essential for the conservation of the species.[45]

Because the ESA defines *conservation* as the "use of all methods and procedures which are necessary to bring any endangered species or threatened species to the point at which the measures provided [by the ESA] are no longer necessary,"[46] designating critical habitat is directed not only at protecting the habitat a species currently needs to merely survive, but unoccupied areas necessary for the species to recover from its endangered status.[47] This ability to protect unoccupied habitat gives the critical habitat designation process part of its power. In the case of gray wolf recovery in the Southern Rockies, this is particularly important because all wolf habitat remains currently unoccupied by gray wolves. Designating critical habitat would protect these presently unoccupied areas and thus ensure they remain suitable for wolf recovery. Additionally, if wolves reoccur naturally or are reintroduced to the Southern Rockies in the future, critical habitat designation would greatly increase the ESA protection of these wolves. This is particularly true for federal government actions and for all actions on federal lands as discussed immediately below.

The designation of critical habitat comes into play most importantly in the ESA's Section 7 "consultation" process. Under Section 7(a)(2), all federal agencies must consult with the secretary of the Department of the Interior to "insure that any action authorized, funded, or carried out by [federal agencies] is not likely to jeopardize the continued existence of any endangered species or threatened species or result in the destruction or adverse modification of [its critical habitat]."[48] If critical habitat is not designated, then the no "adverse modification" standard of the Section 7 consultation requirement "becomes unenforceable."[49]

It is easy to see how the no "adverse modification" of critical habitat standard is likely to be more enforceable and effective than the no "jeopardy" standard. The "jeopardy" standard concerns the immediate survival of a species, while the "adverse modification" standard addresses long-term conservation and recovery.[50]

By defining *critical habitat* in terms of conservation, the ESA uses the prohibition of "adverse modification of critical habitat" as a means of ensuring that federal agency action does not hinder a species' recovery. Thus, "adverse modification" is a much broader concept and higher standard than the protection afforded under the "jeopardy" prohibition, which focuses on "mere survival."[51] This distinction is perhaps best explained by way of analogy. The "jeopardy" standard asks the ultimate question: Is this *the* straw that breaks the camel's back? The "adverse modification" standard asks a much simpler question: Is this *a single* straw that makes it more likely that the camel's back will break? The second question is easier to answer. Accordingly, the substantial legal and ensuing practical benefits of designating critical habitat for the gray wolf should not be quickly discounted.

Section 4 of the ESA: Recovery Planning

ESA Section 4 contains a third important provision that could influence gray wolf recovery in the Southern Rockies: the recovery planning requirement. Indeed, developing a gray wolf ESA recovery plan for the Southern Rockies seems to be exactly what is required to meet this end.

Section 4(f) requires the Fish and Wildlife Service to "develop and implement" recovery plans for "the conservation and survival of endangered species and threatened species," unless the agency finds that "such a plan will not promote the conservation of the species."[52] To the "maximum extent practicable," each recovery plan should include "a description of such site-specific management actions as may be necessary to achieve the plan's goal," "objective measurable criteria which, when met, would result in a determination…that the species be removed from the list," and "estimates of the time required and the cost to carry out those measures needed to achieve the plan's goal."[53]

A recovery plan can consider actions to reintroduce species and also unlocks federal funds to assist "appropriate public and private agencies and institutions, and other qualified persons" to help in developing and implementing the recovery plan.[54] The service itself has

stated that "recovery planning under section 4(f) of the Act is the 'umbrella' that eventually guides all [ESA] activities and promotes a species' conservation and eventual delisting."[55] The service should use its "umbrella" and prepare a recovery plan to guide wolf recovery efforts in the Southern Rockies.

Section 5 of the ESA: Land Acquisition

Though it is quite likely that gray wolves could be recovered in the Southern Rockies on existing extensive federal land holdings in the region, it should be noted that ESA Section 5 authorizes both the secretaries of Interior and Agriculture to carry out a program of land acquisition to benefit listed threatened or endangered species.[56]

Section 6 of the ESA: Cooperation with States

ESA Section 6 authorizes the Fish and Wildlife Service to "cooperate to the maximum extent practicable with the States" in implementing the ESA. Section 6 has the potential to influence gray wolf recovery in the Southern Rockies while allowing the states to play a significant role.[57]

At the outset, Section 6 requires the service to consult "with the States concerned before acquiring any land" for the purpose of conserving endangered or threatened species.[58] Section 6 also allows the service to enter into management agreements with any state "for the administration and management of any area established for the conservation of endangered species or threatened species."[59]

The most significant aspect of Section 6, however, is that it authorizes the Fish and Wildlife Service to enter into "cooperative agreements" with "any State which establishes and maintains an adequate and active program for the conservation of endangered species and threatened species."[60] The service is required to determine if any such state program is "in accordance" with the ESA. If the program is "in accordance" with the ESA, the

Fish and Wildlife Service must enter into the cooperative agreement and assist the state to implement its program.[61] To determine if a state program is "an adequate and active program for the conservation of endangered species and threatened species," the service must find "and annually thereafter reconfirm such finding" that under the state program:

(A) authority resides in the state agency to conserve resident species of wildlife determined by the state agency or FWS [Fish and Wildlife Service] to be endangered or threatened;
(B) the state agency has established acceptable conservation programs, consistent with the purposes of the ESA, for all resident species of wildlife in the state which are deemed by the Secretary to be endangered or threatened, and has furnished a copy of such plan and program together with all pertinent details, information, and data requested to FWS;
(C) the state agency is authorized to conduct investigations to determine the status and requirements for survival of resident species of wildlife;
(D) the state agency is authorized to establish programs, including the acquisition of land or interests therein, for the conservation of resident endangered or threatened species of wildlife; and
(E) provision is made for public participation in designating resident species of wildlife endangered or threatened; or (i) the requirements of sections (C), (D), and (E) are met, and (ii) plans are included under which immediate attention will be given to those resident species of wildlife which FWS and the state agency agree are most urgently in need of conservation programs, subject to additional limitations.[62]

ESA Section 6 then authorizes significant federal financial assistance to any state entering into an approved conservation agreement to help implement the state program.[63] Accordingly, Section 6 could be used effectively by states to assist gray wolf recovery and to take advantage of federal funding.

Section 7 of the ESA: Duty to Conserve
ESA Section 7 contains two substantive duties that could influence wolf recovery in the Southern Rockies: Sections 7(a)(1) and 7(a)(2).[64] Although the latter is much more widely known than the former, Section 7(a)(1) should not be neglected, for its potential to assist wolf recovery is strong.

As discussed above, the ESA establishes that "it is...the policy of Congress that all federal...agencies shall seek to conserve [listed] species and shall utilize their authorities in furtherance of the purposes of this Act."[65] Section 7(a)(1) implements this congressional policy by requiring that "all...federal agencies shall...utilize their authorities in furtherance of the purposes of [the ESA] by carrying out programs for the conservation of endangered species and threatened species."[66] Both the legislative history and the language of the ESA lend credence to the assertion that ESA Section 7(a)(1) is a substantive duty similar to those duties imposed by Section 7(a)(2). Indeed, courts have interpreted Section 7(a)(1) as "a specific, rather than a generalized duty to conserve species,"[67] and have held that federal agencies "must utilize all [of their] authorities"[68] to conserve threatened and endangered species. Courts have further interpreted Section 7(a)(1) to mean that "the ESA mandates that [federal agencies] place conservation above any of the agency's competing interests."[69]

Accordingly, the substantive duty imposed by Section 7(a)(1) is a distinct duty, completely separate from the duty to consult and to avoid "jeopardy" or "adverse modification" of critical habitat found in Section 7(a)(2).[70] Courts have held that the "recovery" duty under Section 7(a)(1) is broader than the "no jeopardy" duty of Section 7(a)(2), requiring more attention to the species than would be necessary to merely avoid extinction.[71] "[An agency] must do far more than merely avoid the elimination of protected species. [It] must bring these species back from the brink so that they may be removed from the protected class, and [it] must use all methods necessary to do so."[72]

Section 7(a)(1) could be used by litigants to force any federal agency to pursue active measures to recover gray wolves in the Southern Rockies. However, collectively the case law considering Section 7(a)(1) suggests that a litigant likely will be more successful in forcing the Section 7(a)(1) conservation duty upon an agency whose own directives also contain provisions for conserving listed species. For example, in 1992 the Federal Energy Regulatory Commission (FERC) successfully avoided a judicially imposed affirmative ESA conservation duty by persuading a court that such an imposition would be an excessive expansion of the agency's powers as delegated by Congress.[73] On the other hand, in a 1997 case in which the US Forest Service wished to proceed with a timber sale that would harm an endangered bat species, the court looked at the agency's forest plan, which provided that "[c]onservation and recovery of federally listed endangered, threatened, and proposed species is given top priority in management," and the general ESA Section 7(a)(1) duty to hold that "defendants are bound by the ESA and their own forest Plan, to place the Indiana bat, an endangered species, at the top of the priority list."[74] The court explained that the Forest Service had "failed to comply with its affirmative duty by placing the sale of 199 acres worth of trees before the protection of an endangered species."[75]

Section 7 of the ESA: Duty to Avoid Jeopardy and Adverse Modification of Critical Habitat

Section 7(a)(2) of the ESA has received much more attention than Section 7(a)(1) discussed immediately above. In a nutshell, through Section 7(a)(2) Congress heeded the wisdom of the old saw that "when you are in a hole, stop digging," and required all federal agencies to "insure that any action authorized, funded or carried out by such agency... is not likely to jeopardize the continued existence of any endangered species or threatened species or result in the destruction or adverse modification of [critical] habitat of such species."[76] To satisfy this requirement, all federal agencies must consult with the Fish and Wildlife Service when any activity they authorize, fund, or carry out could affect listed species.[77]

Although the "jeopardy" and "adverse modification" prohibitions apply only when a federal agency is involved, this limitation is much narrower than it seems. The ESA prohibitions on "jeopardy" and "adverse modification" are actually quite broad, because they apply in any situation where a federal agency funds, authorizes, or carries out an action. This includes situations in which a private actor wishes to engage in activity that requires a federal permit or license or receives federal funding. As a result of federal permitting, it applies to any activity on federal land. For a detailed explanation of the consultation process, one may find the US Fish and Wildlife and National Marine Fisheries Service's Endangered Species Consultation Handbook under "Endangered Species" on the US Fish and Wildlife Service's home page.[78]

The service's most important role in the consultation process is formulating biological opinions through formal consultation. In its biological opinions, the service determines "whether the action, taken together with cumulative effects, is likely to jeopardize the continued existence of listed species or result in the destruction or adverse modification of their critical habitat."[79] As discussed above, answering the question of whether or not an action destroys or adversely modifies critical habitat should be substantially easier than concluding whether or not it jeopardizes the continued existence of a species.

If the service determines that "the action is likely to jeopardize the continued existence of a listed species or result in the destruction or adverse modification of critical habitat," the agency must formulate reasonable and prudent alternatives to the proposed action "which [it] believes would not violate [Section 7(a)(2)] and can be taken by the Federal [action] agency[80] or applicant in implementing the agency action."[81] "Reasonable and prudent alternatives" refer to alternative actions that can be implemented in a manner consistent with the intended purpose of the action, that can be implemented consistently with the scope of the federal action agency's legal authority and jurisdiction, that are economically and technologically feasible, and that the service believes would avoid the likelihood of jeopardizing the continued existence of listed species or resulting in the destruction or "adverse modification" of critical habitat.[82] For the purposes of Section 7(a)(2) consultation, the service is the expert agency. Therefore, in identifying reasonable and prudent alternatives, the service must use its own expertise, the expertise of the federal action agency, and that of any applicant.[83] If the service cannot develop any reasonable and prudent alternatives to the proposed action, then it must indicate that to the best of its knowledge, there are no such alternatives.[84] If there are no reasonable and prudent alternatives to the proposed action, then that action likely cannot proceed without violating Section 7(a)(2) and the ESA's "take" prohibitions discussed below.

However, Sections 7(b)(4)[85] and 7(o)(2)[86] of the ESA authorize the service to include "incidental take statements" as part of its biological opinions rendered for federal action agencies through the Section 7 consultation process. These statements allow a federal agency or applicant subject to Section 7(a)(2) that is planning to engage in an activity not likely to jeopardize the continued existence of a species, to take members of that species if the taking is not the purpose of the action and is therefore incidental to the action. In effect, these "incidental take statements" amount to get-out-of-jail-free cards, which authorize violating the ESA Section 9's "take" prohibition, discussed below.

If, after Section 7 consultation, the service concludes that the proposed action will not jeopardize the species and that the "incidental taking" is not likely to jeopardize the species, then the service must "formulate a statement concerning the incidental take."[87] This statement must specify the extent of the incidental take, those reasonable and prudent measures necessary to minimize the impact, the terms and conditions with which the action agency and any applicant must comply in order to implement the reasonable and prudent measures, and the procedures for handling or disposing of taken species.[88] Section 7(o)(2) provides that any taking in compliance with a Section 7(b)(4) incidental take statement "shall not be considered to be a prohibited taking of the species concerned.[89] This is the functional get-out-of-jail-free card: a permit to kill endangered species.

The benefit of consultation for an action agency is the strong likelihood that it will receive an incidental take statement and thus be immunized from Section 9 "take" liability. On the other hand, failure to consult can result in dramatic consequences, including blanket injunctions against federally authorized actions. For example, in 1994 the US District Courts for Oregon and Idaho and the Ninth Circuit Court for the far western United States enjoined a broad range of human activity on the national forests in

Oregon and Idaho to protect endangered salmon.[90] In 1995, the US District Court for Arizona imposed a similar injunction on all national forests in Arizona and New Mexico as result of the Forest Service's failure to consult on actions affecting the Mexican spotted owl.[91]

Accordingly, in many respects the Section 7(a)(2) consultation process is protective of both endangered species and other federal agencies that want to undertake actions that might harm endangered species, because it allows the service to modify these actions to reduce harm to species and allows the actions to proceed without risk of dramatic legal interruptions.

Section 9 of the ESA: Take

ESA Section 9 prohibits the "take" of endangered species.[92] While the Section 7 "jeopardy" prohibition applies only to federal agencies, the Section 9 "take" prohibition applies to every person within the jurisdiction of the United States and protects every member of every species of endangered fish or wildlife.[93]

"The term 'take' means to harass, harm, pursue, hunt, shoot, wound, kill, trap, capture, or collect, or attempt to engage in any such conduct."[94] *Harass* and *harm* are further defined by regulation: "Harass in the definition of 'take' in the Act means an intentional or negligent act or omission which creates the likelihood of injury to wildlife by annoying it to such an extent as to significantly disrupt normal behavioral patterns which include, but are not limited to, breeding, feeding or sheltering."[95] "Harm in the definition of 'take' in the Act means an act which actually kills or injures wildlife. Such act may include significant habitat modification or degradation where it actually kills or injures wildlife by significantly impairing essential behavioral patterns, including breeding, feeding or sheltering."[96] The definitions of the terms *harass* and *harm* extend the "taking" prohibition to

cover protected species' members and their essential habitat. The degree to which the harm regulation protects essential habitat has been a subject of legal dispute. However, in 1995 the US Supreme Court specifically upheld the authority of the service to promulgate regulations including "habitat takings" within the definition of *harm*.[97]

Because it has been specifically upheld by the Supreme Court, the *harm* definition has received the most attention. However, in considering gray wolf recovery in the Southern Rockies, the potential power of the *harass* definition should not be discounted. To harass is potentially broader than to harm in three significant ways:

1. *Harass* applies to intentional or negligent acts or omissions. *Harm* is limited to acts, presumably requiring an overt act.
2. *Harm* requires actual death or injury. *Harass* can be found based on the "likelihood of injury."
3. *Harm* includes acts of "significant habitat modification or degradation" that actually kill or injure by "significantly impairing essential behavioral patterns, including breeding, feeding or sheltering." On the other hand, *harass* includes annoying wildlife "to such an extent as to significantly disrupt normal behavioral patterns which include, but are not limited to, breeding, feeding or sheltering." In short, the *harm* definition's discussion of "significant habitat modification or degradation" is absent from the harass regulation. Harass also extends beyond "breeding, feeding or sheltering."

By its own terms, the Section 9 "take" prohibition applies only to endangered species; however, ESA Section 4(d)[98] gives the service discretionary authority to apply Section 9(a)(1)'s "take" prohibition to threatened fish or wildlife species and Section 9(a)(1)(G)[99] makes it unlawful to violate a regulation concerning such threatened species.

The service has by a blanket regulation applied the Section 9 "take" prohibitions to all threatened wildlife species.[100] The agency may, however, vary its blanket prohibition of the taking of threatened wildlife species by a special individualized rule, a so-called 4(d) Rule.[101] At present, because gray wolves in the Southern Rockies are listed as endangered, these regulations are not relevant; however, were the wolf down-listed to threatened status, the service could adjust the level of its take protection through a Section 4(d) rule.

Though it is often asserted that it is difficult to prove take, this is not necessarily true. There are several straightforward ways to prove it. Evidence that a defendant killed a listed species is obviously sufficient.[102] Similarly, any evidence that a defendant pursued, hunted, shot, wounded, trapped, captured, or collected a listed species would suffice. Though it is frequently stated that a dead body is required to prove any of these violations, the opposite is true. Because the "take" prohibition includes "attempt" language as discussed above, evidence that a defendant attempted to pursue, hunt, shoot, wound, kill, trap, capture, or collect a listed species should be sufficient to prove a take violation. More important, actual knowledge that the species being taken is a listed species is not required. Take is a general, rather than specific, intent crime. In other words, "the critical issue is whether the act was done knowingly, not whether the defendant recognized what he was shooting."[103] The Supreme Court stated in 1994, "Congress intended 'take' to apply broadly to cover indirect as well as purposeful actions."[104] Accordingly, a take can even be the result of an accident.[105]

Section 9's "take" prohibition applies to any "person." The ESA defines a *person* to mean "an individual, corporation, partnership, trust, association, or any other private entity; or any officer, employee, agent, department, or instrumentality of the Federal Government, of any State, municipality, or political subdivision of a State, or of any foreign government; any State, municipality, or political subdivision of a State; or any other entity subject to the jurisdiction of the United States."[106] This broad definition subjects state and local governments to potential vicarious liability for takings conducted by third parties acting under state and local laws.

The vicarious liability of local governments or permitting authorities for take directly caused by third parties but proximately caused by the permitting or regulatory authority is a hot legal issue. Several courts have found a regulatory agency liable under Section 9 for government-authorized conduct carried out by another party that directly causes the take of listed species.[107] The test appears to be one of "but-for" causation, for example, in a case concerning a state government licensing fishing activity that was causing the take of a listed whale species. In 1988 the court concluded that Section 9 liability attaches "to acts by third parties [the state] that allow or authorize acts that exact a taking and that, but for the permitting process, could not take place."[108]

Section 10 of the ESA: Experimental Populations

ESA Section 10(j) authorizes the release of an experimental population of a threatened or endangered species into the wild, and it is likely to figure prominently in any federal gray wolf recovery efforts in the Southern Rockies. Indeed, the service used this provision of the ESA to reintroduce gray wolves to the Yellowstone ecosystem and red wolves in North Carolina (see chap. 2).[109]

Section 10(j) authorizes the service to "release a population of an endangered or threatened species outside the current range of such species" if the agency "determines that such release will further the conservation" of the species.[110] The ESA defines an *experimental population* as a "population (including any offspring arising solely therefrom) but only when, and at such times as, the population is wholly separate geographically from nonexperimental populations of the same species."[111] Before authorizing the release of any experimental population, the service must identify the population and determine on the basis of the best available information whether or not such population is essential or nonessential to the continued existence of the endangered or threatened species.[112] Thus, there are two types of experimental populations, essential and nonessential.

Each individual member of an experimental population is treated as a threatened species under the ESA.[113] Accordingly, the members of an experimental population are still entitled to Section 9 take protection, but those protections can be reduced as they are for threatened species. Indeed, an individual who shot an experimental wolf from the Yellowstone ESA Section 10(j) experimental population has been convicted of take.[114] However, a nonessential experimental population is not entitled to Section 7 consultation under the ESA unless it occurs in an area within the National Wildlife Refuge System or the National Park System.[115] Section 10(j) also precludes critical habitat designation for any nonessential experimental population.[116] Accordingly, an essential experimental population is entitled to both Section 7 consultation and critical habitat designation, but a nonessential experimental population is not entitled to Section 7 consultation, unless it occurs on a national wildlife refuge or national park, and is not entitled to critical habitat designation. The members of both types of experimental populations are entitled to some level of take protection, though it may be reduced by specific rule.

THE NATIONAL ENVIRONMENTAL POLICY ACT

Policy

The National Environmental Policy Act (NEPA)[117] predates the ESA and is the second major federal statute that will generally influence all federal actions affecting gray wolf recovery in the Southern Rockies. NEPA sets forth a broad national policy "to encourage productive and enjoyable harmony between man and his environment," and it promotes efforts to prevent or eliminate damage to the environment and biosphere.[118] Unlike the ESA, NEPA is primarily procedural in that it does not set forth substantive standards and prohibitions.[119] Instead, NEPA lays out a process for considering environmental impacts and for citizen participation in agency decision making. NEPA requires federal agencies to take a hard look at the environmental consequences of their actions before acting and encourages public involvement in the agency decision-making process.[120]

Applicability of NEPA

NEPA's analytical duty is triggered whenever an agency undertakes a "major federal action" that could "significantly impact the quality of human health or the environment."[121] Because environmental impacts include impacts to wildlife, NEPA provides an up-front opportunity for the federal government to analyze how its projects will impact endangered species like the gray wolf outside of, and distinct from, the ESA Section 7(a)(2) consultation process.[122] Importantly, NEPA's analytical process is a public one in which citizens can participate. The ESA's Section 7(a)(2) process is not public.

Whether an action will have significant impacts to wildlife and other environmental resources is the question to be resolved in the NEPA analysis itself. Before discussing the details of how a NEPA analysis is actually undertaken, however, it is important to discuss when NEPA applies. What exactly constitutes a "major federal action" is a question of law to be resolved, in the last instance, by a court. Nonetheless, the question of what governmental actions meet this standard and thus trigger NEPA has already been considered, if not decided, by the courts for many situations that may arise in wolf recovery efforts.

NEPA WOULD APPLY
TO REINTRODUCTION

All federal species reintroduction programs are subject to NEPA.[123] Therefore, active federal reintroduction of the gray wolf to the Southern Rockies would trigger a NEPA process and public participation.[124] Though reintroduction would likely have positive impacts on the environment, whether those impacts ultimately turned out to be positive or negative is inconsequential. Any reintroduction effort could cause significant impacts to the environment. The nature and magnitude of those impacts must be analyzed by the government under NEPA.

NEPA WOULD APPLY TO AN
ESA SECTION 10(J) RULE

Developing or significantly amending a species ESA Section 10(j) rule triggers the NEPA process.[125] As discussed above, designating a population of an endangered species as experimental alters its legal protections under the ESA. The experimental designation does not, however, alter NEPA's application. This means that if the government develops an ESA Section 10(j) rule for wolf reintroduction into the Southern Rockies, the Section 10(j) rule would require an additional NEPA analysis beyond that required for reintroduction alone, without a Section 10(j) rule.

NEPA WOULD LIKELY APPLY TO
CRITICAL HABITAT DESIGNATION

Designating critical habitat under the ESA *may* trigger the NEPA process, depending on the location of the critical habitat. The Ninth Circuit Court of Appeals has held that NEPA analysis is not required for the designation of critical habitat within its jurisdiction,[126] while the Tenth Circuit Court of Appeals has held exactly the opposite.[127] The

majority of the Southern Rockies Ecoregion (Colorado and New Mexico, but not Arizona) falls in the Tenth Circuit. Accordingly, it is most likely that NEPA would apply to any critical habitat designation in the Southern Rockies.

NEPA WOULD LIKELY APPLY TO THE
DEVELOPMENT OF FOREST PLANS

The development of forest plans *may* trigger the NEPA process. The National Forest Management Act (NFMA)[128] requires the US Forest Service to develop management plans for each national forest,[129] and to promulgate regulations that ensure such forest plans are developed in accordance with NEPA.[130] The purpose of a forest plan is to establish basic guidelines for managing the forest and set forth those planning elements that will be employed by the Forest Service for future site-specific actions within that forest. For forests that contain gray wolves or their critical habitat, engaging in the NEPA process at the forest planning stage lends an opportunity for the government to analyze how forest policies may impact the wolf and for the public to comment accordingly.

Until recently, the Forest Service had a judicially recognized agency-wide policy of conducting NEPA analyses for the development of all forest plans.[131] This policy was set forth in the Forest Service's "planning rules."[132] These rules, however, have undergone a series of amendments since they were first introduced in 1982.[133] The latest installment of planning rules, adopted in 2005, represents a substantial deviation from the former Forest Service planning policy. One of these deviations is a departure from the NEPA process.

The 2005 planning rule "embodies a paradigm shift in land use management planning."[134] Among other things, the 2005 rule categorizes forest plans as "strategic and aspirational in nature" with no "on-the-ground effects that can be meaningfully evaluated."

Because the 2005 rule concludes that forest plans have no direct environmental impacts, it no longer requires NEPA analysis during their development.[135]

A federal court overturned the Forest Service's 2005 planning rule in March 2007.[136] Though this holding may signal problems for the 2005 rule, it did not remove the possibility that this rule may be upheld later. The court declined to decide whether the rule itself was an unlawful deviation from NFMA. Instead, the court overturned the rule because the Forest Services violated NEPA in promulgating the rule in the first instance.[137] The court barred application of the 2005 rule pending the Forest Service's completion of a legally sufficient NEPA analysis.

The effect all of this legal wrangling on the question of whether NEPA applies to forest plans is confusing. To date, however, the Forest Service is still required to comply with NEPA when developing forest plans.

NEPA APPLIES TO
SITE-SPECIFIC ACTIONS

Site-specific federal actions *usually* trigger the NEPA process. Every day, federal land managers approve and/or undertake site-specific actions, such as timber harvests and road construction. Many categories of site-specific agency actions have been deemed to be "major" for the purposes of NEPA.[138] If these actions pose any possible impacts to the environment, a NEPA analysis is appropriate. If wolves roam in or around that area where the site-specific action is proposed (otherwise known as the "action area"), they should be considered within the NEPA analysis. Additionally, the NEPA analysis must consider any critical habitat within the action area of a proposed site-specific action. This includes unoccupied critical habitat.

The one caveat to the general principle that site-specific actions trigger NEPA is the increasing use of "categorical exclusions." Categorical exclusions give land managers a way out of NEPA compliance by categorically excluding a site-specific proposed action from the otherwise legally imposed NEPA process. The authority to categorically exclude site-specific actions from NEPA analysis derives from various sources, depending on the agency that administers the public land at issue and the type of action being contemplated. Currently, categorical exclusions are most often employed for public lands logging and grazing decisions. In almost all cases, the presence of endangered species within or around the action area will preclude the use of a categorical exclusion.[139]

NEPA APPLIES TO
ISSUING FEDERAL PERMITS

Issuing federal permits triggers the NEPA process. Federal land managers issue permits to private citizens, corporate entities, and other governmental bodies to conduct all sorts of activities on public land. From grazing permits to permits for ski resort construction, the issuance of a federal permit is a "major federal action" under NEPA, which triggers the analytical and public participation process.[140] Whenever a federal agency issues a permit to a third party to conduct an action that has the potential to impact threatened or endangered species, the government should complete a NEPA process, and that NEPA analysis must look at impacts to the species and its individual members.

NEPA DOES NOT APPLY
TO RECOVERY PLANS

Recovery planning *probably does not* trigger NEPA. Recovery plans are predecisional in nature, outlining future actions. Because NEPA is designed to evaluate the impacts of agency actions, not merely the plans to implement those actions, NEPA analysis is probably not required for the development of species recovery plans.[141] Additionally, because the impacts to the species at issue should be thoroughly vetted during the recovery planning process and within the content of the planning document itself, it is questionable what added value would come from a NEPA analysis.

Possibly for this reason, courts have declined to address the precise question of whether NEPA applies to species recovery planning.[142] It is important to remember, however, that if and when an agency implements an action recommended in a species recovery plan, that action itself may be subject to NEPA when it is implemented. The issue at that point would be whether the discrete action implementing the recovery plan constitutes a "major federal action" under NEPA.

NEPA DOES NOT APPLY TO LISTING, DELISTING, OR DOWN-LISTING A SPECIES

Listing, delisting, or down-listing a species *does not* trigger NEPA. As discussed above, the ESA sets forth enumerated criteria for when a species can be listed as threatened or endangered. Those same criteria apply to delisting or down-listing. Listing decisions do not have immediate impacts themselves. Rather, the ESA's protective measures that flow from listing might have environmental impacts. Accordingly, it is premature to require a NEPA analysis for a listing decision. Although there is no specific case law dealing with the question of whether NEPA is triggered by an agency decision to delist or down-list a protected species, courts have held that an initial ESA listing decision does not trigger the NEPA process.[143] Because delisting and down-listing decisions rely on the same criteria as initial listing decisions, it is safe to assume that delisting or down-listing a species requires no NEPA compliance.

As this discussion suggests, the NEPA process applies to myriad federal actions, many of which have the potential to significantly impact gray wolf recovery. The next pertinent question is then what constitutes a proper NEPA analysis.

What Does NEPA Require?

In practice, federal agencies examine the environmental consequences of their actions through scientific study, the results of which are set forth in an Environmental Assessment (EA) or Environmental Impact Statement (EIS). EAs and EISs serve not only to document analytical results, but also to put the public on notice of pending federal actions and their potential consequences. The public has the right to comment on any action throughout the NEPA process and, further, has the right to judicially appeal a final agency action that is "arbitrary and capricious, an abuse of discretion, or otherwise not in accordance with law."[144] In federal court, "an agency action taken without observance of the procedure required by law will be set aside."[145]

The Council on Environmental Quality (CEQ) has promulgated generally applicable NEPA regulations.[146] The CEQ, created under NEPA in 1969, provides federal agencies with guidance on NEPA implementation.[147] The CEQ's regulations serve as the foundational building blocks for developing NEPA documents as well as the substantive criteria for challenging them.

EAs and EISs differ slightly in function, but not in form. Due to their brevity, EAs are frequently referred to as "mini-EISs,"[148] and offer the action agency a means for avoiding the often arduous and resource intensive process of completing an EIS.[149] An EA is meant to be a concise public document that serves to provide sufficient evidence and analysis to determine whether the proposed action may significantly impact human health or the environment and thus require preparation of an EIS.[150] Though EAs and EISs vary in depth, both must contain discussions of the following: the need for the proposed action, alternatives to the proposed action, the anticipated environmental impacts of both the proposed action and its alternatives,[151] and the cumulative impacts of the proposed action.[152]

Three of the CEQ's NEPA requirements could prove valuable for assisting wolf recovery and thus deserve more explanation. First, each EA or EIS must discuss the anticipated environmental impacts of the proposed action and its alternatives. Because impacts to the environment encompasses impacts to wildlife in or around the contemplated action area, any NEPA document analyzing a proposed action that will be undertaken in areas occupied by wolves or containing gray wolf habitat should address how the proposed action and alternative actions might impact the wolf or its habitat.

NEPA's alternatives requirement implements the spirit of the act by forcing agencies to assess whether they can carry out a proposed action in a less environmentally damaging manner and whether alternatives exist that make the proposed action unnecessary.[153] Specifically, all agencies must "study, develop, and describe appropriate alternatives to recommended courses of action…"[154] The range of alternatives to be set forth in an EA or EIS is governed by the "rule of reason" and defined by the "purpose and need" of the action itself.[155] The action agency need not consider an infinite range of alternatives in its NEPA analysis. However, it must seriously consider all reasonable and feasible alternatives for fulfilling the project purpose.

The CEQ has described a requirement to consider a reasonable range of alternatives as the "heart" of environmental review, and courts have referred to it as the "linchpin" of the EIS.[156] The alternatives requirement is, however, an equally important component of an EA.[157] Federal agencies are required "to study alternatives to any actions that have an impact on the environment, even if [it is ultimately determined that] the impact is not significant enough to require a full-scale impact statement."[158] A proper alternatives analysis should "rigorously explore" and "objectively evaluate" these alternatives, which means it should "devote substantial treatment to each alternative considered in detail so that reviewers may evaluate their comparative merits."[159]

A discussion of the cumulative environmental effects of a proposed action is also an essential part of the NEPA process;[160] otherwise the combined environmental effect of related actions will not be evaluated. *Cumulative impact* is defined as "the impact on the environment which results from the incremental impact of the action when added to other past, present, and reasonably foreseeable future actions…Cumulative impacts can result from individually minor but collectively significant actions taking place over a period of time."[161]

The CEQ interprets NEPA as requiring analysis and a concise description of the identifiable present effects of past actions. Federal agencies must do this to the extent that these effects are relevant and useful in analyzing whether the reasonably foreseeable impacts of the current agency proposal may have a continuing, additive, and significant relationship to those effects.[162] The courts of appeal have adopted different tests to determine what cumulative impacts must be included in a discussion of environmental impacts. The Ninth Circuit, for example, applies the CEQ regulation that all "reasonably foreseeable" actions that have potential cumulative impacts must be addressed in an EA or EIS.[163]

In the end, because it is procedural and not substantive, NEPA does not require an action agency to make the most environmentally friendly decision. Rather, NEPA sets forth a process of deliberation to ensure that federal agencies are engaged in *informed* decision making. Thus, accurate scientific analysis, expert agency comments, and public scrutiny are essential to implementing NEPA. NEPA documents must concentrate on the issues that are truly significant to the action, while NEPA procedures must ensure that high-quality environmental information is made available to public officials and citizens before decisions are made or actions are taken.[164] Because of NEPA's broad applicability affecting numerous federal actions, it will be a key component of the legal framework governing wolf recovery in the Southern Rockies.

FEDERAL LAWS APPLYING TO SPECIFIC LANDS

As set out above, the ESA and NEPA are generally applicable to wolf recovery. Other federal laws may also come into play for wolf recovery, depending on which lands are involved. If wolves are reintroduced onto or naturally reoccupy the national forests, the National Forest Management Act (NFMA) will influence wolf management on these lands. Similarly, if wolves reoccupy Bureau of Land Management lands, BLM's management practices under the Federal Land Policy Management Act (FLPMA) are relevant. Although these laws will, to some extent, influence how wolves are managed in certain areas, nothing in these statutes supersedes the ESA or its regulations. Rather, these other federal statutes become important for gray wolf recovery only to the extent that they provide additional layers of procedural and substantive protections for wolves, or in the event the wolf is removed from the endangered and threatened species list.

THE NATIONAL FOREST MANAGEMENT ACT

Passed in 1976, the National Forest Management Act (NFMA)[165] sets forth the management policies and procedures to be implemented on the national forests, lands managed by the US Forest Service, an agency under the Department of Agriculture. NFMA contains several provisions that, when implemented, could impact the management of wildlife, including threatened and endangered species. NFMA requires, for example, that the government prepare and adopt a governing forest plan for each forest system unit.[166] As discussed above, the Forest Service may be required to prepare an EA or EIS under NEPA when developing its forest plans. This environmental analysis must consider how the Forest Service's proposed management strategies will impact wildlife.

Each forest plan should have meaningful standards for wildlife management. NFMA directs the Forest Service to promulgate regulations that specify guidelines for how its forest plans will "provide for diversity of plant and animal communities based on the suitability and capability of the specific land area in order to meet overall multiple-use objectives."[167] In 1982, the Forest Service promulgated regulations pursuant to this NFMA provision. These regulations, the original NFMA planning rule, were designed to protect wildlife and other forest resources.

In light of NFMA's statutory direction to provide for species diversity, the 1982 planning rule included a species viability provision. This provision provided that "fish and wildlife habitat shall be managed to maintain viable populations of existing native and desired nonnative vertebrate species in the planning area."[168] To implement this provision, the 1982 planning rules required the Forest Service to select certain wildlife species to be monitored as proxies for the health of broader wildlife populations in each specific ecosystem within the relevant forest. These proxy species are referred to as "management indicator species" (MIS).[169]

As discussed briefly above, the Forest Service has made several confusing attempts to revise its 1982 planning rule. In 2000, the agency promulgated a second set of planning regulations that significantly deviated in substance from the 1982 rule. Importantly, the 2000 planning rule included a change to the species viability requirements. Upon releasing the 2000 regulations, many people, including agency personnel, did not understand when the 1982 planning rule applied as opposed to when the newer, 2000 planning rule applied. Therefore, the Forest Service again amended its planning regulations in 2002 by introducing a "transitional rule." Although the 2002 transitional rule was supposed to provide clarity on this point, by 2004 the Forest Service was still conceding "considerable uncertainty" around the effect of the 2000 planning rule and its transition. Thus, the Forest Service next issued an "interpretive rule" for its planning regulations. The 2004 interpretive rule stated that the 1982 regulations, along with their species viability provision, were no longer in effect.[170] The Forest Service has since issued new, final planning regulations. The 2005 forest planning rule conclusively eliminated the species viability and diversity requirements created by previous Forest Service planning regulations.

However, in March of 2006, a California federal court overturned the NFMA 2005 planning rule for violating NEPA.[171] The court's holding has reinvigorated the 1982 planning rule and its species viability provisions. Unless and until the Forest Service completes a legal NEPA analysis for its rule-making proposal, the agency is still legally bound to implement its MIS policy in developing new forest plans. Accordingly, if a forest plan designates gray wolves or their prey species as a management indicator species, NFMA could have important impacts on wolf recovery.

Once a forest plan is in place, that plan is implemented through site-specific actions. Here NFMA offers an additional substantive standard. The Forest Service can undertake site-specific actions only if the effects of those actions are consistent with the goals and objectives of the relevant forest plan.[172] Because forest plans must be developed with the interests of species viability and diversity in mind, they often include some meaningful provisions for promoting wildlife health.

Forest Service actions that diminish or otherwise harm species viability or diversity could therefore be challenged as contrary to the applicable forest plan and NFMA.

THE FEDERAL LAND POLICY AND MANAGEMENT ACT

The Federal Land Policy and Management Act (FLPMA)[173] governs the management of all public lands held by the Bureau of Land Management (BLM), an agency of the US Department of the Interior. FLPMA establishes a policy "in favor of retaining public lands for multiple use management."[174] The term *multiple use* has somewhat of an unwieldy definition, but contemplates, in part, the balancing of wildlife with other uses on BLM lands.[175] Because multiple use is a "deceptively simple term that describes the enormously complicated task of striking a balance among many competing uses,"[176] multiple-use management is more of a goal than a defined mandate.

Like NEPA, FLPMA is "primarily procedural in nature."[177] While FLPMA is full of management policies and objectives, it provides few nondiscretionary agency duties.[178] BLM must conform to FLPMA to the extent that its actions, taken as a whole, carry out the statute's goals. How the BLM reaches those goals, however, is left to the agency's discretion.

Rather than dictating outcomes, the multiple-use principle simply requires that the BLM "informedly and rationally" balance the multiple-use values on its lands.[179] In practice, this means that the BLM must use some sort of a balancing test each time it approves site-specific actions in order to determine whether the proposed activity in question is actually in the public interest. In short, the BLM "must give consideration to the relative values of the resources" in a given area before authorizing conflicting uses there.[180] Wildlife and threatened and endangered species are one of the "resources" that the BLM must weigh.

FLPMA also requires that the BLM "shall, in managing the public lands, take any actions necessary to prevent unnecessary or undue degradation."[181] Though this sounds like a nondiscretionary duty, "unnecessary or undue degradation" remains undefined by the statute or BLM's regulations, leaving the decision as to what magnitude of degradation is unnecessary or undue for any particular area largely up to the BLM. It is possible that litigants could successfully challenge a site-specific, discrete agency action on the grounds that that action was causing unnecessary or undue degradation to BLM lands or the resources on those lands, including degradation to wildlife populations. Deference to the agency's decision making, however, would create a steep burden for the litigant to overcome. It seems that such a challenge could be successful only where the degradation was egregious and directly flowed from the BLM's action. In such a case, one may be able to force the BLM to stop doing something only if a court agreed that the BLM was allowing unnecessary or undue degradation. However, a court will not order the BLM to take an action not otherwise planned in order to prevent degradation that has not yet occurred.[182]

The BLM implements its multiple-use mandate through its various resource management plans (RMPs).[183] RMPs are similar to forest plans and are adopted only after the conclusion of a NEPA process and potentially Section 7(a)(2) consultation under the ESA if the plan affects listed species. RMPs are "designed to guide and control future management actions" of the BLM.[184] In general, an RMP will describe the allowable uses, goals for future land condition, and specific next steps for a particular area.[185]

FLPMA directs the BLM to manage the public lands in accordance with its resource management plans when those plans are available."[186] Like the Forest Service's NFMA consistency requirement, this BLM statutory directive prevents the agency from taking actions inconsistent with the provisions of its plans. Unless and until an RMP is amended, such actions can be set aside as contrary to law.[187] It should be noted, however, that "will do" projections of agency action set forth in land use plans do not constitute legally binding, enforceable agency commitments.[188]

STATE AND LOCAL LAWS

LAWS THAT CONFLICT WITH THE ESA ARE PREEMPTED

As mentioned at the outset of this chapter, currently any gray wolves in the Southern Rockies are federally protected as endangered species under the ESA. So long as gray wolves remain listed under the ESA, the Supremacy Clause of the US Constitution[189] mandates that federal law trumps all state and local laws on wolf management to the extent that those laws offer a lower level of protection than that afforded by the ESA. States are free, however, to provide higher levels of species protection than that given by the federal government. Therefore, to the extent that state or local laws provide additional protections to wolves beyond that afforded to them by the ESA, those additional protections will apply for wolf management within that state or local government's respective borders. All state and local laws that conflict with the ESA are preempted and irrelevant so long as the federal government retains management control of the species under the ESA.

The question of who holds the power to regulate wildlife within a state is not a new or underdebated question. After many historical legal twists and turns, our modern regulatory framework for wildlife management is now well-settled and firmly rooted in constitutional law. The federal government derives its authority to regulate threatened and endangered species through the ESA from the Commerce Clause of the US

Constitution.[190] While the Commerce Clause gives the federal government authority to regulate wildlife, it does not, in and of itself, take regulatory authority away from states and local governments. That is to say, wildlife regulation in general, and the regulation of threatened and endangered species specifically, is not necessarily beyond the purview of the states. States and local governments may, in certain circumstances, legislate for wildlife and listed species so long as their laws do not run afoul of the Supremacy Clause.

THE STATES RETAIN LIMITED POWER

Although Congress has legislative power over threatened and endangered species through the Commerce Clause, states still may exercise their police power to regulate wildlife within their boundaries through the Tenth Amendment of the US Constitution. Under the Tenth Amendment, those "powers not delegated to the United States... are reserved to the States respectively, or to the people."[191] The Tenth Amendment "expressly declares the constitutional policy that Congress may not exercise power in a fashion that impairs the States' integrity or their ability to function effectively in a federal system."[192] The Supreme Court has long recognized the power of a state to regulate its "police, its domestic trade, and to govern its own citizens."[193] This "police power" includes the power to protect the public health, safety, morality, and general welfare. Wildlife conservation is "a proper function of the state government, as tending directly to promote the public welfare."[194]

State authority to regulate threatened and endangered species under the police power is well recognized today. Indeed, all fifty states offer wildlife protection through the adoption of state-specific endangered species lists and other wildlife regulation. Both Colorado and New Mexico have undertaken both of these strategies. These states have adopted their own respective endangered species lists,[195] and have legislated for threatened and endangered species through state laws. Because the laws of these two states are those most likely to come into play for Southern Rockies wolf reintroduction and recovery, they are discussed here briefly.

Colorado

The Colorado Revised Statutes contain provisions applying to threatened and endangered species.[196] These provisions are very similar to ESA Sections 4 and 9 in that they authorize the state to compile a list of protected species and set forth "take" prohibitions: "Except as otherwise provided in this article, it is unlawful for any person to take, possess, transport, export, process, sell or offer for sale, or ship and for any common or contract carrier to knowingly transport or receive for shipment any species or subspecies of wildlife appearing on the list of wildlife indigenous to this state determined to be [threatened or] endangered within the state."[197]

New Mexico

Similarly, New Mexico has legislated for threatened and endangered species through the New Mexico Wildlife Conservation Act of 1978 (NMWCA).[198] The NMWCA also largely mirrors the purposes and prohibitions set forth in the ESA. The New Mexico legislature has found and declared that "species of wildlife indigenous to the state that may be found to be threatened or endangered should be managed to maintain and, to the extent possible, enhance their numbers within the carrying capacity of the habitat,"[199] and that "the state should assist in the management of species of wildlife that are deemed to be endangered elsewhere by prohibiting the taking...of species of wildlife listed on the United States lists of endangered fish and wildlife, unless such actions will assist in preserving or propagating the species."[200] Furthermore, the NMWCA makes it "unlawful for any person to take...any species of wildlife" appearing on the state or federal lists of endangered species.[201]

As these state laws indicate, Colorado and New Mexico have established some level of endangered species protection. However, neither state offers gray wolves more protection than does the ESA and in many respects both offer less. For example, neither protects critical habitat or has anything analogous to ESA Section 7 protection. This means that unless and until gray wolves are taken off the federal list of threatened and endangered species, these state laws need not be considered when contemplating Southern Rockies wolf reintroduction. Should the gray wolf be delisted in the future, however, management authority over their populations could be turned over to the states.

LOCAL LAW

If state laws are inconsequential for wolves at this point, the legislative hierarchy demands that local laws are even less influential. However, because state counties and municipalities do possess some authority to regulate wildlife, those powers are discussed here briefly.

Local governments are creatures of the state, and state-imposed constraints on local governments define the state-local relationship. State legislatures have complete control over local governments, except as limited by federal or state constitutional clauses.[202] This is because local governments are simply political subdivisions of the state and are not sovereigns with inherent powers.

Generally, counties only possess those powers expressly granted, those necessarily or fairly implied from the express powers, and those essential to accomplish the purposes of the county.[203] Such powers are conferred upon a local government either in the state constitution or in its statutes. Under this structure, a local government will only have the power to regulate threatened and endangered species if it is expressly granted or fairly implied from an express grant of power.

The State of Colorado has expressly granted its counties power over wildlife only in the context of land use regulation, such as the adoption of zoning ordinances. Specifically, Colorado counties may "regulate the use of land by protecting those lands from activities which would cause immediate or foreseeable material danger to significant wildlife habitat and would endanger a wildlife species."[204] New Mexico has declined to grant its counties any power over wildlife regulation, though that power may be implied from the state's general grant of police power to its counties.[205]

When a county has been delegated police power authority under state law, it can exercise those powers whenever reasonably necessary to protect and safeguard the public health, safety, or general welfare.[206] Once granted, the police power is a legitimate support for a variety of regulations related to the health, safety, and welfare of the community. Should wildlife, including threatened and endangered species, need to be regulated in order to protect public safety, one can safely assume that this type of regulation could properly fall under a county's police power. Even so, such local regulations enacted pursuant to the police power may be subject to preemption by either the federal or state government. This means that in the same way conflicting state laws are trumped by the ESA, so too are conflicting local laws. Even if wolf management is someday turned over to the states, no county or municipality may regulate for threatened or endangered species in a way that is more restrictive than the laws of their parent state.

NOTES

1. The ESA is codified at 16 U.S.C. §§ 1531 et seq.
2. NEPA is codified at 42 U.S.C. §§ 4321 et seq.
3. NFMA is codified at 16 U.S.C. §§ 1604 et seq.
4. FLPMA is codified at 43 U.S.C. §§ 1701 et seq.
5. 16 U.S.C. §§ 1531(a)(1) & (2).

6. 16 U.S.C. § 1531(a)(3).
7. 16 U.S.C. § 1531(b).
8. 16 U.S.C. § 1531(c).
9. *Tennessee Valley Authority v. Hill*, 437 U.S. 153, 180 (1978).
10. Ibid., 184.
11. 16 U.S.C. § 1532(15).
12. See 50 C.F.R. § 17.11 (list of endangered and threatened wildlife); 50 C.F.R. § 17.12 (list of endangered and threatened plants).
13. See, e.g., *Federation of Fly Fishers v. Daley*, 131 F. Supp., 2nd 1158, 1163 (N.D.Cal. 2000) (holding that "listing is critically important because it sets in motion the [ESA's] other provisions, including the protective regulation, consultation requirements, and recovery efforts").
14. 16 U.S.C. § 1533.
15. S. Rep. No. 418, 97th Cong., 2nd sess., at 10; see also H. Rep. No. 567, 97th Cong., 2nd sess., at 10 (stating that "the listing process under Section 4 is the keystone of the [ESA].").
16. The Mexican gray wolf (*Canis lupus baileyi*) is a genetically distinct subspecies of the gray wolf (*Canis lupus*) species.
17. 16 U.S.C. § 1532(16).
18. 61 Fed. Reg. 4722.
19. Ibid.
20. Ibid.
21. See 72 Fed. Reg. 14760 (Designating the Northern Rocky Mountain Population of Gray Wolf as a Distinct Population Segment and Removing This Distinct Population Segment From the Federal List of Endangered and Threatened Wildlife).
22. 16 U.S.C. § 1532(6).
23. 16 U.S.C. § 1532(20).
24. 16 U.S.C. § 1533.
25. Ibid.
26. 16 U.S.C. §§ 1533(a)(1)(A)-(E).
27. Ibid.
28. Ibid.
29. 16 U.S.C. § 1533(b)(1)(A).
30. 16 U.S.C. § 1540.
31. 16 U.S.C. § 1532(5)(B).
32. See 5 U.S.C. § 553(e) (stating that "each agency shall give an interested person the right to petition for the issuance, amendment, or repeal of a rule").
33. *Tennessee Valley Authority v. Hill*, 437 U.S. 153, 179 (1978) (quoting S. Rep. No. 93–307, at 2 (1973), reprinted in 1973 U.S.C.C.A.N. 2989, 2990).
34. Ibid.
35. H. R. Rep. No. 94–887, at 3 (1976).
36. 16 U.S.C. § 1533(a)(3)(A)(i); *see also* 16 U.S.C. § 1533(b)(6)(C).
37. 16 U.S.C. § 1533(b)(6)(C)(ii).
38. Ibid.
39. H. R. Rep. No. 1625, 95th Cong., 2nd sess., 17, reprinted in 1978 U.S.C.C.A.N. 9453, 9467.
40. The term *take* means" to harass, harm, pursue, hunt, shoot, wound, kill, trap, capture, or collect, or to attempt to engage in any such conduct." 16 U.S.C. § 1532(19).
41. 50 C.F.R. § 424.12(a)(1).
42. See, e.g., *Natural Resources Defense Council v. US Department of the Interior*, 113 F.3d 1121 (9th Cir. 1997) (rejecting Fish and Wildlife Service [FWS] argument that designation of critical habitat for coastal California gnatcatcher was not prudent); *Conservation Council of Hawai'i v. Babbitt*, 2 F. Supp. 2d 1280 (D. Haw. 1998) (rejecting FWS decision not to designate critical habitat for 245 species of Hawaiian plants); *Building Industry Association of Southern California v. Babbitt*, 979 F. Supp. 893 (D.D.C. 1997) appeal dismissed by 161 F.3d 740 (D.C. Cir. 1998) (rejecting argument that designating critical habitat for various species of fairy shrimp not prudent).
43. 16 U.S.C. § 1533(a)(3)(A)(ii).
44. 16 U.S.C. § 1533(b)(2).
45. 16 U.S.C. § 1532(5)(A).
46. 16 U.S.C. § 1532(3).
47. See, e.g., *Northern Spotted Owl v. Lujan*, 758 F.Supp. 621, 624–25 (W.D.Wash. 1991) (holding that "designation of critical habitat is a central component of the legal scheme developed by Congress to prevent the permanent loss of species.").
48. 16 U.S.C. § 1536(a)(2).
49. *Forest Guardians v. Babbitt*, 174 F.3d 1178, 1185–86 (10th Cir. 1999); see also *Greenpeace v. National Marine Fisheries Service*, 273 F.Supp.2d 1181, 1193 n. 11 (W.D.Wash. 2002) (holding that "the concepts of jeopardy and adverse modification...are two separate standards and are to be analyzed separately"); *Conservation Council of Hawaii v. Babbitt*, 2 F.Supp.2d 1280, 1287 (D.Haw. 1998) (holding that the ESA "clearly established two separate considerations, jeopardy and adverse modification").
50. See 16 U.S.C. § 1532(5)(A) and § 1532(3) (giving the definitions of *critical habitat* and *conservation*).
51. *Sierra Club v. US Fish and Wildlife Service*, 245 F.3d 434, 441–42 (5th Cir. 2001); see also *Gifford Pinchot Task Force v. US Fish and Wildlife Service*, 378 F.3d 1059, 1070 (9th Cir. 2004) (holding that "the requirement to preserve critical habitat is designed to promote both conservation and survival").
52. 16 U.S.C. § 1533(f)(1).
53. 16 U.S.C. §§ 1533(f)(1)(B)(i),(ii), and (iii).
54. 16 U.S.C. § 1533(f)(2)
55. 59 Fed. Reg. 4845 at 4846.
56. 16 U.S.C. § 1534.
57. 16 U.S.C. § 1535(a).
58. Ibid.
59. 16 U.S.C. § 1535(b).
60. 16 U.S.C. § 1535(c)(1).
61. Ibid.
62. 16 U.S.C. § 1535(c)(1)(A)-(E).
63. 16 U.S.C. § 1535(d).
64. 16 U.S.C. §§ 1536(a)(1) and (2).
65. 16 U.S.C. § 1531(c)(1).
66. 16 U.S.C. § 1536(a)(1).

67. *Sierra Club v. Glickman*, 156 F.3d 606, 618 (5th Cir. 1998); *Defenders of Wildlife v. Secretary, US Dept. of the Interior*, 354 F.Supp.2d 1156 (D.Or. 2005).

68. *Rio Grande Silvery Minnow v. Keys*, 2002 WL 32813602 (D.N.M. 2002).

69. *House v. US Forest Service*, 974 F.Supp. 1022, 1027 (E.D. Ken. 1997) (holding that the Forest Service was bound by both the ESA and its own Forest Plan to place an endangered bat species at the top of its priority list).

70. *Defenders of Wildlife v. EPA*, 420 F.3d 946 (9th Cir. 2005) (holding that Sections 7(a)(1) and 7(a)(2) impose separate and distinct requirements to mandate and authorize all federal agencies to conserve endangered species and their ecosystems).

71. *Carson-Truckee Water Conservancy District v. Watt*, 549 F.Supp. 704 (D.Nev. 1982), aff'd sub nom; *Carson-Truckee Water Conservancy District v. Clark*, 741 F.2d 257 (9th Cir. 1984), cert. denied sub nom.; *Nevada v. Hodel*, 470 U.S. 1083 (1985).

72. *Defenders of Wildlife v. Andrus*, 428 F.Supp. 167 (D.D.C. 1977).

73. *Platte River Whooping Crane Trust v. FERC*, 962 F.2d 27 (D.C. Cir. 1992).

74. *House v. US Forest Service*, 974 F.Supp. 1022, 1027 (E.D. Ken. 1997)

75. *House v. US Forest Service*, 974 F.Supp. 1022, 1027 (E.D. Ken. 1997)

76. 16 U.S.C. § 1536(a)(2).

77. Ibid. Once consultation has been initiated, the federal agency involved and any permit or license applicant involved may not make any irreversible or irretrievable commitment of resources. 16 U.S.C. § 1536(d).

78. www.fws.gov/endangered/consultations/s7hndbk/s7hndbk.htm.

79. 50 C.F.R. § 402.14(g)(4). The biological opinion must include the following: (1) a summary of the information on which the opinion is based; (2) a detailed discussion of the effects of the action on listed species or critical habitat; and (3) the FWS's opinion on whether the action is likely to jeopardize the continued existence of a listed species or result in the destruction or adverse modification of critical habitat; or, an opion on whether the action is not likely to jeopardize the continued existence of a listed species or result in the destruction or adverse modification of critical habitat. 50 C.F.R. § 402.14(h).

80. For the purposes of ESA Section 7(a)(2) consultation, the federal agency wanting to undertake the proposed action is known as the "action agency," while the FWS is known as the "expert agency."

81. 16 U.S.C. § 1536(b)(3)(A); 50 C.F.R. § 402.14(h).

82. 50 C.F.R. § 402.02.

83. 50 C.F.R. § 402.14(g)(5).

84. 50 C.F.R. § 402.14(h)(3).

85. 16 U.S.C. § 1536(b)(4).

86. 16 U.S.C. § 1536(o)(2).

87. 50 C.F.R. § 402.14(g)(7).

88. 50 C.F.R. § 402.14(i)(1). Reasonable and prudent measures, along with the terms and conditions that implement then, cannot alter the basic design, location, scope, duration, or timing of the action and may involve only minor changes. 50 C.F.R. § 402.14(i)(2). The action agency must report the progress of the action and its impact on the species to FWS, and if the amount or extent of incidental taking as specified in the incidental take statement is exceeded, the federal action agency must reinitiate consultation immediately. 50 C.F.R. §§ 402.14(i)(3) & (4).

89. Under some circumstances, issuance of an incidental take statement can be a major federal action significantly affecting the quality of the human environment and subject to the requirements of NEPA. See, e.g., *Ramsey v. Kantor*, 96 F.3d 434 (9th Cir. 1996).

90. See *Pacific Rivers Council v. Thomas*, 854 F.Supp. 713 (D.Or. 1994) aff'd in part, rev'd in part by 30 F.3d 1050 (9th Cir. 1994).

91. *Silver v. Thomas*, 924 F.Supp. 976 (D.Ariz. 1995).

92. 16 U.S.C. § 1538.

93. 16 U.S.C. § 1538(a)(1).

94. 16 U.S.C. §1532(19).

95. 50 C.F.R. § 17.3.

96. Ibid.

97. See *Babbitt v. Sweet Home Chapter of Communities for a Greater Oregon*, 515 U.S. 687 (1995).

98. 16 U.S.C. § 1533(d).

99. 16 U.S.C. § 1538(a)(1)(G).

100. 50 C.F.R. § 17.31(a).

101. See 50 C.F.R. §§ 17.40–17.48.

102. See, e.g., *US v. Mckittrick*, 142 F.3d 1170 (9th Cir. 1998) (defendant shot wolf, conviction upheld).

103. *US v. St. Onge*, 676 F.Supp. 1044, 10465 (D. Mont. 1988); see also *US v. Mckittrick*, 142 F.3d 1170, 1176 (holding that the ESA "requires only that Mckittrick knew he was shooting an animal and that the animal turned out to be a protected gray wolf.").

104. *Babbitt v. Sweet Home Chapter of Communities for a Greater Oregon*, 515 U.S. 687, 704 (1995). See also, *Palila v. Haw. Dep't of Land and Natural Resources*, 852 F.2d 1106, 1108 (9th Cir. 1988) (holding that "'take' is defined…in the broadest possible manner to include every conceivable way in which a person can 'take' or attempt to 'take any fish or wildlife.'").

105. *NWF v. Burlington Northern Railroad, Inc.*, 23 F.3d 1508 (9th Cir. 1994).

106. 16 U.S.C. § 1532(13).

107. See e.g. *Strahan v. Coxe*, 127 F.3d 155, 163 (1st Cir. 1997), cert. denied, 525 U.S. 830 (1988) (holding that "we believe that…a government third party pursuant to whose authority an actor directly exacts a taking of an endangered species may be deemed to have violated the provisions of the ESA."); *Defenders of Wildlife v. Administrator, EPA*, 882 F.3d 1294 (8th Cir. 1989) (recognizing ESA liability where a "regulatory entity purports

to make lawful activity that allegedly violates the ESA."); *Loggerhead Turtle v. County Council of Volusia Co.*, 148 F.3d 1231, 1253 (11th Cir. 1998), cert. denied, 526 U.S. 1081 (1999) (holding that the plaintiff has "standing to proceed against Volusia County for lighting-related 'harm'…even though the actions or inactions of those 'third parties not before the court' may be another 'cause of the harm.'").

108. *Strahan v. Coxe*, 127 F.3d 155, 163 (1st Cir. 1997), cert. denied, 525 U.S. 830 (1988).

109. 59 Fed. Reg. 60252.

110. 16 U.S.C. § 1539(j)(2)(A).

111. 16 U.S.C. § 1539(j)(1).

112. 16 U.S.C. § 1539(j)(2)(B).

113. 16 U.S.C. § 1539(j)(C).

114. See *US v. Mckittrick*, 142 F.3d 1170 (9th Cir. 1998) (defendant shot wolf, conviction upheld).

115. 16 U.S.C. § 1539(j)(C)(i).

116. 16 U.S.C. § 1539(j)(C)(ii).

117. 42 U.S.C. §§ 4321 et seq.

118. See 42 U.S.C. § 4321.

119. See *Save the Yaak Comm. v. Block*, 840 F.2d 714, 717 (9th Cir. 1998).

120. See *Robertson v. Methow Valley Citizens Council*, 490 U.S. 332, 348 (1989).

121. 42 U.S.C. § 4332(C).

122. See, e.g., *Sierra Club v. US Department of Energy*, 287 F.3d 1256 (10th Cir. 2002).

123. See, e.g., *Wyoming Farm Bureau Federation v. Babbitt*, 199 F.3d 1224, 1240 (10th Cir. 2000).

124. Because NEPA is triggered only when the government undertakes a major action, natural recolonization of the Southern Rockies Ecoregion or elsewhere by wolves would not trigger the NEPA process.

125. See *Sierra Club v. Penfold*, 857 F.2d 1307, 1313 (9th Cir.1988) (holding that "actions" within the term "major federal actions" include new or revised agency rules, regulations, plans, policies or procedures, and that whether a federal agency is required to follow NEPA depends upon the magnitude of that action). Because any court would likely find that a rule substantially altering those protections otherwise afforded to a population of endangered species under the ESA may significantly impact that population, it is assumed that the *Sierra Club* ruling would apply specifically to an ESA § 10(j) rule making.

126. See *Douglas County v. Babbitt*, 48 F.3d 1495, 1503 (9th Cir. 1995) (holding that Congress intended to exempt the process under which a critical habitat is designated from the purview of NEPA because the ESA furthers the goals of NEPA without requiring an Environmental Impact Statement).

127. See *Catron County Board of Commissioners v. US Fish and Wildlife Service*, 75 F.3d 1429, 1439 (10th Cir. 1996) (holding that the designation of critical habitat does not displace NEPA requirements).

128. 16 U.S.C. §§ 1600 et seq.

129. 16 U.S.C. § 1604(a).

130. 16 U.S.C. § 1604(g)(1).

131. See, e.g., *Colorado Off-Highway Vehicle Coalition v. US Forest Service*, 357 F.3d 1130, 1131–32 (10th Cir. 2004) (holding that because the creation or revision of a forest plan constitutes a major federal action impacting the environment, a forest plan must be supported by NEPA analysis).

132. Forest Service planning regulations may be found at 36 C.F.R. § 219.

133. The original Forest Service planning regulations were adopted in 1982. Since that time, the Forest Service has issued "transitional" forest planning regulations in 2000, "proposed" forest planning regulations in 2002, "interpretive" forest planning regulations in 2004, and then, finally, new, "final" forest planning regulations in 2005.

134. 70 Fed.Reg. 1024.

135. 70 Fed. Reg. 1024, at 1031–1032.

136. *Citizens for Better Forestry v. US Department of Agriculture*, 481 F.Supp.2d 1059 (N.D.Cal. 2007).

137. Final agency rule making is a "major federal action," which triggers NEPA compliance.

138. See, e.g., *Robertson v. Methow Valley Citizen's Council*, 490 U.S. 332 (1989) (holding that a timber harvest on Forest Service lands is a "major federal action" for the purposes of NEPA).

139. PL 108–447, the authority for grazing categorical exclusions, for example, states that categorical exclusions cannot issue for areas with "extraordinary circumstances," which includes the presence of threatened and endangered species.

140. See, e.g., *Ramsey v. Kantor*, 96 F.3d 434, 444–446 (9th Cir. 1996) (holding that if a federal permit is a prerequisite for a project with adverse impacts on the environment, issuance of that permit constitutes a "major federal action" and the federal agency involved must conduct a NEPA analysis before granting it).

141. See generally *National Wildlife Federation v. National Park Service*, 669 F.Supp. 384, 388 (D. Wyo. 1987) (stating that because a relevant House report said that recovery plans are implicit in the ESA but not mandated, the court won't second-guess the Secretary's motives for not following the species recovery plan at issue).

142. See *Defenders of Wildlife v. Lujan*, 792 F. Supp. 834, 836 (D.D.C. 1992) (in declining to decide as a matter of law that NEPA may not stand as a prerequisite to implementation of a recovery plan, the court stated that NEPA analysis is "perhaps unnecessary or not legally required" for such implementation); see also *Fund for Animals v. Babbitt*, 903 F. Supp. 96, 110 (D.D.C. 1995) (stating that "the Court need not address plaintiffs' argument respecting the applicability of NEPA to recovery plans").

143. See *Pacific Legal Foundation v. Andrus*, 657 F.2d 829, 836 (6th Cir. 1981).

144. This standard of review is provided by the Administrative Procedures Act (APA), 5 U.S.C. § 706(2)(A).

145. *Save the Yaak Comm. v. Block*, 840 F.2d 714, 717 (9th Cir. 1998).

146. Although the CEQ regulations explicitly apply to EISs, the courts readily apply these regulations to EAs. See, e.g., *Blue Mountains Biodiversity Project v. Blackwood*, 161 F.3d 1208 (9th Cir. 1998); *American Canoe Ass'n v. White*, 277 F. Supp. 2d 1244 (N.D. Ala. 2003); 40 C.F.R. § 1508.9; and 40 C.F.R. § 1508.8.

147. See 42 U.S.C. § 4342.

148. See, e.g., *Fund for Animals, Inc. v. Thomas*, 932 F. Supp. 368 (D.D.C. 1996), aff'd by *Fund for Animals, Inc. v. Thomas*, 127 F.3d 80 (D.D.Cir. 1997).

149. It should be noted that many agencies begin their NEPA process with what is known as a "scoping notice." This beginning NEPA document is used to alert the public that the NEPA process has begun, and solicits up-front comments on the proposed action to be integrated, if they are applicable, into the upcoming EA. Because scoping is not a legal requirement, it is not discussed in detail here.

150. Should the action agency determine through the EA process that its proposed action will not significantly affect the quality of the environment, it will issue a finding of no significant impact (FONSI), which then ends the NEPA process, thus constituting final agency action for the purposes of administrative appeal and subsequent litigation.

151. 40 C.F.R. § 1508.9.

152. See, e.g., *Kern v. BLM*, 284 F.3d 1062 (9th Cir. 2002); *Hall v. Norton*, 266 F.3d 969 (9th Cir. 2001); *Blue Mountains Biodiversity Project*, 161 F.3d 1028 (9th Cir. 1998); and *Idaho Sporting Cong. v. Thomas*, 137 F.3d 1146 (9th Cir. 1998).

153. See *Environmental Def. Fund. Inc. v. United States Army Corps of Eng's*, 492 F.2d 1123, 1135 (5th Cir. 1974) (holding that the purpose of NEPA § 102(2)(E) is "to insist that no major federal project would be undertaken without intense consideration of other more ecologically sound courses of action, including shelving the entire project…").

154. 42 U.S.C. § 4332(2)(E).

155. 40 C.F.R. § 1502.13.

156. 40 C.F.R. § 1502.14. dismissed

157. See, e.g., *Monroe County Conservation Council, Inc. v. Volpe*, 472 F.2d 693 (2nd Cir. 1972).

158. *City of New York v. United States Department of Transportation.*, 715 F.2d 732 (2nd Cir. 1983), appeal, 465 U.S. 1055 (1984).

159. 40 C.F.R. § 1502.14(b); see also Council on Environmental Quality, "Forty Most Asked Questions Concerning CEQ's National Environmental Policy Act Regulations," 46 Fed. Reg. 18026, 18027, 18028 (1981): Questions 5 & 7; see also 40 C.F.R. §§ 1502.2(d), 1505.1(e), & 1503.25(b).

160. See *Tomac v. Norton*, 433 F.3d 852 (D.C. Cir. 2006).

161. 40 C.F.R. § 1508.7; see also *Inland Empire Pub. Lands Council v. United States Forest Serv.*, 88 F.3d 754 (9th Cir. 1996); and *Coalition on Sensible Transportation, Inc. v. Dole*, 826 F.2d 60 (D.C. Cir. 1987).

162. See 40 C.F.R. § 1502.22.

163. See, e.g., *Blue Mountains Biodiversity Project v. Blackwood*, 161 F.3d 1208 (9th Cir. 1998) (Environmental Assessment for timber sale must address cumulative effects of other "reasonably foreseeable" timber sales in the forest); *Kern v. BLM*, 284 F.3d 1062 (9th Cir. 2002) (timber sales); *Muckleshoot Indian Tribe v. United States Forest Serv.*, 177 F.3d 800 (9th Cir. 1999) (land exchange); *City of Tenakee Springs v. Clough*, 915 F.2d 1308 (9th Cir. 1990) (logging in forest); *Northern Alaska Environmental Center v. Norton*, 361 F. Supp. 2d 1069 (D. Alaska 2005) (oil and gas leasing, must analyze effects of proposed plan amendment).

164. See 40 C.F.R. § 1500.1(b).

165. 16 U.S.C. §§ 1600 et seq.

166. 16 U.S.C. § 1604(a).

167. 16 U.S.C. § 1604(g)(3)(B).

168. 36 C.F.R. § 219.19(a)(1) & (6) (1982).

169. 36 C.F.R. § 219.19(a)(1).

170. See 69 Fed.Reg. 58057.

171. See *Citizens for Better Forestry v. US Department of Agriculture*, 481 F.Supp.2d 1059 (N.D. Cal. 2007).

172. 16 U.S.C. § 1604(i).

173. 43 U.S.C. §§ 1701 et seq.

174. *Lujan v. National Wildlife Federation*, 497 U.S. 871, 877 (1990); see also 43 U.S.C. § 1732(a).

175. The definition of *multiple use* may be found at 43 U.S.C. § 1702.2(c).

176. See *Norton v. Southern Utah Wilderness Alliance*, 524 U.S. 55 (2004).

177. *Center for Biological Diversity v. Veneman*, 394 F.3d 1108, 1111 (9th Cir. 2005).

178. See generally *Norton v. Southern Utah Wilderness Alliance*, 524 U.S. 55, 67 (2004) (holding that BLM's FLPMA duty for managing Wilderness Study Areas is "mandatory as to the object to be achieved, but it leaves BLM a great deal of discretion in deciding how to achieve it").

179. *Sierra Club v. Butz*, 3 Envtl. L. Rprtr. 20292 (9th Cir. 1973).

180. See *National Wildlife Federation v. US Bureau of Land Management*, 140 IBLA 95 (1997).

181. 43 U.S.C. § 1732(b).

182. See *Norton v. Southern Utah Wilderness Alliance*, 524 U.S. 55, 64 & 66 (2004) (holding that a failure to act claim under 5 U.S.C. § 706(1) can proceed only where a plaintiff asserts that an agency failed to take a discrete agency action that it is required to take…as such, courts do not have the authority to "enter general orders compelling compliance with broad statutory mandates").

183. 43 C.F.R. § 1601.0-5(k).

184. 43 C.F.R. § 1601.0-2.

185. 43 C.F.R. § 1601.0-5(k).

186. 43 U.S.C. § 1732(a).

187. *Norton v. Southern Utah Wilderness Alliance*, 524 U.S. 55, 69 (2004) (holding that such an action lies in the Administrative Procedures Act (APA), 5 U.S.C. § 706(1)).

188. *Norton v. Southern Utah Wilderness Alliance*, 524 U.S. 55, 72 (2004).

189. U.S. Const. art. VI, § 3 cl. 2 provides that the "Constitution, and the Laws of the United States...shall be the supreme Law of the Land." It is from this constitutional source that the federal government's ability to preempt conflicting state and local law is derived.

190. U.S. Const. art. I, § 8, cl. 3. empowers the federal government "to regulate Commerce with foreign Nations, and among the several States..." See also *Hughes v. Oklahoma*, 441 U.S. 322, 326 (1979) (holding that because states do not own the wildlife within their borders, state laws regulating wildlife are circumscribed by Congress's commerce power)

191. U.S. Const. Amend. X.

192. *Fry v. United States*, 421 U.S. 542, 547 n. 7 (1975).

193. *Gibbons v. Ogden*, 22 U.S. 1 (1824).

194. *West Point Water Power & Land Improvement Co. v. Moodie*, 66 N.W. 6 (Neb. 1896).

195. The Colorado state endangered species list, which includes the gray wolf, may be found at http://wildlife.state.co.us/WildlifeSpecies/SpeciesOf Concern/ThreatenedEndangeredList/ListOf ThreatenedAndEndangeredSpecies.htm. The New Mexico state endangered species list, which likewise includes the gray wolf, may be found at www.fws.gov/southwest/es/EndangeredSpecies/lists/ListSpecies.cfm.

196. See C.R.S. § 33-2-105 (2005).

197. C.R.S. §§ 33-2-105(3) and (4).

198. N.M.S. §§ 17-2-37—17-2-46.

199. N.M.S. § 17-2-39(a).

200. N.M.S. § 17-2-39(b).

201. N.M.S. § 17-2-41(c).

202. Sandra M. Stevenson, Antieau on Local Government Law § 13.01 (2nd ed. 1999).

203. See *El Dorado at Santa Fe, Inc. v. Bd. of County Commissioners*, 89 N.M. 313, 317 (1976) (holding that "a county is but a political subdivision of the State, and it possesses only such powers as are expressly granted to it by the Legislature, together with those necessarily implied to implement those express powers").

204. C.R.S. § 29-20-104(1)(b), also known as the Local Government Land Use Control Enabling Act.

205. See generally N.M.S.A. § 4-37-1. See also *Brazos Land, Inc. v. Board of County Commissioners*, 115 N.M. 168, 174 (1993) (referring to the power contained in Section 4-37-1 as "police powers").

206. Sandra M. Stevenson, Antieau on Local Government Law at § 35.01 (1st ed. 1999) (when not reasonably related to these legitimate purposes, county regulatory ordinances are void as *ultra vires*, though county ordinances passed in the exercise of the police power are presumed to be reasonable and valid).

Chapter 8

Policy: Integrated Problem Solving as an Approach to Wolf Management

Susan G. Clark, Brian Miller, and Richard P. Reading

INTRODUCTION

Wolf (*Canis lupus*) recovery and management is typically a high-profile subject that is contentious and complex. If we want to reach a broadly supported decision to restore (or not to restore) wolves in the Southern Rocky Mountains, we must employ much more integrative approaches than the methods used thus far. Successful management requires an effective problem-solving approach—an approach that is rational, practical, and justified.

Traditional approaches to wolf recovery and management have focused almost exclusively on biology. Yet the root cause of wolf extirpation in the past, as well as opposition to wolf restoration currently, rests with human perceptions, values, and practices. Individuals, governments, and nongovernmental organizations (NGOs) institutionalized past perceptions and values into basic societal beliefs. However, the modern general public is slowly changing its beliefs to recognize the value of fully functioning native ecosystems (see chap. 6). As such, we now need a new approach to recovery that comprehends the social, political, and organizational aspects of wolf management policy in a contemporary world. An integrative approach can help us address issues of wolf biology and at the same time the human dimensions of wolf restoration and management (see chap. 5 and 6). Fortunately, as we shall see, a science of integration exists that can aid wolf conservation For example, a science of integration was used to analyze

wolf management policy in the Greater Yellowstone Ecosystem by Wilmot and Clark (2005), and was used more broadly for all the large carnivores in the region (Clark et al. 2005).

This chapter looks at the wolf management process in general terms and how it could be improved, offers an introduction to integrated (often called interdisciplinary) problem solving that could help wolf recovery, and lists basic individual, organizational, and policy problems in wolf management policy and what might be done to address them.

WHAT IS THE WOLF MANAGEMENT POLICY AND WHY IMPROVE IT?

Carefully analyzing wolf biology and the human aspects of wolf management helps professionals working within agencies, field researchers, and all concerned members of the public to understand and improve wolf management policy.

WHAT IS THE WOLF MANAGEMENT POLICY PROCESS?

At times, conflict among competing values appears to have hopelessly mired the policy process for wolf management. Perhaps the best way to describe the current policy process is to outline our perception of its major shortfalls.

Individuals, NGOs, and government agencies struggle to influence and/or determine policy. They come to the issue from various sectors of society with vastly different perspectives. Politics, the ecology of the species, economic considerations, power skirmishes, conflicting values, agency loyalties, divergent strategies, and much more enter the fray. As a result, many battles over wolf management have degenerated into "zero-sum" or "winner-take-all" games. For a variety of reasons outlined below, the current wolf management process is problematic for many, perhaps most, people involved.

A problem can be defined as a discrepancy between what you prefer to happen and what is actually happening (or about to happen). In other words, a problem is a conflict between a goal and a trend and condition not leading to that goal. From the perspective of people who value a naturally functioning ecosystem, the absence of wolves in the Southern Rockies Ecoregion is a problem (see Soulé et al. 2003a, 2005). The solution for them would be to restore wolves where there is an adequate prey base. However, little consensus exists among groups wanting to restore wolves. Some factions may be content with the presence of several populations of wolves that represent the species, but they would restrict those wolves to national parks or remote areas (e.g., wilderness areas) to reduce conflict. Others believe wolves should be restored to all suitable habitats within their former range and in sufficient numbers to fulfill their ecological function. Some people favor killing wolves that create problems for livestock owners. Other people favor letting wolves be wolves, even if they kill livestock or pets. Of course, many people opposed to wolves see any form of restoration as a problem.

The policy process with respect to wolf management is a human social dynamic in which we have been unable to clarify, secure, and sustain an outcome that represents the common interest of divergent groups. An integrated approach incorporating biological, social, organizational, and political components is necessary to help us map, understand, and improve the entire process and find common ground.

Public problems such as wolf restoration and management result from a decision process of some sort. That decision process represents a sequence of events through which an issue passes, beginning when a problem is recognized and ending when decision makers resolve or redefine the problem and people move on to the next problem of interest (Clark et al. 2000, 2001a, 2001b).

By "policy making" we refer to a series of actions by individuals and organizations in the decision process (Ascher and Healy 1990). A policy is a commitment, a program, and a process that aims for a preferred outcome. It represents an alternative to the context and processes that produced the problem in the first place. Often, descriptions of the management policy process avoid or downplay the analytic, coordination, communication, and political challenges of creating a successful policy. Yet all of these factors comprise the policy process. Recognizing and effectively dealing with each of these factors can spell the difference between success and failure in species and ecosystem conservation.

The US Fish and Wildlife Service develops formal wolf management policies through region-specific recovery plans and other documents associated with the recovery plan, all of which come out of an unfolding decision process. Will the policy process produce viable populations of wolves in a region with long-lasting public support (see Clark et al. 2001a)? What actions professionals and other stakeholders actually take matter far more than what people write in formal government documents. Real policy making occurs in the field, through the collective actions of many people. The key is to make the decision process for wolf restoration more effective, efficient, and equitable.

WHY IMPROVE THE WOLF MANAGEMENT POLICY PROCESS?

Efficiency (time and money), effectiveness (results), and equability (fairness) should drive the wolf management policy process. An effective program makes more efficient use of resources, and if it is successful, more resources may become available to help other deserving species. A poorly performing program or policy may consume scarce resources, including time, money, animals, expertise, and goodwill. If we increase efficiency, agencies could apply the savings to other equally pressing conservation problems. Indeed, insufficient funding already hinders most deserving conservation programs. Alternatively, effective and efficient programs move more rapidly toward recovery.

Effective and efficient programs result from good planning, inclusivity, and enhanced learning processes. If a species occurs in the jurisdiction of more than one agency, a comprehensive plan can enhance communication, cooperation, and coordination. Joint problem solving offers many advantages. Without a clear plan, conflicting goals may arise and people may duplicate effort, omit important tasks, and even engage in opposing actions. Poorly defined programs can also create friction among representatives from different groups, resulting in antipathy, distrust, and unnecessary delays in future decisions for that program or for the next program involving the same agencies. Better learning improves effectiveness and efficiency. Yet learning often has been hampered by inadequate or noncomparable scientific designs in many programs that reintroduced or translocated species. Programs spanning agency jurisdictions or geographic and political boundaries may not be designed to produce the statistically comparable information necessary to recover species rapidly or to pass lessons along for future benefits. Better, more efficient programs often serve as prototypes, or models, that personnel from other recovery projects try to imitate.

Integrated problem solving can help meet the objective of improved wolf management; this approach differs significantly from current single-agency-dominated approaches, or even multidisciplinary approaches, and it draws on systems thinking and the policy sciences (Lasswell 1971). An integrated approach requires that people merge information from different disciplines and experiences systematically and explicitly. In contrast, multidisciplinary approaches use information from many disciplines, but collection, evaluation, and application of that information occurs independently and piecemeal. As a result, recommendations emanating from different disciplines are often not fully compatible or can be contradictory. This approach fails to achieve integration as described in the next section of this chapter.

INTEGRATED PROBLEM SOLVING

Policy makers and other stakeholders require an analytic framework for integrated or interdisciplinary problem solving to be successful in wolf management. Such a framework has been used effectively on several endangered species in the United States and abroad by helping program participants see the whole picture—biological, social, political, and organizational—so they can systematically improve problem solving. In Lasswell's (1971, 181) words, this framework enables users to "study the process of deciding or choosing and evaluate the relevance of available knowledge for the solution of particular problems." Although directly applicable to wolf management, the framework has not yet been fully employed. The approach and framework are described in detail and examples given in Clark et al. (2000, 2001b) and Clark (2002). The following description of key elements in the framework is stated in general terms and applies to all kinds of problems and species.

Three key perspectives—rational, political, and moral—characterize any management policy problem (Clark 2000). We can examine the first perspective (rational) using a problem orientation, which asks, "Is the management policy process reasonable?" To examine the second perspective (political), we can construct a cognitive map of the current social and decision processes that focuses on the values different participants embrace, use, and promote and on the conflicts that arise among those participants. The political perspective considers those values and asks, "Is the process feasible?" The third perspective (moral) considers the underlying assumptions or beliefs that participants use to justify their positions. This perspective asks, "Is the process moral or justified?" No person or organization, not even the US Fish and Wildlife Service in its recovery plan (US Fish and Wildlife Service 1987a), has employed all three perspectives to understand and plan for wolf conservation. Yet we could realize significant increases in efficiency and effectiveness if policy makers utilized integrated problem solving in wolf management.

PROBLEM ORIENTATION: IS WOLF MANAGEMENT POLICY RATIONAL?

Problem orientation is a strategy for constructing a rational policy. In the rush to solve problems, conservation activists, politicians, and other stakeholders are typically solution oriented rather than problem oriented. A solution-oriented frame of reference to endangered species conservation tends to recycle a misconceived conservation problem over and over in ways that consistently fail (Wallace and Clark 1999). Decision makers must define, analyze, and understand problems to construct effective solutions. Being solution oriented, also called "problem blind," leads people to promote solutions before they fully understand the problem. Thus, being solution oriented can be a major problem itself.

Five interrelated tasks help address any problem (Clark 2000):

1. Clarify goals: What events or processes do you want as preferred outcomes (e.g., a reestablished wolf population or a landscape that continues to be wolf free)?
2. Describe trends: What are the historic and recent events that can affect goals (e.g., predator control programs, large ungulate population trends, rancher attitudes)?
3. Analyze conditions: What factors shape the trends you described (e.g., attitudes toward wolves, agricultural policies)?
4. Make projections: What future developments are likely under various circumstances (e.g., elk [Cervus elaphus] population projections given current management with or without a reintroduced wolf population)?
5. Invent, evaluate, and select alternatives: What course of action will likely help you realize your goals (e.g., reintroducing wolves only in wilderness areas, passing legislation that prohibits reintroduction)?

If decision makers carry out these five tasks fully, in an interactive fashion, they can establish rational choices using trends, conditions, and projections to "choose the alternative that you expect...to be the best means of realizing your goals" (Brunner 1995, 3). By "best," we mean the most effective, efficient, and equitable alternative.

This approach implies that striving for a rational policy is the preferred ideal, but in reality, we must always consider other relevant information. No matter how hard or long you work to solve a problem, achieving perfect rationality is impossible. In addition, unanticipated events can (and do) undermine what we consider rational policy. The point is that the actual practice of problem solving proceeds by a series of approximations. Using this process helps us construct ever more rational policies rather than remaining committed to one initial policy. Thus, achieving rationality is procedural and ongoing. In other words, to be rational a person must carry out certain procedures, namely the five interrelated steps in problem orientation in the sequence listed above (Clark 2000). These five operations should be conducted repeatedly to gain greater insight into the nature of the problem and potential solutions. Subsequent iteration should reconsider previous findings in light of new information and changing circumstances.

The sequence of the five activities is important. Begin by clarifying goals. Without goals, we have no rational basis for deciding which trends, conditions, and projections are important. We must analyze selectively because it is impossible to consider everything. At first, goals should be tentative. As we learn more about trends, conditions, and projections, we will likely want to revisit our goals. Perhaps they should be reevaluated. This iterative process promotes individual and group learning and is extremely important in real problem solving. Failed policies commonly result from downplaying clarifying goals and describing trends in the rush to get on with the high-profile implementation tasks that follow.

Problem orientation is essential not only to construct our own policy, but also to appraise an argument made by another person. In fact, evaluating other policy position(s) is necessary to construct our own policy stance. We must specifically look for and find the goals, trends, conditions, projections, and alternatives upon which others base their policy arguments. If any of the five elements are not explicitly stated, then we should raise questions about them and demand responses.

When decision makers omit or poorly treat one or more of the five tasks, a gap exists in the policy argument (Clark 2000). Sometimes the omission is a sign of propaganda or censorship designed to manipulate viewpoints on controversial issues (Brunner 1995). For example, a person promoting wolf reintroduction into the Southern Rockies may censor methods of reintroduction that permit lethal control of problem animals to prevent consideration of that tactic. This, in effect, "captures" expressed goals by associating them with the promoter's alternative. In addition, people can misrepresent decisions in order to cover hidden motives. For example, they can portray value-based decisions as science based. While good analysis thrives on alternatives, politics often depend on restricting consideration of alternatives to control policy outcomes.

THE SOCIAL AND DECISION PROCESS: IS WOLF REINTRODUCTION FEASIBLE?

The second perspective concerns the social and decision processes or the means by which we resolve conflicts and agree on policy. Politics are inevitable in policy because people have special interests based upon their values and they tend to promote their interests to the exclusion of other alternatives. No single interest has a complete or completely objective picture of any issue (Brewer and Clark 1994). Yet people must reconcile their differences to find some degree of common ground.

Politics develop as participants, each with their particular perspectives, interact in complex ways and changing situations. Each participant brings certain skills, characteristics, and values (e.g., power, wealth, knowledge, enlightenment, well-being, skill, affection, respect, and rectitude) to the table and uses them to promote their own interests (Lasswell 1971). The players each advocate an alternative that will improve their situation. A selected policy should represent a public consensus on rules that hold people accountable for behaviors that violate the policy. Unfortunately, policy often reflects the special interests of those who pushed the policy through rather than consensus among all stakeholders.

A consensus in conservation does not mean that special interests have gone away, nor does it mean that all parties agree with the rules of conduct. What consensus does mean is that everyone sees some benefit in the new policy and can support it. Everyone more or less expects leaders to enforce the rules fairly, regardless of whether or not they agree with all of them or with the purpose of all the rules. For example, everyone expects that a poacher of legally reintroduced wolves should be prosecuted to the full extent of the law. "More or less" is an important qualification here. After all, consensus is never perfect and rules are seldom perfectly clear.

Wolf conservation is a mandate of the US Fish and Wildlife Service under the Endangered Species Act, and Congress has legislated guidelines to support this goal (see chap. 7). For wolves, however, these rules are contingent upon where they are located. People visiting the Yellowstone region tend to comply with laws designed to protect wolves, in part because of a basic respect for the law, but also due to concern for wolves (positive sanctions). People also comply with the rules because they do not want to be arrested (negative sanctions). However, if enforcement becomes lax or nonexistent, people will gradually change their expectations and do what they like. Because enforcement and compliance are not perfect, effective rules are more lenient (as opposed to formal rules, which tend to be more stringent).

BASIC BELIEFS: IS WOLF MANAGEMENT POLICY MORALLY JUSTIFIED?

The third perspective, the morality of a policy, can best be understood by examining basic beliefs (see chap. 6). Basic beliefs are fundamental assumptions about the way society should function, and they serve as guidelines on how a community or society uses power. Policy and political conflicts usually stem from differences in basic beliefs. We can better understand a wolf policy process by examining how people justify divergent policy positions (i.e., who appeals to which beliefs to justify a political stance). For example, disagreeing about whether or not to kill wolves that depredate livestock is rooted in opposing basic beliefs. Social scientists recognize that basic beliefs and premises form the foundation of political myths; a myth is the underlying worldview of communities of individuals, rather than a fictitious story (see chap. 6). People accept myths or basic beliefs as a matter of faith; most people do not question myths or challenge the assumptions behind them because myths are so deeply ingrained in our psyches. Greater appreciation of the doctrines, formulae, and symbols that one follows can liberate individuals previously unaware of their own myths.

The three perspectives on the policy process—rationality, politics, and morality—are interdisciplinary tools for critical thinking and practical problem solving. Simply knowing about these elements does not guarantee reaching consensus; however, using the concepts can result in considerable insight into and understanding of the policy process. With this as background, we turn to the issue of the individual standpoint that each professional brings to the policy process.

FREQUENT PROBLEMS IN SPECIES CONSERVATION

A number of recurring problems plague species and ecosystem conservation, including wolf restoration. We can group these problems into individual problems, organizational problems, and problems in the management policy process. Further, we can remedy these problems largely by standpoint clarification exercises as described below and by using integrated problem-solving methods.

INDIVIDUAL PROBLEMS

People involved in wolf conservation have a standpoint, which we define as "an individual's value orientations and biases resulting from personality, disciplinary training, experiences, epistemological assumption, and organizational allegiances" (Clark and Willard 2000, 21). Some standpoints support wolf recovery, others oppose it; some people are aware of their standpoint, others are not. Common problems arise when, for example, wildlife professionals are at the center of wolf management. They have substantial biological knowledge that is important to wildlife conservation. While their knowledge is necessary, it needs to be complemented by another kind of knowledge, knowledge that deals with the socioeconomic, organizational, and political aspects of wolf management policy.

Policy scientists are skilled in integrating this kind of knowledge, and while some wildlife professionals have these skills, most do not. People skilled at both tasks explicitly and systematically use integrated problem solving to address practical challenges like wolf conservation. Biology majors at universities seldom learn integrated problem solving, including standpoint clarification, and policy makers have yet to apply a fully integrated approach that adequately incorporates social as well as biological considerations to wolf conservation.

Much of the knowledge about wolf conservation management policy is fragmented. Individuals hold knowledge partitioned according to disciplines, organizations, and basic beliefs. Such compartmentalization can impede communication, cooperation, and coordination. Consequently, a wildlife biologist, sociologist, agricultural economist, federal official, and state administrator may have entirely different views on wolf conservation, as will citizens. Indeed, where one faction sees a problem, another may see a desirable situation. Often, issues of power and control drive one discipline or managing organization to dominate policy development at the expense of other legitimate views. The way those holding power define the problem may limit options for solutions. An integrative approach can minimize such fragmentation.

In the management policy process, the term *participant/observer* means that professionals both participate in the process and simultaneously observe it from their particular standpoint. This dual role is critical to developing the greatest understanding of the process. It is important to remember that all participant/observers have biases based on experience, culture, education, and values. Yet each stakeholder assumes that they are objective, neutral, and acting in the public interest.

There are two kinds of standpoint: conventional and functional. A combination of the two best serves species conservation.

Conventional Standpoint

A conventional person tends to see situations, events, values, and decisions in customary, ordinary, everyday, and even habitual ways; they may devalue, ignore, or silence alternative ways of understanding the world, even if based on fact. Indeed, people selectively remember information better when it supports their preferred belief and ignore information contradicting that belief (Tessler and Shaffer 1990; Olsen and Zanna 1993; see chap. 6).

We contend that much of the conflict surrounding wolf conservation arises from participants drawing only on their standards and basic beliefs, i.e., conventional standpoints. Thinking within such a narrow paradigm encourages partial blindness about wolf management policy. For example, biologists often believe that more and better information will automatically improve the decision-making process (Clark 2000). People with conventional frameworks often restrict their attention to facts and ignore the process. Typically, they overlook or disregard the values of other participants. At best, this makes the decision process fuzzy and leaves participants with only an anecdotal understanding of the overall management policy process. At worst, confusion and misdirection lead to unproductive conflict, power struggles, and failure to conserve the wolf and its ecosystems.

Functional Standpoint

One should seek to move beyond a conventional standpoint to understand the overall structure and functioning of the management policy process (Clark 2000). Each person must appreciate his or her own biases and myths. He or she should explicitly and systematically employ conceptual tools in decision making to take on an anthropological role of sorts, by living in a society while simultaneously describing and analyzing it (Clark 2000).

Many specialists and/or interest groups try to justify their activities by alleging contributions to a common goal. Their actions are most likely to be effective if they and other participant/observers become knowledgeable and skillful in addressing the four elements of policy: rationality, politics, basic beliefs, and standpoint, that is, if they take a functional standpoint (Clark 2000).

To be successful, professionals should provide knowledge useful in the policy process and at the same time have their finger on the pulse of those processes (Clark 1997, 2000). Unfortunately, some professionals worry about losing credibility within their discipline if they become policy oriented. Yet becoming policy oriented does not mean giving up traditional professionalism, but instead it means benefiting from command of the conceptual tools (Clark 1997, 2000).

ORGANIZATIONAL PROBLEMS

Formal organizational structures in general and rigid vertical hierarchies in particular cause problems (Miller et al. 1994; Clark 1997). Less obvious but equally important are informal organizational structures. The latter often represent the real chain of command and the way people in organizations actually accomplish tasks. If not managed well, informal organizational structures can also interfere with progress.

Many federal and state agencies charged with endangered species management employ rigid hierarchical structures, including a long chain of command, that inhibit adaptive responses to problems (Miller et al. 1994, 1996). Although most states have instituted nongame programs, game and fish agencies originated to regulate hunting and fishing, and their primary focus is to establish harvest limits and enforce game laws. When an agency's tasks are routine, a rigid hierarchical structure can be productive and efficient. That is why they developed. However, endangered species programs must react quickly in an uncertain and complex environment influenced by factors outside a traditional organization's experience, conditions that require rapidly assimilating new information and implementing creative, cost-effective solutions. When managing such programs, rigid agencies often demonstrate limited effectiveness, especially when they organize a program using inflexible templates derived from long-standing standard operating procedures.

All organizations have their own cultures in which members view and respond to the tasks and world they face. An organization's culture influences how its members perceive goals and even what goals they seek (Warwick 1975; Reading et al. 1991). Members of an organization consciously or unconsciously select, indoctrinate, and advance people with similar perspectives (Janis 1972). A homogeneous workforce minimizes conflict, but it also reduces creativity. Built-in strategies for hiring, indoctrinating, and promoting perpetuate organizational cultures indefinitely (the good-old-boy system). Eventually, internal rules, regulations, standard operating procedures, rewards, and sanctions institutionalize an organization's culture, making it more rigid and difficult to change (Miller et al. 1996). In his study of organizational behavior, Harrison (1972) found three typical cultures: task-oriented cultures that reward achieving goals; power-oriented cultures that strive to consolidate control of programs, power, and money; and role-oriented cultures that support legitimacy, hierarchy, and status. The last two are typical of rigid bureaucracies that place procedural correctness above performance as the primary goal (Clark et al. 1989). Rigid bureaucracies enable individuals to hide from accountability under the organizational umbrella and to find scapegoats when failure looms. Biological problems notwithstanding, these and other structural and cultural problems impede species recovery and conservation.

A flexible, high-performance team can function as a parallel body to a rigid managing agency to integrate the best available information and to supply managers with options (Clark and Westrum 1989). The team that shares information, values equality and flexibility, and is motivated by a task-oriented culture has the best chance of success. A free flow of ideas facilitates discussing criticism in a neutral, constructive way. Subsequently, the team can evaluate ideas rationally. It is often difficult to unify divergent perspectives and keep everyone on equal footing. The coordinator must represent the task and not a particular agency.

PROBLEMS IN THE MANAGEMENT POLICY PROCESS

Knowledge of the decision part of the policy process enables people to identify patterns within successful and failed programs. Some policies result in undesirable, unplanned, and often unanticipated impacts. Some weaknesses or pitfalls characteristic of each decision phase (outcome) recur time after time, regardless of the technical details of the conservation issue. Knowing about these common process pitfalls can help others anticipate

and avoid them. Of all the factors influencing recovery, organizational and management process issues are perhaps the least understood among the people involved. Common problems (Miller et al. 1996) include:

+ Slow decision making;
+ Decision making without the benefit of expertise from outside the lead organization;
+ Decision making based on issues of control at the expense of scientific and management goals and priorities;
+ Rewarding organizational loyalty while penalizing creativity and initiative;
+ Faulty information flow through communication channels or conscious communication blockage;
+ Failing to develop plans with clear objectives that people can use to evaluate progress toward a goal;
+ Deviating from established plans during implementation for political reasons;
+ Impeding effective action with an overly rigid, or conservative, organizational hierarchy.

Insufficient knowledge for developing a competent course of action often characterizes the early stages of endangered species recovery programs. When biological data are scarce, dominant personalities, issues of program control, unequal power distribution, rigid organizational hierarchies, and administrative philosophies often play a more significant role in policy setting, to the detriment of the program.

Simply avoiding problems and controversies can hinder a recovery program. People sometimes delay action until an emergency clearly exists. Crisis management is more expensive, has a lower probability of success, and deflects funds from proactive strategies that could prevent future catastrophes (Wemmer and Derrickson 1987).

Stacking advisory teams to benefit agency policies lends a veneer of credibility and legitimacy, but it negatively affects planning.

When a conflict arises between biological and political goals, political agendas may subvert recovery needs—a phenomenon known as goal displacement or substitution. This can be used to gain program control. Thus, recovery programs can become powerful tools for legitimizing and enhancing organizational and individual power (Warwick 1975). Reducing the influence of outside specialists assures control of information and provides a tool for legitimizing an established doctrine. Occasionally, those involved even redefine the problem to fit political goals and philosophies. People with alternative ideas may threaten a dominant individual or organization and thereby find themselves evicted from the recovery program. When self-legitimization is a goal, there are rarely methods available for constructively resolving conflicts.

Results ultimately depend on executing a conservation or management plan (Miller et al. 1994, 1996). Often, people formulating plans leave details about implementation vague. Implementation can change intended policy, often substantially, leaving a great deal of power in the hands of the implementing organizations and personnel (Yaffee 1982; Clark and Cragun 1991). Organizations implementing policy can reduce efficiency in a variety of ways, including deliberate delay tactics, failing to allocate sufficient funding, allocating funding to tangential work, intentionally failing to collect necessary data, and by suddenly producing last-minute obstacles that easily could have been resolved earlier. In addition, they can yield to parochial political pressures and prevent critical review. Therefore, it is important that decision makers clearly define management policy and commit to ongoing critical performance reviews (Miller et al. 1994, 1996). Local political officials under economic pressure may not perceive recovery as beneficial, and that too can affect implementation (Greenwalt 1988; Rohlf 1991).

In the United States, the Endangered Species Act ostensibly precludes agencies from considering economic or political factors during the process of identifying species in danger of extinction, but it fails to preclude these same inhibitive factors from affecting implementation.

EVALUATION

Evaluation is critical to improving the effectiveness of conservation programs (Kleiman et al. 2000). Without proper evaluation, learning and change are difficult or impossible. Assessment is also important for enforcing accountability. Evaluations should address the process used to achieve the primary biological goals as well as whether those responsible achieved those goals. For example, how did those involved establish the goals? Did leaders organize the program to address the challenge and did they use innovative problem solving? Did the decision makers use science in an efficient manner? Did they even use science? How efficiently did participants use resources? Was there public support for the program? Did individual and organizational learning occur? Periodic evaluations followed by program adjustments result in adaptive management and continually improve prospects for success (Kleiman et al. 2000). Indeed, without evaluation, adaptive management is impossible. Evaluations should be both internal and external (Backhouse et al. 1996; Kleiman et al. 2000). Comprehensive evaluations should include all participants. Programs that improve over time by using periodic reviews can serve as prototypes to guide future conservation efforts.

Individuals or organizations may be reluctant to critically review their own performance if self-legitimization is a priority (Kleiman et al. 2000). Those who oppose critical evaluation can close communication channels that permit outside critiques or they can impede the critique by presenting huge quantities of paperwork coupled with a brief time period for evaluation and comment. Another ploy is intentionally selecting a biased evaluation team whose purpose is to legitimize a program and discredit critics. When leaders do not permit honest, impartial evaluation of performance, accountability suffers. Recovery plan implementation may then be inefficient, ineffective, or actually be diverted from the plan goals (Miller et al. 1994, 1996).

CONCLUSIONS

Restoring large carnivores is a complex activity involving many individuals, many federal, state, and local governmental agencies, and public and private organizations with a variety of desires, positions, and power (see, for example, Maehr et al. 2001). It is especially so with wolves. Very few people within organizations agree on the parameters of wolf reintroduction. Government agencies (some responsible for actual reintroduction) typically have rigid hierarchical organizational structures, many with internal agendas having nothing to do with their potential role in wolf restoration. Further, there will be a large number of conservation organizations involved, and no two may have the same concerns. Then there are other interest groups, such as livestock growers associations, with yet other agendas.

Often, wildlife biologists and other participants mistakenly believe that their recovery effort is unique (Clark et al. 1994), but in reality, the structure of the managing organization may account for 50 to 75 percent of the way that individuals behave in any group (Galbraith 1977). Put more simply, similar behavior will appear in programs with a similar organizational design regardless of the endangered species, geographic area, or personnel involved. Although politics, personalities, and personal motivations influence programs, careful attention to organizational arrangements and management policy processes can prevent or ameliorate such problems. Unless biologists explicitly recognize and address organizational and policy process issues, those stakeholders who support other outcomes may alter, misuse, or avoid even self-evident solutions to wolf conservation problems. These common problems can afflict all conservation efforts (Miller et al. 1994, 1996).

Miller et al. (1994, 1996) offer advice for improving performance in conservation process, including: (1) learn from experience as quickly and thoroughly as possible; (2) maintain flexibility at all times; (3) remember that science is essential in nearly all efforts to improve policy; and, (4) know there is never enough science available at the time of decision.

Integrated problem solving offers a practical, rational, and validated way forward. Clearly, dealing only with the biology of wolf restoration without addressing the concerns of the multiplicity of people and organizations involved has little hope of success. Rather, the restoration approach must comprehend and effectively deal with not only the complicated biology of restoration, but also the political, social, and organizational aspects of the problem. That is, we need a much more integrative process.

Over the last fifty-plus years, the policy sciences have developed as a discipline to address just this sort of multifaceted challenge (Lasswell 1971). People skilled in policy sciences are problem oriented, and the discipline seeks to understand the various standpoints and basic beliefs of the people and organizations involved. This discipline looks for common ground among participants by clarifying goals, describing trends, analyzing conditions, making projections, and inventing, evaluating, and selecting alternatives. If these processes are applied over time, the prospects for reducing conflict in wolf restoration and management would greatly improve.

Ecological Assessment

Chapter 9

Natural Landscapes of the Southern Rockies

Doug Shinneman, Brian Miller, and Kyran Kunkel

INTRODUCTION

The Southern Rockies Ecoregion is a ruggedly beautiful, diverse, and complex landscape with a rich pattern of landforms that support an equally rich array of plant and animal communities and species. Although the Southern Rockies have lost several native species including the gray wolf (*Canis lupus*) as a result of human settlement, persecution, and overuse of natural resources, and while many species and ecosystems are at risk, a significant portion of the ecoregion's natural landscapes remain relatively intact. These remaining communities of plants and animals are important to regional and global conservation goals because they represent biological elements unique to, and representative of, the Southern Rockies. Moreover, they offer increasingly rare opportunities to restore wild nature and native species. In short, although humans have mined, logged, developed, farmed, dammed, and grazed livestock throughout the ecoregion, conservation opportunities still abound in the Southern Rockies.

To assess the Southern Rockies for their potential to support a restored population of gray wolves, it is essential that we place this assessment within an appropriate ecological context. In this chapter, we briefly describe the natural environment and discuss the condition of the ecoregion's many natural communities and species.

GEOLOGICAL AND LANDFORM BACKGROUND

The land currently occupied by the Southern Rockies changed dramatically over eons as it was subjected to an ancient and complex geologic history. Oceans covered the ecoregion for billions of years until the Ancestral Rockies arose roughly 300 million years ago near the earth's equator. At that time, the land was part of the supercontinent Pangaea. These ancient mountains were leveled over time, and the current Southern Rockies rose roughly 70 million yeas ago as a result of the Laramide Orogeny, a period of mountain building that occurred toward the end of the Cretaceous period (Benedict 2008; Knight 1994). Post-Laramide erosion, deposition, uplift, and volcanism continued to modify the Southern Rockies' mountainous landscape. During the last 2 million years, localized volcanism and extensive glaciation were the main forces, with as many as seventeen major glacial episodes during the Pleistocene epoch (Benedict 2008; Blair 1996; Flannery 2001).

The result of these powerful geologic forces is the complex physiography we see in the Southern Rockies today, largely dominated by mountain ranges with dramatic high peaks (figure 9.1). The numerous ranges comprising the Southern Rockies generally run in a north–south direction, and they are mainly folded and faulted uplifts interspersed with volcanics (Benedict 2008). These include the Laramie Mountains, Medicine Bow Mountains, Park Range,

Front Range, Wet Mountains, Elk Mountains, Gore Range, Sawatch Range, San Juan Mountains, Sangre de Cristo Mountains, Jemez Mountains, and many others. The mountainous landscapes contain an assortment of igneous and metamorphic rock, but younger sedimentary rock is common along the ecoregion's margins, and volcanic rock is found throughout south-central Colorado and northern New Mexico (Ellingson 1996).

The Southern Rockies are the highest ecoregion on the North American continent, with 20 percent of land above the elevation of 3,017 m (9,900 ft.) (Shinneman et al. 2000). There are fifty-four peaks that rise above 4,267 m (14,000 ft.), all in Colorado. The highest point is Mount Elbert, which rises to 4,402 m (14,433 ft.). Colorado also has the lowest elevation of the Southern Rockies, roughly 1,393 m (4,570 ft.), along the Gunnison River on the Western Slope.

The ranges of the Southern Rockies show classic high-mountain topographical features such as alpine cirques and tarns, glacial moraines, broad U-shaped valleys, and glacial-outwash plains at lower elevations. Today, glaciers are small in extent and limited to high-elevation cirques (the basins holding a glacier), but periglacial activity (i.e., influences along a glacier's edge), gravity, water flow, and wind continue to erode and shape the ecoregion's mountainous landscape (Benedict 2008; Blair 1996).

On the Eastern Slope, the Southern Rockies descend into a complex assortment of mesas, foothills, hogbacks, parallel ridges, and rocky outcroppings. The topography then unfolds into the short-grass prairie, a drought-driven system in the rain shadow of the mountains (Flores 1996). On the Western Slope, the mountains and the headwaters to the Colorado, Rio Grande, Yampa, and Green rivers give way to rugged canyons and mesas, including the massive White River and Uncompahgre plateaus, contradicting the ecoregion's popular image of a

land of jagged high peaks. Ancient volcanic activity, especially in places like the San Juan and Jemez mountains, has created large calderas, ancient lava flows, volcanic dikes, and extinct, eroded volcanic domes (Ellingson 1996). The post-Laramide erosion and deposition created several large, relatively flat intermountain basins within rifts created by geologic faulting, such as the San Luis Valley and South Park (Benedict 2008). Streams and rivers have further shaped the landscape by cutting deep rocky gorges and narrow V-shaped canyons.

DRAINAGE BASINS AND AQUATIC SYSTEMS

As moisture-laden weather systems pass over the Southern Rockies, the mountains squeeze out rain and snow, creating an ecoregion that is generally wetter than surrounding areas. This high-elevation moisture collects in rivulets and streams to form the headwaters of some of the continent's major river systems (figure 9.1). West of the Continental Divide, water flows to the Pacific Ocean via the Colorado River to the Gulf of California. On the Eastern Slope, water travels to the Atlantic through the Gulf of Mexico by two main routes: the Rio Grande drains directly into the gulf, while the North and South Platte rivers and Arkansas River empty their aquatic loads indirectly via the greater Mississippi and Missouri river systems.

The Southern Rockies have nearly 48,280 km (30,000 mi.) of perennial creeks, streams, and rivers scattered throughout the ecoregion (Shinneman et al. 2000), ranging from clear, cold, fast high-mountain creeks to relatively slow-moving, wide lower elevation rivers. Natural deepwater lakes are numerous, but roughly 90 percent are found above 2,743 m (9,000 ft.) (Colorado Water Resources Research Institute 2001). Wetlands of various types are found throughout the Southern Rockies, from willow (*Salix* spp.) wetlands, known as carrs, scattered throughout the high country to large playa lakes such as those in the San Luis Valley. Groundwater and aquifers occur throughout the ecoregion, and the largest is the San Luis Valley Aquifer, which supports numerous shallow wetlands and springs (Pearl 1974).

CLIMATE

On a regional level, the climate of the Southern Rockies is classified as a temperate, semiarid steppe regime, with generally sunny weather, warm summers, and cool winters (McNab and Avers 1994). Regional climate is influenced by interrelated factors, including the latitude, mid-continent location, north–south alignment of mountain ranges, and major weather patterns, such as winter storm tracks and jet stream locations (Benedict 2008). These regional factors are influenced locally by topographic aspect and elevation (Benedict 2008; Knight 1994). Lower elevations tend to have hot summers and cool winters with semidesert levels of moisture, while higher elevations are cooler and wetter with short growing seasons (figure 9.2). The highest elevations experience long, harsh, snowy winters.

Due to prevailing westerly weather patterns, the western mountains tend to be wetter than eastern slopes, with most precipitation coming in the form of snow (Neely et al. 2001). In fact, while roughly 60 percent of the Southern Rockies' surface area drains eastward, more than 75 percent of the precipitation falls on the Western Slope (Benedict 2008). This influences the distribution of aquatic and riparian ecosystems in the Southern Rockies as well as how people use and redistribute water, which has had a dramatic impact on aquatic ecosystems by altering stream flows.

Climate differences can be quite pronounced over short distances. For example, portions of the San Luis Valley in Colorado average about 18 cm (7 in.) of precipitation a year, while some locations in the nearby San Juan Mountains, at the valley's western edge, receive more than 140 cm (55 in.), mainly in the form of snow. Wolf Creek Pass averages about 11 m (36 ft.) of snow per year. Temperatures can also vary greatly over relatively short distances. Boulder, Colorado, at 1,640 m (5,382 ft.) has an average July high temperature of 30.5°C (86.9°F), while at Berthoud Pass, at 3,500 m (11,484 ft.), the average July high temperature is only 16.5°C (61.7°F) (Western Regional Climate Center Database 2001).

NATURAL PROCESSES AND LANDSCAPE PATTERN

Natural processes play important roles in maintaining ecological integrity, and they include energy flows, nutrient cycles, hydrologic cycles, disturbance regimes, succession of natural community types, pollination, and predator-prey relationships (Noss and Cooperrider 1994). These processes make ecosystems diverse, dynamic, resilient, and naturally evolving. Fires, floods, windstorms, landslides, insect infestations, and diseases help to create landscape mosaics over space and time by influencing the composition, physical structure, and function of ecosystems. Spatial and temporal characteristics of such natural disturbances within an ecosystem type define a disturbance regime (Pickett and White 1985).

In the Southern Rockies, fire is a particularly important disturbance agent. In general, the dense, continuous crown cover in upper montane and subalpine forests supports occasional but extensive stand-replacing fires, while many lower montane and foothill forests experience low-intensity surface fires carried by fine surface fuels such as grasses (Veblen 2000). The ecoregion's grassland and shrubland fire regimes are less well-understood than those associated with forests (Knight 1994). However, within many community types, fires vary in intensity and size over space and time, creating a shifting mosaic of patch age structures and patch types (Pickett and White 1985). Disturbed patches typically go through various successional stages over time, until a relatively stable stage, such as an old-growth forest, eventually returns (Knight and Wallace 1989). In other cases, such as old-growth ponderosa pine (*Pinus ponderosa*) forests, a regime of low-intensity surface fires may actually maintain relatively steady-state conditions over long periods by thinning forest stands and maintaining large, old trees and grassy understories (Covington and Moore 1994). Yet even these forests experience stand-replacing disturbances occasionally, and for some ecosystems, these less predictable and more variable disturbance regimes may even be the norm (Reice 1994).

Natural disturbances support dynamic and healthy ecosystems and provide habitat for native species. Thus, human alteration and disruption of natural disturbance regimes in the Southern Rockies is of concern for many ecologists (e.g., Veblen and Lorenz 1991; Kipfmueller and Baker 2000; Romme et al. 2000). One way to assess natural conditions is to examine how the mosaic of natural communities are spatially distributed across a landscape such as an ecoregion or a watershed; important indexes include patch size, patch configuration, boundaries between patches, and connectivity (Forman and Godron 1986). However, depending on the ecological element or process of interest, the appropriate scale, detail, and resolution at which to measure landscape structure may vary (Wiens 1997). For instance, in the Southern Rockies, subalpine forests often cover hundreds of thousands of contiguous hectares (1 hectare equals 2.47 acres) and, in a rough sense, can be viewed as one large patch or matrix community that dominates a given landscape area. Yet within the forest

matrix, smaller patches of different forest ages (e.g., old-growth stands, dense pole-sized stands) and cover types such as aspen forest or montane riparian shrublands will exist due to disturbance histories and environmental gradients.

Recognizing that these different landscape patterns exist at different scales has great relevance for species conservation. While a habitat generalist such as an elk (*Cervus elaphus*) or wolf moves easily through the subalpine forest landscape matrix, a pine marten (*Martes americana*) is sensitive to the natural or human-induced patchiness within the forest matrix. The amount of connected forest habitat with dense stands of old trees and downed snags limits pine marten dispersal success (Buskirk and Ruggiero 1994). Although much of the landscape before European colonization was patchy, other areas consisted of extensive expanses of forest that represented continuous habitat for many interior-dependent species (Knight and Reiners 2000). The loss and fragmentation of such large interior habitat due to logging, road building, and residential development increasingly concerns scientists, land managers, and conservationists in the Southern Rockies Ecoregion (e.g., Knight et al. 2000).

ECOSYSTEMS AND NATURAL COMMUNITIES

An ecosystem is an area where plants, animals, and other organisms interact with each other and the nonliving physical environment, such as soil, rock, dead organic matter, air, and water. The distribution of ecosystem types, as well as the plants and animals associated with each, depends on numerous environmental variables, including climate, water availability, topography, geology, soils, and elevation. Within the Southern Rockies, elevation and aspect are particularly influential because these environmental factors strongly affect temperature, moisture availability, wind, and solar radiation levels (Knight 1994). Latitudinal gradient is also relevant to ecosystem distribution, as illustrated by the tree line elevation in the Southern Rockies, which varies from 3,200 m (10,560 ft.) in the north to 3,800 m (12,540 ft.) in the south (Benedict 2008).

Ecologists have long classified ecosystems into broad elevation life zones (e.g., Merriam 1890), and this classification system remains in use today. In the Southern Rockies, the major life zones and their general elevations include the alpine (more than 3,200 m, or 10,560 ft.), subalpine (2,800 to 3,200 m, or 9,240 to 10,560 ft.), upper montane (2,300 to 2,800 m, or 7,590 to 9,240 ft.), and lower montane foothills (less than 2,300 m, or less than 7,590 ft.) (Neely et al. 2001). The US National Vegetation Classification system represents a much more standardized and hierarchical way to classify ecosystem types (Grossman et al. 1998). The assemblages of species that occur together and are capable of interacting define native ecosystems or communities. We describe the Southern Rockies' ecosystems within fourteen major community types (figure 9.3).

PLAINS STEPPE AND GREAT BASIN GRASSLANDS (LOWLAND GRASSLAND)

These grassland ecosystems generally occur below 1,800 m (5,940 ft.). Short-grass prairie and occasional mixed-grass and tall-grass prairie communities occur along the eastern and northern edges of the Southern Rockies (Benedict 2008; Knight 1994), while Great Basin semiarid grasslands dominate lower elevations along the western fringes (Dick-Peddie 1993) (figure 9.3). The eastern short-grass prairie of the Great Plains can be characterized by blue grama grass (*Bouteloua gracilis*), buffalo grass (*Buchloe dactyloides*), western wheatgrass (*Pascopyrum smithii*), needle-and-thread grass (*Hesperostipa comata*), galleta (*Pleuraphis jamesii*), Indian rice grass

(*Achnatherum hymenoides*), fringed sage (*Artemisia frigida*), yucca (*Yucca glauca*), prickly pear cactus (*Opuntia polyacantha*), and cholla (*Cylindropuntia imbricata*) (Benedict 2008; Knight 1994). Semiarid grasslands of the Western Slope are dominated by many of the same grass species, as well as *Poa* spp., black grama (*Bouteloua eriopoda*) in the southwest, and many shrub species (Dick-Peddie 1993).

These grassland ecosystems, although peripheral to the Southern Rockies, have many close ecological ties to the Southern Rockies due to animal migration, water and nutrient flows, and other natural processes. Because snowfall is relatively light and snowpack intermittent, elk from the mountains historically wintered in these lower elevations (Fitzgerald et al. 1994).

In the past, top predator species such as wolves and grizzly bears (*Ursus arctos*) greatly influenced ungulate and other prey species populations (see chap. 3). Burrowing by prairie dogs (*Cynomys* spp.) improved nutrient cycling and increased habitat diversity (Whicker and Detling 1988). Large prairie dog towns and heavy grazing by bison (*Bison bison*) provided habitat for numerous other species, such as western rattlesnakes (*Crotalus viridis*), burrowing owls (*Athene cunicularia*), black-footed ferrets (*Mustela nigripes*), badgers (*Taxidea taxus*), ferruginous hawks (*Buteo regalis*), and mountain plovers (*Charadrius montanus*) (Miller at al. 1996). Fire also regulated these ecosystems (Knight 1994).

People have largely converted the grassland ecosystems bordering the eastern portion of the Southern Rockies to farmland and urban landscapes (Dick-Peddie 1993; Shinneman et al. 2000; Theobald 2000). Where large grassland areas still exist, they are subjected to heavy livestock grazing and fire exclusion (The Nature Conservancy 1998), which alters plant composition and may lead to invasion by woody plant species (Wright and Bailey 1982). Spreading nonnative plants such as leafy spurge (*Tithymalus esula*) and knapweed (*Acosta diffusa*) are problematic in many areas (Sebastian and Beck 2000).

Settlers extirpated wild bison, grizzly bears, wolves, and black-footed ferrets from the grasslands surrounding the Southern Rockies (Fitzgerald et al. 1994; Shinneman et al. 2000). Human activity has reduced black-tailed prairie dogs (*Cynomys ludovicianus*) to less than 2 percent of their original geographic range (Mac et al. 1998), and elk and pronghorn (*Antilocapra americana*) are scarce or absent from many areas (Fitzgerald et al. 1994).

Bison are an important foundation species of the prairie (playing an important ecological role through numerical abundance), and their grazing, wallowing, and effects on cycling of nutrients greatly affected grassland diversity (Detling 1998; Truett et al. 2001). Prairie dogs are a keystone species, and thus their role in regulating the ecosystem is often disproportionately larger than their numerical abundance (Miller et al. 1996, 2000; Detling 1998; Kotlier et al. 1999). In contrast to grasslands that lack prairie dogs, those inhabited by prairie dogs provide a greater mosaic of vegetation structure, an abundance of prey for predators, burrow systems, and altered ecological processes (increased nitrogen content, succulence, and productivity of plants, and macroporosity of soil). Such changes enrich patterns of species diversity for prairie plants and animals (Coppock et al. 1983; Ingham and Detling 1984; Whicker and Detling 1988; Outwater 1996; Detling 1998). The matrix of ecological boundaries created by prairie dog colonies improves overall diversity of life across a landscape (*s.s.*, Paine 1966). Without prairie dogs and bison, the prairie is ecologically poorer.

SEMIDESERT AND SAGEBRUSH SHRUBLANDS

Semidesert and sagebrush shrubland types collectively comprise about 12 percent of the Southern Rockies land area (table 9.1, figure 9.3). Semidesert shrublands are generally found on poorly drained saline soils below 2,300 m (7,590 ft.) where summer temperatures are hot and precipitation is sparse. These ecosystems cover an extensive area in the San Luis Valley, Upper Rio Grande Basin, and portions of the lower Gunnison Valley. Dominant species include greasewood (*Sarcobatus vermiculatus*), fourwing saltbush (*Atriplex canescens*), shadscale (*Atriplex confertifolia*), and winterfat (*Krascheninnikovia lanata*) (Dick-Peddie 1993; Knight 1994). Sagebrush shrublands at low to midelevations are often dominated by basin big sagebrush (*Artemisia tridentata* ssp. *tridentata*) or Wyoming big sagebrush (*Artemisia tridentata* ssp. *wyomingensis*), while mountain sagebrush (*Artemisia tridentata* var. *vaseyana*) communities often occur in cooler, more mesic mid-elevations up to 3,000 m (9,900 ft.) (Knight 1994). Sagebrush shrublands can form extensive areas covering hundreds of thousands of hectares, especially in major valleys and intermountain basins such as the Gunnison Basin, North Park, Middle Park, and the San Luis valleys in Colorado (Neely et al. 2001).

Although the disturbance history is not well known, fires historically played a role in sagebrush shrubland ecology, but fire rotation may greatly exceed 100 years, depending on ecosystem conditions (Welch 2005; Baker and Shinneman 2004). Historically, sagebrush steppe was probably a mosaic of productive grasses, other shrub cover, and sagebrush patches of varying ages because site conditions encouraged a variable mix of species and because sagebrush is easily killed by fire (Knight 1994). Other leading disturbance agents include heavy feeding (herbivory) by grasshoppers, bison, and ungulates, as well as severe drought. Shrublands are important winter range for native deer (*Odocoileus* spp.) and elk, which provide prey for native predators such as coyote (*Canis latrans*), puma (*Puma concolor*), and for grizzly bears and wolves in the past (Fitzgerald et al. 1994; Bennett 1994).

Various shrubland ecosystems contain significantly different plant and animal communities due to the variable broad ranges in environmental conditions; however, common plant species include rabbitbrush (*Chrysothamnus* spp.), black sagebrush (*Artemisia nova*), snakeweed (*Gutierrezia sarothrae*), and bitterbrush (*Purshia tridentata*). Lightly grazed sagebrush shrublands may have well-developed, diverse grass and forb (herbaceous nongrass) cover.

Representative animal species may include western rattlesnake, collared lizard (*Crotaphytus collaris*), ferruginous hawk, golden eagle (*Aquila chrysaetos*), sage grouse (*Centrocercus urophasianus*), sage sparrow (*Amphispiza belli*), green-tailed towhee (*Pipilo chlorurus*), loggerhead shrike (*Lanius ludovicianus*), coyote, pronghorn, elk, mule deer (*Odocoileus hemionus*), desert cottontail (*Sylvilagus audubonii*), black-tailed jackrabbit (*Lepus californicus*), Wyoming ground squirrel (*Spermophilus elegans*), deer mouse (*Peromyscus maniculatus*), white-tailed prairie dog (*Cynomys leucurus*), and Gunnison's prairie dog (*Cynomys gunnisoni*).

In many areas, livestock overgrazing has decreased palatable forbs and grasses favored by wildlife and increased unpalatable or woody plants (Knight 1994). Other human disturbances include removal of sagebrush to increase grazing forage for livestock, conversion to cropland, oil and gas exploration, and invasion of nonnative species, especially cheatgrass (*Bromus tectorum*) (Welch 2005). Because shrubs catch blowing snow that eventually melts and replenishes soil water, loss of sagebrush from these ecosystems can also result in lowered soil moisture (Knight 1994).

These perturbations have collectively replaced, fragmented, and altered the species composition and disturbance regimes of sagebrush communities, causing population declines of shrubland-dependent species, especially sage grouse, sage sparrow, Brewer's sparrow (*Spizella breweri*), white-tailed prairie dog, and Gunnison's prairie dog (Braun 1995; Johnson and Braun 1999; Knick and Rotenberry 1995; Neely et al. 2001). Bison, grizzly bear, and wolves were extirpated (Fitzgerald et al. 1994). Sagebrush shrublands are poorly represented in Southern Rockies' protected areas, with less than 3 percent of their total area in national parks, research natural areas, and designated wilderness areas (table 9.1).

PIÑON-JUNIPER WOODLAND

Piñon-juniper woodlands cover extensive areas in the southern and western foothills and mesa tops, and comprise almost 13 percent of the Southern Rockies (table 9.1, figure 9.3). They generally occur between 1,700 and 2,400 m (5,610 and 7,920 ft.), but occasionally reach 2,700 m (8,910 ft.) on south-facing slopes. Piñon-juniper woodlands may occur as sparsely wooded savannas within lower elevations due to hot and dry conditions (Dick-Peddie 1993). In contrast, at their upper elevational range, these woodlands occur in relatively dense stands, often interspersed with ponderosa pine, Gambel oak (*Quercus gambelii*), and other mixed-mountain shrub species. In northern New Mexico, periodic fires may have thinned these woodlands and prevented their encroachment into neighboring grasslands and shrublands (Jacobs et al. 2002). However, in western Colorado infrequent, large crown fires characterize both the modern and historical fire regime of piñon-juniper woodlands (Baker and Shinneman 2004).

Piñon-juniper woodlands have variable species compositions depending on site conditions, but dominant species include piñon pine (*Pinus edulis*), one-seed juniper (*Juniperus monosperma*), Utah juniper (*Juniperus osteosperma*), and Rocky Mountain juniper (*Juniperus scopulorum*). Juniper is widespread, while piñon pine reaches its northern terminus in an isolated patch along the Colorado-Wyoming border. Alligator juniper (*Juniperus deppeana*) occurs only in the very southern portions of the Southern Rockies. Grassy understories often include June grass (*Koeleria macrantha*), mutton grass (*Poa fendleriana*), and Indian rice grass, and numerous cacti and shrub species also inhabit these ecosystems.

Animal species include eastern fence lizard (*Sceloporus undulatus*), tree lizard (*Urosaurus ornatus*), collared lizard, golden eagle, piñon jay (*Gymnorhinus cyanocephalus*), bushtit (*Psaltriparus minimus*), blue-gray gnatcatcher (*Polioptila caerulea*), coyote, gray fox (*Urocyon cinereoargenteus*), puma, ringtail (*Bassariscus astutus*), Townsend's big-eared bat (*Plecotus townsendii*), pallid bat (*Antrozous pallidus*), mule deer, Mexican woodrat (*Neotoma mexicana*), rock squirrel (*Spermophilus variegatus*), Colorado chipmunk (*Tamias quadrivittatus*), and piñon mouse (*Peromyscus truei*). Piñon nuts are an important food source for many species of wildlife and were sought by native people as well.

Overgrazing by livestock in these semiarid ecosystems reduced plant species diversity and forage for wildlife, decreased biological soil crust cover, and exposed easily eroded soils (Flores 1996). Chaining and roller-chopping (practices in which large tracts of piñon-juniper woodlands are mechanically removed to improve land for domestic livestock) eliminated large areas of old piñon-juniper woodlands). Collectively, grazing, mechanical removal, harvesting trees for firewood, and housing development have greatly altered and fragmented piñon-juniper woodlands in some areas. Less than 6 percent of the total area of piñon-juniper woodlands/savannah fall within protected lands (table 9.1).

MOUNTAIN SHRUBLAND
Mountain shrublands make up slightly more than 8 percent of the ecoregion (table 9.1,

figure 9.3). These shrubland ecosystems typically occur below montane forests and above grasslands, semidesert shrublands, or piñon-juniper woodlands. They mostly develop in semiarid sites between 1,700 and 2,600 m (5,610 and 8,580 ft.), although they may occur above 3,000 m (9,900 ft.) on south-facing slopes (Benedict 2008). Gambel oak shrublands (and sometimes the woodland form) dominate the western and southern portions the Southern Rockies, while mountain mahogany (*Cercocarpus montanus*) dominates the semiarid foothills in the northeastern portion of the ecoregion. These ecosystems can form extensive cover in portions of the Southern Rockies.

Other common mountain shrubland species include serviceberry (*Amelanchier utahensis*), snowberry (*Symphoricarpos oreophilus*), skunkbrush (*Rhus trilobata*), bitterbrush; ninebark (*Physocarpus* spp.), and several currant species (*Ribes* spp.). These shrublands can be quite dense, with little understory, but can also contain well-developed herbaceous understories of bunchgrasses and forbs.

Characteristic animals include eastern fence lizard, western rattlesnake, Virginia's warbler (*Vermivora virginiae*), scrub jay (*Aphelocoma californica*), spotted towhee (*Pipilo maculatus*), rock wren (*Salpinctes obsoletus*), sharp-shinned hawk (*Accipiter striatus*), red fox (*Vulpes vulpes*), ringtail, bobcat (*Lynx rufus*), western small-footed myotis (*Myotis ciliolabrum*); mule deer, bushy-tailed woodrat (*Neotoma cinerea*), brush mouse (*Peromyscus boylii*), mountain cottontail (*Sylvilagus nuttallii*), and rock squirrel. Due to their mid-elevation position, these shrublands often contain a mix of species from different elevation life zones, and several species, such as elk and deer, winter here (Benedict 2008).

Fire encourages the establishment and spread of mountain shrubland ecosystems as an early seral stage (i.e., an intermediate community in ecological succession) (Floyd-Hannah et al. 1996), although evidence suggests they may also exist as stable communities where dry climate and soil conditions permit (Benedict 2008). Mountain mahogany leaves are heavily grazed by native herbivores, and oak acorns represent an important food source for deer, elk, wild turkey (*Meleagris gallopavo*), squirrel (*Sciurus* spp.), black bear (*Ursus americanus*), and many other wildlife species (Knight 1994; Fitzgerald et al. 1994). Many shrublands also support a rich array of insects, which attracts high numbers of insectivorous birds and reptiles (Floyd-Hannah et al. 1996).

Development in mountain shrubland ecosystems reduces and fragments thousands of hectares of valuable wildlife habitat, especially along Colorado's Eastern Slope and portions of the San Juan Mountains (Shinneman et al. 2000). Fire exclusion may eventually alter community composition, and trees may displace native shrub communities. In addition, if not regenerated by fire, Gambel oak woodlands start to decline, become senescent, and acorn production declines. Montane shrublands are not well represented in protected areas, especially oak woodlands, for which less than 3 percent of the total area exists in nature preserves in the Southern Rockies (table 9.1).

PONDEROSA PINE
FOREST AND WOODLAND

Ponderosa pine forests cover about 12 percent of the ecoregion and are found throughout the Southern Rockies in the foothill and montane zones between 1,500 and 2,700 m (4,950 and 8,910 ft.). Ponderosa pine forests exist in variable patch sizes but form large matrix communities along the Eastern Slope of the Front Range and the foothills of southern Colorado and northern New Mexico. Ponderosa pine forests may extend above 2,700 m (8,910 ft.) where thin, dry soils occur on south-facing slopes. These forests are typically dry and warm, and snowfall usually does not accumulate appreciably during the winter. At lower

elevations, ponderosa pine trees are often interspersed with piñon, juniper, and oak; in other cases, open ponderosa pine woodlands dominate the landscape at the grassland-foothill ecotone, or boundary (Dick-Peddie 1993; Knight 1994). At higher elevations and in mesic (wet) sites, stands can grow fairly dense, often mixing with other tree species such as lodgepole pine (*Pinus contorta*), Douglas fir (*Pseudotsoga menziesii*), or aspen (*Populous tremuloides*) (Veblen et al. 2000).

Frequent, low-intensity surface fires historically thinned many ponderosa pine forests, maintaining fire-adapted trees that grow old and large in open, parklike conditions with grassy understories (Veblen and Lorenz 1991; Covington and Moore 1994). However, in some locations in the Southern Rockies, especially on cooler, more mesic sites, denser stands of ponderosa pine also experienced a mixed-fire regime with occasional stand-replacing fires (Veblen et al. 2000; Brown et al. 1999). Ponderosa pine is also susceptible to mountain pine beetle (*Dendroctonus ponderosae*) outbreaks that are capable of killing trees over large areas (Schmid and Mata 1996).

Understory shrubs include kinnikinnick (*Arctostaphylos uva-ursi*), common juniper (*Juniperus communis*), mountain mahogany, wax currant (*Ribes cereum*), and numerous herbaceous plants and other understory plants such as mountain muhly (*Muhlenbergia montana*), Arizona fescue (*Festuca arizonica*), Oregon grape (*Mahonia repens*), wild geranium (*Geranium* spp.), pasqueflower (*Pulsatilla patens*), and mountain ball cactus (*Pediocactus simpsonii*).

Ponderosa pine forests also support a rich diversity of animals. Characteristic species include the bullsnake (*Pituophus melanoleucus*), eastern fence lizard, flammulated owl (*Otus flammeolus*), Mexican spotted owl (*Strix occidentalis lucida*), Lewis's woodpecker (*Melanerpes lewis*), Williamson's sapsucker (*Sphyrapicus thyroideus*), Steller's jay (*Cyanocitta stelleri*), mountain bluebird (*Sialia currucoides*), western tanager (*Piranga ludoviciana*), red crossbill (*Loxia curvirostra*), pygmy nuthatch (*Sitta pygmaea*), mountain chickadee (*Poecile gambeli*), solitary vireo (*Vireo solitarius*), black bear, puma, long-eared myotis (*Myotis evotis*), mule deer, porcupine (*Erethizon dorsatum*), Abert's squirrel (*Sciurus aberti*), least chipmunk (*Tamias minimus*), and golden-mantled ground squirrel (*Spermophilus lateralis*).

Historical and current logging has substantially reduced old-growth ponderosa pine forest; probably less than 5 percent remain in the Southern Rockies (Shinneman et al. 2000), and most remain in small, isolated patches (Romme et al. 2000). Old forest conditions support species such as Abert's squirrel and Mexican spotted owl. In many areas, logging, fire exclusion, and overgrazing have created dense stands of younger trees susceptible to unnaturally large, catastrophic fires and insect outbreaks (Harrington and Sackett 1992; Romme et al. 2000). Managers have used thinning techniques (logging) and prescribed fire to return some of these altered forests to their presettlement structures and composition (Covington and Moore 1994), especially around residential development (US Forest Service 1997a, 2000; City of Boulder 1999). However, this approach may be ecologically misguided in areas where naturally dense forests exist that historically experienced stand-replacing fires, especially in more mesic sites and at upper elevations (Veblen et al. 2000; Brown et al. 1999). Vegetation restoration efforts should retain remaining old trees; not increase road densities or edge habitat; maintain interior habitat, roadless areas, and landscape structures; and prevent the spread of weedy species (Shinneman and Baker 2000; Romme et al. 2000).

Other significant human impacts in ponderosa pine forests include heavy recreation, extensive road networks, and rapidly increasing residential development that significantly fragments ponderosa pine forest habitats in places such as Colorado's Front Range foothills (Shinneman et al. 2000; Theobald 2000). Only about 4 percent of these forests fall under protected land status in the ecoregion (table 9.1).

DOUGLAS FIR FOREST

Douglas fir forests cover just over 2 percent of the ecoregion. They generally occur between 1,700 and 2,700 m (5,610 and 8,910 ft.), usually on cooler and less xeric (dry) sites than ponderosa pine, although the two trees often occur together (Goldblum and Veblen 1992) (table 9.1, figure 9.3). At the higher end of its elevation range and on north-facing slopes at lower elevations, Douglas fir forms pure stands, but it can also be found with blue spruce (*Picea pungens*), aspen, Rocky Mountain juniper, and lodgepole pine (Benedict 2008). In the southern part of the ecoregion, Douglas fir is often codominant with white fir (*Abies concolor*) (Dick-Peddie 1993). On exposed ridgetops and dry south-facing slopes, Douglas fir can exist in open, park-like stands along with limber pine (*Pinus flexilis*) and bristlecone pine (*Pinus aristata*) (Benedict 2008; Knight 1994).

Historically, low-intensity surface fires occurred regularly, maintaining stands of large, old, fire-tolerant trees on drier sites (Goldblum and Veblen 1992). In addition, occasional large stand-replacing fires occurred when sufficient moisture supported dense forest stands (Veblen et al. 2000). Other disturbance agents include outbreaks of western spruce budworm (*Choristoneura occidentalis*) and Douglas fir bark beetles (*Dendroctonus pseudotsugae*), which are capable of defoliating or killing Douglas fir trees over large areas (Schmid and Mata 1996).

Several shrub species commonly thrive in these forests, including common juniper, ninebark, snowberry, Rocky Mountain maple (*Acer glabrum*), mountain lover (*Paxistima myrsinites*), thimbleberry (*Rubacer parviflorus*), Oregon grape (*Berberis repens*), and wild rose (*Rosa woodsii*). Herbaceous understories often include heart-leaved arnica (*Arnica cordifolia*) and Arizona fescue, while in more moist locations, especially north-facing slopes and narrow ravines, numerous species of lichen and mosses, such as old man's beard (*Usnea hirta*), are found.

Animal species are similar to those found in other montane coniferous forests. Characteristic species include northern goshawk (*Accipter gentilis*), hairy woodpecker (*Picoides villosus*), hermit thrush (*Catharus guttatus*), dark-eyed juncos (*Junco hyemalis*), ruby-crowned kinglet (*Regulus calendula*), elk, pine squirrel (*Tamiasciurus hudsonicus*), and red-backed voles (*Clethrionomys gapperi*).

Similar to ponderosa pine, these Douglas fir forests suffer from the effects of historical fire suppression, logging and loss of old-growth habitat, heavy recreation, and residential development. Only about 4 percent of these forests are protected in the ecoregion (table 9.1).

LODGEPOLE PINE FOREST

Lodgepole pine forests cover almost 7 percent of the Southern Rockies, mainly in the northern half of the ecoregion, where they are extensive (table 9.1, figure 9.3). These forests exist in only scattered patches in southern Colorado and not at all in northern New Mexico (except where planted). They generally occur between 2,600 and 3,000 m (8,580 and 9,900 ft.). Lodgepole pine grows under a variety of conditions but can dominate on cool, dry sites while co-occurring with spruce and fir on more mesic sites (Knight 1994). Snowfall can be heavy at these elevations, while summers are typically warm with intermittent periods of drought (Knight 1994).

Lodgepole pine forests are often considered pioneer forests (in an early successional stage), though recurring stand-replacing fires may perpetuate lodgepole pine over other tree species that grow in the understory of mature stands, such as Douglas fir, Engelmann spruce (*Picea engelmannii*), and subalpine fir (*Abies lasiocarpa*) (Knight 1994). Fires vary in size and intensity in these forests, creating spatially complex mosaics of mature forest and relatively open, unevenaged stand conditions (Knight 1994). Infrequent stand-replacing fires can burn tens of thousands of hectares, and subsequent regeneration, especially when coupled with phenotypes (the physical form of the trees) possessing serotinous cones (cones that remain closed until opened by intense heat), often results in large patches of even-aged forest with dense stands of sapling and pole-sized trees (Kipfmueller and Baker 2000). Foresters often refer to such forest stands as doghair stands.

Other disturbance agents capable of destroying stands over large expanses include windthrow, mountain pine beetle (previously called bark beetles), and disease (Knight 1994; Schmid and Mata 1996). Dwarf mistletoe (*Arceuthobium americanum*), a parasitic plant, can deform and reduce vigor in individual trees over large areas, but it also provides an important source of food, cover, and nesting sites for many species of wildlife (Kipfmueller and Baker 1998).

Because these forests often grow as dense stands with closed-canopy conditions, lodgepole understory may be sparse; however, common forbs and shrubs include heart-leaved arnica (*Arnica cordifolia*), pine drops (*Pterospora andromedea*), grouse whortleberry (*Vaccinium scoparium*), wild rose; kinnikinnick, common juniper, and buffaloberry (*Shepherdia canadensis*).

Typical animal species include sharp-shinned hawk, Steller's jay, gray jay (*Perisoreus canadensis*), white-breasted nuthatch (*Sitta carolinensis*), Clark's nutcracker (*Nucifraga columbiana*), downy woodpecker (*Picoides pubescens*), brown creeper (*Certha americana*), pine siskin (*Carduelis pinus*), ruby-crowned kinglet, elk, black bear, pine marten, mule deer, pine squirrel, southern red-backed vole (*Myodes gapperi*), and porcupine.

Clear-cutting and shelterwood logging (i.e., leaving selected trees to provide seeds for regeneration and shelter for seedlings) combined with extensive road building have severely fragmented many of the ecoregion's lodgepole pine forests (Reed et al. 1996) (see spruce-fir forests, below, for associated ecological effects). In addition, people continue to build homes in and near these mountain forest habitats, restricting the ability of land managers to allow naturally occurring large fires to burn unimpeded. The presence of these homes leads to fire exclusion, controlled burns, and thinning, all of which may alter forest composition, structure, and natural function. Roughly 14 percent of these forests exist on protected lands (table 9.1), but it is unlikely that the full diversity of the lodgepole pine community is represented within these areas. In addition, many protected forests are not large enough or sufficiently connected to provide for unimpeded natural disturbance regimes or movement of native species.

ASPEN FOREST

Aspen forests comprise 8 percent of the Southern Rockies (table 9.1, figure 9.3). Aspen forests are deciduous and are most common between 2,400 and 3,000 m (7,920 and 9,900 ft.). They can occur under a wide range of site conditions, but forests of large aspen trees generally occur in moist, cool sites. Aspen forests often occur in small groves but can form extensive stands, especially in the southern and western portions of the Southern Rockies.

Aspen often become established after a disturbance such as fire destroys other forest types. They typically precede (in successional stage) conifer species such as Douglas fir and spruce, which grow in the understories of shady aspen groves (Romme et al.

2001). However, under certain conditions, aspen also form stable, pure stands and sometimes maintain old forest conditions for long periods (Knight 1994; Romme et al. 2001). Aspen are susceptible to fungal diseases, numerous leaf-eating insects, and browsing by deer and elk, which eat aspen bark and sprouts.

Species composition varies depending on site conditions; in drier areas stands often have grassy understories, while under moist conditions thick forb cover develops, including lupine (*Lupinus* spp.), columbine (*Aquilegia* spp.), wild geranium, heartleaf arnica, and cow parsnip (*Heracleum sphondylium*).

Aspen forests support a rich diversity of mammals and birds (DeByle 1985), including black bear, silver-haired bat (*Lasionycteris noctivagans*), elk, mule deer, deer mouse, western jumping mouse (*Zapus princeps*), northern pocket gopher (*Thomomys talpoides*), long-tailed vole (*Microtus longicaudus*), and masked shrew (*Sorex cinereus*). Beaver (*Castor canadensis*) depend on aspen for food and dam-building material. Dozens of songbird species prefer to nest in old aspen forests, including many cavity nesting birds such as the red-naped sapsucker (*Sphyrapicus nuchalis*), purple martin (*Progne subis*), mountain bluebird, violet-green swallow (*Tachycineta thalassina*), white-breasted nuthatch, and house wren (*Troglodytes aedon*). Aspen forests also support a rich diversity of insects (Jones et al. 1985).

Increased interest in logging old aspen forests, especially on Colorado's Western Slope, may eliminate large stands of mature trees upon which many cavity nesting songbirds, hawks, and owls depend (Finch and Ruggiero 1993). Livestock grazing, overgrazing by elk, and fire exclusion may negatively alter stand structure, composition, and regeneration (Knight 1994). For instance, overgrazing on winter range by overabundant elk herds in portions of Rocky Mountain National Park in Colorado—perhaps exacerbated by the sedentary behavior of elk in the absence of coursing predators (e.g., wolves)—contributes to the mortality of established aspen trees and prevents regeneration of new stands (Baker et al. 1997; Singer and Zeigenfuss 2002). Increased levels of residential development fragment and replace these forests (Theobald 2000). Roughly 9 percent of aspen forests are protected in the ecoregion (table 9.1).

MIXED-CONIFER AND GENERAL-CONIFER FOREST

Broadly defined, mixed-conifer forests occur throughout the Southern Rockies, but ecologists apply the term to the ecoregion's middle elevation (2,270–2,900 m, or 7,491–9,504 ft.) conifer stands in southern Colorado and northern New Mexico (figure 9.3). These mixed-conifer stands cover about 4 percent of the ecoregion (table 9.1) and a variety of tree species dominate them, including ponderosa pine, white fir, Douglas fir, southwestern white pine (*Pinus strobiformus*), bristlecone pine, corkbark fir (*Abies lasiocarpa* var. *arizonica*), Engelmann spruce, and blue spruce.

Mixed-conifer forests generally grow under more mesic and cool conditions than do foothill forests, but site conditions dictate the various combinations and abundances of conifer species that may occur. Due to their relatively mesic conditions and dense stand structures, these forests were historically subjected to less frequent fires than many ponderosa pine forests and experienced a mixed fire regime with occasional stand-replacing fires (Jamieson et al. 1996; Dick-Peddie 1993). Western spruce budworm and Douglas fir bark beetle infections also create significant disturbances (Lynch and Swetnam 1992). Because of the diversity of conifers, understory plant species and animal composition are also diverse and somewhat characteristic of other conifer forests. Animal species include Abert's squirrel, pine squirrel, white-breasted nuthatches, pygmy nuthatches, Mexican spotted owl, black bear, mule deer, and porcupine.

Similar to ponderosa pine and Douglas fir forests, these forests suffer from the effects of fire exclusion, logging, road building, loss of old-growth habitat, heavy recreation, and residential development. Roughly 11 percent of these forests are protected (table 9.1).

MONTANE AND INTERMONTANE GRASSLANDS

Montane and intermontane grasslands make up about 8 percent of the ecoregion (table 9.1). While these ecosystems are generally dominated by grasses, they may also blend with sagebrush communities or transition into meadows with significant forb cover (table 9.1). Montane grasslands are generally found as small to medium-sized patches among forest ecosystems (figure 9.3). Fires and other disturbances create some meadows, but most likely result from dry, cold growing conditions and nutrient-poor soils that won't support trees (Knight 1994). Intermontane grasslands typically occur in large mountain valleys and mountain "parks" characterized by dry and cold growing conditions. These grasslands can cover hundreds of square kilometers, such as in South Park, North Park, the Wet Mountain Valley, and grasslands along the fringes of the San Luis Valley in Colorado.

Plant species include bunchgrasses such as Idaho fescue (*Festuca idahoensis*) and Thurber fescue (*Festuca thurberi*) in the north and Arizona fescue to the south. Other common grasses include Junegrass, needle-and-thread grass, oat grass (*Danthonia* spp.), and mountain muhly. Many shrubs are common, especially big sagebrush species. These grasslands also often contain numerous wildflowers such as lupine, yarrow (*Achillea lanulsa*), golden banner (*Thermopsis montana*), Colorado loco (*Oxytropis lambertii*), paintbrush (*Castilleja* spp.), harebell (*Campanula* spp.), false hellbore (*Veratrum tenuipetalum*), penstemon (*Penstemon* spp.), and monkshood (*Aconitum columbianum*).

Bird species include red-tailed hawk (*Buteo jamaicensis*), mountain bluebird (*Sialia currucoides*), and broad-tailed hummingbird (*Selasphorus platycercus*). South Park's large grassland patches support breeding populations of the imperiled mountain plover.

These grassland ecosystems often provide important forage for mammal species such as elk, mule deer, and pronghorn. Carnivore species include coyotes, badgers, and historically a heavy presence of wolves (Fitzgerald et al. 1994; Bennett 1994). Other species include mountain cottontail, white-tailed jackrabbit (*Lepus townsendii*), northern pocket gopher, long-tailed vole, masked shrew, Gunnison's prairie dog, white-tailed prairie dog, and Wyoming ground squirrel. Fire and drought were likely the major natural disturbances in these ecosystems, and many grasslands evolved with herbivory by bison, elk, deer, and antelope (Neely et al. 2001; Knight 1994).

Intermountain grasslands probably did not evolve under heavy herbivory by bison, as occurred on the Great Plains. Heavy livestock grazing thus has reduced forage cover and production in many areas. It has also spread nonnative weeds such as Kentucky bluegrass (*Poa pratensis*), Russian thistle (*Salsola australis*), and cheatgrass (Fleischner 1994; Weddel 1996).

Off-road vehicles, housing development, and fire exclusion have also degraded and fragmented intermountain grasslands. Only about 4 percent of intermontane and 1 percent of montane grasslands are protected, leaving these grasslands poorly represented in protected areas (table 9.1).

LIMBER PINE AND
BRISTLECONE PINE FOREST

The area of unique limber and bristlecone pine forests amounts to less than 1 percent of the ecoregion (table 9.1). They are usually found from 2,300 m (7,590 ft.) up to tree line and grow under harsh conditions, typically on high-elevation south-facing slopes, exposed ridges, and rocky outcrops with windy, dry, sunny exposures and short growing seasons (figure 9.3) (DeVelice et al. 1986; Benedict 2008; Dick-Peddie 1993). Limber pine and bristlecone pine occur in relatively pure stands, together as codominants or with other conifer species such as Douglas fir, lodgepole pine, Engelmann spruce, and subalpine fir. Bristlecone pine is found mainly in the southern two-thirds of the ecoregion. While these forests do not typically form extensive stands, they do occasionally occur in large patches in places such as the Sangre de Cristo Mountains. Due to severe growing conditions, these forests are often sparse with open canopies. Bristlecone pine trees can live 2,000 years or longer in the Southern Rockies (Benedict 2008).

The understory is generally sparse, with herbaceous species such as Arizona fescue, Junegrass, mountain muhly, sedum (*Amerosedum lanceolatum*), and common alumroot (*Huechera parvifolia*) and characteristic shrubs such as serviceberry, common juniper, and sticky laurel (*Ceanothus velutinus*). Limber pine seeds are an important food source for Clark's nutcrackers and gray jays. Clark's nutcrackers are important to the reproduction and dispersal of five-needle pines. In general, animal species found in these forests are similar to those of other mountain coniferous forests.

Many of these forests remain relatively unaltered because the trees are generally undesirable as timber due to twisted wood grain and because the rugged, inhospitable sites make development and road building difficult. However, in some areas overgrazing has denuded fragile soils and the already sparse understory plant communities. Roughly 6 percent of these forests are protected in the ecoregion (table 9.1). Blister rust, a disease of five-needled pines, has now arrived from Eurasia, and some researchers anticipate that it will eliminate 98 percent of the five-needled pines before it runs its course (J. Mitten, pers. comm.). The mutualistic relationship between jays and five-needled pines may be broken during this decline, costing the pines their method of dispersal and the jays and nutcrackers a critical food source.

ENGELMANN SPRUCE AND SUBALPINE FIR FORESTS

Spruce-fir forests often form vast high-elevation matrix communities and make up nearly 14 percent of the Southern Rockies (table 9.1, figure 9.3). They generally occur from 2,700 m (8,910 ft.) to tree line on cool, moist sites where most precipitation falls as abundant snow. Found throughout the ecoregion, Engelmann spruce and subalpine fir sometimes grow in pure stands of either species, but they are typically codominate tree species (Knight 1994). In other cases, spruce-fir forests are interspersed with lodgepole pine, limber pine, or aspen. Stunted, windswept versions of these forests, called krummholz, intersperse with alpine tundra at tree line.

Spruce-fir forests experience stand-replacing crown fires, capable of burning thousands of hectares, every few hundred years on average. In addition, spruce beetle (*Dendroctonus rufipennis*) outbreaks can kill most mature trees over hundreds of thousands of hectares (Baker and Veblen 1990; Veblen et al. 1994; Schmid and Mata 1996; Kipfmueller and Baker 2000). Windthrow and wood-rotting fungi are other notable disturbance agents. Due to variability in disturbance, presettlement spruce-fir forest landscapes probably contained a complex mosaic of various stand ages, including substantial old growth (Rebertus et al. 1992). Old-growth forest stands have complex forest structures with various-sized standing trees and numerous downed dead trees, with many large canopy trees 300 to 500 years old (Veblen

et al. 1994; Mehl 1992). Large patches of old-growth forests probably existed in many locations prior to Euro-American settlement, especially in topographically sheltered locations less susceptible to windthrow and fire (Knight and Reiners 2000).

Depending on stand conditions, understory vegetation ranges from dense to open and patchy and includes blueberry (*Vaccinium* spp.), common juniper, mountain lover, wild rose, and numerous herbs such as heart-leaved arnica, wood nymph (*Moneses uniflora*), and lady's slipper (*Cypripedium fasciculatum*).

Representative animal species include boreal owl (*Aegolius funereus*), northern goshawk, mountain chickadee, red crossbill, blue grouse (*Dendragapus obscurus*), Townsend's solitaire (*Myadestes townsendi*), olive-sided flycatcher (*Contopus cooperi*), golden-crowned kinglet (*Regulus satrapa*), hermit thrush (*Catharus guttatus*), elk, black bear, pine marten, southern red-backed vole, pine squirrel, and snowshoe hare (*Lepus americanus*). The ecoregion's historic populations of Canada lynx (*Lynx canadensis*) and wolverine (*Gulo gulo*) also inhabited these forests (Seidel et al. 1998).

Logging and associated road building have fragmented and reduced formerly extensive interior forest habitat and old growth and have altered forest stand structure and composition (Reed et al. 1996; Knight and Reiners 2000). Much of the Medicine Bow National Forest in Wyoming and portions of the Rio Grande National Forest in southern Colorado offer good examples of harvest levels that led to extensive habitat fragmentation (Reed et al. 1996; US Forest Service 1998; Shinneman et al. 2000). In addition, inappropriate clear-cutting practices often inhibit stand regeneration (Reed et al. 1996; US Forest Service 1998).

Recreation is a concern in many areas, including summer and winter use by off-road vehicles and ski-area development and expansion (Knight 2000). In some areas, highly fragmented forests and loss of old growth have led to subsequent declines in populations of old growth and forest-interior-dependent species, including the goshawk, boreal owl, and pine marten (Reynolds et al. 1992; Hayward 1994; Buskirk and Ruggiero 1994).

Because people have long appreciated these scenic high-mountain forests, roughly 30 percent fall within protected land management categories (table 9.1). Land managers should give more consideration to including the full diversity of spruce-fir associated species and natural communities, maintaining natural processes, restoring old forest conditions and interior habitat, and connecting forest habitats across the regional landscape.

ALPINE SYSTEMS

Alpine systems are found throughout the ecoregion above tree line, about 3,000 m (9,900 ft.) (figure 9.3). These cold, windswept ecosystems receive substantial precipitation, mostly in the form of snow. In many cases, however, persistent high winds sweep snow away, limiting moisture availability. Alpine conditions are typically patchy, with localized topographic diversity and different plant communities occurring under different site conditions resulting in a rich mosaic of alpine wetlands, dry meadows, snowfields, fell-fields, talus and scree slopes, rock faces, and krummholz forests (Knight 1994; Benedict 2008). Alpine habitats represent approximately 6 percent of the ecoregion (table 9.1).

In general, alpine ecosystems remain relatively stable, but natural disturbances include soil movement, spring snowmelt, expanding snowfields, and burrowing impacts from small mammals such as pocket gophers (Knight 1994). Grizzly bears also historically foraged in alpine areas, digging for roots, rodents, and other food sources (Fitzgerald et al. 1994). Due to the harsh and brief growing season, succession after disturbance often takes hundreds of years.

Plant communities vary with moisture availability, snow cover duration, solar radiation, and wind exposure. Plants are dominated by low-growing shrubs and perennial herbs, including cushion plants, forbs, sedges, and grasses. Representative species include barren ground willow (*Salix brachycarpa*), Arctic willow (*Salix arctica*), planaleaf willow (*Salix planifolia*), tufted hairgrass (*Deschampsia cespitosa*), alpine bluegrass (*Poa alpina*), kobresia (*Kobresia myosuroides*), Rocky Mountain sedge (*Carex scopulorum*), moss campion (*Silene acaulis*), alpine avens (*Acomastylis rossii*), Parry's clover (*Trifolium paryii*), alpine phlox (*Phlox pulvinata*), alpine sorrel (*Oxyria digyna*), snowlover (*Chionophila jamesii*), American bistort (*Bistorta bistortoides*), Arctic gentian (*Gentianodes algida*), alpine lousewort (*Pedicularis scopulorum*), marsh marigold (*Psychrophila leptosepala*), and rose crown (*Clementsia rhodantha*). Lichens and mosses are also common.

Characteristic animal species include white-tailed ptarmigan (*Lagopus leucurus*), brown-capped rosy finch (*Leucosticte australis*), white-crowned sparrow (*Zonotrichia leucophrys*), American pipit (*Anthus rubescens*), horned lark (*Eremophila alpestris*), common raven (*Corvus corax*), golden eagle, short-tailed weasel (*Mustela erminea*), bighorn sheep (*Ovis canadensis*), elk, yellow-bellied marmot (*Marmota flaviventris*), pika (*Ochotona princeps*), northern pocket gopher, and montane shrew (*Sorex monticolus*).

In many areas, especially in the southern portion of the ecoregion, grazing by domestic sheep has damaged fragile native alpine vegetation. Dramatic increases in recreation, especially off-road vehicle use and "peak bagging" by hikers, can also trample and destroy alpine vegetation and cause severe erosion. Formerly, wolverines roamed alpine habitats and the grizzly bear played a major ecological role in alpine areas; both are considered extirpated from the ecoregion (Fitzgerald et al. 1994). Alpine systems are generally well represented in protected areas, exceeding 50 percent (table 9.1).

WETLAND AND
RIPARIAN SYSTEMS

The Southern Rockies contain a diverse but uncommon range of aquatic, wetland, and riparian ecosystem types (table 9.1). These terms are sometimes used interchangeably because these ecosystems are often ephemeral, overlapping, and transitional in nature. For instance, the shallow and ephemeral playa lakes in the San Luis Valley are typically classified as wetlands. Although aquatic ecosystems tend to be small patches and linear features on the landscape and collectively constitute a small portion the ecoregion's surface area, one thing is clear: despite their small size, these ecosystems are among the most valuable to native species in the Southern Rockies.

The Southern Rockies contain thousands of kilometers of streams and rivers dispersed throughout the ecoregion, from fast, clear high-mountain streams to slower-moving low-elevation rivers. Natural lakes, called tarns, in the Southern Rockies generally occur above 2,700 m (8,910 ft.) and were formed behind terminal moraines or in depressions left by past glacial activity (Benedict 2008). Ponds are also abundant at higher elevations. In addition, there are hundreds of reservoirs, some quite deep, covering thousands of hectares, many in lower elevations that were historically devoid of deepwater lakes (Shinneman et al. 2000).

Wetlands occur throughout the ecoregion. A wetland can be defined as an area that is covered by water for at least part of the year. There, plants and animals are adapted to life in water or in saturated soils (Cowardin et al. 1979). Wetlands in the Southern Rockies include forested wetlands, willow carrs, fens, marshes, bogs, alpine snow glades, wet meadows, salt meadows, bottomland shrublands, shallow ponds, and playa lakes. Many of the wetlands in the Southern Rockies are seasonal, resulting from spring snowmelt and high water tables. Wet meadows account for the largest acreage of wetlands in Colorado (Jones and Cooper 1993).

Riparian ecosystems are a special type of wetland occurring along the upland margins of streams, rivers, and lakes, and they represent the meeting place of aquatic and terrestrial ecosystems. Riparian ecosystems are distributed throughout the ecoregion at all elevations, from narrow linear communities in deep canyons to more extensive forests in broad floodplains. Roughly 3 percent to 8 percent of the Southern Rockies occur within streamside riparian habitat (Shinneman et al. 2000).

All of these different aquatic ecosystem types are actually interconnected hydrologic systems influenced by the ecoregion's geology, soils, topography, weather, plant communities, and even animals. For instance, during spring peak flow, streams overflow their channels and inundate adjacent floodplains, providing water to wetlands. Water from wetlands and streams replenishes groundwater reserves. In a reciprocal fashion, during times of low precipitation, riparian areas and wetlands serve as sources of water recharge for creeks and streams, and groundwater may supply water to streams and wetlands via seeps, springs, and direct stream-water recharge (Maxwell et al. 1995).

The beaver, an aquatic keystone species (ecosystem engineer), also contributes to aquatic habitat, by creating ponds that benefit and support diverse assemblages of species and natural communities. These ponds trap and store organic material, nutrients, and sediment that build up over time and transform areas into riparian communities, marshes, wet meadows, and eventually even dry meadows. Streams with more beaver dams also maintain higher late-summer stream flows, which benefit fish, wildlife, and even landowners in the Southern Rockies (Knight 1994).

Aquatic-dependent species and communities have adapted to and depend on dynamic and interconnected hydrologic systems. For example, groundwater recharge to streams and wetlands is often crucial to the survival of aquatic plants and animals in the Southern Rockies during dry periods (Cooper 1993; Power et al. 1997). Meandering stream flows and periodic high river flows (especially floods) alter riparian habitats by both destroying and rebuilding streamside landforms such as oxbows, cut banks, point bars, islands, and terraces. These hydrologic processes provide the main vehicle for establishing cottonwood (*Populus* spp.) riparian forests by building new point bars with nutrient-rich sediment layers that are beneficial to seedling development and by distributing cottonwood seeds onto these new landforms (Knight 1994). The dynamic mosaics of riparian and floodplain habitat in various successional stages are also required by many other aquatic and riparian-associated species (Gutzwiller and Anderson 1987; Baker and Walford 1995).

Riparian vegetation in turn provides shade for rivers and streams, creating cooler air and water temperatures that aquatic species such as native fish require. Riparian vegetation that falls into streams provides sources of food and nutrients for fish, insects, and other organisms. Riparian root systems deter stream bank erosion by decreasing the velocity of water flow and by trapping nutrients and sediments that build stream banks and form nutrient-rich wet meadows and floodplains (Cheney et al. 1990).

Native species compositions vary considerably among the many types of aquatic ecosystems in the region. Lower elevation shallow lakes and ponds in the Southern Rockies, which tend to be richer in oxygen, organic matter, and other nutrients, support species such as yellow pondlily (*Nuphar luteum*), arrowhead (*Sagittaria* spp.), duckweed (*Lemna* spp.), northern leopard frog

(*Rana pipiens*), wood frog (*Rana sylvatica*), tiger salamander (*Ambystoma tigrinum*), and numerous macroinvertebrates such as crayfish, insects, snails, clams, and leeches. Plant and animal plankton also populate these waters. Deep, cold mountain lakes typically provide habitat for fewer but no less-important species, including the ecoregion's native cutthroat trout (*Oncorhynchus clarki*).

Streams support different species compositions depending on factors such as channel width and depth, oxygen availability, velocity, turbidity, volume, and temperature. For instance, native greenback (*Oncorhynchus clarki stomias*), Colorado River (*Oncorhynchus clarki pleuriticus*), and Rio Grande cutthroat trout (*Oncorhynchus virginalis*) depend on the clear, cold, well-oxygenated streams with riffles and pools that occur at higher elevations. In contrast, slower, more turbid, less oxygen-rich, and warmer rivers at lower elevations contain native fish such as the roundtail chub (*Gila robusta*), razorback sucker (*Xyrauchen texanus*), and Colorado pikeminnow (*Ptychocheilus lucius*).

The river otter (*Lutra canadensis*) depends on larger streams and rivers, and the beaver plays an important role by affecting stream habitats and hydrology. Species such as the American dipper (*Cinclus mexicanus*), muskrat (*Ondatra zibethicus*), and water shrew (*Sorex palustris*) are also found in streams. Macroinvertebrate insect species such as caddisfly, mayfly, and stonefly nymphs fulfill important roles in the aquatic food web, as do numerous microinvertebrate species and algae.

The many types of wetlands in the ecoregion offer diverse, important, and varied habitat for numerous plants and animals, including a wide variety of plant species such as bog birch (*Betula glandulosa*), bitter cress (*Cardimine cordifolia*), crowfoot (*Ranunculus* spp.), reedgrass (*Calamagrotis* spp.), horsetail (*Equisetum* spp.), bog orchid (*Limnorchis* spp.), and yellow pondlily, as well as numerous species of willows (*Salix* spp.), sedges

(*Carex* spp.), rushes (*Juncus* spp.), and pond-weeds (*Potamogeton* spp.).

These wetlands host amphibian species such as northern leopard frog, tiger salamander, and boreal toad (*Bufo boreas*). Many lower elevation wetlands, including the San Luis Valley's marshes and playa lakes, provide important stopover sites for thousands of migratory waterfowl and shorebirds such as sandhill crane (*Grus canadensis tabeda*), avocet (*Recurvirostra americana*), snowy egret (*Egretta thula*), green-winged teal (*Anas crecca*), and northern pintail (*Anas acuta*). Numerous insect species and other macroinvertebrates also inhabit the ecoregion's wetlands, such as clams, fairy shrimp, flatworms, water striders, and mosquito larvae. Microscopic plant and animal plankton are also abundant, especially in nutrient-rich waters.

As with other aquatic ecosystems, the species composition of riparian communities varies with soils, landforms, and elevation. Whether riparian areas are narrow willow communities in steep mountain canyons or extensive cottonwood forests in broad low-elevation valleys, they tend to be extremely rich in species diversity relative to surrounding upland communities. More deciduous tree and shrub species occur in riparian ecosystems than in any other ecosystem in the Southern Rockies and include narrowleaf cottonwood (*Populus angustifolia*), plains cottonwood (*Populus deltoides*), box elder (*Negundo aceroides*), Rocky Mountain maple, red-osier dogwood (*Swida sericea*), mountain alder (*Alnus incana tenuifolia*), gooseberry (*Ribes inerme*), river birch (*Betula fontinalis*), bog birch (*Betula glanulosa*), New Mexican locust (*Robinia neomexicana*), shrubby cinquefoil (*Pentaphylloides floribunda*), and dozens of species of willows. Conifer species such as blue spruce and white fir are often found. Numerous species of forbs, grasses, sedges, rushes, mosses, lichens, fungi, and liverworts also typify many riparian areas.

Riparian communities support up to 80 percent of all animal species in the ecoregion. These species depend on riparian habitats for food, water, shelter, and other important life history needs, such as breeding or nesting (Olson and Gerhart 1982; Floyd-Hannah et al. 1996). Characteristic reptiles and amphibians include tiger salamander; northern leopard frog; wood frog; bull snake (*Pituophis* spp.); and smooth green snake (*Opheodrys vernalis*).

Characteristic birds include red-tailed hawk, northern harrier (*Circus cyaneus*), kingfisher (*Ceryle alcyon*), great blue heron (*Ardea herodias*), western grebe (*Aechmophorus occidentalis*), green-winged teal, American dipper, Lincoln's sparrow (*Melospiza lincolnii*), northern oriole (*Icterus galbula*), yellow warbler (*Dendroica petechia*), Wilson's warbler (*Wilsonia pusilla*), and tree swallow (*Tachycineta bicolor*). More songbird species nest in riparian habitat than in any other mountain ecosystem (Mutel and Emerick 1992; Jones and Cooper 1993).

Mammals are also abundant, and include black bear, river otter, mink (*Mustela vison*), mule deer, beaver, meadow jumping mouse (*Zapus hudsonius*), water shrew, and montane vole (*Microtis montanus*). Riparian areas also support a rich assortment of insects, including numerous butterflies and dragonflies.

Human development and water use have destroyed or dramatically altered most species-rich aquatic and riparian ecosystems in the Southern Rockies. As a result, many species at risk of extinction or extirpation in the ecoregion are aquatic-dependent or riparian species. In the American Southwest, for example, although riparian areas comprise only 5 percent of the lands managed by the US Forest Service, 70 percent of the federally threatened and endangered species are dependent upon riparian and aquatic ecosystems (US Forest Service 1997b). In the Southern Rockies, representative riparian and aquatic-dependent species at risk include the boreal toad, Preble's meadow jumping mouse (*Zapus hudsonius preblei*), Rio Grande cutthroat trout, and Ute ladies' tresses (*Spiranthes diluvialis*). There are also hundreds of rare and imperiled wetland and riparian plant communities in the ecoregion (Neely et al. 2001).

Some streams, mountain lakes, and ponds in the Southern Rockies are distant from human-dominated landscapes and remain relatively unpolluted. However, acid deposition from nearby power plants, pesticides and herbicides from agriculture, acid and heavy-metal mine drainage, excess nutrients from septic systems or livestock waste, and increased sedimentation from land uses such as logging, road building, and recreation pollute many other systems. In many areas, overgrazing has destroyed riparian habitat and caused stream bank erosion, thus leading to warmer, more ephemeral, and more sediment-filled waters, which are harmful to native aquatic species (Belsky et al. 1999).

Thousands of water storage and diversion projects in the Southern Rockies have significantly altered stream hydrology, often limiting or eliminating floodwaters. Dams and diversions alter sediment loads, oxygen levels, and water temperatures, and these changes have harmed native aquatic species such as downstream warm-water fish (Osmundson et al. 1995). Dams in the Southern Rockies have also damaged many riparian forest communities by impeding flooding and thus preventing regeneration within aging cottonwood communities. Under the relatively static hydrologic conditions created by dams, shrubby and nonnative species such as tamarisk (*Tamarix* spp.) have invaded and outcompeted cottonwood seedlings. Thus in many places, old cottonwood forests are being replaced by less biologically diverse and weedy species (Somers and Floyd-Hannah 1996). In other cases in the Southern Rockies, engineers have channelized streams, damaging stream ecosystems and destroying riparian habitat.

Before Euro-American settlement, wetlands covered about 3 percent of what is now the state of Colorado, but we have now lost roughly one-third to one-half of the original wetland acreage in Colorado, New Mexico, and Wyoming to human development and conversion to croplands (Dahl 1990; Wilen 1995). Lowered groundwater levels may also lead to the destruction of groundwater-fed springs and seeps that provide water for wildlife and sustain wetland communities. For instance, thousands of hectares of marsh wetlands in the San Luis Valley may be destroyed by existing and proposed groundwater pumping that will lower water tables just one or two meters (three to six feet) (Cooper 1993). Loss of groundwater may also threaten some riparian forests, which depend on the groundwater supply when stream levels have dropped (Cooper 1993; Power et al. 1997).

In addition, several nonnative species threaten native aquatic species in the Southern Rockies. Agencies stock many streams and lakes with nonnative fish species (e.g., sport fish) that alter the food chain by preying upon, outcompeting, or hybridizing with native fish. These exotic fish species threaten all three species of native cutthroat trout (Young 1995). Other nonnative species of concern include the eastern bullfrog (*Rana catesbeiana*), which threatens native frogs, and plants such as purple loosestrife (*Lythhrum salicaria*) (Rosen and Schwalbe 1995; Rutledge and McLendon 1996).

OTHER NOTEWORTHY ECOSYSTEMS
There are many other natural communities nested within the major ecosystems described above (table 9.1), a number of which are rare, highly localized, or limited in extent. For example, regionally unique, active sand dune complexes occur in the San Luis Valley and in North Park. Those in the San Luis Valley, mostly within Great Sand Dunes National Park and Preserve, are composed of

active sand dunes (some more than 200 m, or 660 ft., high) and stabilized sand dune and swale complexes covering thousands of hectares that support numerous unique natural communities and species, including several endemic species of plants and insects (Neely et al. 2001). Other important natural features are the many cliffs, canyons, and barren rock faces scattered throughout the ecoregion. Many birds nest in cliff habitats, such as the peregrine falcon (*Falco peregrinus*) and black swift (*Cypseloides niger*), and unique species of plants are found in these rocky habitats. Fortunately, many of the best examples of the ecoregion's unique, rare, and imperiled communities have been targeted for further conservation action (Neely et al. 2001).

Human-dominated landscapes in the Southern Rockies are also noteworthy. While they extend across less than 6 percent of the land area (table 9.1), they are interspersed throughout the ecoregion (figure 9.3) and exert influences disproportionate to their area. Because the pace of development in the Southern Rockies is rapid and increasing (Theobald 2000, 2001), human-dominated landscapes will continue to exert disproportionate influence over the dynamics of the Southern Rockies Ecoregion.

DIVERSITY AND DISTRIBUTION OF PLANTS AND WILDLIFE

The Southern Rockies are a biological meeting place where species of high-elevation Rocky Mountain ecosystems converge with species from adjacent lowland prairie and semidesert ecosystems to form unique natural communities. The ecoregion is well known for species such as elk, puma, and ponderosa pine, but thousands of lesser-known species also call the Southern Rockies home. Some of these are abundant and widespread throughout almost every major habitat type in the ecoregion. For example, Colorado has the continent's largest elk population, with an estimated 291,960 individuals in 2007 (Colorado Division of Wildlife 2008). The state also supported approximately 614,000 deer in 2005 and a predicted post-hunt population of about 621,000 in 2006 (Kahn 2006). In contrast, other species in the ecoregion are narrowly restricted to particular habitats and locations, like the dependence of Abert's squirrels on dense, old ponderosa pine stands (Fitzgerald et al. 1994).

Shinneman et al. (2000) estimated that there were at least 328 extant native vertebrate species closely associated with the Southern Rockies' mountain habitats, including 203 birds, 90 mammals, 18 fish, 10 reptiles, and 7 amphibians; only two other ecoregions in the United States and Canada have a higher total number of mammal species (Ricketts et al. 1999; Shinneman et al. 2000; Neely et al. 2001). When we add peripheral vertebrate species to the list (i.e., those species more closely associated with the neighboring short-grass prairie or Colorado Plateau regions but occupying the margins of the Southern Rockies), well over 500 vertebrate species inhabit the ecoregion (Shinneman et al. 2000).

Colorado alone boasts more than 2,596 native vascular plants, and lesser-known taxonomic groups may contain thousands more species awaiting recognition or discovery (Weber and Whitman 1992; Stucky-Everson 1997; P. Opler, pers. comm.).

Compared to other ecoregions, the Southern Rockies are rich in bird species. The ecoregion supports the second highest number of lepidopteran species north of Mexico. There are more than 270 species of butterflies and an estimated 5,200 species of moths; this represents over 40 percent of North America's known moth and butterfly species (Kocher et al. 2000; Paul Opler, pers. comm.).

In addition, hundreds of these species are globally rare and many are limited to the Southern Rockies. Examples of species endemic to the Southern Rockies include the San Luis Dunes tiger beetle (*Cicendela theatina*), Jemez Mountains salamander (*Plethodon neomexicanus*), Weber monkeyflower (*Mimulus gemmiparus*), Uncompahgre fritillary (*Boloria improba acrocnema*), greenback cutthroat trout (*Oncorhynchus clarki stomias*), brown-capped rosy finch (*Leucosticte australis*), and even mollusks, such as the banded physa (*Physa utahensis*).

In general, species richness in the Southern Rockies is greatest within lower elevation ecosystems, culminating in low-elevation riparian and aquatic ecosystems. For comparison, more than 450 vertebrate species are associated with Colorado's wetland and riparian communities, 129 with foothill ponderosa pine forests, and 51 with alpine habitat (Shinneman et al. 2000). However, another important consideration is that 40 percent of the ecoregion is within private lands, and these lands typically contain biologically rich lower elevation landscapes. Theobald et al. (1998) determined that in Colorado, species richness is 46 percent higher on private versus public lands.

SPECIES AND COMMUNITIES AT RISK

Persecution, intensive and extensive levels of natural resource use, pollution, and erupting human population levels have led to the extinction of at least four species that once inhabited the ecoregion. These include the yellowfin cutthroat trout (*Salmo clarki macdonaldi*), the Eskimo curlew (*Numenius borealis*), the Carolina parakeet (*Conuropsis carolinensis*) (which visited the southern foothills and plains), and the New Mexico sharp-tailed grouse (*Tympanuchus phasianellus hueyi*) (Shinneman et al. 2000; Neely et al. 2001).

The grizzly bear, gray wolf, wild populations of bison, black-footed ferret, and wolverine are considered extirpated from the Southern Rockies (Shinneman et al. 2000).

The last known wild gray wolf in the ecoregion was shot in the south-central portion of Colorado (Conejos County) by a state hunter in 1945 (Bennett 1994), although in 2004 one of the Yellowstone wolves was killed west of Denver by a car. The Canada lynx was considered extirpated in the ecoregion until a recent restoration effort by the Colorado Division of Wildlife led to the reintroduction of 218 animals from 1999 to 2006. As of August 2008, between 45 and 106 of the reintroduced lynx survived and 116 kittens were born, but there is no information on kitten survival and no litters were produced in 2007 or 2008 (Shenk 2008). At this point, no more lynx reintroductions are planned.

The Rio Grande bluntnose shiner (*Notropis simus simus*), Rio Grande silvery minnow (*Hybognathus amarus*), American eel (*Anguilla rostrata*), freshwater drum (*Aplodinotus grunniens*), sturgeon (*Scaphirhynchus platorynchus*), blue sucker (*Cycleptus elongatus*), Rio Grande shiner (*Notropis jemezanus*), and speckled chub (*Macrhybopsis aestivalis aestivalis*) have also been extirpated (Neely at al. 2001). At least four species of birds that historically bred in the ecoregion no longer do so, including the marbled godwit (*Limosa fedoa*), harlequin duck (*Histrionicus histrionicus*), merlin (*Falco columbarius*), and ring-billed gull (*Larus delawarensis*) (Andrews and Righter 1992; Neely et al. 2001).

At least eight plants, two invertebrates, and ten vertebrate species from the ecoregion are currently listed as threatened or endangered under the Endangered Species Act (Shinneman et al. 2000; US Fish and Wildlife Service 2001a). State natural heritage programs track 101 species native to the Southern Rockies that are globally imperiled, and nearly 300 other species are considered species of special concern due to restricted ranges, population declines, and other vulnerability factors (Neely et al. 2001). Shinneman et al. (2000) reported that of the 328 species closely linked to Southern

Rockies' mountain habitats, the Colorado Natural Heritage Program lists about one-half of the amphibians, one-half of all fish, one-quarter of all birds, and one-fifth of all mammals as vulnerable, imperiled, or critically imperiled.

Finally, as discussed, many natural communities are greatly reduced in extent, natural composition, and function due to activities such as logging, fire exclusion, overgrazing, housing development, agricultural conversion, water use and dams, and pollution. Habitats particularly at risk include old-growth ponderosa pine forest, old aspen forest, low-elevation riparian communities, sagebrush shrublands, montane grasslands, and most wetlands and aquatic systems (Noss et al. 1995; Shinneman et al. 2000; Neely et al. 2001). Fortunately, there is increasing interest in restoring and protecting these ecosystems.

CONCLUSIONS

In the Southern Rockies, few if any ecosystems remain significantly unaltered by humans. Some, such as aquatic and riparian communities, have been severely degraded. Hundreds of native species are of conservation concern. In addition, rapidly increasing human population and development in the Southern Rockies will degrade more ecosystems.

Yet, compared to other areas in the United States, the Southern Rockies Ecoregion still contains many opportunities to protect and restore its vast biological wealth and diversity. Large matrix communities such as subalpine forests remain relatively intact throughout the ecoregion and in similar patterns of distribution as when Euro-Americans first settled the ecoregion.

Despite the negative effects of fire exclusion in some fire-dependent ecosystem types, fifty years of effective fire suppression have probably not significantly altered the forests, woodlands, and other natural communities with long-rotation fire regimes, which typically experience stand-replacing events on the order of hundreds of years (Romme and Despain 1989). Moreover, many areas that experienced significant anthropogenic disturbance in the Southern Rockies such as logging, road building, overgrazing, and even damming and fire exclusion can be restored, especially if they exist on public lands.

As Gosnell and Shinneman (chap. 5) point out, roughly 60 percent of the ecoregion is within public ownership; about 10.5 percent lies within strictly protected reserves, and another 13 percent remains in an unprotected roadless condition. Thus collectively, nearly a quarter of the ecoregion (about 4 million hectares, or 9.9 million acres) remains in a wild or protected condition, and roughly two-thirds (about 10 million hectares, or 25 million acres) receives at least some minimal level of protection as publicly owned lands. Moreover, these public lands are configured in a pattern of relative connectivity across the landscape.

Thus, a key strategy for protecting and restoring wide-ranging species such as wolves and large landscape natural processes in the Southern Rockies includes protecting ecologically strategic public landscapes that remain at risk, such as roadless lands and wetlands. Also, working with willing landowners would conserve biologically important habitat areas on private lands. Finally, restoring chokepoints that sever the region's connectedness, such as sections of highways, would enhance wildlife movement.

Ecosystem Type	Area (ha)	% of Southern Rockies Land Area	% on Public Lands	% in Protected* Lands	% in Protected & Roadless** Lands
Semidesert and Sagebrush Shrublands					
-Winterfat Shrub Steppe	297,956	1.80%	60.50%	7.00%	10.70%
-Sagebrush Steppe	246,608	1.50%	52.60%	2.20%	7.40%
-Greasewood Flat and Ephemeral Meadow Complex	180,668	1.10%	24.10%	14.70%	14.80%
-Mountain Sagebrush Shrubland	1,278,653	7.70%	50.10%	2.50%	7.20%
Piñon-Juniper Woodland					
-Piñon-Juniper Woodland	1,783,025	10.70%	54.70%	4.70%	12.20%
-Juniper Savanna	311,859	1.90%	55.10%	5.90%	17.50%
Mountain Shrublands					
-Lower Montane-Foothills Shrubland	768,274	4.60%	54.80%	9.50%	19.60%
-Gambel Oak Shrubland	641,792	3.80%	42.80%	2.70%	12.30%
-Ponderosa Pine Forest/Woodland	1,988,765	11.90%	50.20%	4.10%	11.60%
-Douglas Fir/Ponderosa Pine Forest	384,613	2.30%	74.20%	3.90%	24.60%
-Lodgepole Pine Forest	1,108,372	6.60%	85.50%	14.30%	38.50%
-Aspen Forest	1,336,616	8.00%	75.00%	9.20%	38.00%
-Montane Mixed Conifer Forest	616,173	3.70%	61.70%	11.30%	22.70%
-Limber Pine and Bristlecone Forest and Woodland	77,994	0.50%	47.50%	5.80%	10.40%
-Spruce/Fir Forest	2,252,216	13.50%	90.20%	30.10%	56.70%
Montane and Intermontane Grasslands					
-Intermontane-Foothill Grassland	833,883	5.00%	29.60%	4.30%	4.70%
-Montane Grassland	497,947	3.00%	37.20%	1.20%	3.70%
Alpine Tundra					
-Alpine Dry Tundra and Moist Meadow	679,726	4.10%	77.80%	34.10%	55.90%
-Alpine Tundra—Dwarf Shrub and Fell Field	125,329	0.80%	97.40%	63.30%	84.30%
-Alpine Substrate—Ice Field	206,537	1.20%	95.10%	70.50%	85.20%
Wetland/Riparian*					
-Marsh and Wet Meadow	18,990	0.10%	40.70%	4.10%	12.20%
-Upper Montane Riparian Forest and Woodland	19,063	0.10%	24.80%	5.70%	14.60%
-Montane Riparian Shrubland	13,244	0.10%	51.00%	28.30%	31.60%
-Foothills Riparian Woodland and Shrubland	5,283	0.00%	14.40%	0.10%	0.10%
Other Natural Landscape Features					
-Active Sand Dune and Swale Complex	10,834	0.10%	92.00%	90.20%	90.20%
-Stabilized Sand Dune	38,336	0.20%	44.00%	46.00%	46.00%
-Montane-Foothill Cliff and Canyon	20,570	0.10%	70.80%	17.70%	46.10%
Heavily Altered/Human-Dominated Landscapes					
-Agriculture—Dry	59,146	0.40%	12.60%	0.40%	0.50%
-Agriculture—Irrigated	741,714	4.40%	4.90%	1.50%	1.70%
-Recent Clearcut Conifer Forest	68,721	0.40%	93.60%	0.10%	3.70%
-Water	35,347	0.20%	65.40%	1.80%	2.70%
-Urban	26,761	0.20%	19.50%	0.60%	2.60%
-Mining Operation	4,951	0.00%	5.40%	0.00%	0.80%
Totals	**16,679,966**	**100.00%**		**11.70%**	**24.80%**

* All land management types that are within class one and two protected areas

** Includes all USFS inventoried roadless areas, and areas identified by conservationists and included in the Colorado Citizen's Wilderness proposal. Other areas surveyed by conservationists are not included.

*** Due to small patch and narrow linear spatial characteristics, GAP Analysis mapping represents the region's larger wetland and riparian features and, thus, the area and percent values in this table should be considered incomplete.

Table 9.1—Percentages of Southern Rockies ecosystem types by land use designations.

Source: Colorado Gap Analysis Program. 1998. Land cover map. Scale: 1:100,000

Chapter 10

Disease and Translocation Issues of Gray Wolves

Colin M. Gillin and Dave Hunter

INTRODUCTION

This overview of pathogens of North American wolves includes health management considerations for translocations. These health issues encompass potential direct effects of a specific pathogen on wolves. It is also a discussion of pathogens present at potential relocation sites (referred to as endemic or enzootic pathogens or diseases), and the potential to move new diseases via translocation to a naive (i.e., unexposed) population, causing a new disease in existing populations. These diseases are referred to as epidemic (in people) or epizootic (in other animal species) pathogens or diseases. Once a new or novel pathogen is introduced into a wildlife population, control of the pathogen is problematic. We never just translocate a species; we translocate biological packages containing all the external and internal parasites, bacteria, fungi, and viruses associated with that animal. There is concern that an introduced disease will move beyond a local pack to the rest of the new environment and then spread to other packs and species. Disease movement by natural dispersal, dispersal via human intervention, and movement corridors into historic habitat is well documented.

Diseases and health anomalies in carnivores have occurred throughout recorded history and generally have a minimal impact on humans. Rabies is an exception. Severe and widespread rabies epizoodemics (i.e., rapid and severe disease outbreaks that occur in both people and other animals simultaneously) were reported in the late eighteenth century (1796) in the Americas in foxes and dogs, and distemper outbreaks occurred in dogs and cats as early as the late nineteenth century (Fleming 1975).

Diseases that influence species at the top of the food chain not only affect predator numbers directly but also indirectly, by spreading diseases that cause changes in prey populations. Describing each disease entity will provide insight into the transmission pathways that pathogens might travel between or within populations. The movement of disease via animal translocation can play a major role in the persistence of that disease in a population and can be a major concern when making decisions that affect rare endemic (i.e., restricted to one location) or founder animals or those with naive immune systems.

DISEASE OVERVIEW

Wolves (*Canis lupus*) have been exposed to a variety of viral, bacterial, fungal, and parasitic diseases throughout all areas of their range. Several publications have provided extensive overviews of the known diseases that affect free-ranging wolves (Mech 1970; Brand et al. 1995; Kreeger 2003). These authors identified important diseases carried by wolves, including those that cause high numbers of animals to be infected (known as morbidity) and high numbers of animals to die of the disease (in other words, mortality).

Wolves potentially carry diseases that are important in other carnivores but do not appear pathologic in wolves. Multiple publications have documented diseases affecting gray wolves in North America using necropsy (i.e., autopsy of an animal), surveys for blood antibodies (or serological surveys), parasitic surveys, investigations into the factors affecting wolf health and illness (epidemiological investigations), or incidental observations from case reports (Chapman 1978; Todd et al. 1981; Carbyn 1982). Due to the naturally low densities of this top carnivore species, the large home range and distribution among packs within populations, and relatively secretive nature of wolves, large die-offs from disease might go undetected unless specific populations are being intensively monitored (Brand et al. 1995). Diseases and parasites have been shown to have significant impacts on wolf population recovery in Michigan, Minnesota, and Wisconsin (US Fish and Wildlife Service 2000). The risk of disease should be an important consideration in reintroduction decisions regarding founder animals and release sites for North American wolves.

VIRUSES

Viral diseases are the most important to carnivore populations from an epizootic perspective. Viral diseases affecting wolves in North America include rabies, canine parvovirus, canine distemper, infectious canine hepatitis, and oral papillomatosis. Epidemic and endemic rabies is predicted to be capable of causing population declines in wild carnivores. Canine parvovirus may affect wolf pup recruitment, based on circumstantial evidence in a captive wolf colony in Minnesota in which eleven of twelve pups succumbed to the disease (Mech and Fritts 1987). The potential exists for canine parvovirus to affect wolf pup survival and recruitment in wild populations.

Recent published reviews of rabies in North American wolves have been described by Brand et al. (1995) and Johnson (1995).

Murie (1944), Cowan (1949), and Mech (1970) identified this important viral disease as one that could potentially limit population numbers. Rabies is a rhabdovirus (a type of bullet-shaped, enveloped virus with a single strand of RNA) that is generally confined to one species in a geographic area, although extension to other species is not uncommon. New diagnostic tests have enabled researchers to understand endemic and epidemic rabies. However, the role that rabies may play in regulating wolf populations is unknown (Brand et al. 1995). Historic and recent accounts of rabies in wolves (Weiler et al. 1995; Ballard and Krausman 1997) indicate that this disease will likely remain in wolf range for extended periods. Additionally, several authors have shown wolf packs being reduced due to the incidence of rabies (Chapman 1978; Davis et al. 1980; Theberge et al. 1994).

North American wolves are not considered reservoirs of rabies virus. In published cases, wolves were suspected of contracting the disease from other canid species including red foxes (*Vulpes vulpes*) and arctic foxes (*Alopex lagopus*) (Mech 1970; Rausch 1973; Ritter 1981; Theberge et al. 1994). The spread of rabies by wolves, though generally contained within individual packs (Chapman 1978), can occur when infected animals contact members of adjacent packs at their territory boundaries or via dispersing individuals.

Canine parvovirus was first detected in domestic dogs in 1978 and had spread worldwide by 1980 (Pollock 1984). Parvovirus is very stable in the environment and spread by direct contact and fecal contamination of the habitat. Once infected, canids are capable of periodically shedding the virus for many years. Based on retrospective studies of serological (blood serum) data, canine parvovirus likely entered wild coyote (*Canis latrans*) and wolf populations in North America sometime during 1978 or 1979 (Thomas et al. 1982; Barker et al. 1983) and possibly as early 1975 (Goyal et al. 1986).

Testing blood for diseases yields serological titers that indicate whether or not an animal has been exposed to a disease. Though serological titers in wild wolves have been reported as high as 65 percent in Minnesota (Mech 1986), Montana, and southeastern British Columbia (Johnson et al. 1994), no published reports of mortalities or clinical signs have been reported in wild populations (Brand et al. 1995).

Captive studies conducted by J. Zuba and reported by Brand et al. (1995) challenged a cohort of study animals with live canine parvovirus. Only 30 percent developed clinical signs and about 10 percent would have died without supportive care. In captive populations, canine parvovirus has been shown to carry high mortality rates, especially among young animals (Mech and Fritts 1987; Mech and Goyal 1993; Mech et al. 2008). Circumstantial evidence from population crashes in Isle Royale National Park during the 1980s indicates that the disease is capable of limiting wolf populations. This episode was coincidental with a canine parvovirus outbreak among neighboring domestic dogs (R. O. Peterson, unpubl., as reported in Brand et al. 1995). In a Minnesota study of wolves from 1973 to 2004, Mech et al. (2008) found that pup survival was reduced by 40 percent to 60 percent, limiting the population rate of increase to 4 percent compared with increases in other populations of 16 percent to 58 percent. Canine parvovirus was suspected to reduce gray wolf pup survival from 80 percent to 60 percent in populations residing in central Idaho and Yellowstone National Park (Gillin et al. 2000), with similar circumstantial evidence occurring in Glacier National Park, Montana (Johnson et al. 1994).

Canine distemper is another important viral disease of canids and other carnivores (Johnson et al. 1994). The disease is caused by a paramyxovirus (a type of single-strand RNA virus) closely related to measles and rinderpest. This disease affects domestic dogs at three to nine weeks of age (Gillespie and Carmichael 1968), and morbidity and mortality can be high in exposed unvaccinated animals. Despite the ubiquitous distribution of canine distemper, there are only two reports in the literature of mortality occurring in wild populations (Carbyn 1982; Peterson et al. 1984). Because recruitment (i.e., young animals surviving to adulthood) in North American wolf populations is generally good, canine distemper cannot be considered a significant mortality factor (Brand et al. 1995).

Infectious canine hepatitis (ICH) is an important disease in domestic dogs and has been reported via seropositive titers in Alaskan (Stephenson et al. 1982; Zarnke and Ballard 1987; Zarnke et al. 2004) and Canadian wolves (Choquette and Kuyt 1974). A DNA virus, canine adenovirus 1, causes ICH. In Alaskan populations, annual prevalence has reached 100 percent with up to 42 percent of the exposed animals being pups, suggesting exposure at an early age. Although infectious canine hepatitis appears to be enzootic in wolf populations, the percentage of wild wolves that test positive for exposure to this disease, called the seroprevalence, is uncorrelated with its occurrence in domestic dogs. No mortality from this disease has been reported in wolves.

Oral papillomatosis is a disease caused by a small, double-stranded DNA virus of the Papovaviridae family. It has been reported in wild populations of wolves and coyotes (Samuel et al. 1978). Although this disease causes severe oral tumors in coyotes (Trainer et al. 1968), it has not been documented to cause mortality in wild wolves or other canids and is not considered a threat to those populations.

BACTERIAL AND FUNGAL DISEASES

The most noted bacterial disease threats in North American populations of wolves are brucellosis (*Brucella* spp.), Lyme disease

(*Borrelia burgdorferi*), leptospirosis (*Leptospira* spp.), tularemia (*Francisella tularensis*), plague (*Yersinia pestis*), and bovine tuberculosis (*Mycobacterium bovis*). Of these, Lyme disease and plague are spread through the bite of infected fleas and ticks, whereas the other diseases are passed primarily through the exposure to or consumption of mammalian prey.

Lyme disease has the potential to infect wolves, but clinical disease has never been demonstrated (Kazmierczak et al. 1988). The bacterium is spread through the bite of infected ticks, principally of the genus *Ixodes damnii*. It is passed to other species through transmission via a life cycle involving small mammals such as the white-footed deer mouse (*Peromyscus leucopus*) that host immature ticks, and then to white-tailed deer (*Odocoileus virginianus*), the host of the adult ticks. In one study, two of seventy-eight wild wolves sampled in Wisconsin and Minnesota tested positive to exposure (i.e., were seropositive) with *B. burgdorferi* (Kazmierczak et al. 1988). When inoculating captive wolves, Kazmierczak (1988) saw only swollen lymph nodes (or lymphadenopathy) and no evidence of chronic lymph node inflammation (known as lymphadenitis), fever, and arthritis, as seen in domestic dogs (Lissman et al. 1984; Kornblatt et al. 1985). Although the effects on wolf reproduction are not known, abortion and fetal mortality have been reported in humans and horses (Schlesinger et al. 1985; Burgess et al. 1989).

Fungal diseases do not appear to play an important morbidity or mortality role in wild wolf populations. The only reported fatal case occurred in a wolf in Minnesota from the fungal disease blastomycosis (*Blastomyces dermatitidis*) (Thiel et al. 1987). This disease is enzootic and limited to the region encompassing Minnesota and Wisconsin and is most commonly diagnosed in domestic dogs in those states (Archer 1985).

HELMINTHS

Holmes and Podesta (1968), Mech (1970), and Archer et al. (1986) describe an array of parasites for which wolves serve as an important host species. These parasites include three species of spiny-headed worms (acanthocephala), nine species of flukes (trematodes), twenty-one species of tapeworms (cestodes), and twenty-four species of roundworms (nematodes). Craig and Craig (2005) conducted a definitive literature survey of helminth parasites of wolves and identified a total of seventy-two species from forty genera, 93 percent collected from the gastrointestinal tract. They found twenty-eight species of nematode, twenty-seven species of cestode, sixteen species of trematode, and one acanthocephalan. As a general observation, the majority of helminth infections cause little pathology among wolves, and apparently they are not a factor in regulating populations (Brand et al. 1995). Several species of note are described below.

Dog heartworm infection (*Dirofilaria immitis*) is caused by a nematode that inhabits the heart and pulmonary arteries of canid and several felid species, but is most prominent in domestic dogs. Several case history accounts of dog heartworm infection and fatalities from pathologic changes have occurred in wolves held in zoo collections where the parasite occurs enzootically (Hartley 1938; Coffin 1944; Pratt et al. 1981). This disease may have been partially responsible for the decline of red wolves (*Canis rufus*) in the southeastern United States (McCarley and Carley 1979). Mech and Fritts (1987) have expressed concern over the potential effects of *D. immitis* infection in free-ranging wolves in heartworm enzootic areas.

Dog hookworm (*Ancylostoma caninum*) is another internal parasite of canids. It causes ulcerative lesions on intestinal mucosa through its blood-feeding activities. In domestic dogs, emaciation accompanied by anemia (or a deficiency of red blood cells), diarrhea, and occasionally death can occur. Although this parasite has not been reported in gray wolves, it has been suspected of causing infection and deaths in red wolves (McCarley and Carley 1979; Custer and Pence 1981) and coyotes (Mitchell and Beasom 1974). Similar morbidity and mortality may occur in areas inhabited by gray wolves where the parasite is enzootic (Brand et al. 1995).

A liver fluke (*Metorchis conjunctus*) was found in wolves from Alberta (Holmes and Podesta 1968) and Saskatchewan (Wobeser et al. 1983). Spending a portion of its life cycle in fish, this trematode caused pathologic changes to the bile ducts and pancreas in several of the infected wolves. Health effects to infected wolves were not known from these observations (Wobeser et al. 1983), and population effects have not been documented.

Wild canids including wolves harbor a wide variety of cestode (tapeworm) populations, particularly from the genera *Taenia* and *Echinococcus*. *Echinococcus grunulosus* can cause hydatid disease in humans as an intermediate host. After inadvertently ingesting eggs, the eggs hatch and invade the circulatory system and lodge in various organs (liver and lungs). Human infection from *Tinea* spp. and *Echinococcus multiloculares* has also been documented.

Cestode populations within wolves segregate regionally by differences in the prey species they consume. From an individual animal and population perspective, tapeworms do not cause known negative pathologic changes because they do not feed on the host, but rather use nutrients of passing ingested food in the intestinal tract of the host.

Wolves should be monitored for other internal parasites common in wild canid species. *Capillaria* spp. and *Crenosoma* spp. are lungworms that could hinder wolf populations by causing chronic bronchitis or pneumonia.

ECTOPARASITES

Lack of published reports indicates infestations of external parasites (or ectoparasites) are rare in gray wolves. As might be expected in wild canid species, ticks (*Amblyomma americanum*, *Amblyomma maculatum*, *Dermacentor albipictus*, *D. variabilis*, *Ixodes* spp.) (Pence and Custer 1981; Archer et al. 1986), fleas (*Pulex simulans*, *Ctenocephalides canis*) (Skuratowicz 1981; Hristovski and Beliceska 1982), and occasional deerflies (*Lipoptena cervi*) (Itamies 1979) have been reported as pests on wolves. However the most notable ectoparasites occurring in wolf populations are from infestations of lice and mange mites.

Domestic dogs were likely the source of infection of the dog louse (*Trichodectes canis*) on gray wolves (Brand et al. 1995). The louse is transmitted by direct contact between infected and uninfected animals. Infected animals show varying degrees of hair loss (i.e., alopecia). Although dog lice occur throughout most of the wild gray wolf range in North America, there is scant evidence that the parasite causes negative effects on populations (Schwartz et al. 1983; Mech et al. 1985).

Sarcoptes scabei, known commonly as sarcoptic mange (or scabies), is found worldwide and transfers easily among a variety of host species (Sweatman 1971), including the gray wolf. The mite causes skin pathology by burrowing into the epidermis of infected animals. Mites are transferred to new hosts by direct contact between infected and noninfected individuals or contaminated objects such as scratching and rubbing posts. Classic clinical presentation of a severely infected individual usually includes extensive hair loss, lesions with crusting and exudate, and thickened, gray discolored skin. Todd et al. (1981) reported that wolves in advanced levels of infestation might show lower body weight and overall condition. Although the evidence is not substantial, there is reason to believe that sarcoptic mange may be regulating some wild canid populations (Murie 1944; Cowan 1951; Green 1951; Todd et al. 1981).

DISEASES OF PREY SPECIES

Brucellosis, a highly contagious disease in many species, is caused by the bacterium from the genus *Brucella*. Of the five known *Brucella* species, a canine species, *Brucella canis*, is the only species endemic in domestic canids. It has not been documented in wild wolf populations.

The other species of *Brucella* affect domestic and wild hoofed animals (known also as ungulates). However, wolves in Alaska have been tested seropositive to *Brucella suis* biovar 4, which is present in infected caribou (*Rangifer tarandus*) herds (Pinigan and Zabrodin 1970; Neiland 1975; Zarnke and Ballard 1987). The effects of *Brucella* infection in wild wolf populations have not been documented; however, one might expect antibody titers where the disease occurs in their prey, such as the Greater Yellowstone Ecosystem or Wood Buffalo National Park, Alberta and Northwest Territories. Wolves are considered dead-end hosts for *Brucella abortus* because they are unable to transmit the disease.

Under experimental captive conditions, Neiland and Miller (1981) infected two pregnant female wolves with *Brucella suis* biovar 4. Although these animals showed no apparent clinical signs of disease, four of six offspring were born dead. *Brucella suis* biovar 4 was subsequently isolated from various organs and lymph nodes of the pups and bitches. Although *Brucella* was not determined to be the cause of death in the pups, the authors concluded that reproductive failure could possibly occur if infection were present during pregnancy.

Leptospirosis infection, of the bacterium *Leptospira* spp., is endemic in domestic hogs, cattle, and horses in parts of Minnesota and in moose (*Alces alces*) populations (Khan

et al. 1991). Signs of disease in domestic animal populations range from undetectable to mortalities depending on the species, type of microorganism (i.e., serotype), and host (Brand et al. 1995). Wolves in Alaska (Zarnke and Ballard 1987) and in northern Minnesota (Khan et al. 1991) have tested serologically positive to the disease. However, clinical disease has not been documented in wild canids. The disease is spread among carnivores primarily through infected urine or via consumption of infected food (Reilly et al. 1970). Due to the potential of severity of leptospirosis in domestic dogs (Alston et al. 1958) and other species, Brand et al. (1995) felt concern was warranted for wolf reintroduction where leptospirosis was endemic in other carnivore species or in prey.

Tularemia is present in many lagomorph and rodent populations. The disease has caused clinical signs in coyotes and foxes (*Vulpes* spp.) including diarrhea, loss of appetite (or anorexia), and difficulty in breathing (Bell and Reilly 1981). However, clinical disease has not been documented in wolves, although some Alaskan populations have shown seroprevalance. Zarnke and Ballard (1987) felt that healthy adults recover from the disease.

In many areas where tularemia is found, the plague bacterium is also present. Plague is maintained in wild rodent populations and has not been reported in wolves. Antibody titers exist in regions of wolf range where plague is found in their prey. The plague organism is spread by fleas and can be devastating for prairie dog (*Cynomys ludovicianus* and *C. gunnisoni*) populations in the western United States. North America's most endangered mammal, the black-footed ferret (*Mustela nigripes*), is also at risk from a plague epizootic. Humans are also at risk from handling flea-infested animals. In the Greater Yellowstone Ecosystem, coyotes showed positive antibody titers to *Yersinia pestis* without associated disease (Gese et al. 1993).

Tuberculosis is a bacterial disease with three species of potential concern to wolves (*Mycobacterium tuberculosis*, *M. bovis*, and *M. avium*). The bovine bacilli found in domestic cattle and wild ungulates would be the most likely to produce infection in wolves. Any mammal can contract clinical disease through direct exposure (Thoen and Hines 1981; Tessaro 1986) to the bovine, human, or avian types. The only reported occurrence of bovine tuberculosis in wolves was from Riding Mountain National Park, Manitoba (Carbyn 1982). This case history account was limited but fatal to two wolf pups. The source of the infection was not determined. Tuberculosis, among other diseases, was believed to have been partially responsible for a decline in the wolf population from 1975 to 1978 in Riding Mountain National Park (Carbyn 1982).

Neospora caninum is a protozoan parasite identified in dogs and cattle (Bjerkas et al. 1984; Dubey et al. 1988) causing bovine abortions worldwide (Dubey 1999). The disease has more recently been described in other mammalian species including sheep, goats, horses, and deer (Dubey and Lindsay 1996), with more definitive studies identifying transmission of the parasite between wild canids and domestic species (Gondim et al. 2004). Dogs and coyotes were considered the definitive host (McAllister et al. 1998; Gondim 2004, 2006) in the sylvatic transmission cycle between canids and cervids. However, wolves may play a role as a host in areas where the parasite exists in prey species. In an Illinois study, Gondim et al. (2004) found a seroprevalence of 39 percent in free-ranging gray wolves, with lesser prevalences in coyote (11 percent), white-tailed deer (26 percent), and moose (13 percent). The risk of transmitting the parasite to domestic livestock may increase with the infection of multiple wild canid and ungulate species occupying shared ranges with domestic species.

Chronic wasting disease (CWD) is an emerging disease of elk (*Cervus elaphus*), moose, and deer (*Odocoileus* spp.) (Williams and Young 1980, 1982). First identified in northeastern Colorado and southern Wyoming, it is now recognized in wild cervid populations in eleven states and two providences. CWD is a fatal, transmissible spongiform encephalopathy (type of degenerative brain disease) considered unique to native North American cervids. The disease is caused by a prion that alters proteins, which ultimately degenerate specific neural regions of the brain leaving nonfunctional spaces, or spongiform areas.

CWD was first documented in 1968, but to date it has not controlled ungulate populations. Should that change, reduced prey numbers could impact carnivores dependent upon them. Wolves, however, are able to select alternative species from a diverse range of prey. Further, wolves are highly mobile, have large home ranges, and can move to areas of higher prey density. On the other hand, this might increase intraspecific strife. CWD has not been reported in scavengers of diseased ungulate prey species, although translocation of the prion through feces of the scavenger could spread the pathogen via environmental contamination transmission.

Wolves could prey on CWD-affected ungulate species early in the course of the disease. They would differentiate affected prey by their abnormal behaviors and remove them, perhaps before they contaminate the environment and spread the disease to additional animals. If canids are not susceptible to CWD, a hypothetical consequence of wolves in a CWD-infected habitat would be an increase in the health and vitality of the prey species. Model simulations based on conditions at Rocky Mountain National Park (i.e., high elk density) suggest wolves could have "potent effects" on the prevalence of CWD (Wild and Miller 2005).

A similar prion disease, bovine spongiform encephalopathy (BSE), jumped from infected cattle to humans, causing a fatal brain disease (or encephalopathy) known as new variant Creutzfeldt-Jakob disease (known as mad cow disease in cattle). In experiments using BSE-infected food, domestic canids did not appear susceptible to contracting the disease (Southwood n.d.); however, domestic cats did contract the disease. Other carnivores (domestic ferret, *Mustela putorius furo*; raccoon, *Procyon lotor*; and skunks) have been shown to be susceptible to a similar prion disease known as transmissible mink encephalopathy (TME) (Eckroade et al. 1973).

CONCLUSIONS

Wolves or other wildlife species run the risk of becoming infected by diseases from domestic species when their home ranges take them close to human habitation. In Denali National Park and Preserve, Alaska, biologists have witnessed increased stress on wildlife populations due to domestic animal diseases and lice infestations (P. Owens, Denali National Park Research and Resources Division, pers. comm.). Canine parvovirus, canine distemper, and infectious canine hepatitis may have been transmitted to wild carnivores from the large domestic dog population (including sled dogs) outside the park (Elton 1931; Stevenson et al. 1982). This could be a concern for wolves in the Southern Rockies.

Although viral agents (rabies, canine distemper, parvovirus), bacterial agents (tuberculosis), and parasites (sarcoptic mange) have caused mortality with possible declines in local populations (Davis et al. 1980; Carbyn 1982), there appears to be little evidence that any one disease has historically controlled wolf populations. The territorial nature of wolves with minimal mixing of individuals may limit losses to a pack or two and spare most of the population. Many canine diseases originate from domestic sources, and these pathogens may be less well-adapted to wild hosts.

The role of disease and parasites in controlling wolf populations remains relatively unknown. Several authors have suggested a relationship between disease and population density in other canid populations (Todd et al. 1981; Debbie 1991; Fekadu 1991). This has yet to be shown in wolf populations; however, it could become an important factor, particularly in fragmented or island populations.

When animals are moved from one location to another, the bacteria, viruses, and parasites residing with them are also relocated. Disease consequences can be significant on wildlife populations and devastating to relocation or reintroduction programs. The questions then are how to limit disease outbreaks, particularly involving domestic species and wolves, and how to limit transporting diseases with relocated animals. Other important considerations in translocation issues involve wolves as potential carriers of pathogens. Wolves may harbor pathogens without signs of disease but cause morbidity and mortality to endemic animals with naive immune systems. Relocated animals may also be infected by disease pathogens from endemic species or may be affected indirectly either by new or enzootic diseases that cause morbidity and mortality in their prey.

The risks and costs associated with diseases and translocation programs have been documented by several authors: Karesh (1993), Lyles and Dobson (1993), Woodford (1993), Olney et al. (1994), and Woodford and Rossiter (1994). The greatest disease risks occur when species are exposed to new pathogens, are chronically stressed, or when herd immunity is not present (Lyles and Dobson 1993). To understand the basis of risk, fundamental issues to address include: (1) identifying known diseases that could be relocated or acquired at release sites by relocated animals; and (2) the consequences of inadvertent infection.

The ramifications of disease on legal or illegal animal reintroduction can be measured from case histories throughout the literature. These include examples of brucellosis in elk and bison (*Bison bison*) (Mohler 1917; Rush 1932; Tessaro et al. 1990), bovine tuberculosis in elk (Merritt 1991) and bison (Joly et al. 1998), respiratory disease in desert tortoises (*Gopherus agassizii*) (Jacobson et al. 1991), and whirling disease in trout (Hoffman 1970), to name a few. Managers should evaluate the risks involved from translocated disease by familiarizing themselves with occurrences cited in the literature and taking precautions to prevent human-assisted intrusion of a wildlife disease. These important issues of identifying the pathogens that may be released with relocated animals and the variety of related risks can be reduced with good planning.

The most effective preventive measure is to follow strict quarantine protocols (Woodford 2001). This should include identifying the entire range of health hazards associated with the translocation. A complete translocation assessment includes identifying and prioritizing all hazards, then, for each health hazard selected, determining the probability that the event will occur and the magnitude of negative consequences should it arise (Leighton 2002). These risk assessments should include identifying diseases carried within translocated animals and enzootic diseases residing at the release site. Then, following a systematic procedure, quantitative and qualitative health risk assessments can be determined.

Disease issues are also critical in decisions related to planning and designing habitat corridors through which species might travel and migrate. Corridors can function similarly to the physical transportation of an animal from one location to another with the same potential deleterious health effects on populations (Simberloff et al. 1992; Hess 1994).

Introducing diseases into uninfected areas and connecting several populations via habitat corridors can create herd immunity. This immunity is maintained in populations that experience repeated outbreaks of a pathogen (Dobson et al. 1999). Immunity by some or all individuals decreases the potential for a large-scale epidemic that could significantly reduce population numbers (Anderson and May 1991). Outbreaks of a pathogen are less frequent in isolated populations located in habitat islands, but those animals would be more susceptible, causing a high morbidity and mortality. Dobson et al. (1999) surmise that habitat corridors between habitat islands can thus permit the natural flow of pathogens, thereby maintaining a level of herd immunity and reducing the risk of epidemics.

Chapter 11

Potential for and Implications of Wolf Restoration in the Southern Rockies

Michael K. Phillips, Brian Miller, Kyran Kunkel, Paul C. Paquet, William W. Martin, and Douglas W. Smith

INTRODUCTION

A healthy ecosystem requires its full complement of native species, as well as the ecological functions and processes linking those species to their environment, such as fire and predator-prey relationships. An environment able to support a full array of native carnivores for an extended time is likely healthier than one that cannot. We believe the presence of self-sustaining populations of gray wolves (*Canis lupus*) within their native range indicates the healthiest ecosystems. The extirpation of gray wolves distorted ecological and evolutionary relationships well beyond the changes in numbers and behavior of ungulates, because wolves perform several important functions, such as changing pathways of energy flow through an ecosystem, influencing the adaptations with other organisms that evolved with wolves (e.g., prey species, smaller predators, parasites), and affecting the amount (or biomass) and production of plants in the system.

Ecologists have been interested in how wolves affect the broader ecosystem for decades. From 1939 to 1941, Adolph Murie (1944) conducted field studies in Mount McKinley (now Denali) National Park, Alaska, to determine how wolves contributed to the ecology of the park. Murie entertained questions that delved into the relationships between park wolves and other wolves, between wolves and their prey, and between wolves and other predators. During that time, other ecologists, such as S. Charles Kendeigh, Aldo Leopold, Ernest Thompson Seton, and Victor Shelford, began questioning the ecological wisdom of killing wolves.

Recent research suggests that the impact wolves and other large carnivores have on an ecosystem may be more profound than previously expected (see chap. 3). In this chapter, we examine the probability that wolves could live in the Southern Rockies and the implications of that restoration by exploring wolf population dynamics, the interactions of wolves and other carnivores, the potential impact of wolves on native ungulates and livestock in the Southern Rockies, and how wolves might affect land use and human safety in the region.

POTENTIAL FOR WOLVES IN THE SOUTHERN ROCKIES

The wolf has long been gone from the Southern Rockies. When livestock arrived at Jamestown, Virginia, in 1609, the fate of North America's wolves seemed sealed (see chap. 2). By the 1930s, the wolf was nearly extirpated from the Lower 48; in 1945, the last wolf was shot in Colorado (Bennett 1994; Boitani 2003). Yet evidence of the important role wolves play in their ecosystems is mounting rapidly (see chap. 3 and Soulé et al. 2003a, 2005). Important ecological drivers such as wolves must exist at sufficient distribution and density to exert that role. Far more wolves are necessary for the species to play its ecological role than are needed for simple viability of a taxon. While a viable population of wolves may exist in the

Greater Yellowstone Ecosystem, that population does not contribute to the ecological functioning of the Southern Rockies.

Substantial interest has developed in restoring wolves to the Southern Rockies (see chap. 6). This has spurred questions about whether the Southern Rockies can support wolves. Bennett (1994), working with the US Fish and Wildlife Service and the University of Wyoming Cooperative Fish and Wildlife Research Unit, estimated that western Colorado could support around 500 to 1,000 wolves. Martin et al. (1999) and Carroll et al. (2003) identified areas in northwestern, west-central, and southwestern Colorado where wolves could thrive (figures 11.1 and 11.3). In addition, they noted good wolf habitat at the Colorado-Wyoming border and in northern New Mexico (Carroll et al. 2003). Carroll et al. (2003) predicted that perhaps 1,300 wolves could eventually live in the Southern Rockies, with nearly 90 percent of those wolves using public land. The Southern Rockies Ecosystem Project's Southern Rockies Wildlands Network Vision (Miller et al. 2003) outlined a plan to retain and enhance connectivity for wolves among these areas, largely using least-cost path analysis (Fink et al. 2003).

Carroll et al. (2003) further estimated the success of reintroducing wolves to four core areas of 2,500 sq. km (965 sq. mi.) of high-quality habitat (figures 11.2). They predicted that ninety-seven wolves could inhabit a northern New Mexico–south-central Colorado core area (the Carson National Forest, Santa Fe National Forest, Vermejo Park Ranch); seventy-five wolves could live in a southwestern Colorado core area that is probably the wildest area in the Southern Rockies (the San Juan National Forest, Rio Grande National Forest, and the Grand Mesa, Uncompahgre, and Gunnison national forests); 102 wolves could exist in a west-central Colorado core area (northern portions of the Grand Mesa,

Uncompahgre, and Gunnison national forests and the southern portion of the White River National Forest); and 155 wolves could reside in a northwestern Colorado core area (the Flattops, encompassing portions of the White River National Forest and Routt National Forest). Eventually some wolves would disperse from these core areas and promote growth of the population throughout the ecoregion and beyond.

Carroll et al. (2003) also considered the likelihood of wolves inhabiting the Southern Rockies Ecoregion as a result of dispersers arriving from Wyoming, concluding that such movements would produce less than one pack in the Southern Rockies over 200 years. Since Carroll et al.'s analyses, it has become clear that the state of Wyoming will manage wolves aggressively to minimize the size of the population there, including the number of dispersing wolves. While it seems appropriate for the Colorado Division of Wildlife to adopt a management plan that promotes the survival of wolves dispersing from Wyoming, it further seems certain that reintroducing wolves to core areas of high-quality habitat is the most certain and cost-effective way to restore the species to the Southern Rockies Ecoregion.

The message from the models of Martin et al. (1999), Bennett (1994), Phillips et al. (2000), and Carroll et al. (2003) is that the Southern Rockies Ecoregion could support a viable population of around a thousand wolves under current landscape conditions. Those wolves would largely inhabit public lands, and genetic exchange would occur among populations. While the social structure of wolves hastened their decline a century ago, that same social structure can help wolves restore themselves quickly, as evidenced by the results in Yellowstone National Park (Smith and Ferguson 2005).

Wolves likely will leave protected areas such as Rocky Mountain National Park, but populations will remain dependent on those protected areas (Fritts and Carbyn 1995; Haight et al. 1998; Woodruffe and Ginsberg 1998). Even though elk (*Cervus elaphus*) numbers in the Southern Rockies rival prey availability in the Greater Yellowstone Ecosystem, the smaller size of protected areas in the Southern Rockies (figure 5.1) means humans may kill more wolves as wolves move throughout the region. That could slow the rate of wolf establishment in the Southern Rockies. While wolf recovery efforts in the Great Lakes region of the United States suggest that wolves can coexist with high levels of development, people there have lived with wolves for several decades. Wolf reintroduction to the Southern Rockies will likely face heavy initial resistance. Other factors such as states' rights, concerns over possible restrictions from implementing the Endangered Species Act, and fear of change undoubtedly will all come into play (see chap. 6 and 7). It may take years to alter such perceptions. After a decade, the Mexican wolf reintroduction still falters due to human resistance and lack of a core protected area (see chap. 2).

The small size and relative isolation of core areas in the Southern Rockies Ecoregion means connectivity among populations will remain important (Haight et al. 1998). The Southern Rockies Ecosystem Project's Southern Rockies Wildlands Network Vision outlines a plan to retain and enhance such connectivity (Miller et al. 2003). Combined with proposed reintroductions into the Grand Canyon area, a place that enjoys the largest potential for wolves in the southwestern United States (Carroll et al. 2004), reintroducing wolves into the Southern Rockies provides an outstanding opportunity to help recover the animal throughout a significant portion of its range, as mandated by the Endangered Species Act. These two proposed reintroductions would reconnect wolves along the spine of the continent—the Rocky Mountains and Sierra Madre—from Mexico through Canada and into Alaska.

Noted wolf biologist L. D. Mech concluded the following when considering wolf restoration to the Southern Rockies Ecoregion:

> Ultimately then this restoration could connect the entire North American wolf population from Minnesota, Wisconsin, and Michigan through Canada and Alaska, down the Rocky Mountains into Mexico. It would be difficult to overestimate the biological and conservation value of this achievement.

Reintroduction to these two areas would also restore a linkage for wolves along the Colorado River, thus connecting two extremely popular national parks, Grand Canyon and Rocky Mountain (as well as Arches and Canyonlands national parks and the Glen Canyon National Recreation Area, all in Utah). Sufficient habitat and prey for wolves exist in these regions now, and we should not wait.

We have a rare opportunity to re-create the evolutionary potential of wolves, as well as reestablish the role of wolves as a keystone species with strong ecological interactions throughout the Rocky Mountains (see chap. 3). Evolutionary and ecological restoration will not occur if we limit wolf recovery to a few small and isolated populations in the Northern Rockies, north-central United States, and southwestern United States, all of which will come to more closely resemble museum pieces rather than functioning ecological and evolutionary processes (see Soulé et al. 2003a, 2005).

WOLF POPULATION DYNAMICS

In North America, wolf densities vary widely across regions, but they generally remain relatively stable within populations. Wolf populations and the population sizes of their ungulate prey are closely linked (Keith 1983; Fuller 1989). Generally, densities of wolves are highest where prey biomass is highest. Social factors including pack formation, territorial behavior, exclusive breeding, deferring reproduction to dominant individuals, aggression among wolves (i.e., intraspecific aggression), dispersal, and shifts in the primary prey that wolves target can alter how the amount of food affects wolf demography (Keith 1983). Packard and Mech (1980) concluded that social factors and the influence of food supply are interrelated in determining population levels of wolves. Changes in habitat composition and distribution can affect prey densities and distributions, and therefore wolf spatial distribution and abundance (Paquet et al. 1996).

Average annual densities of wolves are around one wolf per 23 sq. km (9 sq. mi.) (see Fuller 1989; Darimont and Paquet 2002). During periods of exceptionally high concentrations of prey, wolf densities may increase dramatically. Kuyt (1972) reported that in some parts of Canada's Northwest Territories (Mackenzie) winter wolf densities increased to about one wolf per 10 sq. km (3.8 sq. mi.) when concentrations of caribou (*Rangifer tarandus*) were high. When deer (*Odocoileus* spp.) reached densities of 64 per sq. km (24.7 sq. mi.) in Superior National Forest (Minnesota), wolves reached a density of one per 14 sq. km (5.4 sq. mi.) (Van Ballenberghe 1974). The highest density of wolves ever recorded was one per about 2 sq. km (0.77 sq. mi.) at a winter deeryard near Algonquin Provincial Park, Ontario (Forbes and Theberge 1995), reflecting a seasonal concentration of wolf packs. The lowest reported density in North America for a stable population occurred in the central Canadian Rocky Mountains, with a density of one wolf per 250 to 333 sq. km (96.5 to 128.6 sq. mi.) over ten years (Paquet et al. 1996).

The amount of prey per wolf, the prey's vulnerability to predation, and the degree of human exploitation of wolves may largely drive wolf population dynamics (Keith 1983;

Fuller 1989). Building on work by Keith, Fuller reviewed twenty-five studies of North American wolf and prey populations and found that availability of ungulate biomass and human-caused mortality affected rates of increase for wolves the most. Ungulate biomass was particularly important for pup survival during the first six months of life (Fuller 1989). Fuller (1989) found the index of ungulate biomass per wolf is highest for heavily exploited (Ballard et al. 1987) or newly protected (Fritts and Mech 1981) wolf populations and lowest for unexploited wolf populations (Oosenbrug and Carbyn 1982; Mech 1986) or those where ungulates are heavily harvested (Kolenosky 1972).

The rates at which wolves consume prey explain the importance of ungulate biomass as a factor limiting wolf populations. Mech (1977a) determined that 3.2 kg (7 lb.) per wolf per day is the minimum rate of consumption required for all wolves of a pack to survive and rear pups successfully. In southwestern Quebec (Messier 1985) and in Minnesota (Mech 1977b), researchers noted that low ungulate biomass increased starvation rates and intraspecific aggression among wolves.

Overall, quantifying the importance of food to population growth is difficult, and results vary among studies. Some researchers have accepted this variability and decided any sign of starvation among adult wolves means food is limiting population growth (Fritts and Mech 1981; Ballard et al. 1997). This assumption is reasonable given that adults typically are the last members of the population affected by food shortages.

Many studies have reported no disease-related mortality (Van Ballenberghe et al. 1975; Mech 1977b; Fritts and Mech 1981; Messier 1985; Hayes et al. 1991; Pletscher et al. 1997). In other studies, disease accounts for 2 to 21 percent of wolf mortality (Carbyn 1982; Peterson et al. 1984; Fuller 1989; Ballard et al. 1997). The link between disease and low availability of food is uncertain, but intuitively the relationship makes sense. A population of wolves lacking food should be more vulnerable to disease than one with food easily available. Furthermore, a food shortage could combine with disease to increase the significance of otherwise innocuous or sublethal disease conditions (Brand et al. 1995).

Human-caused mortality can also be a primary limiting factor for wolf populations (Peterson et al. 1984; Ballard et al. 1997). Large carnivores typically did not need to evolve any response to high levels of mortality from predation. Human-related causes of mortality include legal harvest (Fuller and Keith 1980; Keith 1983; Gasaway et al. 1983; Messier 1985; Ballard et al. 1987, 1997; Peterson et al. 1984; Bjorge and Gunson 1989; Fuller 1989; Hayes et al. 1991; Pletscher et al. 1997), illegal harvest (Fritts and Mech 1981; Fuller 1989; Pletscher et al. 1997), collisions with vehicles on highways (Fuller 1989; Paquet 1993; Forbes and Theberge 1995; Paquet and Hackman 1995; Thiel and Valen 1995; Bangs and Fritts 1996) or collisions with trains (Paquet 1993; Paquet and Hackman 1995; Paquet et al. 1996), and introduced diseases (see chap. 10).

The annual rate of mortality that causes a population decline in wolves remains uncertain. To complicate matters, many researchers consider only harvests (i.e., hunting or trapping) when they calculate mortality rates. Keith (1983) reviewed studies of thirteen exploited populations and determined that populations declined when harvests exceeded 30 percent in autumn. Similarly, Fuller (1989) found that the annual rates at which wolf population increase varies in direct response to rates of mortality; where wolves are killed by humans, harvests exceeding 28 percent of autumn or early winter populations might result in a population decline. He concluded that a population would stabilize with an overall rate of annual mortality of 35 percent or a human-caused

mortality rate of 28 percent. Gasaway et al. (1983), Keith (1983), Peterson et al. (1984), Ballard et al. (1987), and Fuller (1989) found that harvest levels of 20 to 40 percent can limit wolf populations but that lower rates have a more significant effect in areas with low ungulate biomass (Gasaway et al. 1983). Indeed, the effects of mortality also vary over time and with different population structures (Peterson et al. 1984; Fuller 1989). If wolf productivity is high, and consequently the ratio of pups to adults is high, the population can withstand a higher overall mortality because pups (nonreproducers) make up a disproportionate amount of deaths (Fuller 1989). Lastly, net immigration into or emigration out of a wolf population may mitigate the effects of harvest (Fuller 1989).

INTERACTIONS BETWEEN WOLVES AND OTHER CARNIVORES

Wolves profoundly influence other carnivores and scavengers (secondary consumers), and in turn, these species affect ungulates and other prey. Yet researchers have yet to adequately address the extent and full implications of these interactions (Smith et al. 1999). Wolves may change the distribution and abundance of competitors such as coyotes (*Canis latrans*) (Paquet 1989, 1991, 1992; Crabtree and Sheldon 1999). In addition to these competitive interactions, wolves also provide a regular supply of carrion, which is exploited by smaller carnivores. For coyotes, the benefits from scavenging wolf kills can compensate for the associated risk of conflict with wolves (Paquet 1992); Paquet demonstrated that, although wolves occasionally killed coyotes, coyotes nonetheless followed wolves and scavenged at their kills.

Following wolf reintroduction into the northern range of Yellowstone National Park, the ecosystem entered a period of adjustment. During this period, competition among carnivores that exploit similar prey was amplified and thus more easily detected. Such adjustment may occur more slowly during natural recolonization than during reintroductions. During reintroduction, the naiveté of newly coexisting predators probably affects the intensity of interaction (Berger et al. 2001b). Educated coyotes (i.e., those that have learned how to survive in the presence of wolves), for example, have done well in the presence of educated gray wolves, but naive coyotes have fared poorly in Yellowstone, suffering heavy mortality during the early stages of the reintroduction (Crabtree and Sheldon 1999). In some regions, wolves and coyotes have reduced the level of competition between them by focusing on different, nonlimiting (i.e., relatively abundant) prey species (Paquet 1992).

Kunkel et al. (1999) compared patterns of prey selection between wolves and pumas (*Puma concolor*). Their results suggest that wolves and pumas might exhibit the two classic types of competition: exploitation, in which species exploit the same resource, and interference, in which species physically interfere with each other. Both types of competition affect the behavior and population dynamics of each species and of its prey. Wolves in Yellowstone killed several pumas (Kunkel, pers. obs.; Ruth, pers. comm.) and also pushed pumas off their kills, resulting in pumas consuming their prey at lower rates and being forced to kill their prey at higher rates (Kunkel, pers. obs.; Ruth, pers. comm.).

In Yellowstone, grizzly bears (*Ursus arctos*; usually large individual animals that were presumably males) discovered a reliable source of food in wolf kills, and that could happen with black bears (*Ursus americanus*) if wolves are restored to the Southern Rockies. Alternatively, researchers have also observed wolves harassing black bears and grizzly bears, and even killing a grizzly cub and a black bear (Paquet, pers. obs.).

POTENTIAL EFFECTS OF WOLVES ON NATIVE UNGULATES IN THE SOUTHERN ROCKIES

Viable, well-distributed wolf populations depend on abundant, available, and stable ungulate populations. Researchers have heatedly debated the relationship between wolves and their prey (Gasaway et al. 1983; Boutin 1992; Boertje et al. 1996; Ballard and Gipson 2000). Differences notwithstanding, researchers agree that myriad biological and nonbiological factors affect wolf predation, including weather, time of year, habitat area and characteristics, disease, species of ungulate, sex and age structure of the herd, numbers and types of other prey, numbers and types of other carnivores including humans, and size and distribution of the wolf population. Due to complex interactions among factors, it will remain exceedingly difficult to understand the dynamics of wolf-prey numbers and the importance of contributing factors.

GENERAL PREDATOR-PREY INTERACTIONS

Ungulate density, snow depth, weather, and predation all affect the population dynamics of ungulates living in northern latitudes. Studies conducted in areas without predators emphasize density dependence and weather as drivers of ungulate population dynamics (Merrill and Boyce 1991; Singer et al. 1997; Post et al. 1999; Singer and Mack 1999). Increasing ungulate density and severe weather interact to decrease survival. Weather and population density affect adult survival less than juvenile survival, with the former often representing the prime determinant of population growth rate (Singer et al. 1997).

Overall, the lack of large carnivores in North America in recent decades has resulted in low deer mortality rates, likely leaving most populations close to carrying capacity of the vegetation (Crête and Daigle 1999). Consistent with the hypothesis of top-down pressures on ecosystems (Oksanen et al. 2001; see chap. 3), ungulate biomass in North America is much higher without wolves than with them (Crête 1999). Crête (1999) concluded that wherever wolves remained relatively free from human persecution for decades, ungulate densities were low.

Predation by wolves can limit and possibly regulate the growth rate and size of ungulate populations (Skogland 1991; Messier 1994). Anything causing mortality or affecting birthrates can function as a limiting factor (Caughley and Sinclair 1994). Ecologists refer to sources of mortality that occur regardless of the size of the population as density-independent factors. A limiting factor is density dependent if it causes increasing mortality with an increasing population size, such as density-induced starvation (Sinclair 1989). Density-independent sources of mortality are additive to density-dependent mortality. Density-dependent sources of mortality tend to move a population toward equilibrium and thus regulate it (Caughley and Sinclair 1994). If one type of mortality substitutes for another and leaves the overall mortality rate unchanged, ecologists refer to it as compensatory mortality. Sometimes predator populations lag behind prey population, causing a delay in density-dependent mortality. In some circumstances this can result in what ecologists refer to as depensatory mortality, which accentuates a population trend instead of regulating it (Caughley and Sinclair 1994). For example, if predators take an increasing proportion of a declining, secondary prey population as they decline (which might happen if the predators' primary prey population is increasing), they hasten that decline rather than allowing it to recover back toward equilibrium (Caughley and Sinclair 1994).

Despite difficulties in applying rigorous experimental design to predator-prey studies (Boutin 1992; Minta et al. 1999), many researchers report that wolf predation decreases survival or population growth rates of prey (Gauthier and Theberge 1986; Gasaway et al. 1992; Boertje et al. 1996; Jedrzejewska and Jedrzejewski 1998; Kunkel and Pletscher 1999; Hayes and Harestad 2000). The interactions of ungulates and their predators may overshadow the amount of forage as a controlling factor for ungulate populations. Researchers also found that wolf predation increased with snow depth (Nelson and Mech 1986; Huggard 1993; Post et al. 1999), indicating that predation can interact with weather to affect ungulates. In situations where other factors reduce prey populations (e.g., winter weather), predation by wolves may therefore inhibit the recovery of prey populations for long periods of time (Gasaway et al. 1983).

Many studies emphasize the direct effects (e.g., prey mortality) of wolves on the population dynamics of their ungulate prey (Mech and Karns 1977; Carbyn 1983; Gasaway et al. 1983; Messier 1994; Messier and Crete 1985; Peterson et al. 1984; Ballard et al. 1987; Boutin 1992). However, predation can affect prey populations indirectly by influencing their behavior, such as the types of habitat and times of habitat use, activity patterns, foraging mode, diets, mating systems, and life histories. Several studies describe the influence of wolves on the movements, distribution, and habitat selection of caribou, moose (*Alces alces*), white-tailed deer (*Odocoileus virginianus*) (Mech 1977b; Ballard et al. 1987; Nelson and Mech 1981; Messier and Barrette 1985; Messier 1994), and elk (Ripple and Larson 2000; Ripple and Betscha 2003, 2004; Fortin et al. 2005). Berger et al. (2001a) showed that naive moose improved their antipredator behavior after a single aversive experience with wolves.

Prey can lower their mortality rate by preferentially residing in areas with few or no wolves. Several studies suggest that ungulates seek out predator-free refugia to avoid predation by wolves (Mech 1977b; Paquet 1993). Research shows that wolf predation in the Superior National Forest of northern Minnesota affects deer distributions within wolf territories (Mech 1977b). For example, deer existed in higher densities along the edges of wolf territories, where predation was less likely.

Unusually mild or severe winter weather can temporarily increase or depress ungulate populations relative to that predicted by habitat potential (which reflects a long-term average). Wolf packs may react to changing conditions in varying ways, depending on the location of their territories in relation to other packs and on prey distribution. If packs encounter lower prey densities within their territories, they may exploit their territories more intensely. This may be achieved by (1) persevering in each attack; (2) using carcasses more thoroughly; (3) feeding on alternative, possibly less attractive food resources, such as beaver (*Castor canadensis*); and (4) patrolling their territory more intensely (Messier and Crête 1985).

WOLF-UNGULATE INTERACTIONS IN NORTH AMERICA

In western North America, wolves prey primarily on elk, deer, moose, and caribou. As opportunistic predators, wolves typically focus their predation on the most abundant species (Huggard 1993; Kunkel 1997; Smith et al. 2000). Thus, elk and deer would likely comprise the primary diet for wolves in the Southern Rockies. Kill rates by wolves vary greatly, from 2.0 to 7.8 kg (4.4 to 17.2 lb.) per wolf per day (Mech 1966; Fuller 1989; Thurber and Peterson 1993; Ballard and Gipson 2000; Hayes et al. 2000; Jedrzejewski et al. 2002), depending on numerous factors. Wolves generally kill animals most vulnerable to predation because of age, body condition, or habitat and weather conditions (Mech 1996; Kunkel et al. 1999; Kunkel and Pletscher 2001).

Through 1997, wolf packs in Yellowstone killed approximately 130 ungulates per year (Smith et al. 2000). Studies found that elk comprised 90 percent of wolf prey in Yellowstone (the Environmental Impact Statement predicted 53 percent) (US Fish and Wildlife Service 1994). Wolves killed about fifteen elk per wolf per year. Winter severity explained more of the variations in kill rates than did naiveté of prey (Mech et al. 2001). For example, wolves killed 6.1 kg (13.4 lb.) of prey per wolf per day in the mild winter of 1998 and 17.1 kg (37.7 lb.) of prey per wolf per day in the severe winter of 1997 (Mech et al. 2001). From 1995 to 2000, estimated wolf kill rates in Yellowstone National Park were higher in late winter (2.2 kills per wolf per month) compared to early winter (1.6 kills per wolf per month), with an overall estimated rate of 1.9 kills per wolf per month (Smith et al. 2004)

Where wolves and deer coexist in the northern United States and Canada, deer populations remained unstable for the duration of the monitoring period (twenty to forty years) (Potvin et al. 1988; Fuller 1990). The level of predation that affects ungulate populations depends on whether predation is additive or compensatory relative to other sources of mortality. In general, compensatory effects are most likely when prey numbers approach the carrying capacity of the habitat (Bartmann et al. 1992; Dusek et al. 1992; White and Bartmann 1998). In contrast, when prey populations lie well below carrying capacity, we hypothesize that wolf predation acts at least partially additive to other sources of mortality.

Dusek et al. (1992) reported that among heavily exploited deer populations in Montana, hunting mortality by humans was largely additive to other forms of mortality including predation, and there was little opportunity for compensatory mortality in the adult segment of the population. Kunkel and Pletscher (1999) reported similar findings for deer and elk populations in which predation represented the main source of mortality. For calves, however, the situation appears to be different. Singer et al. (1997) reported possible compensation in elk calf mortality for Yellowstone's northern range because predators primarily killed calves with lower birth weights and those born later in the year. These results were similar to those of Adams et al. (1995) for caribou in Denali National Park, Alaska. The significant difference in prey selection by wolves and humans provides a further argument for compensatory mortality (Kunkel et al. 1999). While wolves typically kill the youngest and oldest segment of the prey population, human hunters usually take animals in their prime. For example, since 1995, the average age of wolf-killed ungulates in and around Yellowstone has been fourteen, while the average age for hunter-killed ungulates is six (Smith et al. 2001).

In the Northern Rockies, wolves, pumas, bears, coyotes, and humans are important predators of native ungulates. There, wolf predation, one of many mortality factors affecting cervid (i.e., members of the deer family) survival, may negatively affect hunter harvests (Kunkel and Pletscher 1999). This issue remains a central concern to the public regarding wolf recovery in the region (US Fish and Wildlife Service 1987b, 1994). In northern Minnesota, wolf predation did not affect harvests of white-tailed deer bucks by humans in "good" habitat; however, adjustments to female harvest have been necessary (Mech and Nelson 2000). For more than twenty years at the end of the last century, wolf populations have increased in Minnesota while hunter harvests of deer have also increased, despite variable weather and deer deaths from vehicle collisions, other predators, and other sources (Minnesota Department of Natural Resources 2001). Alternatively, in some areas of Alaska and Canada where game managers or hunters did not reduce wolf numbers, human harvests of moose declined (Gasaway et al. 1992). Mean survival rate of moose calves at locations in Alaska, Canada, Norway, and Wyoming

with wolves and grizzly bears were three times lower than at sites without these predators (Berger et al. 2001b).

Six years after wolf reintroduction, scientists estimated that the northern Yellowstone elk herd included 13,400 animals, a number nearly identical to the twenty-five-year average (1976 to 2001) of 13,890 (Lemke et al. 1998). Similarly, total ungulate numbers in Yellowstone had tripled from 1968 to 1988, with elk alone numbering about 52,000 in 1988 (Singer and Mack 1999). At such high numbers of elk, it makes sense that in the first years after wolf reintroduction, weather remained a dominant factor for ungulate numbers. Ten years after wolf reintroduction to the northern range, however, elk numbers there dropped to 8,335 (White and Garrott 2005). The population continued to drop until 2006 and then leveled off for the next three years, with a population of 6,279 in the northern range in early 2008 (US National Park Service 2008). Yet it remains unclear as to how much of that decline could be attributed to wolf predation (Vucetich et al. 2006). As such, data on elk survival do not provide an early indicator of whether wolves are exerting a top-down role. Yet a change in elk behavior should appear more rapidly than changes in survival. Ripple and Beschta (2004) propose that fear of predation in ungulates can restructure ecosystems because of behavioral changes. Fortin et al. (2005) documented changes in elk behavior following wolf restoration in Yellowstone. As a result of changes in numbers and behavior of prey, studies suggest that wolves are showing signs of ecological effectiveness in Yellowstone National Park already. In the absence of wolves over the last seventy-five years, cottonwoods and willows suffered lower recruitment (Beschta and Ripple 2006). Since the reintroduction of wolves, that recruitment has increased, permitting beavers to reestablish and create additional wetlands (Ripple and Beschta 2004).

ESTIMATED EFFECTS OF WOLVES ON UNGULATES IN THE SOUTHERN ROCKIES

The research being conducted in the Northern Rocky Mountains greatly influenced our assessment of the potential effects of wolf predation on ungulates in the Southern Rockies. We used data from the Yellowstone area to generate reasonable estimates of the effects of wolf predation on prey populations for the Southern Rockies. Although we report our estimates of effects of a possible wolf restoration as single figures (as opposed to ranges), we emphasize that they should be viewed in a relative sense to gain an appreciation of the potential magnitude of wolf predation.

Our hypothetical wolf population for the Southern Rockies includes 100 animals distributed in ten packs (each including ten animals: six adults and four pups). Each hypothetical pack occupies a territory of about 500 sq. km (or 193 sq. mi. or 123,520 acres) in size and kills the equivalent of 230 elk per year (i.e., each wolf would kill the equivalent of twenty-three elk per year). We further assumed that 95 percent of the wolf kills would involve elk and 5 percent would involve deer. We consider three deer to equal one elk (Fuller 1989). Finally, we assumed that of the elk killed, 43 percent would be calves, 28 percent adult females, 20 percent adult males, and 9 percent of unknown age and sex (Smith and Ferguson 2005; Smith et al. 2004). Therefore, the total population of 100 wolves in ten packs would inhabit a total area of about 5,000 sq. km (or 1,930 sq. mi. or 1.23 million acres) and annually kill about 2,185 elk and 345 deer. Of the elk killed, 940 would be calves, 612 would be cows, 437 would be bulls, and 196 would be of unknown age and sex.

Depending on a wide variety of circumstances, a population of more than 100 wolves could proportionately increase the effects on wild ungulates above the figures predicted above. Assuming a directly linear relationship between wolf population size and effects (which is probably overly simplistic), a population of 1,000 wolves (the approximate carrying capacity of wolves in the Southern Rockies as predicted by ecological factors alone; see above) would inhabit a total area of about 50,000 sq. km (19,305 sq. mi.) and annually kill about 22,000 elk and 3,500 deer.

Because of the high elk numbers throughout the Southern Rockies Ecoregion, a combination of factors working simultaneously may be required to reduce large populations of elk to a lower density and keep them there. The elk herds in both Colorado and New Mexico exceed state goals. Recent game management statistics for Colorado indicate that the state hosted approximately 291,960 elk and 538,770 deer in 2007 (Colorado Division of Wildlife 2008). For simplicity, this analysis utilizes the 2007 statewide game population numbers from Colorado, given that the majority of the Southern Rockies fall within the borders of Colorado. The hypothetical area occupied by 100 packs represents approximately 31 percent of the 41,721,141 acres in the Southern Rocky Mountains. We predict a level of wolf predation that takes roughly 7.5 percent of the 2007 elk population and 0.6 percent of the 2007 deer population in the Colorado portion of the Southern Rockies Ecoregion. This may overestimate the actual effect if wolves are restored to the ecoregion, because it seems unlikely that a restored wolf population in the Southern Rockies would reach 1,000 wolves. Social intolerance would likely constrain the size of the wolf population with a consequent reduction in effects on elk and deer.

Regional Deer Population

Generally, deer are doing well in the Southern Rockies as they recover from relatively low populations in the 1990s and early this century. Colorado's mule deer population has been expanding over the past decade, and in 2007 it reached 538,770 (Colorado Division of Wildlife 2008).

Historically, New Mexico's deer population fluctuated dramatically (New Mexico Game and Fish 1999). The deer population in the state reached a peak of about 301,000-plus animals in the mid-1960s, but declined to approximately 200,000 deer in 1999 (New Mexico Game and Fish 1999). Unfortunately, we could not obtain more recent deer population estimates because New Mexico recently moved away from statewide population estimates to regional projections. New Mexico Game and Fish believes that the period of peak numbers represented an anomalous irruption of deer numbers caused by several factors including: (1) abundant growth of high-quality forage due to widespread disturbances (caused by infrequent suppression of fire and extensive clear-cutting of forests); (2) widespread predator control programs; and (3) favorable climatic conditions (B. Hale, New Mexico Department of Game and Fish, pers. comm.). The decline in deer numbers likely resulted from many factors, not the least of which was habitat succession (resulting from more frequent fire suppression) that caused a reduction in shrub forage and an overall reduction in carrying capacity. Other factors included increases in human population and development of deer habitat, weather patterns, increased grass production for cattle, and increased predator densities.

The addition of wolves to the Southern Rockies Ecoregion could exacerbate the effects of other predators on mule deer unless interference competition between wolves and other large carnivores proves to be significant (Ballard et al. 1999, 2001; Crabtree and Sheldon 1999). This would help repress population growth in Colorado, where deer surpass current objectives, but might negatively impact deer recovery efforts in New Mexico.

Alternatively, the presence of wolves may benefit mule deer if wolves differentially prey on elk, which is likely (Smith et al. 2000). If wolf predation helps reduce the size of the elk population in the Southern Rockies, mule deer may benefit from reduced competition with elk for forage and space. This would help deer recovery in New Mexico, but add to the challenge of restraining mule deer population growth in Colorado.

Regional Elk Population

If wolves establish themselves in very high densities in parts of the Southern Rockies (e.g., one wolf per 25 sq. km or 10 sq. mi., though very few locations in the ecoregion could sustain such densities), they might exert enough predation pressure on small, isolated elk herds to prompt wildlife managers to stop or decrease hunting of cow elk in these herds. However, because the region hosts such significant elk numbers, we feel that the likelihood of this scenario is low.

Colorado has the largest elk population of any state. The Colorado Division of Wildlife estimated the total population as being 305,000 in 2002 (Colorado Division of Wildlife 2002). That number far exceeded the state's objective at the time of 188,580 elk (Colorado Division of Wildlife 2002; Burkhead 2006). Since that time, the state has successfully decreased the size of the elk herd through increased hunting pressure. The Division of Wildlife estimated a population of 291,960 elk in 2007 (Colorado Division of Wildlife 2008), which is still higher than the Division of Wildlife's recently revised population objective for elk of 228,000 animals (Kahn 2006).

New Mexico supports the sixth largest elk herd in North America, with an estimated population of 70,000 to 90,000 animals in 2007 (D. Weybright, New Mexico Department of Game and Fish, pers. comm.). The 2002 population exceeded the statewide goal of 62,000 elk by 13 to 45 percent.

Three ecoregions contain 80 percent of the population: north-central (Southern Rockies Ecoregion), with 51 percent; southwestern (Gila Ecoregion), with 23 percent; and south-central (Sacramento Mountain Ecoregion), with 6 percent.

Hunting represents the major source of elk mortality where it is allowed in North America, with predation being second (Ballard et al. 2000). And yet, Colorado and New Mexico have been forced to markedly increase hunting pressure in an attempt to decrease elk numbers toward population targets established by the states. Given that it would take wolves a considerable period of time to reduce the large elk herds of the ecoregion, we predict that wolves would not affect hunter success in the Southern Rockies until years after wolves establish, if ever. This prediction could change, of course, if a local or small elk population declined quickly and precipitously due to habitat problems induced by an overabundance of elk or disease such as chronic wasting disease (see chap. 10).

In summary, for the short term (and possibly longer) following wolf reestablishment, we predict that wolf predation on elk would not negatively affect hunter harvest. Quite simply, there appear to be ample elk in the Southern Rockies for both hunters and wolves. Over the long term (several decades), wolf recovery to the Southern Rockies could cause elk populations to decline. Such reductions, however, seem consistent with objectives established by state game agencies. Moreover, such reductions could help ameliorate the negative effects of high ungulate numbers on other flora and fauna and possibly reduce the spread of infectious diseases such as chronic wasting disease.

Options for Minimizing the Effect of Wolves on Native Ungulates

Managers should recognize the potential for elk and deer populations (especially small and localized herds) to remain low for long periods where wolves, bears, cougars, coyotes, and humans vie for the same prey (Gasaway et al. 1992; National Research Council 1997; Kunkel and Pletscher 1999) and where winter weather can greatly affect ungulate numbers (Bangs et al. 2001; Mech et al. 2001; National Research Council 2002; Smith and Ferguson 2005). Depending on their objectives, managers should be prepared to quickly reduce hunting pressure, especially on adult females, to prevent prey populations in such areas from potentially falling to low levels and remaining there for the long term (Fuller 1990; Gasaway et al. 1992; Boertje et al. 1996).

In addition to managing hunter harvests, predators can be managed. Evidence suggests that under certain circumstances reducing the size and distribution of wolf populations can facilitate an increase in ungulate populations (Mech 1985; National Research Council 1997). For example, Bergerud and Elliot (1998) reported that removing 505 wolves from northern British Columbia resulted in an increase of elk and moose. They argued that predator-prey management allows a greater biomass of wolves and ungulates than a laissez-faire approach. Management guidelines for wolves in the Northern Rocky Mountains permit controlling wolves to reduce predation pressure on local ungulate populations (Bangs 1994). State wildlife agencies, which will eventually acquire primary responsibility for wolf management, are considering recreational wolf harvests to control wolf numbers and their effects on prey species. If wolf control is being considered, we suggest that managers follow the recommendations of the National Research Council (1997). Most important, we agree with the council that decisions on wolf control require a comprehensive science-informed process that considers the effects of control on the entire ecoregion. Past decisions based only on the interaction of two species have proven disastrous for the larger system (Terborgh et al. 1999; Estes et al. 2001; see chap. 3).

Alternatives other than direct predator control exist for reducing the effects of wolf predation on ungulates (Boetje et al. 1995; Kunkel and Pletscher 2000; Kunkel and Pletscher 2001). For example, improving habitat and manipulating alternative prey may prove more effective at generating benefits for some prey populations than wolf control (Boertje et al. 1995; Kunkel 1997). Managers should strive to maintain wolf population dynamics within the variability seen in natural systems.

POTENTIAL EFFECTS OF WOLVES ON LIVESTOCK

Wherever wolves occur in the conterminous United States, conflicts with livestock (and pets) have occurred. Problems caused by these conflicts have been controversial, complex, and challenging (Mech 1995, 1996, 1999, 2001; Mech et al. 1996, 2000; Clark et al. 1996; Phillips and Smith 1998; Paquet et al. 2001). Assessing factors that predispose livestock to depredation by wolves is notoriously difficult. Some factors include the size and nature of livestock operations, the intensity of monitoring of livestock, age and health of the livestock, livestock carcass management practices, presence or absence of guard animals, size of the resident wolf pack(s), distance cattle graze from a residence, remoteness and habitat characteristics of pastureland or rangeland, and presence of elk in the pasture (Bradley and Pletscher 2005). Clear understanding of the patterns that characterize wolf depredations remains elusive (Mech et al. 2000; Oakleaf 2002). Consequently, we consider the issue of wolf and livestock interactions in the Southern Rockies Ecoregion in general terms.

DEPREDATION DATA FROM OCCUPIED WOLF HABITAT

It is critically important to note that the relatively high frequency of wolf control belies the actual magnitude of the wolf-livestock problem. For example, within the farm and ranch industry in the Great Lakes states (Minnesota, Michigan, Wisconsin) and the Northern Rockies, losses to wolf depredation have been insignificant compared to overall losses. Only about 1 percent of farms in wolf range in Minnesota experience verified wolf depredations (W. J. Paul, unpublished report, 1998, as cited by Mech et al. 2000).

Similarly, between 1987 and 2003, wolf depredations in northwestern Montana averaged seven cattle and five sheep annually (US Fish and Wildlife Service 2004). In contrast, between the years 1986 and 1991, livestock producers in Montana reported losing an average of 142,000 sheep and 86,000 cattle to all causes annually (Bangs et al. 1995; Montana Agricultural Statistics 1992). In the two reintroduction areas in the Northern Rockies, from 1995 to 2003 the average annual confirmed losses to wolves have been slight: thirteen cattle and forty-six sheep in the Greater Yellowstone Area and eight cattle and thirty-four sheep in Idaho (US Fish and Wildlife Service et al. 2004). Between 300,000 and 400,000 sheep and cattle graze summer pasture on public lands in each of these areas annually, and losses from all causes prior to wolf reintroduction ranged from 8,000 to 12,000 cattle and 9,000 to 13,000 sheep (US Fish and Wildlife Service 1994). A small fraction of these were predator-caused. While the number of livestock that are lost varies annually based on myriad factors, it is clear that wolf depredations are only a very small part of the challenge of raising livestock. The general pattern of wolf depredation on livestock notwithstanding, it is important to point out that some individual operators do experience significant problems.

IMPLICATIONS FOR THE
SOUTHERN ROCKIES ECOREGION

The livestock industry in the Southern Rockies continues to dwindle as a share of the region's economic base. For example, recent data indicate that the entire agricultural sector (crops, livestock, forestry, and fisheries) accounted for roughly 0.5 percent of Colorado's gross output in 2006 (Colorado Office of Economic Development and International Trade 2006; see chap. 5). Nonetheless, resolving conflicts between wolves and livestock undoubtedly would be the most challenging management task if wolves are ever restored to the Southern Rockies Ecoregion. Patterns of low-density public lands grazing in the western United States increase the potential for livestock depredations, which would fuel animosity toward wolf recovery by livestock producers. A recent opinion survey indicates that public support for wolf restoration is maximized if these conflicts can be resolved in a manner that promotes wolf recovery and is respectful of the needs and concerns of ranchers (Meadow 2001; Meadow et al. 2005; see also chap. 6).

Extrapolating from the experience of other regions where wolves and livestock coexist, we do not expect that wolf depredations of livestock would affect the general economy of the Southern Rockies Ecoregion. Moreover, because on average wolf depredations of livestock are insignificant, we predict the economy of the regional livestock industry would not be affected by wolf recovery. Nonetheless, if not addressed quickly, wolf depredations can cause significant losses for individual producers and create great animosity toward wolf recovery.

Our assessment of the effects of wolves on livestock was greatly influenced by the work being carried out in the Northern Rockies. A detailed analysis of the potential effects of wolf reintroduction to central Idaho and the Greater Yellowstone Ecosystem predicted that 100 adult-sized wolves would kill about ten to twenty cattle and fifty to seventy sheep in each area annually (US Fish and Wildlife Service 1994). Depending upon their distribution, more than 100 adult-sized wolves would proportionally increase effects above those predicted in the Environmental Impact Statement (EIS) (US Fish and Wildlife Service 1994). The EIS for the central Idaho and Yellowstone projects further predicted that resolving conflicts with livestock would result in killing about 10 percent of the wolf population annually. Using cost estimates from Alaska, the cost of killing a wolf from the air can range from $770 to $873, excluding personnel costs (Ballard and Stephenson 1982 in Ballard et al. 2001). While the EIS predictions represent overestimates of actual livestock losses to date by 33 to 50 percent (US Fish and Wildlife Service 2002), they are nonetheless useful for describing the likely magnitude of effects of wolf-caused losses of livestock in the Southern Rockies.

We used the EIS predictions because throughout wolf range, wolves kill more livestock than are verified (Roy and Dorrance 1976; Fritts 1982; Bangs et al. 2001; Oakleaf 2002). Oakleaf (2002) determined the cause of death and detection rate of 231 radio-tagged livestock calves (out of 700 calves) on large, remote, and heavily forested US Forest Service grazing allotments near an active wolf den. After two years, natural mortality (pneumonia, etc.) killed the most calves (64 percent), but wolf predation was the second leading cause of death (29 percent). While the number of radio-collared calves that died each year was very small (nine calves in 1999 and five calves in 2000), wolves may have killed from two to six calves for every one detected by normal livestock herding practices (Oakleaf 2002). The calves killed by wolves were relatively small, less well guarded by people, and inhabited the most heavily forested areas closest to the wolf den. Oakleaf (2002) concluded that it was possible that wolves tested the calves and preyed on the most vulnerable animals.

We predict that a population of 1,000 wolves in the Southern Rockies Ecoregion (the approximate predicted biological carrying capacity of the region) (Carroll et al. 2003, 2006) would kill about 100 to 200 cattle and 500 to 700 sheep annually. As of 1997, the sixty-four counties in the Southern Rockies supported 2,181,389 cattle and 788,888 sheep (Oregon State University, 2003). Consequently, we predict that wolves would kill a maximum 0.009 percent of the cattle and 0.1 percent of the sheep in the Southern Rockies annually. The value of these losses would depend upon the market value for these animals at the time of depredation, which varies dramatically depending upon the type and age of the animal and current market conditions. If lethal control is used against depredating wolves, these conflicts could result in the killing of 100 wolves. If airplanes and helicopters were used for control activities, the annual cost could range from about $75,000 to $90,000 (excluding personnel costs). This level of depredation may overestimate the actual values. It seems unlikely that a restored wolf population in the Southern Rockies would achieve the size set by the biological carrying capacity of the ecoregion of about 1,000 wolves. Rather, we believe that the wolf population size would be set at a much lower level by human intolerance, with a consequent reduction in effects on livestock.

OPTIONS FOR MINIMIZING THE EFFECTS OF WOLVES ON LIVESTOCK PRODUCERS

We argue that the tension between promoting wolf survival and population expansion and killing wolves to resolve conflicts with livestock has been and will continue to be the greatest challenge to wolf recovery and conservation. Even though wolf depredations are relatively uncommon, livestock producers demand immediate and definitive action when problems arise. For example, as the Minnesota wolf population increased during the last several decades, the number of wolves killed to resolve conflicts with livestock increased from 21 animals in 1980 to 216 in 1997, but the number subsequently declined to an average of 128 wolves per year from 2000 to 2004 (Paul 2001; US Fish and Wildlife Service 2007a). From 1987 through 2005, 396 wolves were killed in control actions in the Northern Rockies (US Fish and Wildlife Service 2007b). These control actions represent by far the largest percentage of all wolf mortalities in that region (Bangs et al. 1998; US Fish and Wildlife Service 2007b). The second largest source of mortality has been illegal killings, of which there have been thirty (US Fish and Wildlife Service 2007b).

Nonlethal techniques for resolving wolf-livestock conflicts include translocating problem wolves, hazing, aversive conditioning, using guard animals to protect livestock, intensive monitoring of livestock, modifying livestock husbandry practices, and fladry, the practice of hanging flags around livestock use areas to deter wolves. For myriad reasons these techniques must continue to be viewed favorably, improved, and applied whenever practicable. Two nonlethal techniques seem to hold special promise. First, intensive monitoring of livestock has proven useful at reducing conflicts, but it has not been widely practiced because of logistic and cost constraints. Through a range riders program, young adults from local ranching communities could be hired to ride the range and closely monitor livestock to reduce conflicts with wolves (and other predators). The second management approach of note employs fladry, a technique based on the proper spacing of red flags to restrict and direct wolf movements. Fladry is a traditional technique for hunting wolves (by funneling them toward hunters) in Eastern Europe and Russia and recently has been used to live-trap wolves (Okarma and Jedrzejewski 1997). Musiani and Visalberghi (2001) contend that fladry has the potential to reduce conflicts between wolves and livestock. Fieldwork conducted in Alberta and southwestern Montana support this contention, and additional work is under way.

To date, however, both lethal and nonlethal options for managing wolf-livestock conflicts largely have been ineffective, cost prohibitive, and/or logistically unwieldy when applied over a large scale (Cluff and Murray 1995; Mech et al. 1996; Musiani et al. 2005). Musiani et al. (2005) found that wolf depredations were seasonal in Canada and the Northern Rockies and that lethal control did little to prevent future depredation of livestock. As such, they recommended more intensive use of nonlethal methods during seasons of high risk, although they add that in the long term, "eliminating 'problem individuals' (sensu Linnell et al. 1999)… might play a management role by facilitating elimination of genetic or behavioral traits conducive to depredation" (Musiani et al. 2005, 883). They go on to suggest that lethal control may help build support for wolf restoration among livestock producers. Similarly, Mech observed that

> because wolf-taking by landowners or the public is the least expensive and most acceptable to people who do not regard the wolf as special, there will be greater local acceptance for wolf recovery in areas where such control is allowed. Thus, if wolf advocates could accept effective control, wolves could live in far more places. (1995, 276)

Mech's observation may be valid, but only if livestock producers actually do increase their acceptance of wolf recovery, which remains dubious, especially given that lethal control does not appear to decrease livestock depredation.

Many livestock producers have cooperated with wolf recovery because they believed that wolf-induced problems would be resolved equitably. In this regard, monetary compensation for livestock losses has proven useful for reducing animosity toward wolves (Fischer 1989; Fischer et al. 1994). From 1987 to 2007, Defenders of Wildlife paid $769,455 in compensation to livestock producers in Montana, Wyoming, and Idaho who had experienced confirmed or highly probable wolf-caused losses (M. Johnson, Defenders of Wildlife, pers. comm.). This compares to an estimated $45 million in annual losses to all causes for livestock producers in Montana alone (Bangs et al. 1998). Defenders' average annual costs for compensation in the Northern Rockies and Arizona and New Mexico are about $42,000, which amounts to a little more than the 3 percent of the annual total spent by the Wildlife Services Division of the US Department of Agriculture to protect livestock from wolves (about $1.3 million). Even if officials document only one out of ten livestock depredations by wolves, the annual losses would amount to only $420,000. Wildlife Services in the Northern Rockies spends more than three times that on wolf management.

In areas where wolves and livestock coexist, ranchers sometimes report greater losses than can be confirmed. Under current management schemes, however, an instance of missing livestock does not initiate wolf control or compensation by Defenders of Wildlife. Even with intensive monitoring, for various reasons some wolf-induced losses will be unconfirmed. However, without some type of agency-confirmation process, any control or compensation program could be subject to widespread abuse. State-administered compensation programs for livestock losses to pumas, black bears, and grizzly bears in Idaho and Wyoming (Bangs et al. 1998) and to wolves in Minnesota (Fritts et al. 1992) require agency confirmation of reported losses. It is likely that some sort of compensation program would be an important component of any wolf-livestock management scheme in the Southern Rocky Mountains.

Finally, incentives promoting ecologically sound management practices benefit society as a whole (Farraro and Kiss 2002). But there must be a direct link between incentives and the cause of the problem. Incentives should thus aim to change underlying negative attitudes regarding issues such as threats to lifestyles, issues of control over public and private grazing lands, or traditional notions of land stewardship. Incentives that merely replace lost income only reinforce the notion that wolves are pests.

THE EFFECTS OF GRAY WOLVES ON LAND USE

A common concern voiced about wolf recovery is that it inevitably leads to public or private land use restrictions to ensure wolf survival. Yet land use restrictions have largely not been needed to advance wolf survival and recovery, primarily because the gray wolf is an ecological generalist that can survive in myriad settings. Indeed, human tolerance is probably the most important component of habitat quality for the gray wolf. Nonetheless, many opponents to wolf recovery believe that wolf restoration will lead to significant changes in land use. Some people believe that wolf restoration represents a battle in the War on the West that they claim environmentalists are waging. These individuals predict that the federal government will close vast areas of public land to promote wolf conservation.

Nothing in the rules governing reintroduced wolves supports fears of widespread land use restrictions. For example, plans governing the wolf reintroduction projects in the Northern Rockies only provide the option of restricting the use of public land beyond the boundaries of national parks or national wildlife refuges in the immediate area of active den sites (e.g., within about 1.6 km, or 1 mile) for a forty-five-day window of time during spring (mid-April through June) (Bangs 1994). Any such closures are not implemented when the wolf population exceeds six packs in the reintroduction area. Except for restrictions placed on the use of M44 cyanide devices used to kill coyotes, the presence of wolves has not changed public or private land use in the Northern Rockies (Bangs et al. 1998). Draft and approved state wolf management plans similarly do not require sweeping changes to public land use. Further, nothing in federal or state wolf recovery or management plans provides for restricting lawful activities on private land (see chap. 7).

In 1978, about 25,000 sq. km (9,653 sq. mi., or 6.2 million acres) of public land in Minnesota (about 11 percent of the total area of the state) was designated as critical habitat for the gray wolf per Section 4 of the Endangered Species Act (Nowak 1978; see chap. 7). Local offices of federal land management agencies in the area, including the US Forest Service and National Park Service, supported this designation. In 1992, the Eastern Timber Wolf Recovery Team recommended changes to the critical habitat designation (US Fish and Wildlife Service 1992). The designation of critical habitat in Minnesota did not impose any new restrictions on the movement or activities of private citizens or state agencies.

Although it might be necessary to restrict activities within the immediate vicinity of active wolf den sites for short periods of time during spring when the wolf population lies below some predetermined threshold (e.g., less than six packs), we predict that wolves would not affect lawful uses of public land. We also predict that wolf restoration in the Southern Rockies Ecoregion would have very little effect on current and lawful uses of private land.

POTENTIAL EFFECTS OF WOLVES ON HUMAN SAFETY

The following data are based on information compiled by the International Wolf Center (www.wolf.org), a nonprofit education organization that focuses on the wolf. Much of the original work can be found in Mech (1990, 1996a, 1998) and Route (1999).

Debate has raged over whether or not wolves pose a danger to humans. The Alaska Department of Fish and Game (2002) has documented only twenty-eight cases of humans being injured by wolf attacks since 1890, even though more than 60,000 wolves exist in Alaska and Canada. In North America from 1900 to 2000, no healthy wolf killed a human being (Alaska Department of Fish and Game 2002); however, wolves killed a Canadian man in northern Saskatchewan in 2005. Overall, the Alaska Department of Fish and Game (2002) found that wolves present very little threat to human safety.

Humans have historically persecuted wolves throughout much of their range. Perhaps because of this, most wolves remain shy and avoid humans. Yet, in rare cases wolves have become fearless of humans, leading to serious injury and, in some countries, even death. Fearless wolves represent a concern in India, where they roam freely around remote villages. In 1996, sixty-four children were seriously injured or killed on the outskirts of small villages in one area of the country. In some of these cases, evidence collected by a US-trained wolf biologist from India points to one or more wolves being involved. In 1997, officials implicated wolves in the deaths of nine or ten children in the same region.

It is important to keep wolf-human encounters in perspective. Most wolves are not dangerous to humans. Lightning strikes, bee stings, or car collisions with deer present a much greater chance of death than wolves do. Nonetheless, like bears and cougars, wolves are instinctive predators that people should respect and keep wild.

OPTIONS FOR MINIMIZING THE EFFECTS OF WOLVES ON HUMAN SAFETY

Because wolves generally avoid humans, most people will never see a wolf, let alone have a conflict with one. However, wolves can lose their fear of people through habituation and may approach camping areas, homes, or humans, increasing the possibility for conflict. The following guidelines help decrease the chance of wolf habituation to and conflict with people living in or visiting wolf country.

We recommend that people living in areas inhabited by wolves adhere to the following guidelines:

- Do not feed wolves or other wildlife (attracting any prey animal may attract wolves).
- Hang suet feeders at least 2 m (7 ft.) above the ground surface or snow.
- Feed pets indoors and leave no food outdoors.
- Dispose of all food and garbage in cans with secure lids.
- Do not leave pets unattended outside (dogs and cats are easy targets for wolves).
- If you must leave pets unattended in a yard, keep them in a kennel with a secure top.
- Install motion sensor lights, as they may help keep wolves away.

The following guidelines apply to camping in areas inhabited by wolves:

- Cook, wash dishes, and store food away from sleeping areas.
- Pack out or dispose of garbage and leftover food properly.
- Suspend food, toiletries, and garbage out of reach of any wildlife.
- Keep pets near you at all times.

Outdoor enthusiasts should adhere to the following guidelines when observing wolves:

- Do not feed wolves.
- Do not entice wolves to come closer.

- Do not approach wolves.
- Leave room for the wolf to escape.
- Do not allow a wolf to approach any closer than 91 m (300 ft.).

If a wolf acts aggressively (e.g., growls, snarls, or fearlessly approaches at a close distance) take the following actions:

- Raise your arms and wave them in the air to make yourself look larger.
- Back away slowly; do not turn your back on the wolf.
- Make noise and throw objects at the wolf.

CONCLUSIONS

Several factors influence wolf population dynamics, but research suggests that the two most important are the ungulate biomass in a region and the amount of human-caused mortality. Wolves also influence the population dynamics of other species, especially their prey and other carnivores with which they compete for prey. Interactions between wolves and competitors remain poorly understood, but carnivores do compete through direct interference and by exploiting mutually important resources.

Predator-prey interactions are somewhat better studied. Research from the Northern Rockies helps us predict that the Southern Rockies might support up to 1,000 wolves, but people probably would not tolerate that many. We predict that these wolves would consume a maximum of 22,000 elk and 3,500 deer each year. Yet, because the Southern Rockies boast such large populations of both elk and deer, we predict small if any impacts on hunter harvest. This is especially true because both Colorado and New Mexico are currently trying to reduce their elk herds.

Once restored, wolves in the Southern Rockies would likely depredate on livestock; however, evidence from other areas with established wolf populations suggests that the impacts would remain relatively low and localized. Of course, a small number of livestock operations affected by wolf depredation might experience significant losses. In such cases, a variety of mitigation actions are possible, including lethal control of depredating animals, a variety of nonlethal control actions, and compensation programs to pay for losses due to wolves. Finally, wolves generally pose little threat to human safety, but people should still adhere to certain readily available guidelines for minimizing conflict when living in or visiting wolf country.

Southern
Rockies
Ecoregion

| 0 | 105 | 210 | | 420 Miles |
| 0 | 130 | 260 | | 520 Kilometers |

Figure I.1—Location of the Southern Rockies Ecoregion (outlined in green) within North America.
Source: Southern Rockies Ecosystem Project

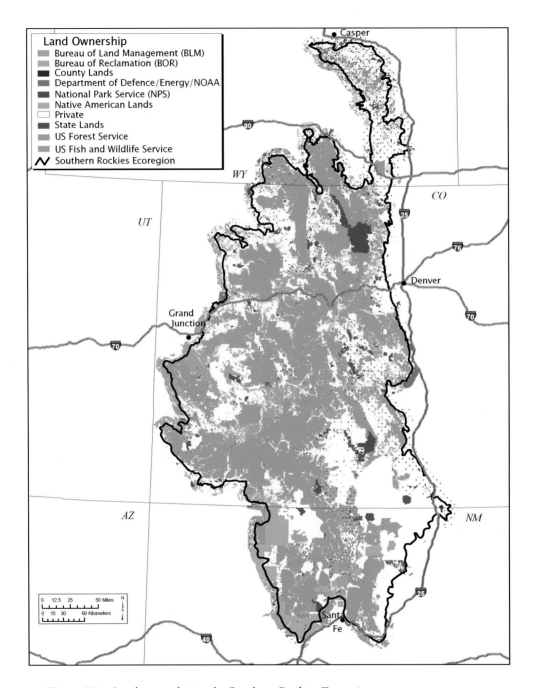

Figure 5.1—Land ownership in the Southern Rockies Ecoregion.

Source: US Geological Survey's Gap Analysis Project, The Nature Conservancy, and the Southern Rockies Ecosystem Project

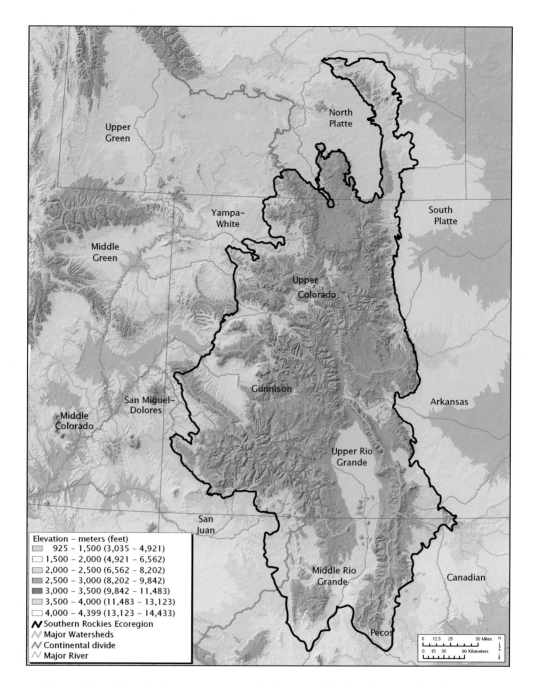

Elevation – meters (feet)
- 925 – 1,500 (3,035 – 4,921)
- 1,500 – 2,000 (4,921 – 6,562)
- 2,000 – 2,500 (6,562 – 8,202)
- 2,500 – 3,000 (8,202 – 9,842)
- 3,000 – 3,500 (9,842 – 11,483)
- 3,500 – 4,000 (11,483 – 13,123)
- 4,000 – 4,399 (13,123 – 14,433)

⋀ Southern Rockies Ecoregion
⋀ Major Watersheds
⋀ Continental divide
⋀ Major River

Figure 9.1—Watersheds, major rivers, and elevation of the Southern Rockies Ecoregion and surrounding area.

Source: US Geological Survey

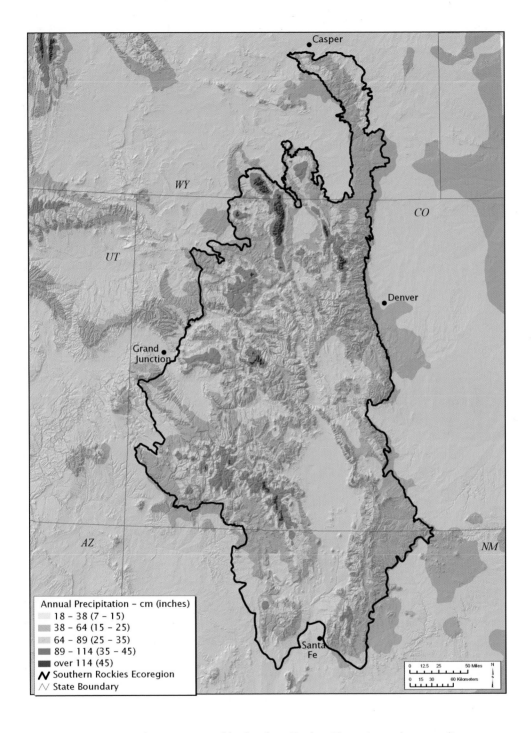

Figure 9.2—Annual precipitation of the Southern Rockies Ecoregion and surrounding area.

Source: PRISM Project, Oregon State University, 1994

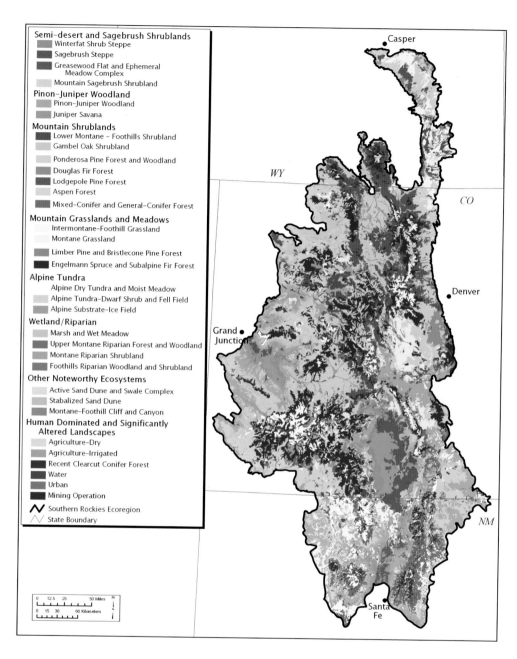

Semi-desert and Sagebrush Shrublands
- Winterfat Shrub Steppe
- Sagebrush Steppe
- Greasewood Flat and Ephemeral Meadow Complex
- Mountain Sagebrush Shrubland

Pinon–Juniper Woodland
- Pinon–Juniper Woodland
- Juniper Savana

Mountain Shrublands
- Lower Montane – Foothills Shrubland
- Gambel Oak Shrubland

- Ponderosa Pine Forest and Woodland
- Douglas Fir Forest
- Lodgepole Pine Forest
- Aspen Forest
- Mixed-Conifer and General-Conifer Forest

Mountain Grasslands and Meadows
- Intermontane–Foothill Grassland
- Montane Grassland

- Limber Pine and Bristlecone Pine Forest
- Engelmann Spruce and Subalpine Fir Forest

Alpine Tundra
- Alpine Dry Tundra and Moist Meadow
- Alpine Tundra-Dwarf Shrub and Fell Field
- Alpine Substrate–Ice Field

Wetland/Riparian
- Marsh and Wet Meadow
- Upper Montane Riparian Forest and Woodland
- Montane Riparian Shrubland
- Foothills Riparian Woodland and Shrubland

Other Noteworthy Ecosystems
- Active Sand Dune and Swale Complex
- Stabalized Sand Dune
- Montane–Foothill Cliff and Canyon

Human Dominated and Significantly Altered Landscapes
- Agriculture-Dry
- Agriculture-Irrigated
- Recent Clearcut Conifer Forest
- Water
- Urban
- Mining Operation

Southern Rockies Ecoregion
State Boundary

WY

CO

NM

Casper

Denver

Grand Junction

Santa Fe

0   12.5   25   50 Miles
0   15   30   60 Kilometers

Figure 9.3—Vegetation communities within the Southern Rockies Ecoregion.
Source: The Nature Conservancy

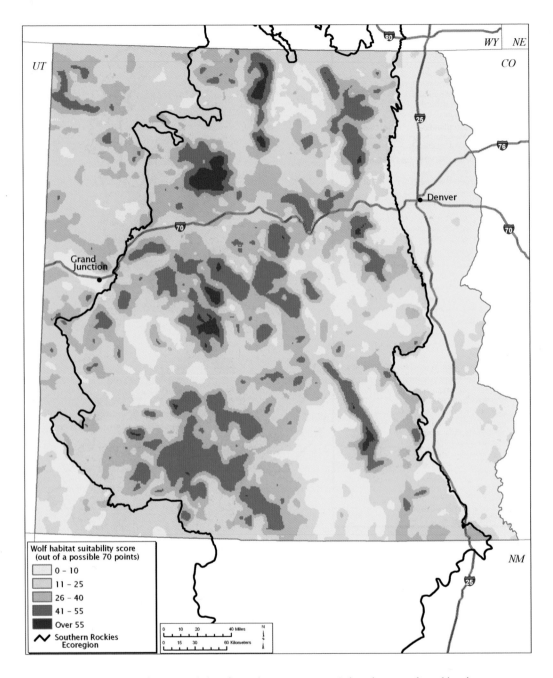

Figure 11.1—Habitat suitability for wolves in western Colorado as predicted by the conceptual model of Martin et al. (1999).

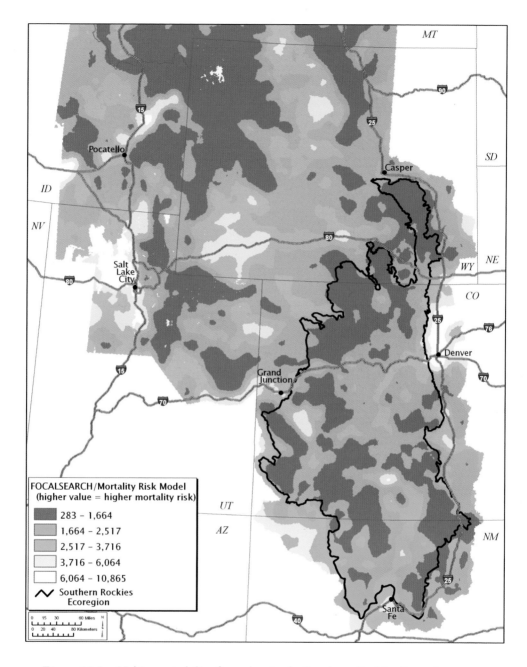

Figure 11.2—Habitat suitability for wolves in the Southern Rockies Ecoregion as predicted by a conceptual model modified from Martin et al. (1999) and Carroll et al. (2001b).

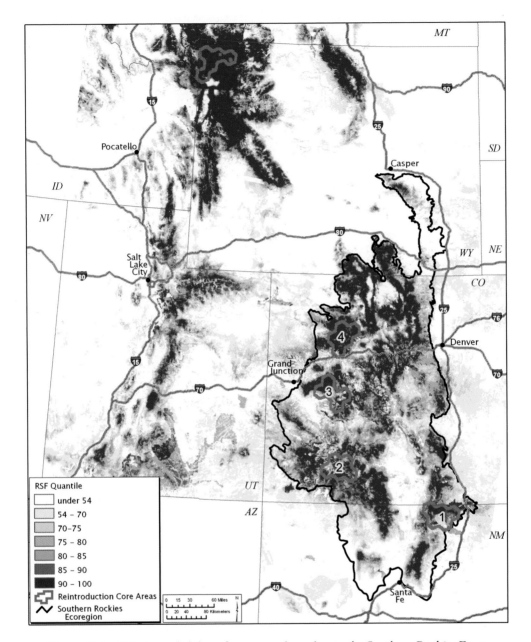

Figure 11.3—Relative probability of occupancy by wolves in the Southern Rockies Ecoregion as predicted by a resource selection function developed from wolf distribution data in the Greater Yellowstone Ecosystem. The four areas of the ecoregion that we selected as reintroduction core areas total 2,500 km2 (976 mi2, or 625,000 acres) and exhibited the highest long-term occupancy rates as determined by patch modeling. These areas are outlined in dark pink: 1) northern New Mexico-south-central Colorado, 2) southwestern Colorado, 3) west-central Colorado, and 4) northwestern Colorado (source: Carroll et al. 2003).

References

Please note that references for chapter 7 are contained within that chapter.

Abbott, C., S. J. Leonard, and D. McComb. 1982. *Colorado: A history of the centennial state*. Rev. ed. Boulder: Univ. Press of Colorado.

Adams, L. G, F. J. Singer, and B. W. Dale. 1995. Caribou calf mortality in Denali National Park, Alaska. *Journal of Wildlife Management* 59:584–94.

Agenbroad, L. D. 1984. New World mammoth distribution. In *Quaternary extinctions: A prehistoric revolution*, ed. P. S. Martin and R. G. Klein, 90–108. Tucson: Univ. of Arizona Press.

Allen, C. D. 1994. Ecological perspective: Linking ecology, GIS, and remote sensing to ecosystem management. In *Remote sensing and GIS in ecosystem management*, ed. V.A. Sample, 111–39. Washington, DC: Island Press.

Alvarez, K. 1993. *Twilight of the panther: Biology, bureaucracy, and failure in an endangered species program*. Sarasota, FL: Myakka River Publishing.

Alverson, W. S., W. Kuhlmann, and D. M. Waller. 1994. *Wild forests: Conservation biology and public policy*. Covelo, CA: Island Press.

Alverson, W. S., D. M. Waller, and S. L. Solheim. 1988. Forests too deer: Edge effects in northern Wisconsin. *Conservation Biology* 2:348–58.

Anderson, A. 1984. The extinction of moa in southern New Zealand. In *Quaternary extinctions: A prehistoric revolution*, ed. P. S. Martin and R. G. Klein, 728–40. Tucson: Univ. of Arizona Press.

Anderson, E. 1984. Who's who in the Pleistocene: A mammalian bestiary. In *Quaternary extinctions: A prehistoric revolution*, ed. P. S. Martin and R. G. Klein, 40–89. Tucson: Univ. of Arizona Press.

Anderson, E., S. C. Forrest, T. W. Clark, and L. Richardson. 1986. Paleobiology, biogeography, and systematics of the black-footed ferret, *Mustela nigripes* (Audubon and Bachman, 1851). *Great Basin Naturalist Memoirs* 8:11–62.

Andrews, R. R., and R. R. Righter. 1992. *Colorado birds*. Denver: Denver Museum of Natural History.

Anonymous. n.d. Chronology of Ute history, Ignacio, Colorado. www.southern-ute.nsn.us/chronology .html (accessed April 14, 2009).

———. 2007. Yellowstone wolves and the regional economy. *Yellowstone Park Foundation* 8 (2):1–2.

Arendt, H. 1958. *The human condition*. Chicago: Univ. of Chicago Press.

Arizona-Sonora Desert Museum. *Mexican wolf international studbook annual update: 1 January 2000 to 31 December 2000*. Tucson: Arizona-Sonora Desert Museum.

Arjo, W. M., and D. H. Pletscher. 1999. Behavioral responses of coyotes to wolf recolonization in northwestern Montana. *Canadian Journal of Zoology* 77:1919–27.

Arnold, M. L., and S. A. Hodges. 1995. Are natural hybrids fit or unfit relative to their parents? *Trends in Ecology and Evolution* 10:67–71.

Ascher, W., and R. Healy. 1990. *Natural resource policymaking in developing countries*. Durham, NC: Duke Univ. Press.

Avise, J. C. 1989. A role for molecular genetics in the recognition and conservation of endangered species. *Trends in Ecology and Evolution* 4:279–81.

Backhouse, G. N., T. W. Clark, and R. L. Wallace. 1996. Reviewing recovery programs for endangered species: Some considerations and recommendations. In *Back from the brink: Refining the endangered species recovery process*, ed. S. Stephens and S. Maxwell, 170–79. New South Wales, Australia: Surrey Beatty and Sons.

Bailey, R. 1995. Description of the ecoregions on the United States. Misc. pub. #1391. Washington, DC: USDA Forest Service.

Baker, W. L., J. A. Munroe, and A. E. Hessel. 1997. The effects of elk on aspen in the winter range in Rocky Mountain National Park. *Ecography* 20:155–65.

Baker, W. L., and T. T. Veblen. 1990. Spruce beetles in the nineteenth-century subalpine forests of western Colorado. *Arctic Alpine Research* 22:65–80.

Baker, W. L., and G. M. Walford. 1995. Multiple stable states and models of riparian vegetation succession on the Animas River, Colorado. *Annals of the Association of American Geographers* 85:320–38.

Baker, W. L. and D. Shinneman. 2004. Fire and restoration of piñon-juniper woodlands in the western United States: A review. *Forest Ecology and Management* 189:1–21.

Ballard, W. B., L. A. Ayres, P. R. Krausman, D. J. Reed, and S. G. Fancy. 1997. Ecology of wolves in relation to a migratory caribou herd in northwest Alaska. *Wildlife Monographs* 135:1–47.

Ballard, W. B., and P. Gipson. 2000. Wolf. In *Ecology and management of large mammals in North America*, ed. S. Demaris and P. R. Krausman, 321–46. Upper Saddle River, NJ: Prentice Hall.

Ballard, W. B., D. Lutz, T. W. Keegan, L. H. Carpenter, and J. C. deVos Jr. 2001. Deer-predator relationships: A review of recent North American studies with emphasis on mule and black-tailed deer. *Wildlife Society Bulletin* 29:99–115.

Ballard, W. B., and R. O. Stephenson. 1982. Wolf control—take some and leave some. *Alces* 18:276–300.

Ballard, W. B., and V. Van Ballenberghe. 1997. Predator/prey relationships. In *Ecology and management of the North American moose*, ed. A. W. Franzman and C. C. Schwartz, 247–73. Washington, DC: Smithsonian Institution Press.

Ballard, W. B., H. A. Whitlaw, B. F. Wakeling, R. L. Brown, J. C. deVos Jr., and M. C. Wallace. 2000. Survival of female elk in northern Arizona. *Journal of Wildlife Management* 64:500–4.

Ballard, W. B., H. A. Whitlaw, S. J. Young, R. A. Jenkins, and G. J. Forbes. 1999. Predation and survival of white-tailed deer fawns in north-central New Brunswick. *Journal of Wildlife Management* 63:574–79.

Ballard, W. B., J. S. Whitman, and C. L. Gardner. 1987. Ecology of an exploited wolf population in south-central Alaska. *Wildlife Monographs* 98:1–54.

Ballou, J. D. 1997. Effects of ancestral inbreeding on genetic load in mammalian populations. *Journal of Heredity* 88:169–78.

Ballou, J. D., and A. M. Lyles. 1993. Working group report on risk assessment and population dynamics. *Journal of Zoo Wildlife Medicine* 24:398–405.

Bangs, E. E. 1994. Establishment of a nonessential experimental population for gray wolves in Yellowstone National Park in Wyoming, Idaho, Montana central Idaho and southwestern Montana. *Federal Register* 59:60252–81.

———. 1998. *Evaluation of the interim wolf control plan.* Helena, MT: US Fish and Wildlife Service.

———. 2002. Potential impact of wolf predation in the Greater Yellowstone area. Discussion paper, Fish and Wildlife Service, Helena, Montana. www.forwolves.org/impact.html.

Bangs, E. E., T. N. Bailey, and M. F. Portner. 1989. Survival rates of adult female moose on the Kenai Peninsula, Alaska. *Journal of Wildlife Management* 53:557–63.

Bangs, E. E., J. Fontaine, M. Jiminez, T. Meier, C. Niemeyer, D. Smith, K. Murphy, et al. 2001. Gray wolf restoration in the northwestern United States. *Endangered Species Update* 18:147–52.

Bangs, E. E., and S. H. Fritts. 1996. Reintroducing the gray wolf to central Idaho and Yellowstone National Park. *Wildlife Society Bulletin* 24:402–13.

Bangs, E. E., S. H. Fritts, D. R. Harms, J. A. Fontaine, M. D. Jimenez, W. G. Brewster, and C. C. Niemeyer. 1995. Control of endangered gray wolves in Montana. In *Ecology and conservation of wolves in a changing world*, ed. L. N. Carbyn, S. H. Fritts, and D. R. Seip, 127–134. Edmonton, AB: Canadian Circumpolar Institute.

Bangs, E. E., S. H. Fritts, J. A. Fontaine, D. W. Smith, K. M. Murphy, C. M. Mack, and C. C. Niemeyer. 1998. Status of gray wolf restoration in Montana, Idaho, and Wyoming. *Wildlife Society Bulletin* 26:785–98.

Baran, P. 1957. *The political economy of growth.* New York: Monthly Review Press.

Bartmann R. M., G. C. White, L. H. Carpenter. 1992. Compensatory mortality in a Colorado mule deer population. *Wildlife Monograph* 121:1–39.

Bath, A. J. 1987a. Attitudes of various interest groups in Wyoming toward wolf reintroduction in Yellowstone National Park. Master's thesis, Univ. of Wyoming.

———. 1987b. *Countywide survey of the general public in Wyoming in counties around the park toward wolf reintroduction in Yellowstone National Park.* Report to Yellowstone National Park. Mammoth, WY: US National Park Service.

———. 1987c. *Statewide survey of the Wyoming general public attitude towards wolf reintroduction in Yellowstone National Park.* Report to Yellowstone National Park. Mammoth, WY: US National Park Service.

———. 1989. The public and wolf restoration in Yellowstone National Park. *Society and Natural Resources* 2:297–306.

———. 1991. Public attitudes in Wyoming, Montana, and Idaho toward wolf restoration in Yellowstone National Park. *Transactions of the North American Wildlife and Natural Resources Conference* 56:91–95.

Bath, A. J., and T. Buchanan. 1989. Attitudes of interest groups in Wyoming toward wolf restoration in Yellowstone National Park. *Wildlife Society Bulletin* 17:519–25.

Bath, A. J., and C. Phillips. 1990. *Statewide surveys of Montana and Idaho: Resident attitudes toward wolf reintroduction in Yellowstone: Report submitted to Friends of Animals, National Wildlife Federation.* Reston, VA: US Fish and Wildlife Service and US National Park Service.

Bauer, S. B. 1985. Evaluation of nonpoint source impacts on water quality from forest practices in Idaho: Relation to water quality standards. In *Proceedings of perspectives in nonpoint source pollution, a national conference, May 19–22,* 455–58. Kansas City, MO: US Environmental Protection Agency.

Bean, M. J. 1983. *The evolution of national wildlife law.* New York: Praeger Publishers.

Beck, B. B., D. G. Kleiman, J. M. Dietz, I. Castro, C. Carvalho, A. Martins, and B. Rhettberg-Beck, 1991. Losses and reintroduced golden-lion tamarins (*Leontopithicus rosalia*). *Dodo, Journal of the Jersey Wildlife Preservation Trust* 27:50–61

Beck, B. B., L. G. Rapaport, M. R. Stanley-Price, and A. C. Wilson. 1993. Reintroduction of captive-raised animals. In *Creative conservation: Interactive management of wild and captive animals*, ed. P. J. S.

Olney, G. M. Mace, and A. T. C. Feistner, 265–86. London: Chapman and Hall Press.

Beier, P. 1993. Determining minimum habitat areas and habitat corridors for cougars. *Conservation Biology* 7:94–108

Beissenger, S., and D. McCullough. 2002. *Population viability analysis.* Chicago: Univ. of Chicago Press.

Beldon, R. C., and J. W. McCown. 1996. *Florida panther reintroduction feasibility study.* Final Report, Study #7507. Tallahassee: Florida Game and Fresh Water Fish Commission.

Belsky, A. J., A. Matzke, and S. Uselman. 1999. Survey of live-stock influences on stream and riparian ecosystems in the western United States. *Journal of Soils and Water Conservation* 54:419–31.

Bem, D. J. 1970. *Beliefs, attitudes, and human affairs.* Belmont, CA: Brooks/Cole Publishing Company.

Benedict, A. D. 2008. *The naturalist's guide to the Southern Rockies: Colorado, southern Wyoming, and northern New Mexico.* Golden, CO: Fulcrum Publishing.

Bennett, L. E. 1994. *Colorado gray wolf recovery: A biological feasibility study.* Final Report. Laramie: US Fish and Wildlife Service and Univ. of Wyoming Fish and Wildlife Cooperative Research Unit.

Berg, W. E. 1982. Reintroduction of fisher, pine martin, and river otter. In *Midwest furbearer management,* ed. G. C. Sanderson, 159–73. Wichita: Kansas Wildlife Society.

Berger, J., P. B. Stacey, L. Bellis, and M. P. Johnson. 2001a. A mammalian predator-prey imbalance: Grizzly bear and wolf extinction affect avian neotropical migrants. *Ecological Applications* 11:947–60

Berger, J., J. E. Swenson, I. Persson. 2001b. Recolonizing carnivores and naive prey: Conservation lessons from the Pleistocene extinctions. *Science* 291:1036–39.

Bergerud, A. T., and J. P. Elliot. 1998. Wolf predation in a multiple-ungulate system in northern British Columbia. *Canadian Journal of Zoology* 76:1551–69.

Beschta, R. L., and W. J. Ripple. 2006. River channel dynamics following extirpation of wolves in northwestern Yellowstone National Park, USA. *Earth Surface Processes and Landforms* 31:1525–39.

Biggins, D. E., A. Vargas, J. L. Godbey, and S. H. Anderson. 1999. Influence of prerelease experience in reintroduced black-footed ferrets (*Mustela nigripes*). *Biological Conservation* 89:121–29

Bishop, N. G., and J. L. Culbertson. 1976. Decline of prairie dog towns in southwestern North Dakota. *Journal of Range Management* 29:217–20.

Bjerkas, J., S. F. Mohn, and J. Presthus. 1984. Unidentified cyst-forming-sporozoon causing encephalomyelitis and myositis in dogs. *Z. Parasitenkd.* 70:271–74

Bjorge, R. R., and J. R. Gunson. 1989. Wolf, *Canis lupus*, population characteristics and prey relationships near Simonette River, Alberta. *Canadian Field Naturalist* 103:327–34.

Blair, B. 1996. Origin of landscapes. In *The western San Juan Mountains: Their geology, ecology, and history,* ed. B. Blair, 3–17. Niwot: Univ. Press of Colorado, Fort Lewis College Foundation.

Bodley, J. H. 1990. *Victims of progress.* Palo Alto, CA: Mayfield Publishing Company.

Boertje, R. D., D. G. Kellyhouse, and R. D. Hayes. 1995. Methods for reducing natural predation on moose in Alaska and Yukon: An evaluation. In *Ecology and conservation of wolves in a changing world,* Canadian Circumpolar Institute Occasional Publication 35, ed. L. N. Carbyn, S. H. Fritts, and D. R. Seip, 505–13. Edmonton, AB: Canadian Circumpolar Institute, Univ. of Alberta.

Boertje, R. D., P. Valkenburg, and M. E. McKay. 1996. Increases in moose, caribou, and wolves following wolf control in Alaska. *Journal of Wildlife Management* 60:474–89

Boitani, L. 1995. Ecological and cultural diversities in the evolution of wolf-human relationships. In *Ecology and conservation of wolves in a changing world,* Canadian Circumpolar Institute Occasional Publication 35, ed. L. N. Carbyn, S. H. Fritts, and D. R. Seip, 3–11. Edmonton, AB: Canadian Circumpolar Institute, Univ. of Alberta.

———. 2003. Wolf conservation and recovery. In *Wolves: Behavior, ecology, and conservation,* ed. L. D. Mech and L. Boitani, 317–40. Chicago: Univ. of Chicago Press.

Bolger, D. T., A. C. Alberts, and M. E. Soulé. 1991. Occurrence patterns of bird species in habitat fragments: Sampling, extinction, and nested species subsets. *American Naturalist* 105:467–78.

Boutin, S. 1992. Predation and moose population dynamics: A critique. *Journal of Wildlife Management* 56:116–27.

Bowker, J. M., D. English, and H. K. Cordell. 1999. Projections of outdoor recreation participation to 2050. In *Outdoor recreation in the United States: Results from the National Survey on Recreation and the Environment,* ed. H. K. Cordell, C. Betz, and J. M. Bowker, 323–50. Champaign, IL: Sagamore Publishing.

Boyce, M. S., and L. L. MacDonald. 1999a. Relating populations to habitats using resource selection functions. *Trends in Ecology and Evolution* 14:268–72.

Boyce, M. S., A. R. E. Sinclair, and G. C. White. 1999b. Seasonal compensation of predation and harvesting. *Oikos* 87:419–26.

Bradley, E. H., and D. H. Pletscher. 2005. Assessing factors related to wolf depredation of cattle in fenced pastures in Montana and Idaho. *Wildlife Society Bulletin* 33:1256–65

Brand, C. J., M. J. Phybus, W. B. Ballard, and R. O. Peterson. 1995. Infectuous and parasitic diseases of the gray wolf and their potential effects on wolf populations in North America. In *Ecology and conservation of wolves in a changing world,* Canadian Circumpolar Institute Occasional Publication 35, ed. L. N. Carbyn, S. H. Fritts, and D. R. Seip, 419–29. Edmonton, AB: Canadian Circumpolar Institute, Univ. of Alberta.

Braun, C. E. 1995. Distribution and status of sage grouse

in Colorado. *Prairie Naturalist* 27:1–9.

Breitenmoser, U., C. Breitenmoser-Würsten, L. N. Carbyn, and S. M. Funk. 2001. Assessment of carnivore reintroductions. In *Carnivore Conservation*, ed. J. L. Gittleman, S. M. Funk, D. W. MacDonald, and R. K. Wayne, 241–81. Cambridge: Cambridge Univ. Press.

Brewer, G. D., and T. W. Clark. 1994. A policy sciences perspective: Improving implementation. In *Endangered species recovery: Finding the lessons, improving the process*, ed. T. W. Clark, R. P. Reading, and A. C. Clarke, 391–413. Covelo, CA: Island Press.

Bright, A. D., and S. C. Barro. 2000. Integrative complexity and attitudes: A case study of plant and wildlife species protection. *Human Dimensions of Wildlife* 5:30–47.

Brown, D. E., ed. 1983. *The wolf in the Southwest: The making of an endangered species*. Tucson: Univ. of Arizona Press.

Brown, J. H., and A. Kodric-Brown. 1977. Turnover rates in insular biogeography: Effect of immigration on extinction. *Ecology* 58:445–49.

Brown, J. S. 1999. Vigilance, patch use, and habitat selection: Foraging under predation risk. *Evolutionary Ecology Research* 1:49–71.

Brown, J. S., B. P. Kotlier, and T. J. Valone. 1994. Foraging under predation: A comparison of energetic and predation costs in rodent communities of the Negev and Sonoran deserts. *Australian Journal of Zoology* 42:435–48.

Brown, P. J., and M. J. Manfredo. 1987. Social values defined. In *Valuing wildlife: Economic and social perspectives*, ed. D. J. Decker and G. R. Goff, 12–23. Boulder, CO: Westview Press.

Brown, P. M., M. R. Kaufmann, and W. D. Shepperd. 1999. Long-term landscape patterns of past fire events in a montane ponderosa pine forest of central Colorado. *Landscape Ecology* 14:513–32.

Brown, T. C. 1984. The concept of value in resource allocation. *Land Economics* 60:231–46.

Brown, T. L., D. J. Decker, and W. F. Siemer. 2001. Valuing wildlife: Economic perspectives. In *Human dimensions of wildlife management in North America*, ed. D. J. Decker, T. L. Brown, and W. F. Siemer, 57–73. Bethesda, MD: The Wildlife Society.

Brown, W. M., and D. R. Parsons. 2001. Restoring the Mexican gray wolf to the desert Southwest. In *Large mammal restoration*, ed. D. Maehr, R. Noss, and J. Larkin, 169–86. Covelo, CA: Island Press.

Brunner, R. D. 1995. Notes on basic concepts of the policy sciences. Unpublished course notes. Department of Political Science, Univ. of Colorado.

Bryan, H. 1980. Social and psychological approaches to assessing and categorizing wildlife values. In *Wildlife values*, Center for Assessment of Noncommodity Natural Resources Values Institute Series Report No. 1, ed. W. W. Shaw and E. H. Zube, 70–76. Tucson, AZ: University of Arizona.

Buchmann, S. L., and G. P. Nabhan. 1996. *The forgotten pollinators*. Covelo, CA: Island Press.

Burger, J. 1987. *Report from the frontier: The state of the world's indigenous peoples*. Cambridge, MA: Cultural Survival Inc.

Burkhead, L. 2006. Colorado's 2006 elk forecast. *Rocky Mountain Game and Fish*.

Cade, T. J., P. T. Redig, and H. B. Tordoff. 1989. Peregrine falcon restoration: Expectation versus reality. *The Loon* 61:160–62.

Campbell, J. 1988. *The power of myth*. With Bill Moyers, ed. B. S. Flowers. New York: Doubleday.

Caras, R. A. 1966. *The Custer Wolf: Biography of an American renegade*. New York: Holt, Rinehart, and Winston.

Carbyn, L. N. 1982. Incidence of disease and its potential role in the population dynamics of wolves in Riding Mountain National Park, Manitoba. In *Wolves of the world: Perspectives of behavior, ecology, and conservation*, ed. F. H. Harrington and P. C. Paquet, 106–16. Park Ridge, NJ: Noyes Publications.

———. 1983. Wolf predation on elk in Riding Mountain National Park, Manitoba. *Journal of Wildlife Management* 47:963–76.

———. 1987. Gray wolf and red wolf. In *Wild furbearer management and conservation in North America*, ed. M. Novak, J. A. Baker, M. E. Obbard, and B. Malloch, 359–76. Ottawa, ON: Ministry of Natural Resources.

Carroll, C. 2003. *Carnivore restoration in the northeastern US and southeastern Canada: A regional-scale analysis of habitat and population viability for wolf, lynx, and marten*. Progress Report 1: *Wolf viability analysis*. Richmond, VT: The Wildlands Project.

Carroll, C., R. F. Noss, P. C. Paquet, and N. H. Schumaker. 2003. Integrating population viability analysis and reserve selection algorithms into regional conservation plans. *Ecological Applications* 13:1773–89.

Carroll, C., M. K. Phillips, and C. A. Lopez-Gonzalez. 2004. *Spatial analysis of restoration potential and population viability analysis of the gray wolf (Canis lupus) in the southwestern United States and northern Mexico*. Report to the Turner Endangered Species Fund. Bozeman, MT. www.klamathconservation.org/docs/carrolletal2005_text.pdf.

Carroll, C., M. K. Phillips, C. A. Lopez-Gonzalez, and N. H. Schumaker. 2006. Defining recovery goals and strategies for endangered species: The wolf as a case study. *BioScience* 56 (1):25–37.

Carroll, C., M. K. Phillips, N. H. Schumaker, and D. W. Smith. 2003. Impacts of landscape change on wolf restoration success: Planning a reintroduction program based on static and dynamic spatial models. *Conservation Biology* 17:536–48.

Cassels, R. 1984. Faunal extinction and prehistoric man in New Zealand and the Pacific Islands. In *Quaternary extinctions: A prehistoric revolution*, ed. P. S. Martin and R. G. Klein, 741–67. Tucson: Univ. of Arizona Press.

Caughley, G., and A. R. E. Sinclair. 1994. *Wildlife ecology and management*. Cambridge, MA: Blackwell Science.

Chaiken, S., and C. Stangor. 1987. Attitudes and attitude

change. *Annual Review of Psychology* 38:575–630.

Chellam, R., and V. Saberwal. 2000. Asiatic lion (*Panthera leo persica*). In *Endangered species: Conflict and context*, ed. R. Reading and B. Miller, 40–44. Westport, CT: Greenwood Press.

Cheney, E., W. Elmore, and W. S. Platts. 1990. *Livestock grazing on western riparian areas*. Eagle, ID: Northwest Resource Information Center, Inc.

City of Boulder. 1999. City of Boulder forest ecosystem management plan. Unpublished report. City of Boulder Open Space/Real Estate Department and Boulder Mountain Parks Division, Boulder, CO.

Clark, T. W. 1986. Professional excellence in wildlife and natural resource organizations. *Renewable Resources Journal* 4:8–13.

———. 1996. Appraising threatened species recovery processes: Some pragmatic recommendations for improvements. In *Back from the brink: Refining the threatened species recovery process*, Transactions of the Royal Zoological Society of Sydney, ed. S. Stephens and S. Maxwell, 1–22. Canberra: Australian Nature Conservation Agency.

———. 1997. *Averting extinction: Reconstructing endangered species recovery*. New Haven, CT: Yale Univ. Press.

———. 2000. Interdisciplinary problem-solving in endangerd species conservation: The Yellowstone grizzly bear case. In *Endangered animals*, ed. R. P. Reading and B. Miller, 285–301. Westport, CT: Greenwood Press.

Clark, T. W., G. N. Backhouse, and R. P. Reading. 1995. Prototyping in endangered species recovery programmes: The eastern barred bandicoot experience. In *People and nature in conservation: Perspectives on private land-use and endangered species recovery*, Transactions of the Royal Zoological Society of New South Wales, ed. A. Bennet, G. N. Backhouse, and T. W. Clark, 50–62. New South Wales: Surrey Beatty and Sons.

Clark, T. W., and J. R. Cragun. 1994. Organizational and managerial guidelines for endangered species restoration programs and recovery teams. In *Restoration and recovery of endangered species: Conceptual issues, planning and implementation*, ed. M. L. Bowles and C. J. Whelan, 9–33. London: Cambridge Univ. Press.

Clark, T. W., R. Crete, and J. Cada. 1989. Designing and managing successful endangered species recovery programs. *Environmental Management* 13:159–70.

Clark, T. W., A. P. Curlee, and R. P. Reading. 1996. Crafting effective solutions to the large carnivore conservation problem. *Conservation Biology* 10:940–48.

Clark, T. W., D. J. Mattson, R. P. Reading, B. J. Miller. 2001. Interdisciplinary problem-solving in carnivore conservation: An introduction. In *Carnivore conservation*, ed. J. L. Gittleman, S. M. Funk, D. Macdonald, and R. K. Wayne, 223–40. Cambridge: Cambridge Univ. Press.

Clark, T. W., R. P. Reading, and A. L. Clarke. 1994. *Endangered species recovery: Finding the lessons,* improving the process. Covelo, CA: Island Press.

Clark, T. W., R. P. Reading, and R. L. Wallace. 1999. Research in endangered species conservation: An introduction to multi-methods. *Endangered Species Update* 16:90–97.

Clark, T. W., M. B. Rutherford, and D. Casey, eds. 2005. *Coexisting with large carnivores: Lessons from Greater Yellowstone*. Washington, DC: Island Press.

———. 1999. The professional in endangered species conservation: An introduction to standpoint clarification. *Endangered Species Update* 16:9–13.

Clark, T. W., and R. Westrum. 1989. High performance teams in wildlife conservation: A species reintroduction and recovery example. *Environmental Management* 13:663–70.

Clark, T. W., and A. R. Willard. 2000. Learning about natural resources policy and management. In *Foundations of natural resources policy and management*, ed. T. W. Clark, A. R. Willard, and C. M. Cromley, 3–31. New Haven, CT: Yale Univ. Press.

Cluff, H. D., and D. L. Murray. 1995. Review of wolf control methods in North America. In *Ecology and conservation of wolves in a changing world*, Canadian Circumpolar Institute, Occasional Publication 35, ed. L. N. Carbyn, S. H. Fritts, and D. R. Seip, 491–504. Edmonton, AB: Canadian Circumpolar Institute, Univ. of Alberta.

Colorado Division of Wildlife. 2001. *Harvest/population estimate—Elk & deer 1949–2000*. http://wildlife.state.co.us/huntrecap.

———. 2002. *A surplus of elk*. Denver: Colorado Division of Wildlife.

———. 2008. *Post-hunt population estimates by unit*. http://wildlife.state.co.us/Hunting/BigGame/Statistics/.

Colorado Office of Economic Development and International Trade. 2006. Colorado data book: Economic base. www.colorado.gov/cs/Satellite?c=Page&child pagename=OEDIT%2FOEDITLayout&cid=1178 305420531&p=1178305420531&pagename=OED ITWrapper.

Colorado Secretary of State. 2008. www.elections.colo rado.gov/DDefault.aspx?tid=547.

Colorado Water Resources Research Institute. 2001. Colorado Water Knowledge. http://waterknowl edge.colostate.edu.

Colorado Wolf Management Working Group. 2004. Findings and recommendations for managing wolves that migrate into Colorado. Unpublished report. Colorado Division of Wildlife, Denver, CO.

Connell, J. H. 1978. Diversity in tropical rain forests and coral reefs. *Science* 199:1302–10.

Cook, J. R. 1989. *The border and the buffalo: All gone*. Austin, TX: State House Press. Cooper, D. J. 1993. Sustaining and restoring western wetland and riparian ecosystems threatened by or affected by water development projects. In *Sustainable ecological systems: Implementing an ecological approach to land management, July 12–15, 1993*, USDA Forest Service General Technical Report RM-247, techn.

coord., W. W. Covington and L. F. DeBano, 27–33. Fort Collins, CO: USDA Forest Service Rocky Mountain Forest and Range Experiment Station.

Coppock, D. L., J. K. Detling, J. E. Ellis, and M. I. Dyer. 1983. Plant-herbivore interactions in a North American mixed-grass prairie: I. Effects of black-tailed prairie dogs on intraseasonal aboveground plant biomass and nutrient dynamics and plant species diversity. *Oecologia* 56:1–9.

Corbin, B. 1900. *The wolf hunters guide*. Bismarck, ND: The Tribune Company Printers.

Covington, W. W., and M. M. Moore. 1994. Southwestern ponderosa forest structure. *Journal of Forestry* 92:39–47.

Cowardin, L. M., V. Carter, F. C. Golet, and E. T. LaRoe. 1979. *Classification of wetlands and deepwater habitats of the United States*. US Fish and Wildlife Service Report FWS/OBS-79/31. Washington, DC: US Fish and Wildlife Service.

Crabtree, R. L., and J. W. Shelton. 1999. Coyotes and canid coexistence in Yellowstone. In *Carnivores in ecosystems: The Yellowstone experience*, ed. T. W. Clark, A. P. Curlee, S. C. Minta, and P. M. Karieva, 127–64. New Haven, CT: Yale Univ. Press.

Craig, H. L., and P. S. Craig. 2005. Helminth parasites of wolves (*Canis lupus*): A species list and an analysis of published prevalence studies in Nearctic and Palaearctic populations. *Journal of Helminthology* 79 (2):95–103.

Crête, M. 1999. The distribution of deer biomass in North America supports the hypothesis of exploitation ecosystems. *Ecology Letters* 2:223–27.

Crête, M., and C. Daigle. 1999. Management of indigenous North American deer at the end of the 20th century in relation to large predators and primary production. *Acta Veterinaria Hungarica* 47:1–16.

Crête, M., and M. Manseau. 1996. Natural regulation of cervidae along a 1000 km latitudinal gradient: Change in trophic dominance. *Evolutionary Ecology* 10:51–62.

Crooks, K. 2002. Relative sensitivities of mammalian carnivores to habitat fragmentation. *Conservation Biology* 16:488–502.

Crooks, K., and M. Soulé. 1999. In a fragmented system. *Nature* 400:563–66.

Crosby, A. 1986. *Ecological imperialism: The biological expansion of Europe, 900–1900*. New York: Cambridge Univ. Press.

Cunningham, A. A. 1996. Disease risks of wildlife translocations. *Conservation Biology* 10:349–53.

Cutlip, S. M., and A. H. Center. 1964. *Effective public relations*. Englewood Cliffs, NJ: Prentice Hall.

Dahl, T. E. 1990. *Wetland losses in the United States: 1780s to 1980s*. Washington, DC: US Fish and Wildlife Service.

D'Antonio, C. M., and P. M. Vitousek. 1992. Biological invasions of exotic grasses, the grass/fire cycle, and global change. *Annual Review of Ecology and Systematics* 23:63–87.

Darimont, C. T., and P. C. Paquet. 2002. The gray wolves, *Canis lupus*, of British Columbia's central and north coast: Distribution and conservation assessment. *Canadian Field Naturalist* 116:416–22.

Dary, D. A. 1974. *The buffalo book*. Chicago: Swallow Press.

Davies, G. 2002. Bushmeat and international development. *Conservation Biology* 16:507–89.

DeByle, N. V. 1985. Wildlife. In *Aspen: Ecology and management in the western United States*, USDA Forest Service General Technical Report RM-119, ed. N. V. DeByle and R. P. Winokur, 135–52. Washington, DC: USDA Forest Service.

Decker, D. J., T. L. Brown, and W. F. Siemer. 2001. Evolution of people-wildlife relations. In *Human dimensions of wildlife management in North America*, ed. D. J. Decker, T. L. Brown, and W. F. Siemer, 3–22. Bethesda, MD: The Wildlife Society.

Detling, J. K. 1998. Mammalian herbivores: Ecosystem-level effects in two grassland national parks. *Wildlife Society Bulletin* 26:438–48.

DeVelice, R. L., J. A. Ludwig, W. H. Moir, and F. Ronco Jr. 1986. *A classification of forest habitat types of northern New Mexico and southern Colorado*. USDA Forest Service General Technical Report RM-131. Fort Collins, CO: USDA Forest Service Rocky Mountain and Range Experiment Station.

Diamond, J. 1997. *Guns, germs, and steel: The fates of human societies*. New York: W. W. Norton and Company.

———. 2005. *Collapse: How societies choose to succeed or fail*. New York: Penguin Books.

Dicey, A. V. 1926. *Law and public opinion*. London: Macmillan.

Dick-Peddie, W. A. 1993. *New Mexico vegetation: Past, present, and future*. Albuquerque: Univ. of New Mexico Press.

DiSilvestro, R. L. 1985. The federal animal damage control program. In *Audubon wildlife report 1985*, ed. R. L. DiSilvestro, 130–48. New York: National Audubon Society.

Dubey, J. P. 1999. Recent advances in *Neospora* and neosporosis. *Veterinary Parasitology* 84:349–67.

Dubey, J. P., L. Carpenter, A. Speer, M. J. Topper, and A. Uggla. 1988. Newly recognized fatal protozoan disease of dogs. *Journal of the American Veterinary Medical Association* 192:1269–85.

Dubey J. P., and D. S. Lindsay. 1996. A review of *Neospora caninum* and neosporosis. *Veterinary Parasitology* 67:1–59.

Duda, M. D., B. J. Gruver, S. Jacobs, T. Matthews, A. Lanier, O. Augustus, and S. J. Bissell. 1995. *Wildlife and the American mind: Public opinion on and attitudes toward fish and wildlife management*. Harrisonburg, VA: Responsive Management National Office.

Duda, M. D., and K. C. Young. 1995. *New Mexico residents' opinions toward Mexican wolf reintroduction*. Harrisonburg, VA: Responsive Management National Office.

Duffield, J. W., C. J. Neher, and D. A. Patterson. 1992.

Wolves and people in Yellowstone: A case study in the new resource economics. Unpublished report. Missoula, MT: Univ. of Montana.

Duffield, J. W., D. A. Patterson, C. J. Neher, and G. Pumb. 2006. Wolves and people in Yellowstone. Abstract in *18th annual North American Wolf conference, April 4–6, 2006, Chico Hot Springs, Montana, Defenders of Wildlife, Madison Valley Ranchlands Group, Nez Perce Tribe, Yellowstone National Park, and the Wolf Recovery Foundation*, 11. Washington, DC: Defenders of Wildlife.

Dunlap, T. R. 1988. *Saving America's wildlife.* Princeton, NJ: Princeton Univ. Press.

Dusek, G. L., A. K. Wood, and S. T. Stewart. 1992. Spatial and temporal patterns of mortality among female white-tailed deer. *Journal of Wildlife Management* 56:645–50.

Eisenstein, W. 1992. Wolf reintroduction into Yellowstone National Park, an attitudinal survey analysis. Master's thesis, Montana State Univ.

Elias, S. A. 2002. *The natural history of the Rocky Mountains.* Washington, DC: Smithsonian Institution Press.

Ellingson, J. A. 1996. Volcanic rocks. In *The western San Juan Mountains: Their geology, ecology, and history,* ed. B. Blair, 68–79. Niwot: Univ. Press of Colorado, Fort Lewis College Foundation.

Erickson, D. W., and D. A. Hamilton. 1988. Approaches to river otter restoration in Missouri. *Transactions of the North American Wildlife and Natural Resources Conference* 53:404–13.

Estes, J. A., K. Crooks, and R. Holt. 2001. Predation and diversity. In *Encyclopedia of biodiversity,* ed. S. Levin, 857–78. San Diego: Academic Press.

Estes, J. A., and D. O. Duggins. 1995. Sea otters and kelp forests in Alaska: Generality and variation in a community ecology paradigm. *Ecological Monographs* 65:75–100.

Estes, J. A., D. O. Duggins, and G. B. Rathbun. 1989. The ecology of extinctions in kelp forest communities. *Conservation Biology* 3:252–64.

Estes, J. A., N. S. Smith, and J. F. Palmisano. 1978. Sea otter predation and community organization in the western Aleutian Islands, Alaska. *Ecology* 59:822–33.

Estes, J. A., M. T. Tinker, T. M. Williams, and D. F. Doak. 1998. Killer whale predation on sea otters linking oceanic and nearshore ecosystems. *Science* 282:473–76.

Fahrig, L., J. H. Pedlar, S. E. Pope, P. D. Taylor, and J. F. Wegner. 1995. Effect of road traffic on amphibian density. *Biological Conservation* 73:177–82.

Fay, J. J., and M. Nammack. 1996. Policy regarding the recognition of distinct vertebrate population segments under the Endangered Species Act. *Federal Register* 61:4722.

Finch, D. M., and Ruggiero, L. F. 1993. Wildlife habitats and biodiversity in the Rocky Mountains and northern Great Plains. *Natural Areas Journal* 13:191–203.

Fink, M., K. Menke, and D. Shinneman. 2003. Methods for creating the wildlands network. In *Southern Rockies wildlands network,* eds. B. Miller, D. Foreman, M. Fink, D. Shinneman, J. Smith, M. DeMarco, M. Soulé, and R. Howard, 69–79. Golden, CO: Colorado Mountain Club Press.

Finley, B. 1999. High-tech vs. high altitude: Man and machines imperil timberline. *The Denver Post,* February 28, 1999.

Fischer, H. 1989. Restoring the wolf: Defenders launches a compensation fund. *Defenders* 64:9, 36.

Fischer, H., B. Snape, and W. Hudson. 1994. Building economic incentives into the Endangered Species Act. *Endangered Species Technical Bulletin* 19:4–5.

Fitzgerald, J. P., C. A. Meaney, and D. M. Armstrong. 1994. *Mammals of Colorado.* Denver and Boulder: Denver Museum of Natural History/Univ. Press of Colorado.

FitzGibbon, C. D., and J. Lazarus. 1995. Antipredator behavior of Serengeti ungulates: Individual differences and population consequences. In *Serengeti II: Dynamics, management, and conservation of an ecosystem,* ed. A. R. E. Sinclair and P. Arcese, 274–96. Chicago: Univ. of Chicago Press.

Fitzsimmons, N. N., S. W. Buskirk, and M. W. Smith. 1997. Genetic changes in reintroduced Rocky Mountain bighorn sheep populations. *Journal of Wildlife Management* 61:863–72.

Flannery, T. 1996. *The future eaters.* New York: Penguin.

———. 2001. *The eternal frontier.* New York: Atlantic Monthly Press.

Fleischner, T. L. 1994. Ecological costs of livestock grazing in western North America. *Conservation Biology* 8:629–44.

Fleming, T. H. 1975. The role of small mammals in tropical ecosystems. In *Small mammals: Their productivity and population dynamics,* ed. F. B. Golley, K. Petrusewicz, and L. Ryszkowski, 269–98. Cambridge: Cambridge Univ. Press.

Flores, D. L. 1996. A long love affair with an uncommon country: Environmental history and the Great Plains. In *Prairie conservation: Preserving North America's most endangered ecosystem,* ed. F. B. Sampson and F. L. Knopf, 3–18. Covelo, CA: Island Press.

Floyd, M. L., W. H. Romme, and D. D. Hanna. 2000. Fire history and vegetation pattern in Mesa Verde National Park, Colorado, USA. *Ecological Applications* 10:1666–80.

Floyd-Hannah, L., A. W. Spencer, and W. A. Romme. 1996. Biotic communities of the semiarid foothills and valleys. In *The western San Juan Mountains: Their geology, ecology, and history,* ed. B. Blair, 143–58. Niwot: Univ. Press of Colorado, Fort Lewis College Foundation.

Forbes, G. J., and J. B. Theberge. 1995. Influences of a migratory deer herd on wolf movements and mortality in and near Algonquin Park, Ontario. In *Ecology and conservation of wolves in a changing world,* Canadian Circumpolar Institute Occasional Publication 35, ed. L. N. Carbyn, S. H. Frotts, and D. R.

Seip, 303–14. Edmonton, AB: Canadian Circumpolar Institute, Univ. of Alberta.

Foreman, D. 1999. The Pleistocene-Holocene event: 40,000 years of extinction. *Wild Earth* (Winter) 9:1–5.

———. 2004. *Rewilding North America: A vision for conservation in the 21st century.* Washington, DC: Island Press.

Forman R. T. T. 2000. Estimate of the area affected ecologically by the road system in the United States. *Conservation Biology* 14:31–35.

Forman R. T. T., and R. D. Deblinger. 2000. The ecological road-effect zone of a Massachusetts (USA) suburban highway. *Conservation Biology* 14:36–46.

Forman R. T. T., and M. Godron. 1986. *Landscape ecology.* New York: John Wiley and Sons.

Fortin, D., H. L. Beyer, M. S. Boyce, D. W. Smith, T. Duchesne, and J. S. Mao. 2005. Wolves influence elk movements: Behavior shapes a trophic cascade in Yellowstone National Park. *Ecology* 86:1320–30.

Foss, P. O. 1960. *Politics and grass: The administration of grazing on the public domain.* New York: Greenwood Press.

Foster, M. L., and S. R. Humphrey. 1995. Use of highway underpasses by Florida panthers and other wildlife. *Wildlife Society Bulletin* 23:95–100.

Frankham, R. 1995. Conservation genetics. *Annual Review of Genetics* 29:305–37.

Frankham, R., J. D. Ballou, and D. A. Briscoe. 2002. *Introduction to conservation genetics.* Cambridge: Cambridge Univ. Press.

Freemuth, J. 1992. *Public opinion on wolves in Idaho: Results from the 1992 Idaho policy survey.* Boise, ID: Boise State Univ.

Fretwell, S. D. 1977. The regulation of plant communities by food chains exploiting them. *Perspectives of Biology and Medicine* 20:169–85.

———. 1987. Food chain dynamics: The central theory of ecology? *Oikos* 50:291–301.

Fritts, S. H. 1982. *Wolf depredation on livestock in Minnesota.* Research Report 145. Fort Snelling, MN: US Fish and Wildlife Service.

———. 1993. Reintroductions and translocations of wolves in North America. In *Ecological issues on reintroducing wolves into Yellowstone National Park,* Scientific Monograph NPS/NRYELL/NRSM-93/22, ed. R. Cook, 1–2. Denver: US National Park Service.

———. 1994. Memorandum regarding a viable wolf population in the Northern Rocky Mountains. In *The reintroduction of gray wolves to Yellowstone National Park and central Idaho,* Final Environmental Impact Statement, ed. US Fish and Wildlife Service, 6–68—6–78. Denver: US Fish and Wildlife Service.

Fritts, S. H., E. E. Bangs, J. A. Fontaine, W. G. Brewster, J. F. Gore. 1995. Restoring wolves to the Northern Rocky Mountains of the United States. In *Ecology and conservation of wolves in a changing world,* Canadian Circumpolar Institute, Occasional Publication

35, ed. L. N. Carbyn, S. H. Fritts, and D. R. Seip, 107–25. Edmonton, AB: Canadian Circumpolar Institute, Univ. of Alberta.

Fritts, S. H., E. E. Bangs, J. A. Fontaine, M. R. Johnson, M. K. Phillips, E. D. Koch, and J. R. Gunson. 1997. Planning and implementing a reintroduction of wolves to Yellowstone National Park and central Idaho. *Restoration Ecology* 5:7–27.

Fritts, S. H., and L. N. Carbyn. 1995. Population viability, nature reserves, and the outlook for gray wolf conservation in North America. *Restoration Ecology* 3:26–38.

Fritts, S. H., C. M. Mack, D. W. Smith, K. M. Murphy, M. K. Phillips, M. D. Jimenez, E. E. Bangs, et al. 2001. Outcomes of hard and soft releases of wolves in central Idaho and the Greater Yellowstone area. In *Large mammal restoration: Ecological and sociological challenges in the 21st century,* ed. D. S. Maehr, R. F. Noss, and J. L. Larkin, 125–47. Covelo, CA: Island Press.

Fritts, S. H., and L. D. Mech. 1981. Dynamics, movements, and feeding ecology of a newly protected wolf population in northwestern Minnesota. *Wildlife Monographs* 80:1–79.

Fritts, S. F., R. O. Stepheson, R. D. Hayes, and L. Boitani. 2003. Wolves and humans. In *Wolves: Behavior, ecology, and evolution,* ed. L. D. Mech and L. Boitani, 289–316. Chicago: Univ. of Chicago Press.

Fryxell, J. M. 1995. Aggregation and migration by grazing ungulates in relation to resources and predators. In *Serengeti II: Dynamics, management, and conservation of an ecosystem,* ed. A. R. E. Sinclair and P. Arcese, 257–73. Chicago: Univ. of Chicago Press.

Fryxell, J. M., J. Greever, and A. R. E. Sinclair. 1988. Why are migratory ungulates so abundant? *American Naturalist* 131:781–98.

Fuller, T. K. 1989. Population dynamics of wolves in north-central Minnesota. *Wildlife Monographs* 105:1–41

———. 1990. Dynamics of a declining white-tailed deer population in north-central Minnesota. *Wildlife Monograph* 110:1–37.

Fuller, T. K., W. E. Berg, G. L. Radde, M. S. Lenarz, and G. B. Joselyn. 1992. A history and current estimate of wolf distribution and numbers in north central Minnesota. *Wildlife Society Bulletin* 20:42–54.

Fuller, T. K., and L. B. Keith. 1980. Wolf population dynamics and prey relationships in northeastern Alberta. *Journal of Wildlife Management* 44:583–602.

Galbraith, J. R. 1977. *Organizational design.* Reading, MA: Addison-Wesley.

Gasaway, W. C., R. D. Boertje, D. V. Grangaard, D. G. Kellyhouse, R. O. Stevenson, and D. G. Larson. 1992. The role of predation in limiting moose at low densities in Alaska and Yukon and implications for conservation. *Wildlife Monographs* 120:1–59.

Gasaway, W. C., R. O. Stevenson, J. L. Davis, P. E. K. Shepherd, and O. E. Burris. 1983. Interrelationships of wolves, prey, and man in interior Alaska. *Wildlife Monographs* 84:1–54.

Gauthier, D. A., and J. B. Theberge. 1986. Wolf predation in the Burwash caribou herd, southwest Yukon. In *Fourth International Reindeer/Caribou Syposium*, ed. A. Gunn, F. L. Miller, and S. Skjenneberd, 137–44. Cambridge Bay, Northwest Territories: Northwest Territories Department of Renewable Resources.

Gese, E. M., R. L. Ruff, and R. L. Crabtree. 1996. Intrinsic and extrinsic factors influencing coyote predation on small mammals in Yellowstone National Park. *Canadian Journal of Zoology* 74:784–97.

Gilbert, F. F. 1995. Historical perspectives on wolf management in North America with special reference to human treatments in capture methods. In *Ecology and conservation of wolves in a changing world*, Canadian Circumpolar Institute Occasional Publication 35, ed. L. N. Carbyn, S. H. Fritts, and D. R. Seip, 13–18. Edmonton, AB: Canadian Circumpolar Institute, Univ. of Alberta.

Gillin, C. M., G. M. Tabor, and A. A. Aguirre. 2000. Ecological health and wildlife disease management in national parks. In *Conservation medicine: Ecological health in practice*, ed. A. A. Aguirre, R. S. Ostfeld, G. M. Tabor, C. House, and M. C. Pearl, 253–64. Oxford: Oxford Univ. Press.

Gilpin, M. E., and M. E. Soulé. 1986. Minimum viable populations: The processes of species extinction. In *Conservation biology*, ed. M. E. Soulé, 19–34. Sunderland, MA: Sinauer Associates.

Gipson, P. S., W. B. Ballard, and R. M. Nowak. 1998. Famous North American wolf and the credibility of early wildlife literature. *Wildlife Society Bulletin* 26:808–16.

Gittleman, J. L., and S. L. Pimm. 1991. Crying wolf in North America. *Nature* 351:524–25.

Goldblum, D., and T. T. Veblen. 1992. Fire history in ponderosa pine/Douglas fir forest in the Colorado Front Range. *Physical Geography* 13:133–48.

Goldschmidt, T. 1996. *Darwin's dreampond: Drama in Lake Victoria*. Cambridge, MA: MIT Press.

Gondim, L. F. P. 2006. *Neospora* in wildlife. *Trends in Parasitology* 22:6.

Gondim, L. F. P., M. McAllister, W. Pitt, and D. Zemlicka. 2004. Coyotes (*Canis latrans*) are definitive hosts of *Neospora caninum*. *International Journal of Parasitology* 34:159–61.

Gondim, L. F. P., M. M. McAllister, N. E. Mateus-Pinilla, W. C. Pitt, L. D. Mech, and M. E. Nelson. 2004. Transmission of *Neospora caninum* between wild and domestic animals. *Journal of Parasitology* 90 (6):1361–65.

Gordon, J. R. 1983. *A diagnostic approach to organizational behavior*. Boston: Allyn and Bacon.

Graham, R. W., and E. Lundelius. 1984. Coevolutionary disequilibrium and Pleistocene extinctions. In *Quaternary extinctions: A prehistoric revolution*, ed. P. S. Martin and R. G. Klein, 223–49. Tucson: Univ. of Arizona Press.

Graham, R. W., E. Lundelius, M. A. Graham, E. K. Schroeder, R. S. Toomey, E. Anderson, A. D. Barnosky, et al. 1996. Spatial response of mammals to late Quaternary environmental fluctuations. *Science* 272:1601–6.

Greenwalt, L. 1988. Reflections on the power and potential of the Endangered Species Act. *Endangered Species Update* 5:7–9.

Greenwood, P. J. 1980. Mating systems, philopatry, and dispersal in birds and mammals. *Animal Behavior* 28:1140–62

Griffith, B., J. M. Scott, J. W. Carpenter, and C. Reed. 1989. Translocation as a species conservation tool: Status and strategy. *Science* 245:477–480.

Groebner, D. J., A. L. Girmendonk, and T. B. Johnson. 1995. *A proposed cooperative reintroduction plan for the Mexican wolf in Arizona*. Arizona Game and Fish Department Technical Report 56. Phoenix: Arizona Game and Fish Department.

Grossman, D. H., D. Faber-Langendoen, A. S. Weakley, M. Anderson, P. Bourgeron, R. Crawford, K. Goodin, et al. 1998. *International classification of ecological communities: Terrestrial vegetation of the United States*. Vol. I: *The National Vegetation Classification Standard*. Arlington, VA: The Nature Conservancy.

Grumbine, R. E. 1990. Protecting biological diversity through the greater ecosystem concept. *Natural Areas Journal* 10:114–20.

Gutzwiller, K. J., and S. H. Anderson. 1987. Multiscale associations between cavity nesting birds and features of Wyoming streamside woodlands. *Condor* 89:534–48.

Haig, S. M., J. D. Ballou, and S. R. Derrickson. 1990. Management options for preserving genetic diversity: Reintroduction of Guam rails to the wild. *Conservation Biology* 4:290–300.

Haight, R. G., D. J. Mladenoff, and A. P. Wydeven. 1998. Modeling disjunct gray wolf populations in semi-wild landscapes. *Conservation Biology* 12:879–88.

Hairston, N. G., F. E. Smith, and L. B. Slobodkin. 1960. Community structure, population control, and competition. *American Naturalist* 94:421–25.

Halaj, J., and D. H. Wise. 2001. Terrestrial trophic cascades: How much do they trickle? *The American Naturalist* 157:262–81.

Hall, E. R. 1981. *The mammals of North America*, 2nd ed. New York: John Wiley and Sons.

Hall, E. R., and K. R. Kelson. 1959. *The mammals of North America*. Vol. 2. New York: The Ronald Press Co.

Hampton, B. 1997. *The great American wolf*. New York: Owl Books.

Hardy-Short, D. C., and C. B. Short. 2000. Science, economics, and rhetoric: Environmental advocacy and the wolf reintroduction debate, 1987–1999. In *Wilderness science in a time of change conference May 23–27, 1999, Missoula, MT*, Proceedings RMRS-P-15-, vol. 2, *Wilderness within the context of larger systems*, compiled S. F. McCool, D. N. Cole, W. T. Borrie, J. O'Loughlin, 65–72. Ogden, UT: US Department of Agriculture, Forest Service, Rocky Mountain Research Station.

Harrington, M. G., and S. S. Sackett. 1992. Past and present influences on southwestern ponderosa pine old growth. In *Old-growth forests in the Southwest and Rocky Mountain regions: Proceedings of a workshop*, USDA Forest Service General Technical Report RM-213, ed. M. R. Kaufmann, W. H. Moir, and R. L. Bassett, 44–50. Fort Collins, CO: USDA Forest Service Rocky Mountain Forest and Range Experiment Station.

Harrison, D. J., and T. G. Chapin. 1998. Extent and connectivity of habitat for wolves in eastern North America. *Wildlife Society Bulletin* 26:767–75.

Harrison, R. 1972. Understanding your organization's character. *Harvard Business Review* (May–June):119–28.

Hayes, R. D., A. Baer, and D. L. Larson. 1991. *Population dynamics and prey relationships of an exploited and recovering wolf population in southern Yukon*. Yukon Fish and Wildlife Final Report TR-91-1. Whitehorse, YT: Yukon Fish and Wildlife.

Hayes, R. D., A. M. Baer, U. Wotschikowsky, and A. S. Harestad. 2000. Kill rate by wolves on moose in the Yukon. *Canadian Journal of Zoology* 78:60–66.

Hayes, R. D., and A. S. Harestad. 2000. Demography of a recovering wolf population in the Yukon. *Canadian Journal of Zoology* 78:36–48.

Hayward, G. D. 1994. Review of technical knowledge: Boreal owls. In *Flammulated, boreal, and great gray owls in the United States: A technical conservation assessment*, USDA Forest Service General Technical Report RM-217, ed. G. D. Hayward and J. Verner, 92–127. Fort Collins, CO: USDA Forest Service Rocky Mountain Forest and Range Experiment Station.

Hedrick, P. W. 2001. Conservation genetics: Where are we now? *Trends in Ecology and Evolution* 16:629–36.

Henke, S. E., and F. C. Bryant. 1999. Effects of coyote removal on the faunal community in western Texas. *Journal of Wildlife Management* 63:1066–81.

Henry, V. G. 1997. 90-day finding for a petition to delist the red wolf. *Federal Register* 62:64799–800.

———. 1998. Notice of termination of the red wolf reintroduction project in the Great Smoky Mountains National Park. *Federal Register* 63:54151–53.

Hinchman, S., and B. Noreen. 1993. Colorado mining industry strikes again. *High Country News*, January 25, 1993.

Hoogland, J. L. 1995. *The black-tailed prairie dog: Social life of a burrowing mammal*. Chicago: Univ. of Chicago Press.

Hook, D. 1982. A survey of public attitudes toward predators in six Michigan counties. Master's thesis, Northern Michigan Univ.

Hook, R. A., and W. L. Robinson. 1982. Attitudes of Michigan residents toward predators. In *Wolves of the world: Perspectives of behavior, ecology, and conservation*, ed. F. H. Harrington and P. C. Paquet, 382–94. Park Ridge, NJ: Noyes Publications.

Huggard, D. J. 1993. Prey selectivity of wolves in Banff National Park. I. Prey species. *Canadian Journal of Zoology* 71:130–39.

Hunter M. D., and P. W. Price. 1992. Playing chutes and ladders: Heterogeneity and the relative roles of bottom-up and top-down forces in natural communities. *Ecology* 73:724–32.

Idaho Environmental Science Teachers. 1987. Attitude survey (wolf) in McCall. Report, Wildlife Issues Course, Univ. of Idaho.

Idaho Legislative Wolf Oversight Committee. 2002. *Idaho wolf conservation and management plan*. Boise: Idaho Department of Fish and Game.

Ingham, R. E., and J. K. Detling. 1984. Plant–herbivore interactions in a North American mixed-grass prairie: III. Soil nematode populations and root biomass on *Cynomys ludovicianus* colonies and adjacent uncolonized areas. *Oecologia* 63:307–13.

Ingram, K., and J. Lewandrowski. 1999. Wildlife conservation and economic development in the West. *Rural Development Perspectives* 14:44–51.

Isbister, J. 1993. *Promises not kept: The betrayal of social change in the third world*. West Hartford, CT: Kumarian Press.

Isenberg, A. C. 1992. Toward a policy of destruction: Buffaloes, law, and the market, 1803–1883. *Great Plains Quarterly* 12:227–41.

IUCN. 1987. *Translocation of living organisms: Introductions, reintroductions, and restocking*. IUCN Position Statement. Gland, Switzerland: International Union for the Conservation of Nature.

Jacobs, B. F., R. G. Gatewood, and C. D. Allen. 2002. *Watershed restoration in degraded piñon-juniper woodlands: A paired watershed study 1996–1998*. Final report to USGS-BRD Research/NPS-Natural Resource Preservation Program. Los Alamos, NM: Bandelier National Monument.

Jablonski, D. 1995. Extinction in the fossil record. In *Extinction rates*, ed. J. H. Lawton and R. M. May, 25–44. Oxford: Oxford Univ. Press.

Jamieson, D. W., W. H. Romme, and P. Somers. 1996. Biotic communities of the cool mountains. In *The western San Juan Mountains: Their geology, ecology, and history*, ed. B. Blair, 159–73. Niwot: Univ. Press of Colorado, Fort Lewis College Foundation.

Janis, I. L. 1972. *Victims of group-think: A psychological study of foreign-policy decisions and fiascos*. Boston: Houghton-Mifflin.

Janzen, D. H. 1983. The Pleistocene hunters had help. *American Naturalist* 121:598–99.

Jaquish, C. E. 1994. Evidence of hybrid vigor in subspecific hybrids of the saddle-back tamarin (*Saguinus fuscicollis*). *American Journal of Primatology* 33:263–76.

Jedrzejewska, B., and W. Jedrzejewski. 1998. *Predation in vertebrate communities: The Bialowieza Primeval Forest as a case study*. Berlin: Springer Verlag.

Jedrzejewski, W., K. Schmidt, J. Theuerkauf, B. Jedrzejewska, N. Selva, K. Zub, and L. Szymura. 2002. Kill rates and predation by wolves on ungulate populations in Bialowieza Primeval Forest (Poland). *Ecology* 83:1341–56.

Johnson, K. H., and C. E. Braun. 1999. Viability and

conservation of an exploited sage grouse population. *Conservation Biology* 13:77–84.

Johnson, M. R. 1995. Rabies in wolves and its potential role in a Yellowstone wolf population. In *Ecology and conservation of wolves in a changing world*, ed. L. N. Carbyn, S. H. Fritts, and D. R. Seip, 431–39. Edmonton, AB: Canadian Circumpolar Institute.

Johnson, M. R., D. K. Boyd, and D. H. Pletscher. 1994. Serologic investigations of canine parvovirus and canine distemper in relation to wolf (*Canis lupus*) pup mortalities. *Journal of Wildlife Diseases* 30 (2):270–73.

Johnson, O. W., T. A. Flagg, D. J. Maynard, G. B. Milner, and F.W. Waknitz. 1991. Status review for the lower Columbia River coho salmon. National Oceanic and Atmospheric Administration Technical Memoirs F/NWC-202. Seattle, WA: National Marine Fisheries Service.

Jones, J. R., N. V. DeByle, and D. M. Bowers. 1985. Insects and other invertebrates. In *Aspen: Ecology and management in the western United States*, USDA Forest Service General Technical Report RM-119, ed. N. V. DeByle and R. P. Winokur, 107–14. Washington, DC: USDA Forest Service.

Jones, K., and D. Cooper. 1993. *Wetlands of Colorado*. Denver: Colorado Department of Natural Resources.

Jule, K. R., L. A. Leaver, and S. E. G. Lea. 2008. The effects of captive experience on reintroduction survival in carnivores: A review and analysis. *Biological Conservation* 141 (2):355–63.

Kaufman, L. 1992. Catastrophic change in a species-rich freshwater ecosystem: Lessons from Lake Victoria. *BioScience* 42:846–58.

Kay, C. E. 1990. Yellowstone's northern elk herd: A critical evaluation of the "natural regulation" paradigm. PhD diss., Utah State Univ.

———. 1994. Aboriginal overkill: The role of Native Americans in structuring western ecosystems. *Human Nature* 5:359–96.

———. 1995. Aboriginal overkill and native burning: Implications for modern eocystem management. *Western Journal of Applied Forestry* 10:121–26.

———. 2007. Were native people keystone predators? A continuous-time analysis of wildlife observations made by Lewis and Clark in 1804–1806. *Canadian Field Naturalist* 121 (1):1–16.

Kay, C. E., and F. H. Wagner. 1994. Historic condition of woody vegetation on Yellowstone's northern range: A critical test of the "natural regulation" paradigm. In *Plants and their environments: Proceedings of the first biennial conference on the Greater Yellowstone Ecosystem*, US National Park Service Technical Report NPS/NRYELL/NRTR-93/xx, ed. D. Despain, 159–69. Denver, CO: US National Park Service.

Keesing, F. 2000. Crytic consumers and the ecology of an African savanna. *BioScience* 50:205–15.

Keith, L. B. 1983. Population dynamics of wolves. In *Wolves in Canada and Alaska*, Canadian Wildlife Report Series No. 45, ed. L. N. Carbyn, 66–77. Ottawa, ON: Canadian Wildlife Service.

Keller, L. F., and D. M. Waller. 2002. Inbreeding effects in wild populations. *Trends in Ecology and Evolution* 17:199–245.

Kellert, S. R. 1976. Perceptions of animals in American society. *Transactions of the North American Wildlife and Natural Resources Conference* 41:534–37.

———. 1980. Contemporary values of wildlife in American society. In *Wildlife values*, Center for Assessment of Noncommodity Natural Resource Values Institute Series Report No. 1, ed. W. W. Shaw and E. H. Zube, 31–60. Tucson, AZ: Center for Assessment of Noncommodity Natural Resource Values.

———. 1984. Assessing wildlife and environmental values in cost-benefit analysis. *Journal of Environmental Management* 18:355–63.

———. 1985a. Public perceptions of predators, particularly the wolf and coyote. *Biological Conservation* 31:167–89.

———. 1985b. *The public and the timber wolf in Minnesota*. New Haven, CT: Yale Univ. Press.

———. 1986a. The public and the timber wolf in Minnesota. *Transactions of the North American Wildlife and Natural Resources Conference* 51:193–200.

———. 1986b. Social and perceptual factors in the preservation of animal species. In *The preservation of species: The value of biological diversity*, ed. B. G. Norton, 50–73. Princeton, NJ: Princeton Univ. Press.

———. 1990. Public attitudes and beliefs about the wolf and its restoration in Michigan. Internal report, School of Forestry and Environmental Studies, Yale Univ.

———. 1993. *Kinship to master: Biophilia in human evolution and development*. Covelo, CA: Island Press.

———. 1996. *The value of life: Biological diversity and human society*. Washington, DC: Island Press.

———. 1999. *The public and the wolf in Minnesota, 1999: Interim report*. Minneapolis, MN: International Wolf Center.

Kellert, S. R., M. Black, C. R. Rush, and A. J. Bath. 1996. Human culture and large carnivore conservation in North America. *Conservation Biology* 10:977–90.

Kelly, B. T., P. S. Miller, and U. S. Seal. 1999. Population and habitat viability assessment workshop for the red wolf (*Canis rufus*). Apple Valley, MN: Conservation Breeding Specialist Group.

Kelly, B. T. and M. K. Phillips. 2000. Red wolf. In *Endangered animals: A reference guide to conflicting issues*, ed. R. P. Reading and B. Miller, 247–52. Westport, CT: Greenwood Press.

King, J. E., and J. J. Saunders. 1984. Environmental insularity and the extinction of the American mastodont. In *Quaternary extinctions: A prehistoric revolution*, ed. P. S. Martin and R. G. Klein, 315–39. Tucson: Univ. of Arizona Press.

Kipfmueller, K. F., and W. L. Baker. 1998. Fires and dwarf mistletoe in a Rocky Mountain lodgepole pine ecosystem. *Forest Ecology and Management* 108:77–84.

———. 2000. A fire history of a subalpine forest in south-eastern Wyoming, USA. *Journal of Biogeography* 27:71–85.

Kleiman, D. G. 1989. Reintroductions of captive mammals for conservation: Guidelines for reintroducing endangered species into the wild. *BioScience* 39:152–61

Kleiman, D. G., B. B. Beck, J. M. Dietz, L. A. Dietz, J. D. Ballou, and A. F. Coimbra-Filho. 1986. Conservation program for the golden lion tamarin: Captive research management, ecological studies, educational strategies, and reintroduction. In *Primates: The road to self-sustaining populations*, ed. K. Benirschek, 959–79. New York: Springer-Verlag.

Kleiman, D. G., R. P. Reading, B. J. Miller, T. W. Clark, J. M. Scott, J. Robinson, R. L. Wallace, R. J. Cabin, and F. Felleman. 2000. Improving the evaluation of conservation programs. *Conservation Biology* 14:356–65.

Kleiman, D. G., M. R. Stanley-Price, and B. B. Beck. 1993. Criteria for reintroductions. In *Conservation: Interactive management of wild and captive animals*, ed. P. J. S. Olney, G. M. Mace, and A. T. C. Feistner, 287–303. London: Chapman and Hall.

Kloor, K. 1999. Lynx and biologists try to recover after disastrous start. *Science* 285 (5426):320–21.

Knapp, A. K., J. M. Blair, J. M. Briggs, S. L. Collins, D. C. Hartnett, L. C. Johnson, and E. G. Towne. 1999. The keystone role of bison in North American tallgrass prairie. *BioScience* 49:39–49.

Knick, S. T., and J. T. Rotenberry. 1995. Landscape characteristics of fragmented shrubsteppe habitats and breeding passerine birds. *Conservation Biology* 9:1059–71.

Knight, D. H. 1994. Mountains and plains: The ecology of Wyoming landscapes. New Haven, CT: Yale Univ. Press.

Knight, D. H., and W. A. Reiners. 2000. Natural patterns in Southern Rocky Mountain landscapes and their relevance to forest management. In *Forest fragmentation in the Southern Rocky Mountains*, ed. R. L. Knight, F. W. Smith, S. W. Buskirk, W. H. Romme, and W. L. Baker, 15–30. Boulder: Univ. Press of Colorado.

Knight, D. H., and L. L. Wallace. 1989. The Yellowstone fires: Issues in landscape ecology. *BioScience* 39:700–6.

Knight, R. L., ed. 1995. *Wildlife and recreationists: Coexistence through management and research*. Covelo, CA: Island Press.

Knight, R. L. 2000. Forest fragmentation and outdoor recreation in the Southern Rocky Mountains. In *Forest fragmentation in the Southern Rocky Mountains*, ed. R. L. Knight, F. W. Smith, S. W. Buskirk, W. H. Romme, and W. L. Baker, 135–53. Boulder: Univ. Press of Colorado.

Knight, R. L, F. W. Smith, S. W. Buskirk, W. H. Romme, and W. L. Baker, eds. 2000. *Forest fragmentation in the Southern Rocky Mountains*. Boulder: Univ. Press of Colorado.

Kocher, S., and E. H. Williams. 2000. The diversity and abundance of North American butterflies vary with habitat disturbance and geography. *Journal of Biogeography* 27:785–94.

Korten, D. C. 1995. *When corporations rule the world*. West Hartford, CT: Kumarian Press.

Kotler, B. P., J. S. Brown, R. H. Slowtow, W. L. Goodfriend, and M. Strauss. 1993. The influence of snakes on the foraging behavior of gerbils. *Oikos* 67:309–16.

Kotlier, N. B., B. W. Baker, A. D. Whicker, and G. Plumb. 1999. A critical review of assumptions about the prairie dogs as a keystone species. *Environmental Management* 24:177–192.

Krebs, C. J., R. Boonstra, S. Boutin, and A. R. E. Sinclair. 2001. What drives the 10-year cycle of snowshoe hares? *BioScience* 51:25–35.

Krebs, C. J., S. Boutin, R. Boonstra, A. R. E. Sinclair, J. N. M. Smith, M. R. T. Dale, and R. Turkington. 1995. Impact of food and predation on the snowshoe hare cycle. *Science* 269:1112–14.

Kreeger, T. J. 2003. The internal wolf: Physiology, pathology, and pharmacology. In *Wolves: Behavior, ecology, and conservation*, ed. L. D. Mech and L. Boitani, 202–14 Chicago: Univ. of Chicago Press.

Kunkel, K. E. 1997. Predation by wolves and other large carnivores in northwestern Montana and southeastern British Columbia. PhD diss., Univ. of Montana.

Kunkel, K. E., and D. H. Pletscher. 1999. Species-specific population dynamics of cervids in a multipredator ecosystem. *Journal of Wildlife Management* 63:1082–93.

———. 2000. Habitat factors affecting vulnerability of moose to predation by wolves in southeastern British Columbia. *Canadian Journal of Zoology* 78:150–57.

———. 2001. Winter hunting patterns of wolves in and near Glacier National Park, Montana. *Journal of Wildlife Management* 65:520–30.

Kunkel, K. E., T. K. Ruth, D. H. Pletscher, and M. G. Hornocker. 1999. Winter prey selection by wolves and cougars in and near Glacier National Park, Montana. *Journal of Wildlife Management* 63:901–10.

Kurtén, B. 1971. *The age of mammals*. London: Weidenfeld and Nicolson.

Kuyt, E. 1972. Food habits and ecology of wolves on barren-ground caribou range in the Northwest Territories. Canadian Wildlife Service Report Series No. 21:1–36. Ottawa, ON: Canadian Wildlife Service.

Lacy, R. C. 1997. Importance of genetic variation to the viability of mammalian populations. *Journal of Mammalogy* 78:320–35.

Laikre, L., and N. Ryman. 1991. Inbreeding depression in a captive wolf (*Canis lupus*) population. *Conservation Biology* 5:33–40.

Lambeck, R. J. 1997. Focal species: A multi-species umbrella for nature conservation. *Conservation Biology* 11:849–56.

Lasswell, H. D. 1971. *A Pre-view of the policy sciences*. New York: Elsevier.

Lasswell, H. D., and A. Kaplan. 1950. *Power and society: A framework for political inquiry*. New Haven, CT: Yale Univ. Press.

Lawrence, B., and W. H. Bossert. 1967. Multiple character analysis of *Canis lupus, latrans,* and *familiaris,* with a discussion of the relationships of *Canis niger. American Zoologist* 7:223–32.

Legislature of the State of Idaho. 2005. House of Representatives: House Joint Memorial No. 5. 58th Legislature, 1st Regular Session. www3.state.id.us/oasis/2005/HJM005.html (accessed April 15, 2009).

Lehman, N., A. Eisenhawer, A. Hansen, L. D. Mech, R. O. Peterson, P. J. Gogan, and R. K. Wayne. 1991. Introgression of coyote mitochondrial DNA into sympatric North American gray wolf populations. *Evolution* 45:104–19.

Leirfallom, J. 1970. Wolf management in Minnesota. In *Proceedings of a symposium of wolf management in selected areas of North America,* ed. S. E. Jorgensen, C. E. Faulkner, and L. D. Mech, 9–15. Fort Snelling, MN: US Fish and Wildlife Service.

Lenihan, M. L. 1987. *Montanans ambivalent on wolves: The Montana poll.* Report to Bureau of Business and Economic Research. Missoula: Univ. of Montana.

Leopold, A. 1933. *Game management.* New York: Charles Scribner's Sons.

———. 1944. A review—The wolves of North America (by Young and Goldman). *Journal of Forestry* 42:928–29.

———. 1966. *A sand county almanac.* New York: Ballatine Books

Leopold, A. Starker. 1964. Predator and rodent control in the United States. *Transactions of the North American Wildlife and Natural Resources Conference* 29:27–49.

Levi-Strauss, C. 1963. *Totemism.* Boston: Beacon Press.

———. 1966. *The savage mind.* Chicago: Univ. of Chicago Press.

Lewis, N. 1988. *The missionaries: God against the Indians.* New York: Penguin Books.

Licht, D. S. 1997. *Ecology and economics of the Great Plains.* Lincoln: Univ. of Nebraska Press.

Linnell, J. D. C., R. Aanes, J. E. Swenson, J. Odden, and M. E. Smith. 1997. Translocation of carnivores as a method for managing problem animals: A review. *Biodiversity and Conservation* 6:1245–57.

Locke, J. 1690. *The second treatise on government.* London: Awnsham Churchill.

Logan, K. A., and L. L. Sweanor. 2001. *Desert puma: Evolutionary ecology and conservation of an enduring carnivore.* Covelo, CA: Island Press.

Logan, K. A., L. L. Sweanor, T. K. Ruth, and M. G. Hornocker. 1996. *Cougars of the San Andres Mountains, New Mexico.* Unpublished Final Report to New Mexico Department of Game and Fish. Alburqueque: New Mexico Department of Game and Fish.

Loomis, J. 2004. The role of economics in managing natural resources for society. In *Society and natural resources: A summary of knowledge,* ed. M. J. Manfredo, J. J. Vaske, B. L. Bruyere, D. R. Field, and P. J. Brown, 295–304. Jefferson, MO: Modern Litho.

Lopez, B. H. 1978. *Of wolves and men.* New York: Charles Scribner's Sons.

Ludwig, D., R. Hilborn, and C. Walters. 1993. Uncertainty, resources exploitation, and conservation: Lessons from history. *Science* 260:17, 36.

Lynch, A. M., and T. W. Swetnam. 1992. Old-growth mixed-conifer and western spruce budworm in the Southern Rocky Mountains. In *Old-growth forests in the Southwest and Rocky Mountain regions: Proceedings of a workshop.* USDA Forest Service General Technical Report RM-213, ed. M. R. Kaufmann, W. H. Moir, and R. L. Bassett, 66–80. Fort Collins, CO: USDA Forest Service, Rocky Mountain Forest and Range Experiment Station.

Lyon, L. J. 1983. Road density models describing habitat effectiveness for elk. *Journal of Forestry* 81:592–95.

Mac, M. J., P. A. Opler, C. E. Puckett Haeker, and P. D. Doran. 1998. *Status and trends of the nation's biological resources.* Washington, DC: US Geological Survey.

Madsen, T., R. Shine, M. Olssen, and H. Wittzell. 1999. Restoration of an inbred adder population. *Nature* 402:34–35.

Maehr, D. S., R. F. Noss, and J. L. Larkin, eds. 2001. *Large mammal restoration.* Washington, DC: Island Press.

Magdoff, H. 1969. *The age of imperialism: The economics of US foreign policy.* New York: Monthly Review Press.

Manfredo, M. J., A. D. Bright, J. Pate, and G. Tischbein. 1994. *Colorado residents' attitudes and perceptions toward reintroduction of the gray wolf* (Canis lupus) *into Colorado.* Project Report No. 21. Fort Collins: Human Dimensions in Natural Resources Unit, Colorado State Univ.

Manfredo, M. J., J. J. Vaske, G. E. Haas, and D. Fulton. 1993. *The Colorado environmental poll.* CEP #2. Fort Collins: Human Dimensions in Natural Resources Unit, Colorado State Univ.

Marsh, R. E. 1984. Ground squirrels, prairie dogs, and marmots as pests on rangeland. In *Proceedings of the Conference for Organization and Practice of Vertebrate Pest Control, August 30—September 3, 1982, Hampshire, UK,* 195–208. Fernherst, UK: ICI Plant Protection Division.

Martin, B., R. Edward, A. Jones. 1999. Mapping a future for wolves in the Southern Rockies. *Southern Rockies Wolf Tracks* 7 (Winter):1–12.

Martin, P. S. 1984. Prehistoric overkill: The global model. In *Quaternary extinctions: A prehistoric revolution,* ed. P. S. Martin and R. G. Klein, 354–403. Tucson: Univ. of Arizona Press.

Martin, P. S., and D. Burney. 1999. Bring back the elephants! *Wild Earth* 9:57–64

Martin, P. S., and R. G. Klein, eds. 1984. *Quaternary extinctions: A prehistoric revolution.* Tucson: Univ. of Arizona Press.

Martin, P. S., and C. R. Szuter. 1999. War zones and game sinks in Lewis and Clark's West. *Conservation Biology* 13:36–45.

———. 2002. Game parks before and after Lewis and

Clark: Reply to Lyman and Wolverton. *Conservation Biology* 16:244–47.

Maxwell, J. R., C. J. Edwards, M. E. Jensen, S. J. Paustian, H. Parrott, and D. M. Hill. 1995. *A hierarchical framework of aquatic ecological units in North America (nearctic zone)*. USDA Forest Service General Technical Report NC-176. St. Paul, MN: USDA Forest Service North Central Forest Experimental Station.

May, R. M. 1991. The role of ecological theory in planning the reintroduction of endangered species. *Symposium of the Zoological Society, London* 62:145–63.

McAllister, M. M., J. P. Dubey, and D. S. Lindsay. 1998. Dogs are definitive hosts of *Neospora caninum*. *International Journal of Parasitology* 28:1473–78.

McCain, L. A., R. P. Reading, and B. J. Miller. 2002. Prairie dog gone: Myth, persecution, and preservation of a keystone species. In *Welfare ranching: The subsidized destruction of the American West*, ed. M. Wuerthner and G. Wuerthner, 230–35. Washington, DC: Island Press.

McCarley, H. 1962. The taxonomic status of wild *Canis* (Canidae) in the southcentral United States. *Southwestern Naturalist* 7:227–35.

McCarley, H., and C. J. Carley. 1979. *Recent changes in the distribution and status of wild red wolves* (Canis rufus). Endangered Species Report No. 4. Albuquerque, NM: US Fish and Wildlife Service.

McClellan, B., and D. Shackleton. 1988. Grizzly bears and resource-extraction industries: Effects of roads on behaviour, habitat use, and demography. *Journal of Applied Ecology* 25:451–60.

McDonald, J. 1984. The reordered North American selection regime and late Quaternary megafaunal extinctions. In *Quaternary extinctions: A prehistoric revolution*, ed. P. S. Martin and R. G. Klein, 404–39. Tucson: Univ. of Arizona Press.

McIntyre, R., ed. 1995. *War against the wolf: America's campaign to exterminate the wolf*. Stillwater, MN: Voyageur Press.

McLaren, B. E., and R. O. Peterson. 1994. Wolves, moose, and tree rings on Isle Royale. *Science* 266:1555–58.

McNab, W. H., and P. E. Avers. 1994. *Ecological subregions of the United States: Section descriptions*. US Department of Agriculture, Forest Service Report WO-WSA-5. Washington, DC: US Forest Service.

McNaught, D. A. 1985. Park visitors' attitudes towards wolf recovery in Yellowstone National Park. Master's thesis, Univ. of Montana.

McShea, W., and J. Rappole. 1992. White-tailed deer as a keystone species within forested habitats of Virginia. *Virginia Journal of Science* 43:177–86.

McShea, W., H. B. Underwood, and J. H. Rappole, eds. 1997. *The science of overabundance: Deer ecology and management*. Washington, DC: Smithsonian Institution Press.

Meadow, R. 2001. *Southern Rockies wildlife and wilderness survey report*. Washington, DC: Decision Research.

Meadow, R., R. P. Reading, M. Phillips, M. Mehringer, and B. J. Miller. 2005. The influence of persuasive arguments on public attitudes toward a proposed wolf restoration in the Southern Rockies. *Wildlife Society Bulletin* 33 (1):154–63.

Mech, L. D. 1966. *The wolves of Isle Royale*. Fauna Series No. 7. Washington, DC: US National Park Service.

———. 1970. *The wolf: The ecology and behavior of an endangered species*. New York: Natural History Press, Doubleday.

———. 1977a. Population trend and winter deer consumption in a Minnesota wolf pack. In *Proceedings of the 1975 predator symposium*, ed. R. L. Phillips and C. Jonkel, 55–83. Missoula: Montana Forestry and Conservation Experimental Station Univ. of Montana.

———. 1977b. Productivity, mortality, and population trends of wolves in northeastern Minnesota. *Journal of Mammalogy* 58:559–74.

———. 1986. *Wolf population in the central Superior National Forest, 1967–1985*. US Forest Service Research Paper NC-270. St. Paul, MN: US Forest Service.

———. 1989. Wolf population survival in an area of high road density. *American Midland Naturalist* 121:387–89.

———. 1995. The challenge and opportunity of recovering wolf populations. *Conservation Biology* 9:270–78.

———. 1996. A new era for carnivore conservation. *Wildlife Society Bulletin* 24:397–401.

———. 1999. Estimated costs of maintaining a recovered wolf population in agricultural regions of Minnesota. *Wildlife Society Bulletin* 26:817–22.

———. 2001. Managing Minnesota's recovered wolves. *Wildlife Society Bulletin* 29:70–77.

Mech, L. D., and L. D. Frenzel, eds. 1971. *Ecological studies of the timber wolf in northeastern Minnesota*. US Department of Agriculture Forest Service Research Paper NC-52. St. Paul, MN: North Central Forest Experiment Station.

Mech, L. D., and S. H. Fritts. 1987. Parvovirus and heartworm found in Minnesota wolves. *Endangered Species Technical Bulletin* 12:5–6.

Mech, L. D., S. H. Fritts, G. L. Radde, and W. J. Paul. 1988. Wolf distribution and road density in Minnesota. *Wildlife Society Bulletin* 1:195–98.

Mech, L. D., S. H. Fritts, and M. E. Nelson. 1996. Wolf management in the 21st century: From public input to sterilization. *Journal of Wildlife Research* 1:195–98.

Mech, L. D., S. H. Fritts, and R. P. Thiel. 1985. Presence and effects of the dog louse *Trichdectes canis* (Mallophaga, Trichedectidae) on wolves and coyotes from Minnesota and Wisconsin. *American Midland Naturalist* 114:404–405.

Mech, L. D., and S. M. Goyal. 1993. Canine parvovirus effect on wolf population change and pup survival. *Journal of Wildlife Diseases* 29:330–33.

Mech, L. D., S. M. Goyal, W. J. Paul, and W. E. Newton. 2008. Demographic effects of canine parvovirus on a free-ranging wolf population over 30 years. *Journal of Wildlife Diseases* 44 (4):824–36.

Mech, L. D., E. K. Harper, T. J. Meier, and W. J. Paul. 2000. Assessing factors that may predispose Minnesota farms to wolf depredation on cattle. *Wildlife Society Bulletin* 28:623–29.

Mech, L. D., and P. D. Karns. 1977. *Role of the wolf in deer decline in the Superior National Forest.* US Forest Service Research Paper NC-148. St. Paul, MN: US Forest Service.

Mech, L. D., and M. E. Nelson. 2000. Do wolves affect white-tailed buck harvest in northeastern Minnesota? *Journal of Wildlife Management* 64:129–36.

Mech, L. D., D. W. Smith, K. M. Murphy, and D. R. MacNulty. 2001. Winter severity and wolf predation on a formerly wolf-free elk herd. *Journal of Wildlife Management* 65:998–1003.

Mehl, M. S. 1992. Old-growth descriptions for the major forest cover types in the Rocky Mountain region. In *Old-growth forest in the Southwest and Rocky Mountain regions: Proceedings of a workshop, March 9–13, 1992, Portal, AZ,* USDA Forest Service General Technical Report RM-213, ed. M. R. Kaufmann, W. H. Moir, and R. L. Basset, 106–20. Fort Collins, CO: USDA Forest Service, Rocky Mountain Forest and Range Experiment Station.

Menge, B. A. 1992. Community regulation: Under what conditions are bottom-up factors important on rocky shores? *Ecology* 73:755–65.

Menge, B. A., and J. P. Sutherland. 1976. Species diversity gradients: Synthesis of the roles of predation, competition, and temporal heterogeneity. *American Naturalist* 110:351–69.

Mercure, A., K. Ralls, K. P. Koepfli, and R. K. Wayne. 1993. Genetic subdivisions among small canids: Mitochondrial DNA differentiation of swift, kit, and arctic foxes. *Evolution* 47:1313–28.

Merriam, C. H. 1890. Results of a biological survey of the San Francisco Mountain region and desert of the Little Colorado, Arizona. *North America Fauna* 3:1–136.

Merrill, E. H., and M. S. Boyce. 1991. Summer range and elk population dynamics in Yellowstone National Park. In *The Greater Yellowstone Ecosystem: Redefining America's wilderness heritage,* ed. R. B. Keiter and M. S. Boyce, 263–74. New Haven, CT: Yale Univ. Press.

Messier, F. 1985. Social organization, spatial distribution, and population density of wolves in relation to moose density. *Canadian Journal of Zoology* 63:1068–77.

———. 1994. Ungulate population models with predation: A case study with the North American moose. *Ecology* 75:478–88.

Messier, F., and C. Barrette. 1985. The efficiency of yarding behaviour by white-tailed deer as an antipredator strategy. *Canadian Journal of Zoology* 63:785–89.

Messier, F., and M. Crête. 1985. Moose-wolf dynamics and the natural regulation of moose populations. *Oecologia* 65:503–12.

Meyers, C. 2002. Hunters can reap abundance of elk. *The Denver Post,* May 5, 2002.

Michigan Department of Natural Resources. 1997. *Michigan gray wolf recovery and management plan.* Lansing: Michigan Department of Natural Resources.

Middleton, N., P. O'Keefe, and S. Moyo. 1993. *Tears of the crocodile: From Rio to reality in the developing world.* Boulder, CO: Pluto Press.

Miller, B., D. Foreman, M. Fink, D. Shinneman, J. Smith, M. DeMarco, M. Soulé, and R. Howard. 2003. *Southern Rockies wildlands network vision: A science-based approach to rewilding the Southern Rockies.* Golden, CO: Colorado Mountain Club Press.

Miller, B., K. Ralls, R. P. Reading, J. M. Scott, and J. Estes. 1999. Biological and technical considerations of carnivore translocation: A review. *Animal Conservation* 2:59–68.

Miller, B., R. Reading, C. Conway, J. A. Jackson, M. Hutchins, N. Snyder, S. Forrest, J. Frazier, and S. Derrickson. 1994. A model for improving endangered species programs. *Environmental Management* 18:637–45.

Miller, B., R. Reading, and S. Forrest. 1996. *Prairie night: Recovery of the black-footed ferret and other endangered species.* Washington, DC: Smithsonian Institution Press.

Miller, B., R. Reading, J. Hoogland, T. Clark, G. Ceballos, R. List, S. Forrest, L. Hanebury, P. Manzano, J. Pacheco, and D. Uresk. 2000. The role of prairie dogs as keystone species: Reponse to Stapp. *Conservation Biology* 14:318–21.

Miller, B., R. Reading, J. Strittholt, C. Carroll, R. Noss, M. Soulé, O. Sánchez, J. Terborgh, D. Brightsmith, T. Cheeseman, and D. Foreman. 1998. Focal species in design of reserve networks. *Wild Earth* 8:81–92.

Miller, R. F., and J. A. Rose. 1999. Fire history and western juniper encroachment in sagebrush steppe. *Journal of Range Management* 52:550–59.

Minnesota Department of Natural Resources. 1998. 1998 Wolf public information meetings: Public comment summaries. Unpublished report. Minnesota Department of Natural Resources, St. Paul, MN.

———. 2001. *Minnesota wolf management plan.* St. Paul: Minnesota Department of Natural Resources.

Minta, S. C., P. M. Karieva, and A. P. Curlee. 1999. Carnivore research and conservation: Learning from history and theory. In *Carnivores in ecosystems: The Yellowstone experience,* ed. T. W. Clark, A. P. Curlee, S. C. Minta, and P. M. Karieva, 323–404. New Haven, CT: Yale Univ. Press.

Mladenoff, D. J., and T. A. Sickley. 1999. Assessing potential gray wolf restoration in the northeastern United States: A spatial prediction of favorable habitat and potential population levels. *Journal of Wildlife Management* 62:1–10.

Montana Agricultural Statistics. 1992. A summary of results. *Montana Crop and Livestock Reporter* (Helena, MT), May 14, 1992.

Montana Fish, Wildlife, and Parks. 2002. Montana wolf conservation and management planning document—draft. Montana Fish, Wildlife, and Parks, Helena, MT.

————. 2004. Amended record of decision: Montana gray wolf conservation and management plan, May 2004. Unpublished report. Montana Fish, Wildlife, and Parks, Helena, MT.

Moosbruker, J., and D. G. Kleiman. 2001. Forgotten elements: Including structure and process in recovery efforts. *Endangered Species Update* 18:63–68.

Morison, S. E. 1972. *The Oxford history of the American people.* New York: New American Library.

Murie, A. 1944. *The wolves of Mount McKinley.* United States National Park Service Fauna Series No. 5. Washington, DC: US National Park Service.

Musiani, M., T. Muhly, C. C. Gates, C. Callaghan, M. E. Smith, and E. Tosoni. 2005. Seasonality and reoccurrence of depredation and wolf control in western North America. *Wildlife Society Bulletin* 33:867–87.

Mutel, C. F., and J. C. Emerick. 1992. *From grassland to glacier: The natural history of Colorado and the surrounding region.* Boulder, CO: Johnson Books.

Nash, D. 1989. Tourism as a form of imperialism. In *Hosts and guests: An anthology of tourism,* ed. V. L. Smith, 37–52. Philadelphia: Univ. of Pennsylvania Press.

National Research Council. 1997. *Wolves, bears, and their prey in Alaska: Biological and social challenges in wildlife management.* Washington, DC: National Academy Press.

————. 2002. *Ecological dynamics on Yellowstone's northern range.* Washington, DC: National Academy Press.

Nature Conservancy, The. 1998. *Ecoregion-based conservation in the central shortgrass prairie.* Boulder, CO: Central Shortgrass Prairie Ecoregional Planning Team, The Nature Conservancy.

Neely, B., P. Comer, C. Moritz, M. Lammert, R. Rondeau, C. Pague, G. Bell, et al. 2001. *Southern Rocky Mountains: An ecoregional assessment and conservation blueprint.* Boulder, CO: The Nature Conservancy, with support from the US Forest Service, Rocky Mountain region, Colorado Division of Wildlife, and Bureau of Land Management.

Neihardt, J. G. 1972. *Black Elk speaks.* New York: Washington Square Press.

Nelson, M. E., and L. D. Mech. 1981. Deer social organization and wolf predation in northwestern Minnesota. *Wildlife Monographs* 77:1–53.

Nelson, M. E. and L. D. Mech. 1986. Relationship between snow depth and gray wolf predation on white-tailed deer. *Journal of Wildlife Management* 50:471–74.

Nelson, R. 1993. Searching for the lost arrow: Physical and spiritual ecology in the hunter's world. In *The biophilia hypothesis,* ed. S. R. Kellert and E. O. Wilson, 201–28. Washington, DC: Island Press.

New Mexico Department of Game and Fish. 1999. *Mule deer of New Mexico.* Santa Fe: New Mexico Department of Game and Fish.

New Mexico gap analysis. 1996. http://rgis.unm.edu:8080.

New Mexico Secretary of State. 2008. www.sos.state.nm.us/pdf/countystats4.pdf.

Noel, T. J., P. F. Mahoney, and R. E. Stevens. 1994. *Historical atlas of Colorado.* Norman: Univ. of Oklahoma Press.

Noss, R. 1999. *A citizen's guide to ecosystem management.* Louisville, CO: Biodiversity Legal Foundation.

Noss, R. F., and A. Y. Cooperrider. 1994. *Saving nature's legacy: Protecting and restoring biodiversity.* Covelo, CA: Island Press.

Noss, R. F., E. T. LaRoe, and J. M. Scott. 1995. *Endangered ecosystems of the United States: A preliminary assessment of loss and degradation.* Biological Report 28. Washington, DC: USDI National Biological Service.

Nowak, R. M. 1972. The mysterious wolf of the south. *Natural History* 81:51–53, 74–77.

————. 1978. Reclassification of the gray wolf in the United States and Mexico, with determination of critical habitat in Michigan and Minnesota. *Federal Register* 43:9607–15.

————. 1979. *North American Quaternary* Canis. Museum of Natural History Monograph No. 6, Lawrence: Univ. of Kansas.

————. 1983. A perspective on the taxonomy of wolves in North America. In *Wolves in Canada and Alaska: Their status, biology, and management,* Canadian Wildlife Service Report Series No. 45, ed. L. N. Carbyn, 10–19. Ottawa, ON: Canadian Wildlife Service.

————. 1992. The red wolf is not a hybrid. *Conservation Biology* 6:593–95.

————. 1995. Another look at wolf taxonomy. In *Ecology and conservation of wolves in a changing world,* Canadian Circumpolar Institute Occasional Paper 35, ed. L. N. Carbyn, S. H. Fritts, and D. R. Seip, 375–97. Edmonton, AB: Canadian Circumpolar Institute, Univ. of Alberta.

Oakleaf, J. K. 2002. Wolf-cattle interactions and habitat selection by recolonizing wolves in the western United States. Master's thesis, Univ. of Idaho.

Odell, E. A., and R. L. Knight. 2001. Songbird and medium-sized mammal communities associated with exurban development in Pitkin County, Colorado. *Conservation Biology* 15:1143–50.

Oksanen, L., S. D. Fretwell, J. Arruda, and P. Niemela. 1981. Exploitation ecosystems in gradients of primary productivity. *American Naturalist* 118:240–61.

Oksanen, L., and T. Oksanen. 2000. The logic and realism of the hypothesis of exploitation ecosystems. *American Naturalist* 155:703–23.

Oksanen, T., L. Oksanen, M. Schneider, and M. Aunapuu. 2001. Regulation, cycles and stability in northern carnivore-herbivore systems: Back to first principles. *Oikos* 94:101–17.

Olson, J. A., and M. P. Zanna. 1993. Attitudes and attitude change. *Annual Review of Psychology* 44:117–54.

Olson, R. A., and W. A. Gerhart. 1982. *A physical and biological characterization of riparian habitat and its importance in Wyoming.* Cheyenne: Wyoming Game and Fish Department.

Olson, S. F. 1938. Organization and range of the pack. *Ecology* 19:168–70.

Oosenbrug, S. M., and L. N. Carbyn. 1982. Winter predation on bison and activity patterns of a wolf pack in Wood Buffalo National Park. In *Wolves: A worldwide perspective of their behavior, ecology, and conservation*, ed. F. H. Harrington and P. C. Paquet, 43–53. Park Ridge, NJ: Noyes Publications.

Oregon State Univ. 2003. *Census of agriculture: 1987, 1992, 1997.* Corvallis: Oregon State Univ. http://govinfo.kerr.orst.edu/php/agri/index.php.

Osmundson, D. B., P. Nelson, K. Fenton, and D. W. Ryden. 1995. *Relationship between flow and rare fish habitat in the "15-mile reach" of the Colorado River: Final report.* Washington, DC: US Fish and Wildlife Service.

Outwater, A. 1996. *Water: A natural history.* New York: Basic Books.

Owen-Smith, N. 1989. Megafaunal extinctions: The conservation message from 11,000 years B.P. *Conservation Biology* 3:405–12.

Packard, J. M., and L. D. Mech. 1980. Population regulation in wolves. In *Biosocial mechanisms of population regulation*, ed. M. N. Cohen, R. S. Malpass, and H. G. Klein, 135–50. New Haven, CT: Yale Univ. Press.

Paine, R. T. 1966. Food web complexity and species diversity. *American Naturalist* 100:65–75.

Palomares, F., and M. Delibes. 1997. Predation upon European rabbits and their use of open and closed patches in Mediterranean habitats. *Oikos* 80:407–10.

Palomares, F., P. Gaona, P. Ferreras, and M. Delibes. 1995. Positive effects on game species of top predators by controlling smaller predator populations: An example with lynx, mongooses, and rabbits. *Conservation Biology* 9:295–305.

Paquet, P. C. 1989. Behavioral ecology of wolves (*Canis lupus*) and coyotes (*C. latrans*) in Riding Mountain National Park, Manitoba. PhD diss., Univ. of Alberta.

———. 1991. Winter spatial relationships of wolves and coyotes in Riding Mountain National Park, Manitoba. *Journal of Mammalogy* 72:397–401.

———. 1992. Prey use strategies of sympatric wolves and coyotes in Riding Mountain National Park, Manitoba. *Journal of Mammalogy* 73:337–43.

———. 1993. Summary reference document—ecological studies of recolonizing wolves in the central Canadian Rocky Mountains. Unpublished report. John/Paul Associates for the Canadian Parks Service, Banff, AB.

Paquet, P. C., and A. Hackman. 1995. *Large carnivore conservation in the Rocky Mountains.* Toronto, ON, and Washington, DC: World Wildlife Fund Canada and World Wildlife Fund US.

Paquet, P. C., J. Vucetich, M. K. Phillips, and L. Vucetich. 2001. *Mexican wolf recovery: Three-year program review and assessment.* Report for US Fish and Wildlife Service. Apple Valley, MN: IUCN SSC Conservation Breeding Specialist Group.

Paquet, P. C., J. Wierzchowski, and C. Callaghan. 1996. Effects of human activity on gray wolves in the Bow River Valley, Banff National Park, Alberta. In *A cumulative effects assessment and futures outlook for the Banff Bow Valley*, ed. J. Green, C. Pacas, S. Bayley and L. Cornwell. Ottawa, ON: Department of Canadian Heritage.

Parendes, L. A., and J. A. Jones. 2000. Role of light availability and dispersal in exotic plant invasion along roads and streams in the H. J. Andrews Experimental Forest, Oregon. *Conservation Biology* 14:64–75.

Parker, W. T, M. P. Jones, and P. G. Poulos. 1986. Determination of experimental population status for an introduced population of wolves in North Carolina—final rule. *Federal Register* 51:41790–96.

Parker, W. T., and M. K. Phillips. 1991. Application of the experimental population designation to the recovery of endangered red wolves. *Wildlife Society Bulletin* 19:73–79.

Parsons, D. R. 1998. Establishment of a nonessential experimental population of the Mexican gray wolf in Arizona and New Mexico. *Federal Register* 63:1752–72.

Pastor, J., R. J. Naiman, and B. Dewey. 1988. Moose, microbes and boreal forests. *BioScience* 38:770–77.

Pate, J., M. J. Manfredo, A. D. Bight, and G. Tischbein. 1996. Coloradans' attitudes toward reintroducing the gray wolf into Colorado. *Wildlife Society Bulletin* 24:421–28.

Paul, W. J. 2001. Wolf depredation on livestock in Minnesota: Annual update of statistics—2000. Grand Rapids, MN: US Department of Agriculture.

Pearl, R. H. 1974. *Geology of groundwater resources in Colorado.* Denver: Colorado Geological Survey, Department of Natural Resources.

Pearson, M. 2000. Wild San Juans. *Wild Earth* 10:78–83.

Peek, J. M., and P. D. Dalke, eds. 1982. Wildlife-livestock relationships. *Symposium: Proceedings 10.* Moscow: Univ. of Idaho Forest Wildlife and Range Experiment Station.

PEER. 1997. *Grizzly science: Grizzly bear biology in the Greater Yellowstone.* Washington, DC: Public Employees for Environmental Responsibility.

Perrow, C. 1986. *Complex organizations: A critical essay.* 3rd ed. New York: McGraw Hill.

Peterson, R. O. 1977. *Wolf ecology and prey relationships on Isle Royale.* National Park Service Scientific Monograph Series No. 11. Washington, DC: US Government Printing Office.

Peterson, R. O., N. J. Thomas, J. M. Thurber, J. A. Vucetich, and T. A. Waite. 1998. Population limitation and the wolves of Isle Royale. *Journal of Mammalogy* 79:828–41.

Peterson, R. O., J. D. Woolington, and T. N. Bailey. 1984. Wolves of the Kenai Peninsula, Alaska. *Wildlife Monograph* 88:1–52.

Petty, R. E., D. T. Wegener, and L. R. Fabrigar. 1997. Attitudes and attitude change. *Annual Review of Psychology* 48:609–74.

Phillips, M. K. 1990. Measures on the value and success of a reintroduction project: Red wolf reintroduction in the Alligator River National Wildlife Refuge. *Endangered Species Update* 8:24–26.

Phillips, M. K., N. Fascione, P. Miller, and O. Byers. 2000. *Wolves in the Southern Rockies: A population and habitat viability assessment.* Apple Valley, MN: IUCN-SSC Conservation Breeding Specialist Group.

Phillips, M. K, and V. G. Henry. 1992. Comments on red wolf taxonomy. *Conservation Biology* 6:596–99.

Phillips, M. K., V. G. Henry, and B. T. Kelly. 2003. Restoration of the red wolf. In *Wolves: Behavior, ecology, and conservation,* ed. L. D. Mech and L. Boitani, 272–88. Chicago: Univ. of Chicago Press.

Phillips, M. K., and D. W. Smith. 1996. *The wolves of Yellowstone.* Stillwater, MN: Voyageur Press.

———. 1998. Gray wolves and private landowners in the Greater Yellowstone area. *Transactions of the North American Wildlife and Natural Resources Conference* 63:443–50.

Phillips, M. K., R. Smith, V. G. Henry, and C. Lucash. 1996. Red wolf reintroduction program. In *Ecology and conservation of wolves in a changing world,* Canadian Circumpolar Institute Occasional Publication 35, ed. L. N. Carbyn, S. H. Fritts, and D. R. Seip, 157–68. Edmonton, AB: Canadian Circumpolar Institute, Univ. of Alberta.

Pianka, E. R. 1974. *Evolutionary ecology.* New York: Harper and Row.

Pickett, S. T. A., and P. S. White, eds. 1985. *The ecology of natural disturbance and patch dynamics.* Orlando, FL: Academic Press.

Pimlott, D. H. 1966. Review of Farley Mowat's "Never Cry Wolf." *Journal of Wildlife Management* 30:236–37.

———. 1967. Wolf predation and ungulate populations. *American Zoologists* 7:267–78.

Polis, G. A., and D. R. Strong. 1996. Food web complexity and community dynamics. *American Naturalist* 147:813–46.

Post, E., R. O. Peterson, N. C. Stenseth, and B. E. McLaren. 1999. Ecosystem consequences of wolf behavioural response to climate. *Nature* 401:905–7.

Potvin, F., H. Jolicoeur, and J. Huot. 1988. Wolf diet and prey selectivity during two periods for deer in Quebec: Decline versus expansion. *Canadian Journal of Zoology* 66:1274–79.

Power, M. E. 1992. Top-down and bottom-up forces in food webs: Do plants have primacy? *Ecology* 73:733–46.

Power, M. E., S. J. Kupferburg, G. W. Minshell, M. C. Molles, and M. S. Parker. 1997. Sustainability and western riparian ecosystems. In *Aquatic ecosystems symposium: Report to the Western Water Policy Review Advisory Commission, August 1997,* ed. W. L. Minckley, 17–31. Reston, VA: US Geological Survey.

Power, T. M. 1996. *Lost landscapes and failed economies: The search for a value of place.* Covelo, CA: Island Press.

Primack, R. B. 1998. *Essentials of conservation biology.* 2nd ed. Sunderland, MA: Sinauer Associates.

Quammen, D. 1998. Planet of the weeds: Tallying the losses of Earth's animals and plants. *Harpers* 297 (October):57–69.

Quintal, P. K. M. 1995. Public attitudes and beliefs about the red wolf and its recovery in North Carolina. Master's thesis, North Carolina State Univ.

Rabb, G. B., J. H. Woolpy, and B. E. Ginsberg. 1967. Social relationships in a group of captive wolves. *American Zoologist* 7:305–11.

Ralls, K., J. D. Ballou, and A. R. Templeton. 1988. Estimates of lethal equivalents and the cost of inbreeding in mammals. *Conservation Biology* 2:185–93.

Ralls, K., R. Frankham, and J. Ballou. 2001. Inbreeding and outbreeding. In *Encyclopedia of biodiversity,* vol. 3, ed. S. Levin, 427–35. San Diego: Academic Press.

Ralls, K., P. H. Harvey, and A. M. Lyles. 1986. Inbreeding in natural populations of birds and mammals. In *Conservation biology: Science of scarcity and diversity,* ed. M. E. Soulé, 35–56. Sunderland, MA: Sinauer Associates.

Rasker, R. 1994. *Measuring change in rural economies: A workbook for determining demographic, economic, and fiscal trends.* Washington, DC: The Wilderness Society.

Raven, P. H. 2001. Keynote address for the 2001 National AZA Conference on September 8, 2001, St. Louis, MO.

Ray, J. C., K. H. Redford, R. S. Steneck, and J. Berger. 2005. *Large carnivores and the conservation of biodiversity.* Washington, DC: Island Press.

Reading, R. P. 1993. Toward an endangered species reintroduction paradigm: A case study of the black-footed ferret. PhD diss., Yale Univ.

Reading, R. P., and T. W. Clark. 1996. Carnivore reintroduction. In *Carnivore behavior, ecology, and evolution,* ed. J. L. Gittleman, 296–336. Ithaca, NY: Comstock Publishing Association.

Reading, R., T. W. Clark, and B. Griffith. 1996. The influence of valuation and organizational considerations on the success of rare species translocations. *Biological Conservation* 70:217–25.

———. 1997. The influence of valuational and organizational considerations to translocation success. *Biological Conservation* 79:217–25.

Reading, R. P., T. W. Clark, and S. R. Kellert. 1991. Towards an endangered species reintroduction paradigm. *Endangered Species Update* 8:1–4.

———. 1994. Attitudes and knowledge of people living in the Greater Yellowstone Ecosystem. *Society and Natural Resources* 7:349–65.

Reading, R. P., and S. R. Kellert. 1993. Attitudes towards a proposed black-footed ferret (*Mustela nigripes*) reintroduction. *Conservation Biology* 7:569–80.

Reading, R. P., D. Stern, and L. A. McCain. 2006. Attitudes and knowledge of natural resources agency personnel towards black-tailed prairie dogs (*Cynomys ludovicianus*). *Conservation and Society* 4 (4):592–627.

Ream, R. R., M. W. Fairchild, D. K. Boyd, and A. Blakesley. 1989. First wolf den in western United States in recent history. *Northwestern Naturalist* 70:39–40.

Ream, R. R., R. Harris, J. Smith, and D. Boyd. 1985. Movement patterns of a lone wolf, *Canis lupus,* in unoccupied wolf range, southeastern British Columbia. *Canadian Field-Naturalist* 99:234–39.

Ream, R. R., and I. U. Mattson. 1982. Wolf status in the Northern Rockies. In *Wolves of the world: Perspectives on behavior, ecology, and management*, ed. F. H. Harrington and P. C. Paquet, 362–81. Park Ridge, NJ: Noyes Publications.

Rebertus, A. J., T. T. Veblen, L. M. Roovers, and J. N. Mast. 1992. Structure and dynamics of old-growth Engelmann spruce-subalpine fir in Colorado. In *Old-growth forest in the Southwest and Rocky Mountain regions: Proceedings of a workshop, March 9–13, 1992, Portal, AZ*, USDA Forest Service General Technical Report RM-213, ed. M. R. Kaufmann, W. H. Moir, and R. L. Basset, 139–53. Fort Collins, CO: USDA Forest Service Rocky Mountain Forest and Range Experiment Station.

Reed, R. A., J. Johnson-Barnard, and W. L. Baker. 1996. Fragmentation of a forested Rocky Mountain landscape, 1950–1993. *Biological Conservation* 75:267–77.

Refsnider, R. 2000. Proposal to reclassify and remove the gray wolf from the list of endangered and threatened wildlife in portions of the conterminous United States. *Federal Register* 65:43450–96.

Reice, S. R. 1994. Nonequilibrium determinants of biological community structure. *American Scientists* 82:424–35.

Reynolds, R. T., R. T. Graham, M. H. Reiser, R. L. Bassett, P. L. Kennedy, D. A. Boyce Jr., G. Goodwin, R. Smith, and E. L. Fisher. 1992. *Management recommendations for the northern goshawk in the southwestern United States*. USDA Forest Service General Technical Report RM-253. Fort Collins, CO: USDA Forest Service, Rocky Mountain Forest and Range Experiment Station.

Ricketts, T. H., E. Dinerstein, D. M. Olson, and C. Loucks. 1999. Who's where in North America? *Bioscience* 49:369–81.

Riebsame, W. E. 1997. *Atlas of the New West*. New York: W. W. Norton.

Ripple, W. J., and R. L. Beschta. 2004. Wolves and the ecology of fear: Can predation risk structure ecosystems? *BioScience* 54:755–66.

Ripple, W. J., and E. J. Larsen. 2000. Historic aspen recruitment, elk, and wolves in northern Yellowstone National Park, USA. *Biological Conservation* 95:361–70.

Rohlf, D. J. 1991. Six biological reasons why the Endangered Species Act doesn't work—and what to do about it. *Conservation Biology* 5:273–82.

Rokeach, M. 1972. *Beliefs, attitudes, and values: A theory of organization and change*. San Francisco: Josey-Bass, Inc.

Rolston, H., III. 1981. Values in nature. *Environmental Ethics* 3:113–28.

———. 1985. Valuing wildlands. *Environmental Ethics* 7:23–48.

Romme, W. H., and D. G. Despain. 1989. Historical perspective on the Yellowstone fires of 1988. *Bioscience* 39:695–99

Romme, W. H., M. L. Floyd, D. Hannah, and J. S. Redders. 2000. Using natural disturbance regimes as a basis for mitigating impacts of anthropogenic fragmentation. In *Forest fragmentation in the Southern Rocky Mountains*, ed. R. L. Knight, F. W. Smith, S. W. Buskirk, W. H. Romme, and W. L. Baker, 377–400. Boulder: Univ. Press of Colorado.

Romme, W. H., L. Floyd-Hanna, D. D. Hanna, and E. Bartlett. 2001. Aspen's ecological role in the West. In *Sustaining aspen in western landscapes: Symposium proceedings, June 13–15, 2000, Grand Junction, CO*, Proceedings RMRS-P-18, ed. W. D. Shepperd, D. Binkley, D. L. Bartos, T. J. Stohlgren, and L. G. Eskew, 243–59. Fort Collins, CO: USDA Forest Service, Rocky Mountain Research Station.

Rosen, P. C., and C. R. Schwalbe. 1995. Bullfrogs: Introduced predators in southwestern wetlands. In *Our living resources: A report to the nation on distribution, abundance, and health of US plants, animals, and ecosystems*, ed. E. T. LaRoe, G. S. Farris, C. E. Puckett, P. D. Doran, and M. J. Mac, 452–54. Washington, DC: USDI National Biological Service.

Rosen, W. 1997. *Red wolf recovery in northeastern North Carolina and the Great Smoky Mountains National Park: Public attitudes and economic impacts*. Ithaca, NY: Cornell Univ.

Ross, P. I., and M. G. Jalkotzy. 1995. Fates of translocated cougars, *Felis concolor*, in Alberta. *Canadian Field Naturalist* 109:475–76.

Roy, L. D., and M. J. Dorrance. 1976. *Methods of investigating predation of domestic livestock*. Edmonton: Alberta Agriculture.

Roy, M. S., E. Geffen, D. Smith, and R. K. Wayne. 1996. Molecular genetics of pre-1940 red wolves. *Conservation Biology* 10:1413–24.

Ruth, T. K., K. A. Logan, L. L. Sweanor, M. G. Hornocker, and L. J. Temple. 1998. Evaluating cougar translocation in New Mexico. *Journal of Wildlife Management* 62:1264–75.

Rutledge, C. R., and T. McLendon. 1996. An assessment of exotic plant species of Rocky Mountain National Park. Fort Collins: Department of Rangeland Ecosystem Science, Colorado State Univ. Northern Prairie Wildlife Research Center. www.npwrc.usgs.gov/resource/othrdata/explant/explant.htm.

Ryder, O. A. 1986. Species conservation and systematics: The dilemma of subspecies. *Trends in Ecology and Evolution* 1:9–10.

Salwasser, H. 1992. From new perspectives to ecosystem management: A response to Frissell et al. and Lawrence and Murphy. *Conservation Biology* 6:469–72.

Sanford, E. 1999. Regulation of keystone predation by small changes in ocean temperature. *Science* 283:2095–97.

Schadweiler, J. D., and J. R. Tester. 1972. Survival and behaviour of hand-reared mallards released into the wild. *Journal of Wildlife Management* 36:1118–27.

Schaller, G. B. 1996. Carnivores and conservation biology. In *Carnivore behavior, ecology, and evolution*, vol. 2, ed. J. L. Gittleman, 1–10. Ithaca, NY: Comstock Publishing Associates.

Schmid, J. M., and S. A. Mata. 1996. *Natural variability of specific forest insect populations and their associated effects in Colorado.* USDA Forest Service General Technical Report RM-GTR-275. Fort Collins, CO: USDA Forest Service, Rocky Mountain Forest and Range Experiment Station.

Schmidt, J. L. 1978. Early management: Intentional and otherwise. In *Big game of North America: Ecology and management,* ed. J. L. Schmidt and D. L. Gilbert, 257–70. Harrisburg, PA: Stackpole Books.

Schmitz, O. J. 1998. Direct and indirect effects of predation and predation risk in old-field interaction webs. *American Naturalist* 151:327–40.

Schmitz, O. J., P. A. Hamback, and A. P. Beckerman. 2000. Trophic cascades in terrestrial systems: A review of the effects of carnivore removals on plants. *American Naturalist* 155:141–53.

Schoener, T. W., and D. A. Spiller. 1999. Indirect effects in an experimentally staged invasion by a major predator. *American Naturalist* 153:347–58.

Schoenwald-Cox, C., and M. Buechner. 1992. Park protection and public roads. In *Conservation biology: The theory and practice of nature conservation, preservation, and management,* ed. P. L. Fielder and S. K. Jain, 373–79. New York: Chapman and Hall.

Schullery, P., ed. 1996. *Yellowstone wolf: A guide and sourcebook.* Worland, WY: High Plains Publishing Company.

Schultz, T. T., and W. C. Leininger. 1990. Differences in riparian vegetation structure between grazed areas and exclosures. *Journal of Range Management* 43:295–99.

Scott, M. E. 1988. The impact of infection and disease on animal populations: Implications for conservation biology. *Conservation Biology* 2:40–56.

Scott, M. J., F. W. Davis, R. G. McGhie, R. G. Wright, C. Groves, and J. Estes. 2001. Nature reserves: Do they capture the full range of America's biological diversity? *Ecological Applications* 11:999–1007.

Sebastian, J. R., and K. G. Beck. 2000. Leafy spurge and Russian knapweed encroachment on Colorado rangeland. Abstract. *Proceedings—Western Society of Weed Science* 53:7–8.

Seddon, P. J., D. Armstrong, and R. F. Malony. 2007. Developing the science of reintroduction biology. *Conservation Biology* 21:303–12.

Seidel, J., B. Andree, S. Berlinger, K. Buell, G. Byrne, B. Gill, D. Kenvin, and D. Reed. 1998. *Draft strategy for the conservation and reestablishment of lynx and wolverine in the Southern Rocky Mountains.* Colorado Division of Wildlife, US Forest Service, National Park Service, US Fish and Wildlife Service, New Mexico Game and Fish Department, Wyoming Game and Fish Department. Technical Report RM-GTR-256. Fort Collins, CO: USDA Forest Service, Rocky Mountain Forest and Range Experimental Station.

Seton, E. T. 1898. *Wild animals I have known.* New York: Charles Scribner's Sons.

Shaffer, M., and B. Stein. 2000. Safeguarding our precious heritage. In *Precious heritage: The status of biodiversity in the United States,* ed. B. A. Stein, L. S. Kutner, and J. S. Adams, 301–21. New York: Oxford Univ. Press.

Shaw, W. W. 1987. The recreational benefits of wildlife to people. In *Valuing wildlife: Economic and social perspectives,* ed. D. J. Decker and G. R. Goff, 208–13. Boulder, CO: Westview Press.

Shenk, T. 2006. Wildlife commission meeting: November 8, 2006: Lynx fact sheet. Unpublished report. Colorado Division of Wildlife, Denver, CO.

———. 2008. Lynx update, August 27, 2008. Unpublished report. Colorado Division of Wildlife, Denver, CO. http://wildlife.state.co.us/WildlifeSpecies/Species OfConcern/Mammals/Lynx/.

Shepard, P. 1978. *Thinking animals: Animals and the development of human intelligence.* New York: Viking.

Shinneman, D. J., and W. L. Baker. 2000. Impact of logging and roads on a Black Hills ponderosa pine forest landscape. In *Forest fragmentation in the Southern Rocky Mountains,* ed. R. L. Knight, F. W. Smith, S. W. Buskirk, W. H. Romme, and W. L. Baker, 311–35. Boulder: Univ. Press of Colorado.

Shinneman, D. J., R. McClelan, and R. Smith. 2000. *The state of the Southern Rockies Ecoregion.* Nederland, CO: Southern Rockies Ecosystem Project.

Short, J., S. D. Bradshaw, J. Giles, T. I. T. Prince, and G. R. Wilson. 1992. Reintroduction of macropods (Marsupialia: Macropodoidea) in Australia—a review. *Biological Conservation* 61:189–204.

Siminski, D. P. 2008a. *Mexican wolf,* Canis lupus baileyi, *international studbook, 2008.* Palm Desert, CA: The Living Desert.

———. 2008b. *Mexican wolf,* Canis lupus baileyi, *species survival plan, 2008.* Palm Desert, CA: The Living Desert.

Simon, H. 1976. *Administrative behavior.* 3rd ed. New York: Free Press.

Sinclair, A. R. E. 1989. Population regulation in animals. In *Ecological concepts: The contribution of ecology to the better understanding of the natural world,* ed. J. M. Cherrett, 197–241. Oxford: Blackwell Scientific Publications.

Sinclair, A. R. E., and P. Arcese. 1995. Population consequences of predation-sensitive foraging: The Serengeti wildebeest. *Ecology* 76:882–91.

Sinden, J., and A. Worrel. 1979. *Unpriced values: Decisions without market values.* New York: John Wiley and Sons.

Singer, F., A. Harting, K. K. Symonds, and M. B. Coughenour. 1997. Density dependence, compensation, and environmental effects on elk calf mortality in Yellowstone National Park. *Journal of Wildlife Management* 61:12–25.

Singer, F., and J. A. Mack. 1999. Predicting the effects of wildfire and carnivore predation on ungulates. In *Carnivores in ecosystems: The Yellowstone experience,* ed. T. W. Clark, A. P. Curlee, S. C. Minta, and P. M. Karieva, 189–237. New Haven, CT: Yale Univ. Press.

Singer, F., and L. C. Zeigenfuss, eds. 2002. *Ecological evaluation of abundance and effects of elk herbivory in Rocky Mountain National Park, Colorado, 1994–1999*. Report 02-208. US Department of Interior, US Geological Survey, and Fort Collins, CO: Colorado State Univ. Natural Resources Lab.

Skogland, T. 1991. What are the effects of predators on large ungulate populations? *Oikos* 61:401–11.

Slotkin, R. 1992. *Gunfighter nation: The myth of the frontier in twentieth-century America*. New York: Harper Perennial.

Smith, A. 1902. *The wealth of nations*. New York: Collier.

Smith, B. L., and S. H. Anderson. 1996. Patterns of neonatal mortality of elk in northwest Wyoming. *Canadian Journal of Zoology* 74:1229–37.

Smith, D. W., and G. Ferguson. 2005. *Decade of the wolf: Returning the wild to Yellowstone*. Guilford, CT: Lyons Press.

Smith, D. G., F. W. Lorey, J. Suzuki, and M. Abe. 1987. Effect of outbreeding on weight and growth rate of captive infant rhesus macaques. *Zoo Biology* 6:201–12.

Smith, D. W., W. G. Brewster, and E. E. Bangs. 1999. Wolves in the Greater Yellowstone Ecosystem: Restoration of a top carnivore in a complex management environment. In *Carnivores in ecosystems: The Yellowstone experience*, ed. T. W. Clark, A. P. Curlee, S. C. Minta, and P. M. Karieva, 103–26. New Haven, CT: Yale Univ. Press.

Smith, D. W., T. D. Drummer, K. M. Murphy, D. S. Guernsey, S. B. Evans. 2004. Winter prey selection and estimation of wolf kill rates in Yellowstone National Park, 1995–2000. *Journal of Wildlife Management* 68 (4):153–66.

Smith, D. W., L. D. Mech, M. Meagher, W. E. Clark, R. Jaffe, M. K. Phillips, and J. A. Mack. 2000. Wolf-bison interactions in Yellowstone National Park. *Journal of Mammalogy* 81:1128–35.

Smith, D. W., T. J. Meier, E. Geffen, L. D. Mech, L. G. Adams, J. W. Burch, and R. K. Wayne. 1997. Is incest common in gray wolf packs? *Behavioral Ecology* 8:384–91.

Smith, D. W., K. M. Murphy, and D. S. Guernsey. 2001. *Yellowstone wolf project: Annual report, 1999*. Yellowstone National Park: US National Park Service, Yellowstone Center for Resources.

Sneed, P. G. 2000. *Gray wolf reintroduction feasibility study: Grand Canyon Ecoregion*. Second progress report, submitted to Grand Canyon Wildlands Council and Defenders of Wildlife.

Snyder, N. R. F., S. R. Derrickson, S. R. Beissinger, J. W. Wiley, T. B. Smith, W. D. Toone, and B. Miller. 1996. Limitations of captive breeding in endangered species recovery. *Conservation Biology* 10:338–48.

Somers, P., and L. Floyd-Hanna. 1996. Wetlands, riparian habitats, and rivers. In *The western San Juan Mountains: Their geology, ecology and human history*, ed. R. Blair, 175–89. Niwot: Univ. Press of Colorado.

Soulé, M. E. 1995. An unflinching vision: Networks of people defending networks of lands. In *Nature conservation 4: The role of networks*, ed. D. A. Saunders, J. L. Craig, and E. M. Mattiske, 1–8. Sydney: Surrey Beatty and Sons Limited.

———. 1996. The end of evolution. *World Conservation* (Originally *IUCN Bulletin*) 1 (96):24–25.

Soulé, M. E., D. T. Bolger, A. C. Alberts, R. Sauvajot, J. Wright, and S. Hill. 1988. Reconstructed dynamics of rapid extinctions of chaparral-rearing birds in urban habitat islands. *Conservation Biology* 2:75–92.

Soulé, M. E., J. A. Estes, J. Berger, and C. M. del Rio. 2003a. Ecologically effective numbers of endangered keystone species: Theory and practice. *Conservation Biology* 17:1204–9.

———. 2003b. Ecological effectiveness: Conservation goals for interactive species. *Conservation Biology* 17:1238–50.

Soulé, M. E., J. A. Estes, B. Miller and D. C. Honnold. 2005. Strongly interacting species: Conservation policy, management, and ethics. *BioScience* 55 (2):168–76.

Soulé, M. E., and J. Terborgh, eds. 1999. *Continental conservation: Scientific foundations of regional reserve networks*. Covelo, CA: Island Press.

Southern Rockies Ecosystem Project. 2000. *Summary of base data and landscape variables for wolf habitat suitability on the Vermejo Park Ranch and surrounding areas*. Bozeman, MT: Turner Endangered Species Fund.

Southwood, Sir T. R. Undated. Statement to the BSE Inquiry. BSE Inquiry, London, England. www.bseinquiry.gov.uk/files/ws/s001.pdf.

Sovada, M. A., A. B. Sargeant, and J. W. Grier. 1995. Differential effects of coyotes and red foxes on duck nest success. *Journal of Wildlife Management* 59:1–9.

Stanley Price, M. R. 1989. *Animal reintroductions: The Arabian oryx in Oman*. Cambridge: Cambridge Univ. Press.

Stark, M. 2006. UM economist: Wolves a big moneymaker, Yellowstone Park survey finds animals have a $70M effect. *Billings Gazette* (Billings, MT), April 7, 2006.

Steinhoff, H. W. 1980. Analysis of major conceptual systems for understanding and measuring wildlife values. In *Wildlife values*, Center for Assessment of Noncommodity Natural Resource Values Institute Series Report No. 1, ed. W. W. Shaw and E. H. Zube, 11–21. Fort Collins, CO: Center for Assessment of Noncommodity Natural Resource Values.

Stenlund, M. H. 1955. *A field study of the timber wolf (Canis lupus) on the Superior National Forest, Minnesota*. Minnesota Department of Conservation Technical Bulletin No. 4. Minneapolis: Minnesota Department of Conservation.

Stenseth, N. C., W. Falck, K. S. Chan, O. N. Bjornstad, M. O'Donoghue, H. Tong, R. Boonstra, S. Boutin, C. J. Krebs, and N. G. Yoccoz. 1998. From patterns to processes: Phase and density dependencies in the Canadian lynx cycle. *Proceedings of the National Academy of Sciences* 95:15430–35.

Stucky-Everson, V. 1997. *Mushrooms of Colorado and the Southern Rocky Mountains.* Denver: Denver Botanic Gardens.

Swem, T. 1994. Removal of the arctic peregrine falcon from the list of endangered and threatened wildlife. *Federal Register* 59:50796–805.

Tear, T. H., J. M. Scott, P. H. Hayward, and B. Griffith. 1993. Status and prospects for success of the Endangered Species Act: A look at recovery plans. *Science* 262:976–77.

Teel, T. L., R. S. Krannich, and R. H. Schmidt. 2002. Utah stakeholders' attitudes toward selected cougar and black bear management practices. *Wildlife Society Bulletin* 30:2–15.

Terborgh, J. 1988. The big things that run the world—a sequel to E. O. Wilson. *Conservation Biology* 2:402–3.

———. 1999. *Requiem for nature.* Covelo, CA: Island Press.

Terborgh, J., and J. A. Estes. Forthcoming. *Trophic cascades.* Washington, DC: Island Press.

Terborgh, J., J. Estes, P. Paquet, K. Ralls, D. Boyd, B. Miller, and R. Noss. 1999. Role of top carnivores in regulating terrestrial ecosystems. In *Continental conservation: Scientific foundations of regional reserve networks,* ed. M. Soulé and J. Terborgh, 39–64. Covelo, CA: Island Press.

Terborgh, J., L. Lopez, P. Nuñez, M. Rao, G. Shahabuddin, G. Orihuela, M. Riveros, R. Ascanio, G. H. Adler, T. D. Lambert, and L. Balbas. 2001. Ecological meltdown in predator-free forest fragments. *Science* 294:1923–25.

Terborgh, J., L. Lopez, J. Tello, D. Yu, and A. R. Bruni. 1997. Transitory states in relaxing land bridge islands. In *Tropical forest remnants: Ecology, management, and conservation of fragmented communities,* ed. W. F. Laurance and R. O. Bierregaard Jr., 256–74. Chicago: Univ. of Chicago Press.

Terborgh, J., and M. Soulé. 1999. Why we need large-scale networks and megareserves. *Wild Earth* 9:66–72.

Terborgh, J., and B. Winter. 1980. Some causes of extinction. In *Conservation biology: An evolutionary-ecological perspective,* ed. M. E. Soulé and B. A. Wilcox, 119–33. Sunderland, MA: Sinauer Associates.

Tessler, A., and D. R. Shaffer. 1990. Attitudes and attitude change. *Annual Review of Psychology* 41:479–523.

Theberge, J. B., and M. T. Theberge. 1998. *Wolf country: Eleven years tracking the Algonquin wolves.* Toronto: McClelland & Stewart Inc.

Theobald, D. T. 2000. Fragmentation by inholdings and exurban development. In *Forest fragmentation in the Southern Rocky Mountains,* ed. R. L. Knight, F. W. Smith, S. W. Buskirk, W. H. Romme, and W. L. Baker, 155–74. Boulder: Univ. Press of Colorado.

———. 2001. Technical description of mapping historical, current, and future housing densities in the US using Census block-groups. Fort Collins: Natural Resource Ecology Laboratory, Colorado State Univ.

www.ndis.nrel.colostate.edu/davet/dev_patterns.htm.

Theobald, D. T., H. Gosnell, and W. E. Riebsame. 1996. Land use and landscape change in the Colorado mountains II: A case study of the East River Valley, Colorado. *Mountain Research and Development* 16:407–18.

Theobald, D. T., T. Hobbs, D. Scrupp, and L. O'Brien. 1998. An assessment of imperiled habitat in Colorado. Unpublished report. Colorado Division of Wildlife, Denver, CO.

Thiel, R. P. 1985. Relationship between road densities and wolf habitat suitability in Wisconsin. *American Midland Naturalist* 113:404.

———. 1993. The timber wolf in Wisconsin: The death and life of a magnificent predator. Madison: Univ. of Wisconsin Press.

Thiel, R. P., L. D. Mech, G. R. Ruth, J. R. Archer, and L. Kaufmann. 1987. Blastomycosis in wild wolves. *Journal of Wildlife Diseases* 23:321–23.

Thiel, R. P., and T. Valen. 1995. Developing a state timber wolf recovery plan with public input: The Wisconsin experience. In *Ecology and conservation of wolves in a changing world,* Canadian Circumpolar Institute Occasional Publication 35, ed. L. N. Carbyn, S. H. Fritts, and D. R. Seip, 169–75 Edmonton, AB: Canadian Circumpolar Institute, Univ. of Alberta.

Thompson, T. 1991. *Attitudes of Wyoming residents on wolf reintroduction and related issues.* Cheyenne: Wyoming Game and Fish Department.

Thompson, R. W., and J. C. Halfpenny. 1991. Canada lynx presence on Vail Ski Area and proposed expansion area. Unpublished report. Western Ecosystems, Inc., Lafayette, CO.

Thurber, J. M., and R. O. Peterson. 1993. Effects of population density and pack size on foraging ecology of gray wolves. *Journal of Mammalogy* 74:879–89.

Trombulak, S. C., and C. A. Frissell. 2000. Review of ecological effects of roads on terrestrial and aquatic communities. *Conservation Biology* 14:18–35.

Trotter, M. M., and B. McCulloch. 1984. Moas, men, and middens. In *Quaternary extinctions: A prehistoric revolution,* ed. P. S. Martin and R. G. Klein, 708–27. Tucson: Univ. of Arizona Press.

Tucker, P., and D. Pletscher. 1989. Attitudes of hunters and residents toward wolves in northwestern Montana. *Wildlife Society Bulletin* 17:509–14.

Tysor, R. W., and C. A. Worley. 1992. Alien flora in grasslands adjacent to road and trail corridors in Glacier National Park, Montana (USA). *Conservation Biology* 6:253–62.

US Bureau of Land Management. 1996. Bureau of Land Management surface status map of Colorado. www.usgsquads.com/prod_blm_land_use_maps.htm.

US Census Bureau. 2007a. Population estimates. www.census.gov/popest/datasets.html.

———. 2007b. Current population survey, 2005 to 2007: Annual social and economic supplements. www.census.gov/hhes/www/poverty/poverty06/state.html.

———. 2008. National and state population estimates. www.census.gov/popest/states/NST-pop-chg.html.

US Congress. 1973. *Endangered species act.* 16 U.S.C. 1531–44.

US Department of Agriculture, National Agricultural Statistics Service. 1997. Census of agriculture.

———. 2002. Census of agriculture.

US Department of Commerce. 2008. Bureau of economic analysis, regional economic information system. www.bea.gov/national/index.htm#gdp.

US Fish and Wildlife Service. 1974. *United States list of endangered fauna, May 1974.* Washington, DC: US Fish and Wildlife Service.

———. 1978. *Recovery plan for the eastern timber wolf.* Washington, DC: US Fish and Wildlife Service.

———. 1980. *Northern Rocky Mountain wolf recovery plan.* Denver: US Fish and Wildlife Service.

———. 1982. *Mexican wolf recovery plan.* Albuquerque: US Fish and Wildlife Service.

———. 1984. *Red wolf recovery plan.* Atlanta: US Fish and Wildlife Service.

———. 1987a. *Northern Rocky Mountain wolf recovery plan.* Denver: US Fish and Wildlife Service.

———. 1987b. *Restoring America's wildlife, 1937–1987: The first 50 years of the federal aid in wildlife restoration (Pittman-Robertson) act.* Washington, DC: US Government Printing Office.

———. 1989. *Red wolf recovery/species survival plan.* Atlanta: US Fish and Wildlife Service.

———. 1992a. *Experimental release of red wolves into the Great Smoky Mountains National Park.* Red Wolf Management Series Technical Report No. 8. Atlanta: US Fish and Wildlife Service.

———. 1992b. *Recovery plan for the eastern timber wolf.* Fort Snelling, MN: US Fish and Wildlife Service.

———. 1994. *The reintroduction of gray wolves to Yellowstone National Park and central Idaho: Final Environmental Impact Statement.* Denver: US Fish and Wildlife Service.

———. 1996a. *Report to Congress on the recovery program for threatened and endangered species.* Washington, DC: US Government Printing Office.

———. 1996b. *Reintroduction of the Mexican wolf within its historic range in the southwestern United States: Final Environmental Impact Statement.* Albuquerque: US Fish and Wildlife Service.

———. 1998. Endangered and threatened wildlife and plants: Establishment of a nonessential experimental population of Mexican gray wolf in Arizona and New Mexico. *Federal Register* 63 (7):1752–72.

———. 2001. *Rocky Mountain wolf recovery 2000 annual report.* Helena, MT: US Fish and Wildlife Service.

———. 2004. *Rocky Mountain Wolf Recovery 2004 Annual Report.* Helena, MT: US Fish and Wildlife Service.

———. 2006. Mexican wolf captive management. www.fws.gov/southwest/es/mexicanwolf/cap_manage.shtml (accessed April 15, 2009).

———. 2007a. Endangered and threatened wildlife and plants: Final rule designating the western Great Lakes populations of gray wolves as a distinct population segment and removing the western Great Lakes distinct population segment of the gray wolf from the list of endangered and threatened wildlife, final rule. *Federal Register* 72 (26):6051–103.

———. 2007b. Endangered and threatened wildlife and plants: Final rule designating the Northern Rocky Mountain population of gray wolf as a distinct population segment and removing this distinct population segment from the federal list of endangered and threatened wildlife, proposed rule. *Federal Register* 72 (26):6105–139.

———. 2008a. Endangered and threatened wildlife and plants: Designating the Northern Rocky Mountain population of gray wolf as a distinct population segment and removing this distinct population segment from the federal list of endangered and threatened wildlife. *Federal Register* 73 (209):63426–63432.

———. 2008b. Mexican wolf Blue Range reintroduction project statistics: Causes of documented Mexican wolf mortalities in the Blue Range Wolf Recovery Area, Arizona and New Mexico, 1998–Present. www.fws.gov/southwest/es/mexicanwolf/pdf/MW_mortality.pdf (accessed April 15, 2009).

———. 2009a. Red wolf recovery project. www.fws.goc/redwolf (accessed April 15, 2009).

———. 2009b. Endangered and threatened wildlife and plants: Final rule to identify the Northern Rocky Mountain population of gray wolf as a distinct population segment and to revise the list of endangered and threatened wildlife. *Federal Register* 74 (62):15123–88.

———. 2009c. Mexican wolf Blue Range reintroduction project statistics: Causes of Mexican wolf management removals from the Blue Range Wolf Recovery Area, Arizona and New Mexico, 1998–2008. www.fws.gov/southwest/es/mexicanwolf/pdf/MW_removals.pdf (accessed April 15, 2009).

US Fish and Wildlife Service, Nez Perce Tribe, National Park Service, and USDA Wildlife Services. 2002. *Rocky Mountain wolf recovery 2001 annual report.* Helena, MT: US Fish and Wildlife Service, Ecological Services.

———. 1998. *Final Environmental Impact Statement for the Rio Grande National Forest Revised Land and Resource Management Plan.* Lakewood, CO: USDA Forest Service, Rocky Mountain Region.

———. 1999. *Draft Environmental Impact Statement for the White River National Forest Land and Resource Management Plan.* Lakewood, CO: USDA Forest Service, Rocky Mountain Region.

US General Accounting Office. 1988. *More emphasis needed on declining and overstocked grazing allotments.* GAO/RCED-88-80. Washington, DC: US General Accounting Office.

US National Park Service. 1988. *Management policies.* Washington, DC: US National Park Service.

———. 2008. 2007–2008 winter count of northern Yellowstone elk. www.nps.gov/yell/parknews/08010.htm.

Vale, T. R. 1975. Report to the Bureau of Land Management on range conditions and grazing in Nevada. *Biological Conservation* 8:257–60.

Van Ballenberghe, V. 1972. Ecology, movements and population characteristics of timber wolves in northeastern Minnesota. PhD diss., Univ. of Minnesota.

———. 1974. Wolf management in Minnesota: An endangered species case history. *Transactions of the North American Wildlife and Natural Resources Conference* 39:313–22.

Van Dyke, F. B., R. H. Brocke, H. G. Shaw, B. B. Ackerman, T. P. Hemker, and F. G. Lindsey. 1986. Reactions of mountain lions to logging and human activity. *Journal of Wildlife Management* 50:95–102.

Van Horne, B. 1983. Density as a misleading indicator of habitat quality. *Journal of Wildlife Management* 47:893–901.

Varley, J. D., and W. Brewster, eds. 1992. *Wolves for Yellowstone? A report to the United States Congress*. Vol. 4, *Research and analysis*. Yellowstone National Park: US National Park Service.

Veblen, T. T. 2000. Disturbance patterns. In *Forest fragmentation in the Southern Rocky Mountains*, ed. R. L. Knight, F. W. Smith, S. W. Buskirk, W. H. Romme, and W. L. Baker, 31–54. Boulder: Univ. Press of Colorado.

Veblen, T. T., K. S. Hadley, E. M. Nel, T. Kitzberger, M. Reid, and R. Villalba. 1994. Disturbance regime and disturbance interactions in a Rocky Mountain subalpine forest. *Journal of Ecology* 82:125–35.

Veblen, T. T., T. Kitzberger, and J. Donnegan. 2000. Climatic and human influences on fire regimes in ponderosa pine forests in the Colorado Front Range. *Ecological Applications* 10:1178–95.

Veblen, T. T., and D. C. Lorenz. 1991. *The Colorado Front Range: A century of ecological change*. Salt Lake City: Univ. of Utah Press.

Vickery, P. D., M. L. Hunter Jr., and S. M. Melvin. 1994. Effects of habitat area on the distribution of grassland birds in Maine. *Conservation Biology* 8:1087–97.

Vrijenhoek, R. C. 1996. Conservation genetics of North America desert fishes. In *Conservation genetics: Case histories from nature*, ed. J. C. Avis and J. L. Hamrick, 367–97. New York: Chapman and Hall.

Vucetich, J. A., M. P. Nelson, and M. K. Phillips. 2006. The normative dimension and legal meaning of endangered and recovery in the US Endangered Species Act. *Conservation Biology* 20:1383–90.

Wallace, M. G., H. J. Cortner, M. A. Moote, and S. Burke. 1996. Moving toward ecosystem management: Examining a change in philosophy for resource management. *Journal of Political Ecology* 3:1–36.

Wallace, R. L., and T. W. Clark. 1999. Solving problems in endangered species conservation: An introduction to problem orientation. *Endangered Species Update* 19 (4):81–86.

Ward, P. D. 1997. *The call of the distant mammoths: Why the Ice Age mammals disappeared*. New York: Copernicus.

Wayne, R. K., and S. M. Jenks. 1991. Mitochondrial DNA analysis implying extensive hybridization of the endangered red wolf, *Canis rufus*. *Nature* 351:565–68.

Wayne, R. K., N. Lehman, M. W. Allard, and R. L. Honeycutt. 1992. Mitochondrial DNA variability of the gray wolf: Genetic consequences of population decline and habitat fragmentation. *Conservation Biology* 6:559–69.

Wayne, R. K., and C. Vila. 2003. Molecular genetic studies of wolves. In *Wolves: Behavior, ecology, and conservation*, ed. L. D. Mech and L. Boitani, 218–38. Chicago: Univ. of Chicago Press.

Weaver, J. 1978. *The wolves of Yellowstone*. US National Park Service Natural Resources Report No. 14. Washington, DC: US National Park Service.

Weber, W. A., and R. C. Wittman. 1992. *Catalog of the Colorado flora: A biodiversity baseline*. Niwot: Univ. Press of Colorado.

Wemmer, C., and S. Derrickson. 1987. Reintroduction: The zoologist's dream. In *AAZPA annual proceedings*, 48–65. Wheeling, WV: AAZPA.

Westemeier, R. L., J. D. Brawn, S. A. Simpson, T. I. Esker, R. W. Janzen, J. W. Walk, E. I. Kerschner, J. I. Bouzat, and K. N. Page. 1998. Tracking the long-term decline and recovery of an isolated population. *Science* 282:1695–98.

Western Regional Climate Center Database. 2001. Western US climate historical summaries: Colorado climate summaries, 1948–2000. www.wrcc.sage.dri.edu.

Westrum, R. 1988. Organizational and interorganizational thought. Paper presented at World Bank Conference on safety control and risk management, Washington, DC.

Whicker, A. D., and J. K. Detling. 1988. Ecological consequences of prairie dog disturbances. *BioScience* 38:778–85.

White, C. A., C. E. Olmsted, and C. E. Kay. 1998. Aspen, elk, and fire in the Rocky Mountain national parks of North America. *Wildlife Society Bulletin* 26:449–62.

White, G. C., and R. M. Bartmann. 1998. Effect of density reduction on overwinter survival of free-ranging mule deer fawns. *Journal of Wildlife Management* 62:214–25.

White Jr., L. 1967. The historical roots of our ecological crisis. *Science* 155:1203–7.

White, P. J., and R. A. Garrott. 2005. Northern Yellowstone elk after wolf restoration. *Wildlife Society Bulletin* 33:942–55.

White, P. J., and K. Ralls. 1993. Reproduction and spacing patterns of kit foxes relative to changing prey availability. *Journal of Wildlife Management* 57:861–67.

White, R. 1991. *It's your misfortune and none of my own: A new history of the American West*. Norman: Univ. of Oklahoma Press.

Wiens, J. A. 1997. The emerging role of patchiness in conservation biology. In *The ecological basis of conservation:*

Heterogeneity, ecosystems, and biodiversity, ed. S. T. A. Pickett, R. S. Ostfeld, M. Shachak, and G. E. Likens, 93–107. New York: Chapman and Hall.

Wilcove, D. S., D. Rothstein, D. Dubow, A. Philips, and E. Losos. 1998. Quantifying threats to imperiled species in the United States. *BioScience* 48:607–15.

Wild, M., and M. Miller. 2005. Throw disease to the wolves? *The Denver Post*, August 9, 2005.

Wildt, D., B. Pukazhenthi, J. Brown, S. Monfort, J. Howard, and T. Roth. 1995. Spermatology for understanding and managing rare species. *Reproductive Fertility and Development* 7:811–24.

Wilen, B. O. 1995. The nation's wetlands. In *Our living resources: A report to the nation on the distribution, abundance, and health of US plants, animals, and ecosystems*, ed. E. T. LaRoe, G. S. Farris, C. E. Puckett, P. D. Doran, and M. J. Mac, 473–76. Washington, DC: US Department of the Interior, National Biological Service.

Wiley, J. W., N. F. W. Snyder, and R. S. Gnam. 1992. Reintroduction as a strategy for parrots. In *New World parrots in crisis*, ed. S. R. Beissinger and N. F. R. Snyder, 165–200. Washington, DC: Smithsonian Institution Press.

Wiley, P., and R. Gottlieb. 1982. *Empires in the sun: The rise of the new American West*. Tucson: Univ. of Arizona Press.

Wilkinson, C. F. 1992. *Crossing the next meridian: Land water and the future of the West*. Covelo, CA: Island Press.

———. 1999. *Fire on the plateau: Conflict and endurance in the American Southwest*. Covelo, CA: Island Press.

Williams Jr., R. M. 1979. Change and stability in values and value systems: A sociological perspective. In *Understanding human values: Individual and societal*, ed. M. Rokeach, 15–46. New York: Free Press.

Wilmot, J., and T. W. Clark. 2005. Wolf restoration: A battle in the war over the West. In *Coexisting with large carnivores: Lessons from Greater Yellowstone*, ed. T. W. Clark, M. B. Rutherford, and D. Casey, 138–73. Washington, DC: Island Press.

Wilson, E. O. 1987. The little things that run the world (the importance and conservation of invertebrates). *Conservation Biology* 1:344–46.

———. 1992. *The diversity of life*. Cambridge, MA: Belknap Press.

———. 2002. *The future of life*. New York: Alfred A. Knopf. Wilson, J. Q. 1990. *The politics of regulation*. New York: Harper.

Wilson, P. J., S. Grewal, I. D. Lawford, J. N. Heal, A. G. Granacki, D. Pennock, J. B. Theberge, et al. 2000. DNA profiles of the eastern Canadian wolf and the red wolf provide evidence for a common evolutionary history independent of the gray wolf. *Canadian Journal of Zoology* 78:2156–66.

Wisconsin Department of Natural Resources. 1999. *Wisconsin wolf management plan*. Madison: Wisconsin Department of Natural Resources.

Wolf, C. M., B. Griffith, C. Reed, and S. A. Temple. 1997. Avian and mammalian translocations: Update and reanalysis of 1987 survey data. *Conservation Biology* 10:1142–54.

Woodford, M. H., and P. B. Rossiter. 1993. Disease risks associated with wildlife translocation projects. In *Creative conservation: Interactive management of wild and captive animals*, ed. P. J. S. Olney, G. M. Mace, and A. T. C. Feistner, 178–200. London: Chapman and Hall.

Woodruff, S. 2007. Montana's plan for wolf management much more sensible than Idaho governor's ideas. *Missoulian* (Missoula, MT), January 21, 2007.

Woodruffe, R., and J. R. Ginsberg. 1998. Edge effects and the extinction of populations inside protected areas. *Science* 280:2126–28.

Wright, H. A., and A. W. Bailey. 1982. *Fire ecology: United States and southern Canada*. New York: John Wiley and Sons.

Wright, R. 1992. *Stolen continents: Conquest and resistance in the Americas*. Boston: Houghton Mifflin.

———. 2005. *A short history of progress*. New York: Carroll and Graf Publishers.

Wuerthner, G., and M. Matteson, eds. 2002. *Welfare ranching: The subsidized destruction of the American West*. Washington, DC: Island Press.

Wydeven, A. P., R. N. Schultz, and R. P. Thiel. 1995. Monitoring of a recovering gray wolf population in Wisconsin, 1979–1991. In *Ecology and conservation of wolves in a changing world*, Canadian Circumpolar Institute Occasional Publication No. 35, ed. L. N. Carbyn, S. H. Fritts, and D. R. Seip, 147–56. Edmonton, AB: Canadian Circumpolar Institute, Univ. of Alberta.

Wyoming Game and Fish Department. 2003. Final gray wolf management plan. Unpublished report. Wyoming Game and Fish Department, Cheyenne, WY.

Wyoming gap analysis. 1996. www.sdvc.uwyo.edu/wbn/gap.html.

Wyoming Secretary of State. 2008. *Wyoming voter registration statistics by party*. http://soswy.state.wy.us/Elections/docs/VR-Stats_by_Party.pdf.

Yaffee, S. L. 1982. *Prohibitive policy: Implementing the Endangered Species Act*. Cambridge, MA: MIT Press.

Yellowstone National Park, US Fish and Wildlife Service, Univ. of Wyoming, Univ. of Idaho, Interagency Grizzly Bear Study Team, Univ. of Minnesota Cooperative Park Studies Unit. 1990. *Wolves for Yellowstone? A report to the United States Congress*. Vol. 2, *Research and analysis*. Yellowstone National Park: US National Park Service.

Young, M. K., ed. 1995. *Conservation assessment for inland cutthroat trout*. USDA Forest Service General Technical Report RM-GTR-256. Fort Collins, CO: USDA Forest Service, Rocky Mountain Forest and Range Experiment Station.

Young, S. P. 1970. *The last of the loners*. New York: MacMillan.

Young, S. P., and E. A. Goldman. 1944. *The wolves of North America*. Washington, DC: American Wildlife Institute.

Zarnke R. L., J. M. Ver Hoef, and R. A. DeLong. 2004. Serology survey for selected disease agents in wolves (*Canis lupus*) from Alaska and the Yukon Territory, 1984–2000. *Journal of Wildlife Diseases* 40 (4):632–38.

Zarnke, R. L. and W. B. Ballard. 1987. Serological survey for selected microbial pathogens of wolves in Alaska, 1975–1982. *Journal of Wildlife Diseases* 23:77–85.

Zinn, H. 1980. *A people's history of the United States*. New York: Harper and Row.

Zinn, H. C., and W. F. Andelt. 1999. Attitudes of Fort Collins, Colorado, residents toward prairie dogs. *Wildlife Society Bulletin* 27:1098–1106.

Contributors

Susan G. Clark is the Joseph F. Cullman 3rd professor (adjunct) of wildlife ecology and policy sciences in the School of Forestry and Environmental Studies and fellow in the Institution for Social and Policy Studies, Yale University. Her interests include conservation biology, organization theory and management, natural resources policy, human rights, and the policy sciences. She has worked in diverse large carnivores conservation projects. Yale University, School of Forestry and Environment, 301 Prospect St., New Haven, CT 06511, 203-432-6965, susan.g.clark@yale.edu.

Rob Edward was formerly the carnivore restoration director for WildEarth Guardians, overseeing the scientific, political, and public policy aspects of the organization's efforts to restore wolves, grizzly bears, lynx, wolverine, and other large carnivores to the American West. He now works as a freelance writer. Edward has worked on issues pertaining to the restoration and protection of wolves and other carnivores since 1994. PO Box 270532, Louisville, CO 80027, 720-213-6873, musefire@gmail.com.

James A. Estes is a professor in the Department of Ecology and Evolutionary Biology at the University of California, Santa Cruz. His research addresses the critical role of apex (top level) predators in the marine environment. Estes is a Pew Fellow in marine conservation and a fellow of the California Academy of Sciences. His Pew Fellowship was used to conduct a workshop and produce a book titled *Whales, Whaling and Ocean Ecosystems* (University of California Press). University of California, Santa Cruz, A316 Earth and Marine Sciences Building, Santa Cruz, CA 95064, jestes@ucsc.edu.

Dave Foreman is an environmentalist, writer, and cofounder of a number of organizations, including Earth First!, the Wildlands Project, the New Mexico Wilderness Alliance, and the Rewilding Institute. The Wildlands Project, PO Box 13768, Albuquerque, NM 87192.

Colin M. Gillin is a graduate of the University of Wyoming and Tufts University School of Veterinary Medicine. He previously worked in the field of conservation as a grizzly bear biologist for the Wyoming Game and Fish Department and as a faculty member with Tufts University teaching wildlife diseases while leading a disease ecology research program with the Consortium for Conservation Medicine in the Yellowstone-to-Yukon bioregion. He currently serves as the state wildlife veterinarian for the Oregon Department of Fish and Wildlife. Oregon Department of Fish and Wildlife, 7118 NE Vandenberg Ave., Corvallis, OR 97330, 541-757-4186 ext. 232, colin.m.gillin@state.or.us.

Hannah Gosnell is assistant professor of geography in the Geosciences Department at Oregon State University, where she is affiliated with the Sustainable Rural Communities Initiative. Her research interests have to do with the interconnections between demographic change, rural land use change, and water resource management change in the American West, and the ways in which laws and institutions might evolve to better reflect changing geographies. Oregon State University, Department of Geosciences, 104 Wilkinson Hall, Corvallis, OR 97331-5506, 541-737-1222, gosnellh@geo.oregonstate.edu.

Melissa Hailey is the staff attorney for WildEarth Guardians. Melissa earned her BA in conservation biology from the University of Denver and her JD from Seattle University School of Law. She now works to promote endangered species conservation and habitat protection throughout the American Southwest. Melissa is actively engaged in WildEarth Guardians' campaign to restore wolves to the Southern Rockies Ecoregion and acts as legal counsel on a number of cases to advance Mexican wolf recovery in the wild. WildEarth Guardians, 312 Montezuma Ave., Santa Fe, NM 87501, 505-988-9126, mhailey@wildearthguardians.org.

Dave Hunter has served as the veterinarian for Turner Endangered Species Fund and Turner Enterprises, Inc., since November 1998. He is currently an adjunct or associate professor of research at Boise State University, University of Idaho, Texas A&M University, and Montana State University. Dr. Hunter lectures throughout the world on disease, immobilization, welfare, and health concerns at the livestock/wildlife/human health interface. Turner Endangered Species Fund, 1123 Research Dr., Bozeman, Montana 59718, 406-556-8500, dave.hunter@retranches.com.

Kyran Kunkel is currently a senior fellow for the World Wildlife Fund, and he maintains professorial positions at the University of Alaska, the University of Montana, and Utah State University. He directs the nonprofit Conservation Science Collaborative. Kunkel received his PhD in wildlife biology from the University of Montana in 1997 and his MSc in wildlife conservation from the University of Minnesota in 1991. World Wildlife Fund, 1875 Gateway South, Gallatin Gateway, MT 59730.

William W. Martin is currently the real estate GIS planner for the Colorado State Land Board. He is actively involved with the mapping and land management of over 3 million acres of trust land in Colorado, including the Stewardship Trust program and other open space/natural area designations. Martin lives in Nederland, Colorado, where he is chair of the town's planning commission. Colorado State Land Board, 600 Grant St., Ste. 306, Denver, CO 80203, 303-318-0709, William.Martin@state.co.us.

Amy L. Masching works in the Department of Conservation Biology at the Denver Zoo. She specializes in community outreach and public awareness programs focused on wildlife and habitat conservation issues. Masching's programs have ranged from the peaks of Colorado's highest mountains to the plains of Kenya. Denver Zoological Foundation, 2300 Steele St., Denver, CO 80205, 303-376-4935, amasching@denverzoo.org.

Brian Miller is the conservation and research director of the Wind River Ranch Foundation, a nonprofit dedicated to conservation, education, and research in northern New Mexico. For more information, see www.windriverranch.org. Wind River Ranch Foundation, PO Box 27, Watrous, NM 87753, 505-425-1819, brimill@earthlink.net.

Paul C. Paquet holds a PhD in zoology from the University of Alberta and is an internationally recognized authority on wolves. He is an adjunct professor in the faculty of Environmental Design at the University of Calgary. Conservation Biology Institute, World Wildlife Fund Canada, Box 150, Meacham, SK S0K 2V0 Canada.

Michael K. Phillips has served as the executive director of the Turner Endangered Species Fund since its inception in 1997. Over the last twenty-five years, he has led restoration projects for endangered plants, birds, fishes, and mammals, with an emphasis on wolves. Turner Endangered Species Fund, 1123 Research Dr., Bozeman, MT 59718, 406-556-8500, Fax: 406-556-8501, Mike .Phillips@retranches.com.

Katherine Ralls is a mammalogist and conservation biologist who obtained her PhD from Harvard University in 1965. She is currently studying southern sea otters, island foxes, and San Joaquin kit foxes. She is a senior scientist at the Smithsonian Institution and has received several awards for her scientific work. Center for Conservation and Evolutionary Genetics, Smithsonian National Zoological Park, PO Box 37012, MRC 5503, Washington, DC 20013-7012, rallsk@thegrid.net.

Richard P. Reading is the founder and director of the Denver Zoo's Department of Conservation Biology. He is also an adjoint senior research professor at the University of Colorado at Denver and associate research professor at the University of Denver. Reading holds a PhD in wildlife ecology and three master's degrees from Yale University, and

he focuses on interdisciplinary approaches to conservation. Denver Zoological Foundation, 2300 Steele St., Denver, CO 80205, 303-376-4945, rreading@denverzoo.org.

Doug Shinneman is a research ecologist who focuses on developing a better understanding of how disturbance and land use, such as fire and timber harvest, affect ecosystems in relation to their ranges of natural variability. He is also interested in developing effective strategies for ecological restoration and conservation of biodiversity, and he has helped to develop regional conservation plans for the Southern Rockies. The Nature Conservancy, Minneapolis, MN 55415, dshinneman@tnc.org.

Douglas W. Smith is currently the project leader for the Yellowstone Gray Wolf Restoration Project in Yellowstone National Park. He worked as a biologist for the project from 1994 to 1997 and has been with the program since its inception. Smith has studied wolves for twenty-nine years. Yellowstone Center for Resources, Yellowstone National Park, PO Box 168, Mammoth, WY 82190.

Jay Tutchton is general counsel of WildEarth Guardians. For the better part of the past two decades, he has litigated on behalf of endangered species under the Endangered Species Act and every other federal environmental statute he can think of that might help protect vanishing plants and animals. WildEarth Guardians, 312 Montezuma Ave., Santa Fe, NM 87501, 505-988-9126, jtutchton@wildearthguardians.org.

Index